Praise for *China in Our Time:*

"Ross Terrill has a rare ability to 'seize the hour,' to place himself in China at the moments of high drama. He arrived in Beijing a few hours before Tiananmen and his account of the bloody turmoil is one of the best and most dramatic. He got into China in 1964, well before the Cultural Revolution and beat Nixon and Kissinger to Beijing by more than a year. His memoir provides an attractive series of vignettes which illuminates China's recent past."

—Harrison Salisbury,
author of *The New Emperors*

"*China in Our Time* is in part a memoir of Mr. Terrill's many 'trips' to the Middle Kingdom, a rich autobiographical account of an intellectual's wrestling with the most populous country in the world—and with its officials. *China in Our Time* provides an absorbing history of the Middle Kingdom's traumatic last three decades. Mr. Terrill, who was on hand, writes movingly of the horrors that he witnessed. This is an elegantly written, engaging and knowledgeable book."

—Nicholas Kristof,
The New York Times

"*China in Our Time* combines the experiences of Terrill's many trips to China with that land's turbulent history in the past three decades. The result is an elegantly written book that is both personal and incisive."

—*Seattle Times*

"An incisive and timely depiction of China's evolution over the quarter century."

—Daniel Yergin,
author of *The Prize: The Epic Quest for Oil, Money, and Power*

"Well-informed and vivid . . . a powerful book."

—Annie Dillard,
author of *Pilgrim at Tinker's Creek* and *An American Childhood*

"Terrill interweaves his personal experiences in China with an analysis of the four decades of Chinese history that culminated in the violent rejection of democratic reforms at Tiananmen Square in June 1989. Terrill delivers a blow-by-blow account. He succeeds in capturing the frenzy of the collapse of the democratic movement. Drawing upon his own adventures there—19 trips spread over 26 years—Terrill has pieced together an entertaining and insightful portrait of China in our time. I can think of no better source to prepare us to understand the next chapter in the long, gyrating saga of the Middle Kingdom."

—J. D. Brown,
Chicago Tribune

CHINA
IN OUR
TIME

∎

THE PEOPLE OF CHINA
FROM THE COMMUNIST VICTORY TO
TIANANMEN SQUARE AND BEYOND

∎

ROSS TERRILL

TOUCHSTONE
Simon & Schuster Building
Rockefeller Center
1230 Avenue of the Americas
New York, New York 10020

Copyright © 1992 by Ross Terrill

First Touchstone Edition 1993
TOUCHSTONE and colophon are registered trademarks of
Simon & Schuster Inc.
Designed by Karolina Harris
Manufactured in the United States of America

1   3   5   7   9   10   8   6   4   2

Library of Congress Cataloging-in-Publication Data
Terrill, Ross.
China in our time: the people of China from the Communist
victory to Tiananmen Square and beyond/Ross Terrill.
p.   cm.
Includes bibliographical references and index.
1. China—History—1949–   I. Title.
DS777.55.T4166   1992
951.05—dc20   92-7699
CIP
ISBN: 0-671-68096-X
ISBN: 0-671-86741-5 (PBK)

CONTENTS

	PROLOGUE: CHINA CHANGES	13
1	FIFTEEN YEARS OF LIBERATION	21
2	BARBARIANS AND BIBLES	41
3	"LIGHT UP YOUR CIGARETTE REGARDLESS"	59
4	FROM MARXIST TO MONKEY KING	76
5	AFTER THE STORM	94
6	THE OPENING	113
7	MAO'S BORROWED TIME	125
8	CHANGE	146
9	CHINA, AMERICA, AND FRIENDSHIP	161
10	IN SEARCH OF WEALTH AND POWER	177
11	CATS AND MICE	195
12	REFORM AFTER REVOLUTION?	214
13	WARM SPRING	228
14	POWER AND EMOTION	243

15 MASSACRE   261
16 SHOCK AND FEAR   276
17 FRIENDS LOSE HOPE   297
18 THE PROBLEM OF CHINA   315
    NOTES   339
    INDEX   349

CHINA
IN OUR TIME

The People's Republic of China
(overleaf)

PROLOGUE:
CHINA CHANGES

IN 1949 Mao Zedong, a farmer's son who rose to lead a Communist rebellion that toppled the rule of Chiang Kai-shek's Nationalist party, left the last of his rural bastions and came north to Beijing. The undisputed leader of a "new" China, he settled into a mansion near the Forbidden City amidst red pillars, white marble steps, and golden tiles brushed by gnarled plane trees, once the habitat of emperors of the Ming and Qing dynasties (1368–1911). The fifty-six-year-old semi-intellectual, with his high-pitched voice and serene air, believed he was redirecting history and in a speech in Tiananmen Square, the hundred-acre stage for Chinese political theater at the southern edge of the Forbidden City, he declared his coming to power, after three decades of costly struggle against Chiang, warlords, and Japanese invaders, the "Liberation" of the nation.

In the China that Mao ruled, the phrases "before Liberation" and "after Liberation" were used to demarcate the evils of chaos, injustice, and foreign invasion from the virtues of order, fairness, and national pride under socialism. But over the years since 1949, I wondered if that change could really be so clear-cut; I tried to understand the impact that Mao's Communists have had upon China, and the impact of China upon them. The China that enticed Westerners like me was not only Communist but old and huge to a degree that seemed to dwarf our own existence. Chinese dynasties rose and fell before the founding of Christianity. The entire population of America and Western Europe, added to that of Japan and the former

Soviet Union, together falls short of the population of China. The "People's Republic of China," as Mao rebaptized his country at Tiananmen Square, forms more than a fifth of mankind, borders twelve nations, possesses one of the ten biggest economies in the world, and maintains a huge military force of more than 3 million equipped with nuclear weapons. Here, surely, communism faced its richest opportunity and sternest test yet.

Few Westerners crossed China's threshold in the early years of Mao's reign. But the formidable Chinese Communist military performance in the Korean War of 1950–53, hand in glove with the Soviet Union, crystallized China's position as a rising force and a solid member of the Communist bloc. Indeed, by the mid-1950s Mao could say, "The Soviet Union's today is China's tomorrow." Yet China seemed different from the rest of the Communist bloc. I already knew by the time of the Hungarian uprising of 1956 that Russian communism was oppressive and Eastern Europe was very nearly enslaved to Moscow, but I wondered if Mao's peasant Communists, heirs to a two-thousand-year-old Confucian tradition, might pursue communism as a "social morality," rather than as Marx's "social science" and Lenin's "science of power."

Communism promised to paint beautiful pictures on the vast canvas of Chinese society. The audacious, Promethean Mao made a spine-chilling remark on the malleability of the Chinese masses as he launched his utopian Great Leap Forward in 1958. "The two outstanding things about China's 600 million people are that they are 'poor and blank,' " he said. "On a blank sheet of paper free from any blotches, the freshest and most beautiful characters can be written, the freshest and most beautiful pictures can be painted."[1] Perhaps it would be among China's poor and blank millions that communism would find its true fulfillment?

I was determined to visit Mao's China to see for myself. In Prague, Budapest, Moscow, and Belgrade during the summer of 1964, while I was a student meandering through Europe, I knocked on the tall carved wooden doors of Beijing's embassies (there were few PRC embassies in Western Europe), saying I would like to go to China to see Mao's communism in action. Each time I was received politely and given every possible response except a visa. Warsaw was my last stop in the Communist bloc and there I laced my pleas with urgency and boldly asked to see the Chinese ambassador. Eventually, perhaps to put an end to my daily appearance at the embassy door, a Chinese version of "Why the hell not?" seemed to prevail and one night the telephone in my room at the Bristol Hotel rang and a Chinese voice said my visa could be picked up at eight the next morning.

It is impossible to put myself back in that year of 1964 and say exactly what I sought and expected on my first visit to China. If something was forbidden, my temperament inclined me to a redoubled interest in it, and that was true of Mao's China, for as an Australian I was required (as were Americans) to get special permission from my own government to go there, and the Chinese government treated visas like precious stones. My sense of China at that time was of its "otherness," an extreme manifestation both of greatness and distress in the human condition, a realm of glory and of trouble, which presented itself to the Western world as part Oriental mystery and part Communist challenge.

But Mao's Liberation suggested the birth of a novel social order that would not only revitalize China but also influence the West. I think it was a quest for the right way to live that propelled me to venture from Melbourne via Eastern Europe to Beijing in 1964. A China for a century in turmoil and now apparently tamed and remolded by communism triggered emotions and ideas that bore on the post–World War II quest for a just society. I viewed hope for the future as indivisible, and the Chinese and we Westerners as voyagers together on the same open sea. I wanted to know if China really had been liberated into peace, equality, and a sense of community, and whether China, the "sick man of Asia," was being transmuted into a vibrant country that would enrich the history of our time.

In Beijing and Guangzhou in 1964, I found bristling patriotism, ideological fanaticism, and a conviction among the Chinese Communists that their revolution had indeed transformed world politics. But I did not quite understand that the Communist revolution was a deceptive facade behind which lay a mixture of social change, political repression, and cultural continuity. My student's foray into the unknown was followed by nineteen more trips to China over the next twenty-six years, during which I traversed eighteen provinces by train and car, met leaders, endured propaganda and surveillance, observed the theater of street life, made friends, learned something of Chinese art and drama, saw three of my books published in Chinese-language editions, and came to love the Chinese people and their food. With each successive visit, and the research in between them, answers to my questions about Communist China came slowly and sometimes as a shock.

I would come to possess a healthy respect for geography, since China's size and centrality determine much, as does the presence of the Pacific Ocean between China and America, and the forty-three-hundred-mile border that binds China and the republics of the former Soviet Union into a wary proximity. I would learn the weight of the past in China, the distant past of ancient emperors and legends and the more recent past of collision between China and the West. I would come to understand why the Chinese can be at once so suspicious of anything new and fascinated by anything from the West. I would conclude that Chinese foreign policy is as changeable as Boston weather, because the first priority for the Communist leaders is always domestic control. Events in the world and even a calculus of China's national interest are secondary to the politics of internal power and can be abruptly reinterpreted to suit its imperatives.

The most savage maelstrom of internal politics occurred in the mid-1960s, when Mao launched the Cultural Revolution that shocked even close colleagues who had sat at the table with him for years. Half the Politburo were tossed aside like used paper tissue, millions were harried, beaten, or killed for ideological shortcomings, and Beijing measured the outside world by its opinion of Mao's Thought. Long afterward, it seemed amazing that China did not fall apart in the course of the Cultural Revolution's ructions. Over subsequent years I would tax the friends I made in China with questions about the causes of the Cultural Revolution and why so many Chinese went along with its madness.

Then almost as abruptly as he had whipped his nation into a bloody frenzy, Mao emerged from the abattoirs five years later, wiped the blood off his apron, and sat down on the silk couch of diplomacy with Richard Nixon and other leaders to woo the West with visions of Ping-Pong, the glories of Chinese culture, and the promise of the China market. Washington and the American public, relieved at the prospect of hiding from sight the Vietnam disaster within a glittering package of detente with China, and satisfied to gain leverage against Moscow by courting Beijing, approached the Chinese government with exquisite politeness during this period of the early 1970s and did not focus on its continuing repression of its own citizens. Nor did I.

When I returned to China in 1971, it seemed like a land just emerging from a storm, its landscape scarred, yet lit by rays of a sun that suggested a better tomorrow. The pathology of the Cultural Revolution was not being faced up to, but veiled behind smiles and silence. An aging Mao, now "broad and splendid like a sea elephant,"[2] put away spear and gun and took up his brush to try again to paint beautiful pictures of communism on the "blank" canvas of China.

Mao had crafted not one but three great dramas in Chinese contemporary history: Liberation, the Great Leap Forward, and the Cultural Revolution. But during his slide toward death from Parkinson's disease in the mid-1970s, he wavered between zealotry and doubt, and the core of the Communist party became a snake pit of uncertainty, fear, and maneuver. When I went back on wider journeys to many provinces in 1973 and 1975, I saw ideology rise to fever pitch in public life even as it evaporated behind closed doors. As most of East Asia gave priority to economic progress, lumbering China remained obsessed with ritual, "class struggle," and power. Chinese bureaucrats lapsed into paralysis, unable to take responsibility for any departure from Maoism while Mao himself still had not departed.

After Mao died in 1976, the Chinese Communists faced problems of political credibility and economic development. Change was inevitable, for Mao's revolution could not continue without Mao and in the absence of richer fruits for people's daily lives from revolutionary policies. An "unofficial China" came into view and I found myself involved with the lives of individual Chinese as never before. Yet on the plane of politics, the repertoire of Chinese communism contained no other mode of governance than semimonarchical ideological paternalism.

Nevertheless, when Deng Xiaoping rose to power at the end of the 1970s, the mask of ideology was pulled back from the face of China, family farming returned to the countryside, people breathed a sigh of relief at the easing of controls over mental life, and give and take began with the ideas and products of the world beyond China's doors. All this was called "reform." Deng declared to his people, "To get rich is glorious," and the drums of nationalism were beaten to save the Communist party's face as Maoism was quietly buried. Yet the ultimate goal of the new post-Mao course remained unclear.

It was, in fact, a collision course. During several trips I made across the country in the mid and later 1980s, Chinese friends spoke of the pain and restlessness that came along with the exhilaration of Deng's reform era. It seemed likely that a new post–Cultural Revolution generation—inclined to judge the Communists by today's achievements rather than yesterday's glories—would move away from the political and social conformism and credulity that had been the norm in Communist China. Deng thought that a full belly and some gadgets in the home would satisfy the masses, and no doubt that was true for many. But some young people rebelled at the barrenness and paternalism of it.

Finally, urban youth took action, flocking into Tiananmen Square in the spring of 1989, touching the heart of China and amazing much of the world by their courage and sophistication. Their appeal for a democracy in which free individuals could flourish was met by a hail of bullets. The real tragedy of communism in China became clear when an entire generation's cry for individual self-realization through democracy was silenced by a regime part of whose historic mission had been to free the individual from a prior bondage to a despotic emperor system. Ironically, both Mao's Liberation and Deng's suppression were signaled to the world from that same historic Tiananmen Square.

Watching tanks and bullets brutalizing unarmed people in the shadow of the edifices of China's imperial and Communist history on the night of June 3–4, 1989, was one of the unforgettable experiences of my life. I felt that communism as a faith died as people fled in horror from the army that had come into Beijing as a liberator forty years before. I walked the smoke-filled streets asking myself what the world would think of this desperate Chinese Communist atavism. I thought the end must surely be near for Deng, yet I also recalled the capacity of China, with its strong centralized state, the weight of its past, and its cultural separateness, to stand outside global historical trends.

So it is that three decades after being stirred by Mao's victory, I find myself still pondering the mix of otherness and universality in Chinese ways, the blend of Chineseness and Stalinism in the Communist party of Mao and Deng, the elusiveness of the Chinese individual, and the staggering power of Chinese communism to eclipse private worlds with its own haughty "people's" agenda.

In the world of the 1960s, the challenge of communism had dominated everything, but by the 1990s, if communism was still an issue, the reason was not its advance, or its prestige, or its threat, but its spreading political and philosophical crack-up. Now it is reasonable to ask of the few remaining Marxist regimes, of which China is easily the most important, a question they used to ask of us: can there be a peaceful evolution toward a new system, or will there be a collapse and chaos? China, the world's most populous country and in some ways its largest problem, seems to stand defiant amidst the wreckage of the Communist bloc. But how much longer can Communist party rule survive—and at what cost to China's people and its global prestige?

The date of 1949 as a watershed of liberation does not seem to me as significant as it used to. A hundred years from now, I doubt it will be judged any more important than half a dozen other turning points in China's twentieth-century history. Most of the beautiful Communist pictures painted on the "blank and poor" canvas of Chinese society have faded like an etching on a rockface worn by the pounding of wind and rain. That electric day of October 1, 1949, when Mao stood at Tiananmen Square and proclaimed Liberation by the truth of communism now seems distant indeed. Another date, June 4, 1989, when Tiananmen Square lost its aura of Communist rectitude, has robbed the Chinese Revolution of its historic magic. True liberation remains a dream.

In the early 1960s I was asking *how* China had changed under the Communists, but in the early 1990s I wonder if a still backward and unfree China *can* change much while the Communists sit astride the nation. And if Communist rule is soon to end in Beijing, as seems quite likely, I am drawn to consider the various roads China might travel as it searches for a new social and political identity. Contemplation of the future turns one back to the recent past. From the palaces of Beijing to the alleys and teahouses and classrooms of the nation's twenty-eight provinces, I have found China over the years to be an arena of hope and fate, of idealism and betrayal, of the smile that invites and the sword that rejects. I am a traveler of the mind who remains outside the locked door of many a secret Chinese chamber, yet I have also accrued a storehouse of experiences, listened to the wisdom and testimony of many Chinese people, and witnessed events that illuminate China's character and the next phase in its immemorial story.

CHAPTER ONE

∎

FIFTEEN YEARS OF

LIBERATION

AT Moscow airport one evening early in August 1964, a worn Aeroflot turboprop stirred to life in mist and a piercing wind. Tarmac lights illuminated handsome birch trees, and low grass in front of the trees turned pink from the glow of red lamps on the tips of the Ilyushin's wings. Aloft, cabin windows rattled as a hostess announced it would take three hours to reach Omsk. Electrical wires lay naked by the armrest at my elbow, and the overhead luggage compartment was simply a long thin hammock. Beside me sat two Hungarians holding on their laps string bags full of shiny green melons. Across the aisle a pair of Albanian trade officials, with whom I had dined on meatballs in sour cream at the airport restaurant, began to smile as the plane left Moscow and carried them nearer China; they were going via Peking* to North Korea for a holiday. There were no Americans on board, of course. I was an Australian student on my first trip to Communist China.

Omsk looked like a town in Alaska or the far north of Japan, and in a terminal that was full of sleeping Russians and resembled a railroad station, we sipped sweet-scented Siberian lemonade. After four hours flying east to Irkutsk, on the next leg of my journey, I began to sense the enormousness of the cohabitation of Russia and China, the two of them leaning upon each other for forty-three

---

* As Beijing was known in those years.

hundred miles, their bodies together like reclining dinosaurs, their minds far apart, one in Europe and the other in Asia.

From Irkutsk we were in the hands of the Chinese airline, CAAC, and hostesses served a lunch of rice, "hundred-year-old eggs," and fragrant tea and handed out bamboo fans and tiny plastic bags for the safekeeping of fountain pens at high altitudes. Lake Baikal appeared, its water gleaming in the rays of the August heat and set about with densely wooded hills, and when the last tentacles of the lake had gone, the Gobi Desert came into view and all soon became a barren ginger waste, a sun-baked no man's land where Russia turned into China.

In that summer of 1964, the Vietnam War was expanding and the politics of the Asia-Pacific region were being pulled out of shape on a rack of tension between the hostile poles of the United States and China. Nikita Khrushchev, who had undone Stalin's reputation, was being maneuvered against in the Kremlin and would soon fall, and in a tense Asia-Pacific, the Chinese Communists were talking about nuclear weapons as if they were firecrackers. I, being young, was stimulated rather than weighed down by the troubles.

A stubborn idealist, I wanted to see for myself the new China that had turned off the lights of Treaty Port China and haughtily excluded the West, throwing out the last American diplomats in 1950 and treating each succeeding American president as the world's devil of the moment. The revolution that Mao clinched in 1949 was still a shimmering abstraction for most people around the world, the way the Russian Revolution was for Europeans through the 1920s and 1930s. The American view of China differed from that held in Europe and most of Asia because past romance made the Sino-American divorce in 1950 bitter. To most Americans the Chinese revolution indeed was an abstraction, but a demonic one. People who focused on an abstraction, whether shimmering or demonic, overlooked concrete realities. I was too young to buy an abstraction, and energetic enough to go looking for the realities.

As the CAAC plane headed toward Peking, north China presented itself as yellow streams and peaked mountains of green velvet, a welcome change for the eye from the Mongolian desert. At Peking airport, I discovered that it was not possible to arrive in the People's Republic of China (PRC) privately. Even a traveler of the lowest level, such as a near-penniless Australian student, had to be received by a cheerleader of the China International Travel Service, whose script was to sing the praises of New China. A customs officer sealed up my rolls of film exposed in Eastern Europe, so that I would be able to take them out of China, and made me undertake to have any film used during my stay developed within China. My cheerleader led me past a huge white statue of Mao that dominated the airport terminal and into a Polish car for the horn-tooting drive into Peking. This guide from the China International Travel Service, like other travel officials I was to meet, displayed a cosmopolitan varnish that only made her lack of mental freedom the more unmistakable. Yet, for all her faults, she was essential to my visit, for in those days I spoke no Chinese.

Chang An Avenue, the spine of Peking, swarmed with bicycles and amidst them an occasional vehicle, like a carp among minnows, made a sedate progress. A nonstop stream of buses, hooked together in pairs with a folding canvas connection, giving a caterpillar effect, ploughed forward packed to capacity. The Polish taxi dashed for half a mile at fifty miles an hour, then coasted for a few hundred yards—a maddening way to drive, which I thought at the time meant engine trouble but learned later was adopted to save gasoline. My first vista of Peking was of a huge mass of people in white shirts and blue pants assembled in Tiananmen Square. It was a rally of eight hundred thousand Chinese protesting President Lyndon Johnson's attack on North Vietnamese vessels in the Gulf of Tonkin, just a few score miles from Chinese territory.

During my first week in China, a total of 20 million Chinese citizens attended such anti-American rallies in various of the twenty-eight provinces. I did not then understand the fearsome social organization (through the blandly named "street committees") that ensured a massive turnout for these officially triggered "demonstrations." At one rally Foreign Minister Chen Yi said: "The acts of aggression of the United States Johnson administration demonstrate that Johnson is even worse than John Foster Dulles. While Dulles pursued a policy of brinkmanship, Johnson has gone over the 'brink of war' by taking the road of extending the war in Indochina."

To the Chinese Communists, Indochina seemed but a short step from the war they had fought against the United States–backed Chiang Kai-shek forces. The civil war of 1946–49 brought to a climax the violence and disorder of the decades since the fall of the Qing dynasty in 1911. President Truman's efforts to forestall one more round of armed struggle between Mao and Chiang came to an end with the failure of the Marshall Mission (1945–46). After General George Marshall came home, Washington supported Chiang's fight against the Communist armies. At the end of three devastating years, during which 3 million Chinese died, Chiang fled to Taiwan and Mao took up residence in the shadow of the Forbidden City. An ally of Chiang's China during World War II, America was rudely switched by the Chinese Communists to the role of "imperialist."

This imperialist label had its historical justification, for the British, followed by the French, Americans, and others, had forced their political, commercial, and religious attentions upon a reluctant China in intensifying waves of encroachment from the 1830s. Everyone I met in China made allusion to their nation's modern trauma at the hands of the West. Territory (including Hong Kong) was forced from China's hands, foreign gunboats cruised China's broad muddy rivers, and the Summer Palace in western Peking was burned by the British in a fit of pique with the Chinese government in 1860. By 1900, when the foreign presence in Peking was substantial, the cry "Expel the Barbarians" rent the air as the Boxer Rebellion shook the capital, missionaries were butchered, and American and British troops in retaliation shot at Chinese in Peking streets.

Peking was dry and dusty and flat, a city broad like the stretch of centuries to which it had borne witness. As if to signal that its vocation lay with governance, and not mere commerce, the Chinese capital (for most of the time since Kublai Khan made it such in 1263) was laid out with an eye to the cosmos, its monuments built to partner the planets and stars. In the east stood the Temple of the Sun, and facing it from the west, the Temple of the Moon. The southern flank of the symmetrical city was graced by the Temple of Heaven, its three conical roofs in blue tile like a pile of coolies' hats, rising above a white marble concourse, to whose Hall of Prayer for Good Harvests emperors had come to seek heaven's aid. The south wall of the park around the Temple of Heaven was straight, and the north wall was semicircular, expressing the ancient Chinese view that the earth was square and heaven round.

As Chinese as everything was, with the curved tiles of the Forbidden City's palaces in the hue of a goldfish's skin, the nasal cries of the hawkers and stone-grinders, and the ubiquitous smell of Chinese noodles and sauces and vegetables, Peking nevertheless had the air of the Communist bloc. I stayed in the Russian-style Xin Qiao Hotel, a rectangular cement block that nestled against a remnant of the city wall. My room had no shades—was privacy thought to be a sin?—and sun streamed in upon the bed at 4:30 A.M., as outside my window cicadas sang as if in millions. In the hotel courtyard where the bushes, although lush, exuded heat, old Chinese men and women did rhythmic snakelike *tai ji quan* exercises.

Out in the streets, some buildings were being spruced up for the fifteenth anniversary of the founding of the PRC a couple of months ahead. The few cars, tooting at bicycles like dogs barking at mice, were mostly Russian and Polish, with an occasional battered Morris or Chevrolet from "imperialist" days. "If Peking had one-tenth of the cars Melbourne has," I wrote in my diary, "people would be deaf within the hour from the noise of their tooting."

No longer an abstraction, here was China as crying babies, steel plants, three-thousand-year-old tombs, soldiers with fixed bayonets at the gates of unlabeled buildings, bookstores selling Albanian political pamphlets and the social realist works of Jack London and Mark Twain and Charles Dickens, and a populace with a genius—sometimes born of necessity—for deriving pleasure from simple things. China seemed more ideological than Russia, its citizens more swept up in public purposes. The Communists had eliminated the waste of disorganization—before 1949 poor communications had turned many a food shortage into a famine—and were introducing the waste of superorganization.

No high-rise or international chain hotels existed, nor did any foreign airline other than Aeroflot fly to China. Guests at the Xin Qiao Hotel were mainly from the Soviet bloc, Africa, and Indochina. President Charles de Gaulle had just recognized the PRC, and there were a few French travelers, wearing high fashions in the dust and humidity, pleased to be ahead of the Americans in exploring Mao's kingdom. My floor in the Xin Qiao was dominated by tiny Laotian dancers and cheerful Cambodian Ping-Pong players. A Hungarian engineer, missing the nightlife of Budapest, carried about with him a chart on which he crossed off one by one the days until his departure from China. In the corridors there were constant mysterious knockings, never answered by a voice or followed by the opening of a door. Beside the elevator the hotel staff had pinned up a score of "letters of appreciation" received from guests, the Chinese Communist equivalent during the 1960s of a tip.

The dining room staff used bread as a magic tool to keep non-Orientals content while in Peking. These cheerful young men and women in their food-stained white garments were convinced that no European could eat a meal that did not include a pile of slices of dense, dry, bitter bread. A culture needs pigeonholes for dealing with other cultures, and for these Chinese bread was the key to our civilization (as, for many Westerners, rice was the essence of Oriental civilization). If I ordered a meal that did not include bread, the waitress would look at me as if to say, "Haven't you forgotten something?" flash a knowing smile, and without my requesting bread (the rice was better) write the two Chinese characters for bread on the flimsy paper of her docket book.

Often I took a pedicab, and the delights of this creaking pedaled conveyance were the exhilaration of being in the open air, the leisured pace of advance, which made sightseeing vivid, and the absence of a tooting horn. Most of the pedicabs that had survived until 1964 were patched and propped up in a dozen places. The Communists frowned upon pedicabs as an exploitative relic from pre-Liberation, and they were hoping to phase them out. The pedicab drivers, gnarled and toothless and cheerful, were a tamed breed who did not haggle over the fare in the pre-Liberation way, or expect a tip, let alone swindle the passenger. The drawback of the pedicab was my fear that Chinese pedestrians might think it politically disgusting for a young foreigner to be pedaled around Peking by an old Chinese.

Remaining portions of the Peking city wall were going to be taken down, I was told, and this philosophically driven rush to destroy the old was buttressed with an argument that the wall prevented the "free flow of traffic." I wondered in what way the destruction of an old city wall was intrinsic to the Communist revolution. Did aesthetics not count at all, and would the citizens of Peking really be better off without the wall, or would the Communists just feel purer in their antifeudal zeal by demolishing it? The rush to pull down city walls all over China was in keeping with the Communist aspiration to make a new socialist literature, drama, ethics, and historiography, indeed a new environment and a new human being. Mao said, "Destroy the old, create the new,"[1] as though an old culture could be removed like dead leaves from a tree, and a new culture could be made to blossom overnight from a seedling thrust into the ground.

The Tian Qiao (Bridge of Heaven) folk entertainment area, south of elegant Qian Men (Front Gate), still existed and attracted happy crowds with its painted magicians, expressive storytellers, huge wrestlers, and double-jointed acrobats. Yet Tian Qiao was being pared and squeezed because the Communists had judged it to be tinged with elements from a decadent past and not "revolutionary" enough in its themes. The laughter and applause of the people were not sufficient in Communist eyes to redeem the Bridge of Heaven.

The Maoists were quite right to say that a lot of "the old crap" still remained in the China of the early 1960s. It wasn't forbidden to consult the writings of Confucius (circa 551–479 B.C.) and the Taoist philosopher Lao Zi (a near-contemporary of Confucius), to enjoy the symphonies of Mozart and Beethoven, or to go dressed in a colorful skirt to a dance on Saturday night and prepare for the occasion with a session at a hair salon. Not everyone yet realized—or could say in public—that the new crap (much of it Soviet "socialist realism") was inferior to the old.

The country was poised uneasily among Chinese tradition, Western culture, and the new Communist culture. These three forces had jostled together in the May Fourth Movement of 1919, which was a prelude to China's later twentieth-century convulsions. On that fourth day of May, three thousand Chinese college students marched to Tiananmen Square to protest the reverses dealt out to China at the Paris Peace Conference in January 1919 and to denounce the Chinese government's weak stance toward a Japan that among other things had issued to China the humiliating Twenty-one Demands in 1915. Out of this patriotic demonstration there followed several years of cultural ferment, whose key idea was a call for "science" and "democracy" to replace Chinese society's traditional amateurism, hierarchy, and conformism.

Mao claimed May Fourth as an antecedent to the Communist party founded in Shanghai two years later, but the Nationalist party of Sun Yat-sen (1866–1925) also embraced it and, in truth, the "New Culture Movement," as the ferment of 1919–21 was known, was a push not for the particular doctrine of Marxism, but for cultural iconoclasm and a general vision of national progress based on openness to non-Chinese ideas. One of the New Culture heroes was Professor Chen Duxiu (1879–1942), who was a founder of the Communist party, but a second was the liberal Professor Hu Shi (1891–1962), who took a rational, pragmatic approach to China's problems —and became Chiang Kai-shek's ambassador in Washington in the 1940s.

In Peking it was not only the dilapidated Morrises and Chevrolets that gave me the feeling of an old-fashioned world. My room at the Xin Qiao Hotel was equipped with a chamberpot and a steel-nibbed pen beside a bottle of ink, and in a nearby park older Chinese men played tennis in long white flannels, gravely inching their way through a baseline game. Leading restaurants, hotels, and embassies were staffed by silver-haired veterans with elegant manners owed to imperialist tutelage, and the little shops of the commercial street

Wang Fu Jing and the art shops of the Bohemian lane Liu Li Chang offered lovely antiques from mansions recently turned into schools or offices or dormitories.

Yet the newness was palpable, and gone from Peking at least were the traits of the China depicted in Pearl Buck's novel *The Good Earth* (1931), Theodore White's crisis report *Thunder Out of China* (1946), and Jack Belden's account of the crumbling 1940s, *China Shakes the World* (1949). Inflation, prostitutes, an influential and privileged foreign presence, warlords, Christian missionaries, beggars—all had vanished. Fifteen years after Liberation, I found that the ragged and mysterious feel of a society teetering on the brink of dissolution had given way to the snap and bustle of a confident new order. The Communists traded upon the people's memory of the awfulness of *luan* (chaos) during the warlord, Sino-Japanese war, and civil war periods, and instituted a total control that made typical army life seem lackadaisical by comparison. Collectivism reigned, and its mounting failures were not yet admitted. Tipping had been abolished as a relic of colonialism, and only twenty years later would it come back as a prized badge of competitiveness.

In some ways China in 1964 seemed a courteous and moral society, a contrast to the prerevolutionary China I had read about. When I bought an ice cream, the seller carefully unwrapped it and put the paper in a trash can before handing me the ice with a smile. When I took a taxi to the Summer Palace, the driver, dropping me at the gate, said I would need sunglasses against the glare and lent me his own pair. After lingering longer than planned in the hillside pavilions, I could not find the taxi or the driver. I took another taxi back to the Xin Qiao Hotel and tried to ensure that the sunglasses were returned and full payment was made. I was not able to press upon the taxi cooperative the sixty yuan agreed upon originally for the round trip to the Summer Palace. They would accept only forty yuan plus the return of the glasses—no tip, even if disguised as a rental fee for the sunglasses. "Let us shake hands instead!" said the staff man when I tried to tip.

Not many days later, I was dining with a Canadian journalist—the only North American journalist resident in China—when a barman came into the restaurant and handed me my wallet. It had dropped from my pocket in the hotel bar two hours before. My impulse was to look inside and see if all was intact, but the Canadian, Charles Taylor of the *Toronto Globe and Mail,* put a hand to my wrist. "It's a point of pride with the Chinese to return anything lost," he said. "Look later, and you will find the wallet as you left it." Taylor was right, and he had good reason for his confidence, since he lived in the hotel and left his room unlocked.

Several times I asked the Chinese people I met about this striking honesty and the standard answer went like this: "Our eyes are set on China, not on personal gain." That was simplistic, yet there was in the early 1960s a strong party-inculcated sense of the collective, and a correspondingly weaker sense of the individual self. It produced the disparate results of honesty, conformity, and a suffocating lack of privacy. At the National Library the director startled me by saying, "Generally speaking, only organizations may borrow books—not individuals."

It was a buoyant, highly organized society, and I felt confident I wasn't going to be banged over the head or robbed. But I also felt a pang of anxiety—as a bon vivant might feel when visiting a strait-laced household—that an impulsive action might result in an accusation of decadence. China seemed like a vast Boy Scout troop, cheerful and busy at its summer camp. If the jarring phrase "social machine" had ever been merited—it was used in late Victorian England[2]—I thought Mao's China earned that phrase; it was machinelike in its collectivism and purposefulness. In my diary I mentioned an appealing side of Chinese society as a well-tuned mechanism. "The alleyways are crowded and they are poor," I wrote, "yet no one is in rags, no one is sitting or lying around in that state of hopeless-looking poverty familiar in some Asian cities. The clothing is standardized to an extreme degree, but it is neat and adequate. Everyone seems to have a task, and consequently no one comes running after you, ingratiatingly, to beg something, or even to sell something. In the midst of poverty there is order and a certain dignity."

The public philosophy of the time was largely composed of the twin negatives of antifeudalism and anti-imperialism. The landlords' grip on the countryside had been broken, and the Chinese had pushed out the bullying foreigners. Mao Zedong,* the leader of the Communist party and the revolution that overthrew landlords and imperialists alike, was born in 1893 in the village of Shaoshan in Hunan Province to a comfortable farming family. The boy had the round face and large eyes of his mother, who was a faithful Bud-

---

* At this time, of course, "Mao Tse-tung" was the usual rendition in Roman letters of the three characters of Mao's name.

dhist. At the age of fourteen, while the Qing dynasty still stood, he was made to marry against his will in traditional fashion (he never lived with the girl and probably never touched her), an incident that provoked one of Mao's many conflicts with his stern father. Through his own determination and with help from relatives—none from his father—he attended a good school and then a teachers' training college in the Hunan capital of Changsha. In the era of dislocation that followed the fall of the Qing dynasty in 1911 and the rise of warlord politics, Mao, whose hair was long and appearance often unkempt, taught, read history, did labor organizing, married the daughter of one of his professors, and in 1921 attended the small clandestine gathering in Shanghai that founded the Chinese Communist party.

For most of the 1920s and 1930s, the Communist party did poorly, as it slavishly followed the Soviet model of organizing workers for uprisings in the cities and suffered savage losses. Mao's second wife was one of thousands of Communists slaughtered by Nationalists or warlords in failed uprisings or anti-Communist purges, and he promptly married another young activist, who bore him a daughter to add to his two sons. Mao, the farmer's son, rose in the party and made it flourish by departing from the Bolshevik example and making rural struggle the focus of the Communist movement, a priority expressed in his searching essay "Report on an Investigation of the Peasant Movement in Hunan" (1927). After Japan's assaults on China began in 1931, Mao brilliantly presented the Communist movement as a national crusade against "imperialists" as well as a plan to recast society. Following bitter intraparty conflicts, he climbed to the party leadership during the Long March of 1934–35, when the Communists found their souls while almost losing their bodies in a trek twice the distance of the breadth of the United States, hotly pursued by Chiang Kai-shek's Nationalists and assorted warlords and hostile non-Chinese tribes.

Mao had been the Marx of the Chinese Communist movement as he made an original peasant-based analysis of China's ills, and he became the Lenin of the revolution when he led the military struggle against both Chiang and the Japanese, who launched full-scale war against China in 1937. In the dusty northwestern town of Yan'an, where he was based after 1936, Mao divorced his third wife and married Jiang Qing, an actress with whom he had a new daughter in 1941. In Yan'an he left behind his lean Bohemian appearance, put on weight, and began to develop the moon-faced look and receding hairline of his later years. In this remote town he also wrote his major treatises, including *On Practice* and *On Contradiction* (both in 1937), *On New Democracy* (1940), and his political-moral essays "Serve the People" (1944) and "The Foolish Old Man Who Removed the Mountains" (1945). By the time he took power in Peking in 1949, helped in the end by the Japanese attack on China, which distracted the Chiang Kai-shek forces from the Communist threat, as well as by Chiang's weakness in the countryside, Mao, in the mode of traditional Chinese rulers, still had never set foot outside China and knew no foreign tongue. Coming to China in 1964, I pictured Mao as a modest, principled Eastern sage-revolutionary, but this image missed his vanity, his streak of pragmatism, and his deep respect for Stalin and the Bolshevik Revolution as foundation stones of socialism.

Chiang Kai-shek, born to a landed family in Zhejiang Province in 1907, had been a dashing young general in Sun Yat-sen's circle, a nationalist with few pretensions to theory. He rose to become president of the Republic of China established at Nanking in 1928, which tenuously united China after a period of warlordism. A decade of substantial achievement under Chiang was ended by Japan's massive attack. Throughout its furies, Chiang continued his war with Mao, convinced, as he put it, that "if the Japanese are a disease of the skin, the Communists are a disease of the heart."[3] After the Japanese defeat in 1945, Chiang's republic never regained momentum and following heavy losses to the Communists in 1948, Chiang fled the mainland in December of 1949 and relocated his Republic of China on Taiwan. His wife, Song Meiling, famous as the fiercely anti-Communist and stylish Madame Chiang Kai-shek of the World War II struggle, was a sister of Sun Yat-sen's widow, who lived on in Peking as a ceremonial leader of Mao's regime. The island of Taiwan, liberated from Japanese occupation only in 1945, now was thrust into the middle of a continuing, if largely symbolic, struggle between Mao and Chiang. Thus "two Chinas," one friendly to the United States and the other its sworn enemy, traded acrimonious talk and occasional gunfire up to and beyond Chiang's death in 1975.

I found in Mao's China that antifeudalism and anti-imperialism, negative as they were, still had a certain moral appeal and united scores of millions of Chinese. The result was public-spiritedness and a restraint upon the assertions of the self. The Communist leadership, too, was comparatively united around these twin public philosophies; the severe fights of the Cultural Revolution period had not yet broken out.

Yet antifeudalism and anti-imperialism were no longer the totality of politics because the Communist party now had a post-Liberation record of fifteen years of exercising national power. One highlight of its years in power, the Great Leap Forward, an attempt that began in 1958 to advance swiftly from socialism to communism, had turned into a costly lurch sideways. A blast furnace in every backyard did not result in steel of usable quality, and the organization of the countryside into communes of tens of thousands of farmers blunted incentive and gave priority to ideological purity over economic rationality.

Ever since I began to study China in a political science class at the University of Melbourne in 1958, every facet of that society was filtered in my mind's eye through the powdery dust rising from the picks and shovels of the hundreds of millions of farmers toiling on communes. These utopian communes, established that very year of 1958, intrigued me more than anything else about Communist China, for Russia and Eastern Europe and all of socialist history had nothing quite like them. Yet the communes I visited in 1964 looked just like a collection of villages, with the addition of new buildings —adorned with political posters and slogans extolling collectivist values—erected at a central location for the supervisory activities of zealous commune officials.

But life on the communes was regimented and a sharp departure from the recent Chinese past. Wages depended as much on "correct attitude" as on work performed, "class enemies" from before Liberation were deprived of civil rights, and planting and marketing decisions were made at political meetings on levels far above the tiller's head. Peking set impossibly high targets, the communes falsified output figures in order to meet them, and so mistaken planning decisions at the center became inevitable. Millions had starved to death in the "three bitter years" of 1959–61, in large part because of policy errors, and Mao lost stature with some of his colleagues as a result. Everyone knew that feudalism and imperialism had caused suffering for the Chinese people, but by 1961 many also knew that Mao's utopian and arrogant Great Leap Forward had caused suffering too.

As I toured communes, children's palaces (a Communist term for a glorified kindergarten), and machine-tool plants in the Peking area, always in the shadow of a guide-interpreter, no one mentioned that Mao, chairman of the Communist party, was grudgingly having to share more power with head of state Liu Shaoqi (at this time spelled Liu Shao-ch'i) and party secretary general Deng Xiaoping (Teng Hsiao-p'ing) than before the Leap. Yet this was the case; a Mao accustomed to supreme power for decades was no longer regarded as virtually infallible by all of those who sat with him in the Politburo. The premier was Zhou Enlai (in these years Chou En-lai), a diplomat and balancer who was more deferent to Mao than were Liu and Deng, and who served as the administrative anchor of the vast government bureaucracy.

"They treated me like a dead ancestor," Mao complained of Liu and Deng, after they had opposed aspects of the Great Leap Forward, and, vindicated by the Leap's failure, moved toward the center of power in the early 1960s.[4] Unlike the impish and experimental Mao, this pair of orthodox Leninists believed unswervingly in the politics of order and the economics of results.

Liu Shaoqi was born in 1898 to a prosperous rural family not far from Mao's birthplace in Hunan Province. He studied in Moscow, where he joined the Chinese Communist party in 1921, and became a labor leader in Shanghai and other cities. A grave man with a handsome, horselike face, Liu made the Long March and from the 1940s assumed a status in the Communist party second only to Mao's. Liu esteemed the revolutionary role of the peasants less than Mao did, and he was not obsessed with Soviet failings as Mao was. He thought of socialism as an edifice to be built brick by brick according to a blueprint held close to the chest of party bureaucrats.

Deng Xiaoping, born in Sichuan Province to a comfortable family of farmers in 1904, was touched lightly by the May Fourth Movement as a high-school pupil in the city of Chongqing. At the age of sixteen he sailed for Marseilles and spent six years in France and Russia as student, metalworker, and political activist. He made the Long March as a military commander, and by the 1950s had joined the ranks of the top half-dozen Chinese Communist leaders. A short chunky man who appeared to have no neck, Deng hid his obstinacy and strength of character behind a beatific smile. No theorist, he shared many of Liu's political instincts, but he had a blunter approach to issues and people than did Liu. He went with Mao to Moscow for the fortieth anniversary celebrations of the Bolshevik

Revolution in 1957, and at a reception Mao pointed him out to Khrushchev and said, "See that little man there? He's highly intelligent and has a great future ahead of him."[5]

Mao's problems with Liu and Deng included a clash of views on the issues of Russia and the United States. In 1949 Mao may not have been entirely happy at his limited options, but nevertheless, as his relations with the United States collapsed, he chose to take China into the Communist bloc, signing a treaty with Moscow and putting himself under Stalin's wing. Within months of Mao's return from a supplicatory trip to Moscow in the winter of 1949–50, the Korean War broke out and the anti-American cast of China's foreign policy became dogma.

Yet by the late 1950s Mao was in deep conflict with Stalin's successor, Nikita Khrushchev, over how to deal with America, Sino-Soviet cooperation on nuclear weapons, and Mao's militant approach to the sharp tensions in the Taiwan Strait, where Chiang Kai-shek held the islands of Quemoy and Matsu, less than a hundred miles from China's Fujian Province. Three weeks after a summit with Khrushchev in Peking in 1958, Mao showed his disrespect for Soviet cautionary advice by shelling Quemoy and Matsu. During 1960, intimate cooperation between China and Russia ended as Khrushchev angrily withdrew Soviet specialists from Chinese factories and institutes. "It's impossible to *leap* into communism," Khrushchev complained of the Great Leap Forward, a remark that infuriated Mao.[6]

Deng Xiaoping observed in a speech in the mid-1960s that the Asia-Pacific region was the center of gravity of world tension, a view most people around the world took for granted as the Peking line. But Mao corrected Deng and said Europe was now the key point of tension, for in Mao's eyes the American threat had shrunk and the Russian threat had grown.[7] Liu and Deng, not long after my visit in 1964, would be upbraided by Mao, much to their surprise, as pro-Russian "revisionists."

China in 1964 seemed to be in the mode of recovery, alike from the Great Leap Forward and from the withdrawal of the twelve thousand Russian specialists in 1960. And if the Leap and the three bitter years that followed it were far from forgotten, they were seldom talked about. No major new clash had erupted in the Politburo. Mao and the pragmatists, Liu and Deng, were using similar words even as they thought different thoughts. Yet looks and even public events were deceptive, for just as I was bent on discovering the new China, Mao was maneuvering into position to knock down much of this new China's political establishment. The "new" was not so secure, after all, and in Mao's view at least, it was not even very new.

Liberation was an exciting concept to many Chinese, as it was to some other Asian and African peoples, but it spoke only of an evil to be rolled away, as though the postliberation state of grace would be too obviously glorious to need description. For many Chinese, liberation simply meant getting rid of Chiang Kai-shek. But who was liberated into what? The Communists said it was the nation that was liberated, and in one concrete sense that was true, for under the Communist party the Chinese became free of major foreign interference for the first time in more than a century.

"The Communist victory depended on the fact that it developed in a period of transition," the historian Sun Longji wrote, "at a particular point in the cycle of order and disorder."[8] Perhaps the long-term goals of the Communists never won the support of the majority of the Chinese people; it was enough, for a season, that the Communist party served as a doctor to revive a sick China on the brink of disintegration from famine, foreign invasion, and civil strife. The socioeconomic agenda to follow Liberation was pushed to the periphery of people's minds by the dramatic blood transfusions of the liberating process.

Liberation's fruits varied among social groups. Many poor farmers for a period got land of their own, and factory workers enjoyed the security of a welfare state. But millions of landowners were killed, capitalists in Shanghai were soon jumping out of windows, and the Tibetans before long found themselves, not in a state of liberation, but in a more rigorous bondage to the Han (Chinese) majority as represented by Peking. Prostitutes, homosexuals, former Nationalists, and millions of other deviants from proletarian moral orthodoxy did not feel any warm breeze of liberation.

To my room at the Xin Qiao Hotel each afternoon an attendant brought an English edition of a bulletin from the Chinese government news agency. The main theme of the overheated reports on world events was anticolonialism. Peking viewed itself, and was widely viewed, as the red heart of opposition to colonialism and neocolonialism. In the late 1960s China hid its totalitarianism in a shiny package of anticolonialism. Mao's China often behaved like the self-contained hermit Middle Kingdom of old, yet its rhetoric was internationalist, designed in particular to win the approval of Asia and Africa.

This was the era of the rise of an "Afro-Asian" world (a precursor term for Third World), and back in Australia my interest in China had been sparked by a prior interest in India. My college professors, who were mostly graduates of British universities, readers of the *New Statesman* from London, and admirers of Jawaharlal Nehru and Krishna Menon, presented the idea of democratic India and totalitarian China as two contrasting models of political development in the Third World. In 1960 I went to India as a participant in the Experiment in International Living. It was my first trip outside affluent Australia and I found the poverty of Bombay, Delhi, and other cities shocking and felt the high-minded moralism of the Hindus sat uneasily with India's terrible inequalities. I began to think that totalitarian China could hardly be worse than democratic India, a proposition I was testing firsthand in 1964.

In India I had been struck by the pervasiveness of religion, an accompanying fatalism, and the Britishness of the intellectuals, and on all points I found China a contrast. China in its secularity seemed more rational, more modern than India, and it was imbued with a Promethean spirit. China was less influenced by any part of the West (or East) than India was by Britain. China was at once more insular and more intellectually challenging than post-British India.

India, of course, was the star of the large "neutralist" band of nations, while China, in the aftermath of the Korean War, had a limited number of friends outside the Communist bloc. But from mid-1960 through 1964, seventeen nations recognized it diplomatically, almost all in the Third World. Peking's push of the hour was toward Africa. Premier Zhou Enlai made a long African tour in the winter of 1963–64, and the air was full of warm words about China-Africa solidarity. Nearly one-third of China's forty-eight embassies were in Africa—eight years before there had been none—and in Peking I met visitors from Zanzibar, Kenya, Mali, Guinea, Ghana, and Uganda.

Common opposition to colonialism was the key to this unlikely bond. China, like Africa, was nonwhite, economically behind the West, and recently freed from Western rule or bullying. A definition of the China-Africa bond in terms of negatives tended to obscure any shared positive China-Africa agenda. One morning during breakfast at the Xin Qiao Hotel, four Africans with whom I had flown from Siberia to Peking came into the restaurant. They approached my table and we shook hands and chatted. From the hotel staff there came a murmur of oohs and ahs. I did not understand why at the time, but after further experiences at the opera and in museums of greeting Asians or Africans and evoking a buzz from Chinese bystanders, I saw the point. To the Chinese, schooled in Marxist orthodoxy about imperialism and national liberation forces, human warmth across the chasm of political contradiction between a white person and Third World brothers came as a shock.

The end of colonialism was supposed almost automatically to solve the problems of the Afro-Asian world. My bulletin from the Chinese news agency spoke of "old forces" of the West being swept aside by a tide of "new forces" of Afro-Asian socialism and many people, including to a degree myself, believed in this upward evolution of the oppressed. The fact that China itself was still a mystery made it easier to expect Chinese success, especially as Peking proclaimed its achievements each day shrilly and without a trace of self-doubt. The vibrant talk about "new nations" and a "new man" diverted attention from evils and stupidities, but the people who knew of these—the Chinese rank and file—could not talk candidly to foreigners, and there was no Amnesty International to probe behind the glossy facade, pressing the Chinese government to disclose information and holding it to universal standards of human rights.

Somehow, the nature of the relation between the Chinese government and the Chinese people seemed "China's business," and anyway we knew little of it. The government and people *had* seen eye to eye for a time after the Communist triumph, as the early 1950s brought a sense of justice done and progress made. Years later I asked Liu Binyan, a tenacious investigative journalist who got into deep trouble with the Communist party during the late 1950s, how he had felt about Liberation. "It was immensely exciting," Liu said, every feature of his large, expressive face stirring to life on a cold winter day as we strolled on the Harvard University campus. "I believed in the party so much that when a constitution was drafted in 1954, I felt it wasn't necessary—let the party decide things, I thought, we don't need rules."

Many Chinese I knew believed that at least until the "three bitter years," the time of hunger and shortages following the failure of the Great Leap Forward, they were living in a pure society. An official folk hero of the early 1960s was a soldier and political zealot named

Lei Feng, who was so frugal that he went on using his toothbrush after the bristles had worn away, and who wrote in his diary: "There could be no me without the Communist party."[9] Some people really possessed a naive faith in the Communist party, made possible by memories of the pathetic last years of the Chiang Kai-shek regime and paucity of information about the non-Chinese world during the 1950s and 1960s.

Among those with wider experience of the world, the United States–educated architect who designed some of the new public buildings I saw in Peking, Lin Luoyi, was soon to be assailed for paying too much attention to the merely bourgeois idea of "a pleasing appearance," and in his self-criticism in 1965 he would write: "I always thought that one would be able to design with ease having thoroughly mastered old and new, Chinese and foreign techniques. Now I realize that one can only make a correct design by listening to the party's words."[10] Some of the new public buildings, like the Peking railroad station, had sprouted in the space of a few months during the Great Leap Forward by dint of bursts of energy and organization; the barely finished structures were set about with trees that arrived fully grown in boxes, ready to be lowered dramatically into waiting holes. The Chinese Communists not only thought they had mastered the laws of history, but saw themselves conquering nature as well. They did not want to acknowledge any limitation, whether on the speed of building monumental structures or on the speed of building communism itself.

But edifices such as the Great Hall of the People and the Museum of the Chinese Revolution and the Museum of Chinese History in Tiananmen Square were bland hybrids. They did not look Chinese and they did not look Western. The sight of them was a reminder that Mao's revolution brought an injection of Russian culture into a China not used to give and take with other cultures. As well as Marxism and a heavy architectural style, Moscow's influence brought Western ballet to China's stages, and the ideas of Pavlov and Lysenko to Chinese laboratories. Russia's linguistic impact even led the Chinese Communists—not matched by the Nationalists who fled to Taiwan—to print books and newspapers with the writing running left to right (rather than top to bottom in the Chinese tradition), and with the lines arrayed from the top of the page to the bottom (rather than from the right of the page to the left as had been the Chinese way).

But these Russian trappings did not do much to pull old China in the direction of cosmopolitanism, but rather brought a veneer, a pretense of a solution to the problem of China's cultural insularity. Buildings like the Great Hall of the People and the museums of the Chinese Revolution and of Chinese History seemed to reflect a fake-Soviet stage of Chinese social development, in which pressure to modernize in the Stalinist way covered up deep cultural confusion. The auditoriums and museums looked as if they had been designed by a committee, and in effect they had been.

One day, I asked my guide-interpreter where she lived. "Why, in the dormitory with the others," she replied. "The others" were her office colleagues, and the dormitory was the dwelling allotted to them along with the job; there was no question of choosing a place to live. The dominance of the collective allowed for tight party control and made for the subordination of private plans to public priorities. China had a "people's government," but where were the people? Any request I made to meet a particular person unnerved the travel service. It was as if such requests detracted from my keenness to see China itself, the great organism of socialism in which each individual was significant—like the cardboard figure of hero Lei Feng—mainly as a cell without a name.

It came as a shock to me to find that Peking was quietly doing trade with South Africa, even as it frothed at the mouth in support of black African radicalism. I would have been even more shocked had I known that Peking was trading in opium to earn hard currency.[11] Opium trading had for more than a century been the throbbing heart of Chinese accusations of Western disrespect for their nation and people. In the Museum of the Chinese Revolution I saw exhibits on the Opium Wars with emotive captions flung against the immorality of the British for bringing opium from India to China to pay for tea imports. Yet Peking was furtively selling opium to help pay for imports of wheat from Australia and steel from Japan.

Such paradoxes had a revealing explanation—in no way a justification—which went to the heart of Maoist China's values. The sense of collective solidarity was limited to the Chinese nation, and international values were as slighted as private values. The collective morality that swamped private concerns stopped dead at the Chinese border. The term *Zhongguo* ("China") translates as "middle country," and under the dynasties the realm of the Chinese emperor was known as "all under heaven" *(tian xia),* implying a nonacceptance of other sovereign countries. In this respect Communist China seemed to be cut from the same cloth as dynastic China; most Chinese had absorbed the connotation of the term "middle country" into their bones. The barman at the Xin Qiao Hotel who brought back my wallet didn't care a fig for human life outside China; it was too dim to be real for him. And for Chinese officials, the nobler Chinese society was considered (by themselves) to be, the more they could justify amoral international dealings—selling opium, exploding atom bombs, trading with South Africa—as a means to the beautiful end of strengthening socialist China.

CHAPTER TWO

∎

BARBARIANS AND
BIBLES

ABOUT five hundred foreigners lived in the whole of China in 1964, less than one per million Chinese,[1] and the tiny community of Westerners and "neutrals" in Peking huddled together like sad birds in an unsuitable clime. Separated even from Russian and other Communist bloc foreign residents of Peking, these diplomats and journalists and technicians received me with a warmth that bespoke their isolation. Charles Taylor, the Canadian journalist who lived in the Xin Qiao Hotel, invited me to a Chinese banquet with some other European and Asian residents, and in an atmosphere of almost conspiratorial fraternization everyone at the dinner—there were no Chinese present—bemoaned life in Peking for its lack of excitement, the wall between themselves and the Chinese, and the political propaganda.

Taylor told me that only one Chinese doctor was allowed to go to the residences of foreigners. So rigidly did the Chinese officials "divide and rule" the "barbarians," as foreigners were traditionally called by Chinese, that they would go to a foreign embassy party only if it was clearly understood that foreigners from no other countries would be present. The term for barbarian, ye man, was rarely heard in Mao's China. But a gentler, and yet still pejorative term, "big nose" (da bizi) could sometimes be heard, especially from the mouths of children when they were not being effectively supervised by adults. I asked one guest at Taylor's dinner, Thambi Srinivasan, an Indian diplomat who displayed an irony and stoicism typical of the foreign residents I met, why it was so hard to look a Chinese in the eye. "They would like to speak to you," he replied, "and to smile at you. But the control is so tight they are scared to."

One Briton, Adam Kellett-Long of Reuters, was lucky enough to be living in a Chinese house in the old and stylish part of town, not far from the Forbidden City. Hosting a lunch party one stifling day, he showed me an adjacent watch-making factory, which the balcony of his own apartment overlooked. "The Swiss ambassador likes to come here," he said. "He sits with his binoculars looking down into the factory, observing the way the Chinese make watches, the shape and the size of this part or that, anxious for any clue that they may be catching up to the standards of Swiss watch making." Or perhaps, I thought, because he has little else to do.

Foreigners clung to each other out of a sense of unsettling proximity to, yet also painful distance from, the maddeningly innocent world of a people who did not build any bridges to the non-Chinese world. Signs around Peking said, LET US BUILD UP CHINA BY OURSELVES, and it seemed to me that the Chinese were too proud and too singular to be able to cooperate much with others. I felt a certain wonder, and a feeling of plucking forbidden fruit, in roaming around China before the storm came to destroy the innocence, and before the doors opened to bring back numerous Westerners. That change was inevitable, I thought even then. No large country can live for long in such isolation from the rest of the modern world.

I ran out of money and it wasn't possible to telephone Australia (or most other countries), so I knocked on the office door of the British chargé d'affaires, hoping Australia's semicolonial status could be turned to advantage. A young diplomat named David Wilson received me, just as he was giving his tennis racquet to an Indian courier to be taken to Hong Kong for restringing. Wilson, a craggy, cheerful Scot who was conversant with Chinese culture and the Chinese language, said the British government did take some responsibility for an Australian in distress in China and he arranged for the London treasury to lend me twenty pounds. He also gave me good advice about Peking, and during my stay drove me around the bare wide boulevards of the city in his red Triumph Spitfire sports car.

A French sinologist, Marianne Bastid, who lived in Peking at that time, later recalled the atmosphere of a city in which foreigners were few. "One day David Wilson was driving his smart red vehicle along Chang An Avenue," she said in her study in Paris, "when car trouble occurred. A crowd of Chinese quickly gathered around the low-slung car. To get out and inspect the engine, David simply leaped over the side of the Triumph Spitfire. And he was wearing a kilt!" Bastid's eyes danced with amusement at the memory. "The Chinese almost died of shock at the sight before their eyes, and for months there was talk of this 'Briton in a dress.' "

The young British diplomat in the kilt later became Sir David Wilson, governor of Hong Kong. "We were very cut off then," he said later, in a conversation in Hong Kong, remembering the years 1963–65 when he was a member of the mission of the British chargé d'affaires. "Access to the Chinese was very limited, and there were few occasions indeed to meet Chinese in an informal setting. We could visit few other cities. It was a tremendous coup if you managed to get hold of a local newspaper at some railway station. Only the Peking press was available to us.

"Everything had a political flavor to it," Sir David said, recalling the newspapers, the radio, and the demonstrations at the gate of the British office. "If there was a need for a rally against the Americans, we were the place for it. We were the great representatives of imperialism among the Peking embassies. You could tell a demonstration was coming because the portable latrines were always set in place first."

One Sunday morning late in August 1964, I went to a Protestant service at Rice Market Church in Dong Dan, just a little northeast of Tiananmen Square. About a hundred people, most of them elderly, sat on wooden chairs in an airy room of the former Peking YMCA, singing hymns quietly to a piano accompaniment. The congregation dispersed quickly after the service, but I lingered on the sun-drenched sidewalk. The pastor came out the front door and peeped from behind a veranda post to see if I was still there. Soon he appeared in the street and motioned me in through a back door.

My interest in China was in part that of a young Christian idealist. At Sunday school and Protestant church services in Australia during the 1950s, I learned of China as an infinity of "souls," bound to us white people as fellow children of one universal heavenly Father. Believing in the universal worth of all humans, I was curious about the peoples of the world beyond Australia's shores, including hundreds of millions of "Chinese heathens." Christianity also immunized me against the more far-reaching appeals of Maoism. To a Christian, Marxism was pretentious in putting "historical forces" in the role that only God's plan fulfilled. It canceled the Christian's free will by its proclamation of an objective social destination. It misread the fundamental conflict between good and evil in the human heart as a particular conflict between economic classes—or so I believed at the time.

I was excited by this opportunity to test my beliefs. At Rice Market Church, I told Pastor Lin I wished to find out how Chinese Christians viewed the universalism of Christianity and what opinion they held of Marxist historical theories. He said I should talk to Zhao Fusan, head of the Research Institute of Theology, and a few days later, Zhao, a short, solidly built man in a white cotton shirt and sandals, received me in a parlor of the church. "We must become Chinese again," he said in a reference to the past dependence of Chinese churches on Western missionaries. Around Peking I had noticed churches being used for secular purposes and I asked Zhao about them. "One of the buildings you refer to is a Methodist church," he said, "but the Methodists themselves decided to abandon it as a place of worship and use a room elsewhere instead. The reason was that from 1900 [the period of the Boxer Rebellion] that church was extensively used as an American fortress, from which to fight the Chinese people."

Christianity had indeed come to China in harness with Western consuls and merchants and gunboats. Probably never more than 3 percent or so of the Chinese people ever became Christian, yet because Christianity was associated with Western power and prestige, its doctrines and way of life had influenced key members of the Chinese elite, including Sun Yat-sen and Chiang Kai-shek. China's long-rooted religions were Confucianism, a fairly worldly system of ethics giving much weight to family, order, and balance, named after Confucius; Taoism, a mystical and nature-oriented view of the universe that was also indigenous to China; and Buddhism, which entered China from India beginning in the sixth century and gradually became a major faith as its otherworldliness was sinicized with ideas of filial piety and other Confucian notions. For the time being the coming of communism had subdued all the religions, for Maoism was a philosophy meant to explain everything, as well as an organizational system designed to encompass everyone.

"The People's government," Pastor Zhao said of the Communist regime, "has achieved for China a great measure of material progress. But its greatest achievement has been to give people an aim, a direction, a united sense of dignity." Zhao, who had visited Australia as well as much of Europe as a member of church delegations, added: "In the Western countries as I have observed them, people are living and working to make money for themselves. In the new China, people are building a society; in the West, society is running down." All this had a certain appeal to me at the time, yet I was disturbed that Zhao built no bridges between his political views and Christian morality.

Zhao said the task of the Chinese churches in 1964 was just to preach the gospel. "Before Liberation the churches had many schools, even universities, and other institutions," he said. "But since Liberation the government is caring for these matters. Our task is a religious one." He went on to attack churches in the West for "getting caught up in secular purposes." Zhao seemed to believe that "a religious task" was not viable in an unjust society. "In the old society what I preached was true only in the Bible," he said. "It was not true in concrete terms in society, and it *could* not be true in the old society. Corruption and avarice and poverty were everywhere, and to preach was hollow. In the new China what we preach really has the chance to be practiced."

On no point did Zhao depart from the Communist line. When I asked him his reaction to Liberation fifteen years before, he smiled and replied: "In 1949 we were told that pastors would be beheaded and churches burned." I suppose he felt relieved that this at least had not happened. "Religious freedom is a daily practice," he claimed. "And the government has been good to the pastors. Before Liberation pastors could not afford to educate their children; now that is not a problem." I did not know if Zhao's pro-Communist talk reflected the worldwide intellectual disintegration of Christianity, a clutching at an ideology to replace a theology, or whether he as a Chinese pastor was under particular pressure and discipline.

I was intrigued when Zhao Fusan began to attack the Russian role in the Christian Peace Conference, a leftist organization based in Prague to which I belonged and whose assembly I had recently attended. The Christian Peace Conference was "dominated by men like Archbishop Nikodim of the Russian Orthodox Church," he complained. "We think they want Asians and Africans there just to decorate the platform with their pretty costumes." Zhao's dark vision was of Americans and Russians in collusion against the new forces of the Third World.

At the end of our talk, Zhao said mysteriously with a broad smile, "There is no need to worry about us in China. I cannot understand why many people in the West worry about us." I walked out into a street crowded with shoppers. At the Rice Market Church,

Christianity seemed delimited to the West, and China seemed mon-
olithically Communist. Wasn't Zhao a Communist, I wondered,
weren't all the Chinese in some sense Communists?

The conversation was of its time. Zhao Fusan was not alone in
offering a line of Marxism plus wounded nationalism; there was
virtually no other opinion to be heard. Imperialism *did* seem to dom-
inate the mental world of the Chinese, and even David Wilson, the
British diplomat, said to me a few days after I spoke with Zhao, "In
China it will take a hundred years to live down the connections
between Christianity and imperialism." Nearly everything from the
West, be it pop music or private business or Christianity, was
thought antithetical to Chinese values.

It took seven hours to fly from Peking to Canton, the capital of
Guangdong Province (known then as Kwangtung Province), with
an intermediate stop for the tired little propeller plane to refuel at
Changsha, the Hunan capital where Mao had attended teachers'
training college. As we approached the southern city, I looked down
upon manicured terraced fields, the green rice shoots set in parallel
wavy lines against the red soil. Then a vast shabby urban honeycomb reared into view, inner city buildings leaning against each
other as if squeezed ever closer by some force coming down from
the sky.

Canton was a steamy, cacophonous city, with more vivacity and
ragged edges than chokingly official Peking. A trading port ever
since the second century, when the Mediterranean world knew of it
through Indian and Arab merchants, Canton drew the Portuguese
in the sixteenth century with its silk, tea, porcelain, and wood carvings. The British followed the Portuguese a century later, wielding
a larger stick, and from there had acquired a "barren Island" (Lord
Palmerston's phrase in 1841) whose name was Hong Kong.[2]

On the living room wall of my family's house in Melbourne, two
carved cork Chinese landscapes hung by a thin copper wire at a
forward-tilted angle, gifts to my schoolteacher grandfather from
Cantonese merchants to whom he taught an evening class in the
English language (Australian version!) in Melbourne's Chinatown.
The delicate cork depictions of hills and lakes and willows, of mysterious palaces and grave old Taoists with tapered beards, still smell-
ing of the camphor wood that bordered the landscapes, spoke of the
culture of south China, which had reached Australia's shores at the

time of the gold rushes of the 1850s. The landscapes made me dream about a civilization that seemed a deep mystery. In downtown Melbourne I peered into the lanes of Chinatown and saw elderly Cantonese laundrymen in black and navy blue garments move noiselessly along the sunny sidewalks and glide into shadowy doorways to smoke opium. I watched younger Cantonese stir sizzling woks full of dim sum rich with the flesh of our Australian cats and dogs. Now I was encountering the Cantonese on their own terrain.

I walked by the mustard-colored waters of the Pearl River, alive with sampans that were home to citizens who did not want to live ashore. Watching the endless sea of people moving along the sidewalks—more quickly than people moved along Peking sidewalks—it was not difficult to believe that seventeen hundred Chinese babies were born each hour. Meanwhile, Mao was saying the more babies Chinese mothers had the better, because the imperialists had always been scared of Chinese hordes. "A man is born with one mouth," he had rejoined when warned by an economist about China's soaring birth rate, "but has two hands to feed that mouth."[3]

The Westerner was a little less of a curiosity, and in person a shade less distrusted here than in the north. The city had been designated by the Chinese Communists as a place for foreigners to conduct trade, just as the imperial dynasties used to keep contacts with the non-Chinese world limited to a few points far from Peking. Foreign businessmen, arriving from Hong Kong ninety miles to the south, visited the twice-yearly Chinese Export Commodities Fair, the main vehicle for China's modest foreign trade, giving the Cantonese a glimpse of the ways of the non-Chinese world.

My smiling, talkative interpreter spoke of the supervision of party secretaries over his work. "We sometimes get sick of their control over us, but we admit they are good organizers." This young man said—when I asked—that he would like to become a party member. "Everyone would like to be a party member!" he exclaimed. The Cantonese style was direct. People were not inclined to abstraction, nor likely to have their heads in the clouds. I learned how different commercial south China was from bureaucratic north China, a point that was to grow in importance with time, as China involuntarily decentralized, and the prospect drew near of a vigorous Hong Kong "tail" wagging a lethargic Chinese "dog."

At times in Guangdong Province I heard faintly, in between the happy chimes of Maoism, a sentiment that served to remind me that the entire purpose of the Chinese Revolution, going back to the days of Sun Yat-sen, himself a Cantonese, was to wrench overpopulated China out of economic deprivation. At a commune just outside Canton, a party supervisor spoke a profound truth, if still clothed in the ideology of the day: "The achievement of communism will take a long, long time. China is vast, and still very backward."

In Canton, the Chinese had already developed a Middle-Kingdom-plus-Marxist model of receiving foreign visitors. Africans and East Europeans each evening at the bar of the museumlike Yang Cheng Hotel, where I stayed, related their boredom at the daily round of visits to monuments, textile mills, communes, and palaces of culture, each offering a puffed-up lecture. The problem was Chinese insularity, for the boastful guides and handlers overlooked the fact that China was not the only country with new blocks of apartments, clean kindergartens, and gleaming machinery.

A Briton who had been in China for a year as an adviser to the airline CAAC on the Viscount plane, which the Chinese had bought from London, complained one evening, "The Chinese keep on saying that safety is very important to them, that every precaution must be taken. But there isn't a major airline in the world for which safety isn't at least as important." What was novel for the Chinese, they took to be novel for non-Chinese. Such self-centeredness, born of isolation and an unfree atmosphere, could become tedious.

I discussed the United States with a bright, intense young intellectual named Shi at the top of the Flowery Pagoda Buddhist temple in downtown Canton. There are people who are angry because of something that has happened, and there are people who are angry as a state of being; Shi was the second type. He found the world a dark place in which China was the solitary light. He blamed the United States for many of the troubles of the globe, peppering his talk with phrases like "wave of the future" and "rubbish heap of history."

Shi said the situation in South Vietnam was the same as that in China during the 1940s. "The puppet clique in Saigon will fall just as [Chiang Kai-shek's] Guomintang fell," he declared. To Shi, confident behind his rimless spectacles, history was an escalator, bearing the world up to a predetermined destination regardless of which way anyone moved on the escalator's steps. He could not consider South Vietnam a legitimate nation because he was convinced its destiny was to be absorbed by Hanoi. We spoke of freedom of speech, and I said, "Remember that in Australia if I disagree with something, I say so," to which he gave the perverse reply, "We do not overlook the contradictions of capitalism." Perhaps this young priest of

Maoist politics believed what he said, but the words were so abstracted from any human sense, and so unilateral, that he might have been talking of gravity or fossils rather than of nations and people.

Virtually every political poster I saw expressed a lie, not always easily discerned. WE HAVE FRIENDS ALL OVER THE WORLD—but China still was a pariah on most continents. INVASION OF NORTH VIETNAM IS INVASION OF CHINA—but Peking drew a sharp distinction between its own interests and Vietnam's. UNITY OF THE WORLD PROLETARIAT —but nationalism was proving a stronger force than class solidarity. These dubious certainties were plastered everywhere in huge characters with vivid illustrations, filling the heads if not the minds of 650 million people, and the anti-Western emotion weighed me down. "The stream of hatred which constitutes the daily news here has shocked me," I wrote in a letter to my parents. The worst ideological distortions were about America, of which younger Chinese knew little. The journalist Edgar Snow had visited China in 1960, but virtually no other Americans had set foot in the country since the Korean War broke out. A few American fellow travelers lived in Peking, serving as handmaidens to the Chinese Communist party, and their views only reinforced the equation of America with the headquarters of "imperialist aggression."

In Australia I was not thought of as pro-American in my political views, but the Chinese propaganda against the United States appalled me. The mere fact that I came from a country friendly with the United States required constant defense and explanation. Lyndon Johnson was facing Barry Goldwater in the presidential election that year, and each day I heard the two men cursed as "jackals of the same lair." My efforts to explain them and draw a distinction between them met with derision from every Chinese I spoke with.

In Canton, opposite the gate of the Yang Cheng Hotel, a row of display cases offered a view of American life and foreign policy. A section was devoted to President John F. Kennedy's murder nine months previously, and photos showed Chinese children cheering at the news. As I stood by the display, scores of people stared at me, and I felt terribly alone as a non-Chinese, the one Western person in a universe of hatred and incomprehension of the West. At the same time I felt a burning challenge to try to understand this alien place.

"Four Wicked Men," said a headline over photos of American presidents. They all looked sinister: Truman with a clenched fist and hatred in his eyes, Eisenhower in a shot designed to make him look moronic, Kennedy looking old and bewildered, and Johnson leering into microphones that resembled guns. How did they devise or touch up these pictures, I wondered. I protested to a Chinese official who was with me, but he shrugged his shoulders and said it was not possible to make thorns look like roses. "Look at their deeds," he proposed, striking a Confucian note.

I looked at their deeds, as presented by the Chinese Communists to their people, and saw photos of American merchandise in Japanese shops, illustrating how the United States used its trade with Japan to "dump unwanted items" (an amusing accusation viewed from the 1990s). A picture of a charred body was accompanied by the inscription, "A Japanese soldier was careless and spilled oil on himself. United States soldiers set him alight just for fun." A rational motivation underlay such lies. A China with few friends and many enemies hoped to drive a wedge between Japan and the United States.

I passed farther along the chamber of horrors, with a cluster of people at my elbow, furtively glancing at my face to detect my reactions. I looked at a picture of a starving child in Peru and bananas in Ecuador beneath the caption, "The United States is taking four thousand dollars a minute out of Latin America." Pictures showed protests against the United States in Iraq, Cuba, Cyprus, South Korea, Panama, and Lebanon. Others depicted "race riots" in Chicago, "where the class struggle is sharpening, as Negroes fight against fascist crimes." The first of an array of "crimes" of President Kennedy was that he had "encouraged a new bourgeoisie in socialist countries." I felt I had seen enough and returned to the Yang Cheng Hotel.

Adam Kellett-Long, the Reuters correspondent in Peking, had told me of the moment when news of Kennedy's death came. "It was a terrible day for us in China," he said. "The first we heard of it was a cable from London asking for a Chinese reaction as soon as possible. But there was absolutely nothing in the Chinese press. No facts about the tragedy. Nothing on the funeral. Just a couple of nasty cartoons. And people who knew of the assassination said things like, 'It's a good thing he's dead, because he was an evil man.'"

So I learned quite early that the Cultural Revolution of the later 1960s was by no means the birth of virulent anti-Americanism in Communist China. In Canton I wrote in my diary: "Two hundred million Chinese born since 1949 know nothing of Americans first-hand—their international awareness is being cultivated in the hothouse of extreme Marxism-Leninism-Maoism. In such a hothouse the seeds of hate could readily produce the evil fruit of war."

Yet for all my shock at Peking's anti-Americanism, I was at this time a crusader for diplomatic recognition of the Chinese government, a step resisted by the American, Australian, and other governments, and I wrote in my Canton diary these words: "From the side of the West, one can only be astonished at the continued American policy of isolating China—to the extent of refusing permission to United States citizens, including the late Eleanor Roosevelt and Averell Harriman, to go to China and cut through the cobwebs of cherished myths with a bit of ordinary human communication. Can ignorance benefit anyone? Can it possibly benefit us in the West whose cause is bound up with the irreducible nature of human freedom?"

Idealistic words perhaps, for I knew a little about the harsh realities of China's modern experience with the West. A large part of the Oriental History curriculum at Melbourne University dealt with the encroachment of the European powers into Asia, and I had read with excitement and some indignation about aggressive British merchants and gunboats in Canton and other cities of the China coast in the last century. "Treaty Port China" was just about the totality of China as the West then knew it, and the turbulence in Canton over opium trading and access to China had led to the Treaty of Nanking in 1842, which "opened" China to the West. I knew that both the British and the Americans had disregarded Chinese sensibilities in order to spur commerce. I embraced the guilt of the Western world for having bullied China.

The Western powers—not to speak of Japan—had certainly treated China badly at times from the Opium War of the 1840s through the 1940s. The British had indeed brought opium to Canton and set up public gardens in Shanghai from which Chinese and dogs (among other categories) were excluded. And a century later the United States had sided with Chiang Kai-shek against Mao's Communists in a civil war that left 3 million Chinese dead. But was revulsion and revenge a wise policy, and how long was it to go on?

Of course during the 1950s, the West, especially the United States in its frustration at having "lost China," dealt out to the Chinese Communists almost as much tight-lipped hostility and as many hyperbolic words as Peking directed at Washington. America and China seemed to bring out the worst in each other, as Mao cemented an alliance with Stalin, the Korean War broke out, the Taiwan Strait became one of the world's tensest zones, and the United States kept the PRC excluded from the UN and other international bodies. Washington-Peking relations could not have been nastier short of a declaration of war. By 1964 the United States had added to the historical reasons for the Chinese Communists to hold fast to a passionate anti-Westernism.

While in Canton, I saw on a reclaimed sandbank in the Pearl River the framework of Treaty Port Canton as it had existed in the nineteenth century. Here, after the Arrow War of 1856 produced one more defeat for the proud but weak Chinese, a point of contact was set up between the Qing dynasty and the West. Foreign business houses and consulates and clubs were erected as a bit of Europe away from Europe. On Pearl Island, as it now was called, I saw stately mansions, peaceful esplanades, rich foliage, and tennis courts and playing fields.

Through the imperialist years the sandbank had been forbidden to ordinary Chinese—because of their "stare and impertinence," according to one British government report[4]—but now the graceful old stone and brick buildings were being used as schools, offices, or workers' dormitories. One villa with paint peeling from its walls was headquarters for a Ping-Pong troupe, and another with rows of garments pegged out to dry on its balcony served as a girls' school.

The inequality and violence of Treaty Port Canton had gone, and so had the commerce and fun and mystery. I found echoes of a past and proof of a great social change, but no clue to the future direction of China. To the schoolgirls and ivory carvers and Ping-Pong stars, the sandbank was just one more slice of the metropolis of Canton, but in its regained Chineseness it seemed a symbol of everything the Chinese could be proud of in Mao's era; nothing in its blandness, everything in its Chineseness.

As a Westerner visiting Pearl Island I fell silent with my own thoughts before the carved gargoyles, stately sloped roofs, confident cornices, and huge trees lovingly transplanted from England. Independence at certain moments in the story of a nation or a person is of absolute importance. The subjugated nation that sees the last foreign troops leave its soil, the prisoner who comes out of jail, the adolescent who gains an income and control of his affairs, all have won riches, regardless of what they do with their freedom. But liberation does not guarantee that the new nation will flourish, or that the newly free person will use his freedom wisely. As I walked back into the city, I felt the hold of my tribe and a certain pride in what Europe had achieved on the China coast, and the gulf between China and the West seemed even wider than before.

China was becoming as anti-Soviet as it was anti-American, and in Peking at the Xin Qiao Hotel, the bar and restaurant, the billiard room, lobby, and post office all had free copies in eight or ten tongues of pamphlets like *On Khrushchev's Phony Communism and Its Historical Lessons for the World.* At a rally to express solidarity with North Vietnam, the Hanoi ambassador gave a speech that upbraided United States "aggression"; with each accusation the vast crowd applauded solidly. Then he attacked the Russians for not expressing immediate support for North Vietnam when the Gulf of Tonkin clashes occurred; the crowd roared its support.

Mao's view of the United States was not a highly informed one, but it was not a simpleminded view either. In 1912, the nineteen-year-old Mao, while browsing in the Changsha public library, came upon a map of the world and for the first time realized that China was but one nation among other nations. A vivid memory of his early reading was of opening a book called *Great Heroes of the World* and quoting excitedly to a friend a sentence about George Washington: "Victory and independence only came to the United States after eight long bitter years of fighting under Washington."[5]

Being imbued with the Middle Kingdom's ingrained pride and also a nationalist in the May Fourth tradition, Mao took it for granted that China was important to the United States. This brought him a surprise or two—as when President Truman, entering the Korean War, didn't realize how seriously Mao took America's intervention as a threat to China's interests in Korea.

Mao also saw the United States as one cause of the humiliation of China as it had encountered the West from the 1840s onward. This made him a natural anti-American, an emotion that intensified during the civil war against the Guomintang in the 1940s, when Washington supported Chiang Kai-shek against Mao. But Mao also viewed the United States as the leading exemplar of an economic success that he sought for China. In America's modernity, the Chinese Communist leader saw aspects of the future his revolution was designed to secure for China.

Mao's belief in Marxism, even though it would sag in his later years, also colored his view of the United States. Believing that imperialism would fall from overextension, and that socialism would everywhere in due course replace capitalism, just as capitalism had replaced feudalism, Mao found the Vietnam conflict proof that

American imperialism had feet of clay. Yet, because Mao's view of the United States was far from simpleminded, the vicissitudes of the American effort in Vietnam brought a generally unexpected phase in his view of Washington.

"The Americans are bastards," he once remarked in a typical moralization of a political issue, "but they are honest bastards. The Russians are not only bastards but liars."[6] There was also the consideration that the American bastards were richer and more technologically advanced than the Russian bastards, and so had more to offer China. Mao by 1964 had burned his bridges with Khrushchev, was no longer very worried about the United States, and already envisaged a phase of Sino-American cooperation.

The feud between China and Russia had turned into a battle of ideological insults, although in origin and meaning it was much more than that. Revolutions go through stages, surprising and deceptive stages, and the chimes of the Russian and Chinese socialist clocks simply lost their synchronization. Russia could afford the limited liberalization of "goulash communism," while China as yet could not, and for that reason the policy revisions of Khrushchev's Russia became a threat to Mao's China. Soviet withdrawal of aid turned Chinese irritation into Chinese fury, and soon national security issues would join the array of reasons for Peking to oppose Moscow. A couple of months after I left China, Khrushchev fell and Peking gloated at the news (which it had predicted).

The United States was not quick in responding to the opportunities offered by the Russia-China split, for many Americans stubbornly doubted its existence. Not to understand that Russian and Chinese Communists could fight bitterly between themselves over pride and power was a mistake possible only for idealists who failed to see that Leninism was 90 percent about power, and only 10 percent about ideas. Having received a practical education in Communist tactics in the Labor party in Melbourne, where Laborites and Communists struggled for control of trade unions, and having observed how Communists twisted words and ardently worshiped at the altar of power, I did not find it hard to credit that as their interests diverged Chinese and Russian Communists would come to despise each other.

Peking exploded its first atomic device in October 1964, and Mao shrewdly tailored his nuclear program to suit the available cloth, avoiding useless flourishes, keeping costs fairly low, making only a few weapons. "Six bombs will do," he would remark to André

Malraux in 1965.[7] The gist of his nuclear strategy was "Boost Chinese courage and scare the others," and it made sense for a poor but proud nation. But I found the Chinese reckless on the policy issues of peace and war. "Nuclear bombs cannot destroy China," the bespectacled young ideologue Shi said to me in Canton, "because bombs cannot reverse history."

China still had no sense of give and take within an international community faced with problems common to all humanity. I found absolutely no curiosity about the outside world among the Chinese I met. On any international topic in which they evinced interest— race relations in Chicago, the Australian Aborigines—they had a mind closed as tight as their base of information was small. No fact about the world existed for them unless it had been published in *People's Daily,* the Communist party newspaper.

It was only in 1861 that China had established a ministry of foreign affairs.[8] Before then its relations with the world were handled by an Office of Barbarian Affairs. It haunted me for years after my 1964 visit that the hundreds of millions of Chinese were still by a long measure the least internationally minded of all the major peoples. It was a proof of the power of shared Chineseness, even in the face of ideological antagonism, that when Peking exploded its first atomic bomb, crowds in Chiang Kai-shek's bastion of Taipei poured into the streets to proclaim their delight.

A straw in the wind of Chinese politics during the early 1960s was the emergence of Mao's wife, Jiang Qing, from total obscurity to a modest visibility, and the story was revealing of the modes of Chinese political struggle. Jiang Qing, before she met Mao, had been a stage and screen actress, but as Mao's wife she had given up her career and was unknown to the Chinese public. A year or so before I reached Peking, Madame Sukarno, wife of the Indonesian president, came to China and Liu Shaoqi as head of state was chief host. Tongues were set wagging when the dashing wife of Liu, Wang Guangmei, was also prominent during the meetings, and *People's Daily* carried a photo of Liu, Madame Wang, and Madame Sukarno together. The next day Mesdames Wang and Sukarno appeared together on the paper's front page, and on subsequent days, in an unprecedented exposure for a Chinese spouse, the wives of the two presidents often were seen in a joint photo.[9]

Jiang Qing's jealousy of Wang Guangmei harmonized sufficiently with Mao's dislike of Liu, and with his newfound need of Jiang's support, for a countermeasure to be forthcoming. Five days later

People's Daily ran on its front page a huge photo of Mao, Jiang Qing, and Madame Sukarno. A small picture of Liu, Madame Wang, and Sukarno was run on the second page. This was the way the tip of the iceberg of political conflict showed itself in the Mao years. Jiang's photo had never before appeared in *People's Daily*. For seven years even her name had hardly been mentioned in any Chinese newspaper. In all the years since 1949, no previous photo of her and Mao together had ever officially been released.

Just before I reached Peking in the summer of 1964, a festival of Chinese operas on contemporary themes took place, at which Jiang gave the first major speech of her political life. "Do you eat?" she cried to her audience of theater people, in a vigorous return to her former specialty in the performing arts. "That food came from the farmers. So *serve* the farmers in your plays and operas!"[10] Said Liu Shaoqi of Jiang's new politicized operas, "She is picking melons before they are ripe," and Deng Xiaoping was even blunter: "You just see a bunch of people running back and forth on the stage. Not a trace of art."[11]

Yet while in China I had no idea that debate over the political content of cultural works was a sign of imminent political struggle. "What we failed to see was how divided they were internally," Sir David Wilson later said of the years 1963–65 in Peking. "We were overly given to thinking there was a unified leadership, simply because that was the message put across incessantly [by the Chinese government]."

At the train station on the day of my departure from Canton, I looked out the carriage window and saw my driver from my days in the south pushing along the platform, seeking me out among the throng to say farewell. Just as the train pulled away he reached me and his two hands clasped mine. While the train chugged from ideologically charged Canton to a Hong Kong that seemed as commercial as a fairground, I wrote in my diary: "A certain mixture of sadness and relief that has come over me today brings to mind the cry of Richard Wright when he left the Communist party. 'I knew in my heart,' he said in *The God That Failed,* 'that I should never be able to feel with that simple sharpness about life, never again express such passionate hope, never again make so total a commitment of faith.' "[12]

If that sentiment later seemed overblown to me, leaving China in 1964 really was like coming out of a theater at the end of a performance. At the Hong Kong border, there were pictures of Queen

Elizabeth and notices warning against pickpockets. It was a Saturday afternoon and in Hong Kong it felt like one—in Canton each day had seemed the same—as men tore off their ties and couples headed for shops and cinemas and sporting fields. In China I had a fixed status as a visitor, but in Hong Kong I was an anonymous part of the crowd, battling along with the rest, not part of any pattern that I did not design for myself.

To my diary I entrusted a summary impression of China in 1964: "I felt a mixture of exhilaration, yet separation before the compulsive buoyancy [of China], with its naiveté and also its optimism. This society cannot be compared to our own because we have not known the desperate depths which China recently plumbed, and hence we cannot feel the unqualified assurance about the new that hundreds of millions of Chinese apparently feel. We look at an enthusiastic, still poor society as a grown man looks at an earnest youth, saying to ourselves that he will change."

Yet my too-emotional reaction did not prevent me from concluding that the logic of modernization would triumph over the doctrines of Marxism. Talking with Shi, the young ideologue in Canton, I had suggested that the historical function of Marxism was to be a lever for modernization, and that as modernity was approached Marxist fervor would abate. Shi looked at me with pity. "You always talk of Marxism's role being to help the modernization of a society," he complained, "but actually we are using it to build communism."

"The future doesn't belong to the reds," I predicted in a diary note after my chat with Shi, "it belongs to moderates" (yet I did not know if moderates existed in high places). And I sensed the problem of governance in China, which made the Communists obsessed with order. "When the pressure comes off here [in China], as it must some day," I wrote, swayed too much by religious concerns, "there will be chaos. With a grossly distorted image of the world, and without Christianity as a basis, there will be disorder as well as crisis." But I did not know how much of what Mao had done was deep and how much was reversible. After 1949 the power-holders and wealth-possessors of the pre-Communist period were knocked down, but had the ways of viewing power and wealth changed? And was the materialism of the Chinese people really canceled?

I had only nibbled at the edges of Chinese reality (even the resident foreigners felt they were doing little more). I later realized that the excitement of discovering a truly different society had made me too open-minded, and the feeling of being engaged in counteracting the stupidity of the nonacknowledgment of China had made me insufficiently skeptical of the Chinese Communist party. If I didn't know much about China yet, what I was learning excited me. Outside China I had seen pockets of Chinese society, but only in China could I behold the civilization in its power and its age-old setting. And only in China could I begin to grasp how heavily the Chinese as a race and a nation would weigh in a crowded world.

CHAPTER THREE

■

"LIGHT UP YOUR CIGARETTE REGARDLESS"

TO say "China" in the mid-1960s—more commonly "Communist China"—was to conjure up a pair of related unsettling images: of the Chinese masses as a bottomless pit of support for the Vietnamese Communists in their war to pull Saigon out of America's reach; and of Mao's unique revolution, with its communes, bristling ideology, hostility to the West, and Spartan ways as a sign of the rising power of the East.

In China ideology entwined itself around every outcrop of life and thought, even poetry, and it made for a novel kind of literary criticism that Mao himself was not only the fount of political power and rectitude but the most famous poet in the realm. Brows furrowed in 1964 when a very grand poem of Mao's called "Snow," written way back in 1936, was published for the first time in the PRC. The last line of "Snow" read: "For truly great men, look to this age alone." Mao wrote the poem just after the triumphant completion of the Long March, a retreat that had turned into a spiritual rebirth for Chinese communism. The first lines paid homage to the beauty of China's landscape. Then Mao went on to mention four of China's greatest emperors, from the Qin, Han, Tang, and Song dynasties, only to catalogue the shortcomings of each, and to declare: "All are past and gone!"[1]

The point of the publication of "Snow" in 1964, a quarter-century after Mao wrote it, was to signal the Communist party chairman's ambitious plans to cast aside his high-level enemies and jolt the

Chinese people into a re-embrace of lost revolutionary values. Mao in the mid-1960s disliked much of what he saw around him, and he was determined to pit his will against unacceptable reality. For a truly great man, Mao was hinting, one must look not to the emperors of Chinese history, but to a leader who could address China's current problems.

So alienated from the Peking political establishment had Mao become that he angrily refused to read the party's newspaper, *People's Daily*. Since Mao was the supreme leader and the object of an intense cult of personality, it seemed surprising that editorials of the early 1960s urged the Chinese to study Mao's *and* Liu Shaoqi's writings. Head of state Liu's little volume *How to Be a Good Communist* sold a staggering 15 million copies between its reissue in 1962 and 1966, exceeding in that period the sales of any work by Mao. Number two man Liu was by now one of Mao's many enemies—nearly all of them quite unaware of their perilously plummeting status in his eyes.

André Malraux, minister of culture in the French government, arrived at the Great Hall of the People one summer afternoon in 1965 to present a letter from President Charles de Gaulle to President Liu Shaoqi. In a reception room hung with traditional paintings, the austere organization man Liu stood with a group of his ministers, while to one side stood Mao by himself, looking, Malraux felt, like a bronze emperor. Malraux gave the parchment envelope to Liu, but before the Chinese head of state could say anything Mao took over, and throughout the entire afternoon Liu did not get a chance to speak a single word.

"You've been to Yan'an, I believe," Mao remarked to Malraux. "What is your impression?" It was a question that exposed the ache in Mao's spirit. Remote, sparse, dusty Yan'an, which was the Communist headquarters after the Long March, had been the cradle of Mao's Promethean reinvention of Marxism, and he felt this ideal had been stifled by Liu's and Deng's stress on the politics of order and the economics of results. Malraux, who had not lost the romanticism about China expressed in his 1920s novel *Man's Fate,* was eager to judge the new China a success, but Mao made restless, dissatisfied, nativist remarks. "Villagers so wretched that they ate bark," he said to his French visitor in recalling his wars against Chiang Kai-shek and Japan, "made better fighters than glib Shanghai chauffeurs." The revolution "cannot be simply the stabilization of victory," he declared, implying that the revolutionary values of the Yan'an era had been lost. "Neither the problem of industry nor that of agriculture has been solved," Mao said to the perplexed Malraux. "And the writers are often anti-Marxist."[2]

While Mao offered Malraux a gloomy analysis of China at mid-decade, his haughty treatment of Liu Shaoqi that afternoon showed a return of the ambitiousness that his poem "Snow" expressed. Soon he slipped out of Peking to visit Jinggangshan in the southeast, a sacred site of the revolution where the Communists in 1928–29 had learned how to turn weakness into strength, and there he wrote another poem. It offered an audacious self-confidence: "We can clasp the moon in the Ninth Heaven / And seize turtles deep down in the Five Seas."[3] Mao's explosive dual mood was about to plunge his country into a frenzy of disputation, destruction, and diversion from the daily round of economic activity that China and the world would come to know by the unlikely appellation "Cultural Revolution."

It would be seven years before I was able to secure a visa for a return to China. During this second half of the 1960s, I observed and felt the seismic jolts of Mao's great convulsion from vantage points in Vietnam, Boston, Hong Kong, and Eastern Europe. In 1965, obsessed with the Vietnam War, I went to Saigon, the front line of resistance to Asian communism with its presumed headquarters in Peking, where a crumbling regime reminded Asia hands of the last years of Chiang Kai-shek in China. The same year, wanting to get away from Australia for a while and study the Chinese language and the Chinese Revolution, as well as the theory of social democracy, I began a Ph.D. in political science at Harvard, and from the classrooms and leafy streets of Cambridge, Massachusetts, I watched the Maoist upheaval through the prism of America's own youth rebellion of the late 1960s. I spent the summer of 1967 in the British colony of Hong Kong, where China's upheaval spilled over, like an opera performance gone crazy, out of the amphitheater and into the street beyond. And on visits to Poland and Czechoslovakia in 1968 and 1969, I marveled at the differences between Mao's increasingly idiosyncratic communism and the stability-minded communism of Leonid Brezhnev's sullen gray Communist bloc.

In the fall of 1965 Mao walked into a Shanghai reception room, with his wife Jiang Qing at his side, for a luncheon party to celebrate the eightieth birthday of Anna Louise Strong, an American journalist long resident in China. He stood and peered at bamboo carvings on a wall, oblivious to the guests, and equally so to his wife, all of whom stood in silence waiting for him to speak. Mao's words were as enigmatic as his entry into the party. He said his doctors had told him to give up smoking, then he lit a cigarette and invited other smokers at the luncheon to follow his example. Noticing that smokers were in a minority, he said to them, "Don't be worried by that. Light up your cigarette regardless."[4]

Mao had come to Shanghai from a Peking that displeased him in order to supervise the editing of an article of devastating theater criticism that was the first shot of the Cultural Revolution. The play reviewed, *Hai Rui Dismissed from Office,* was about a worthy minister in the Ming dynasty (1368–1644) who was fired by the emperor for being too critical. It was not a new play and it had been praised in Peking and elsewhere. But Mao's chosen scribe, local journalist Yao Wenyuan, recruited for the job by Jiang Qing, attacked the play as politically lax and anti-Mao.[5]

In a minority, but going ahead with an action regardless, was precisely Mao's own situation. And maintaining long silences, which kept everyone guessing (especially colleagues in Peking), was a favorite mode as he prepared to destabilize China. He spent six months out of Peking starting in September 1965, most of the time with Jiang Qing, and for five of those six months the Chinese public was given no clue as to his activities.

Behind the scenes, Mao was summoning the People's Liberation Army (PLA) to support a revived extreme left-wing line and help provide political theatrics to mobilize people to support that line. The defense minister during this period was the fawning Lin Biao, a brilliant general but a slippery politician. In the late 1950s, Lin's predecessor as defense minister, the candid Peng Dehuai (like Hai Rui, a "worthy minister" who became too critical) had spoken up to Mao on the folly of the Great Leap Forward, and eventually he paid the price of dismissal for that. In the 1960s Defense Minister Lin, aiming to succeed Mao, flattered his chief. He declared the military "a great school of Mao Zedong's Thought," and his officers formed choirs to *sing* Mao's Thought. It also happened that Lin was not opposed to Mao's hostility to Russia, as his predecessor Peng had been, and as Liu Shaoqi was.

Mao, in his view of historical change, had long given almost as much weight to the "superstructure," as Marx called the realm of ideas, as to Marx's "base," the forces of production. Conscious

ideas, Mao believed, determined how people behaved. Such philosophical idealism was more common among Chinese Communists
than among European, probably because of Confucianism's residual
influence on Chinese minds, yet Mao stressed will far more than did
Liu or Deng. "If we do our work on men well," he observed, "we
shall have things in addition."[6] Deng thought pretty much the opposite; if people had material goods, the pragmatic party general
secretary felt, they would be happy and maybe good as well.

It was a coincidence of great import that Jiang Qing was both a
specialist in the performing arts and a resurgent figure within the
Mao court. Jiang was born in 1914 in Shandong Province to a violent
father and a mother who combined domestic service with prostitution. Given to fantasy, she studied music and drama and married a
young businessman who was entranced with her acting in a school
play. Soon politics intruded when in the German-influenced port of
Qingdao she fell in love with a young Communist. After this second
(de facto) husband was arrested, she moved to Shanghai in 1933 and
began a stage and screen career. She played a memorable Nora in
Ibsen's *A Doll's House,* starred in a tear-jerking movie called *Old
Bachelor Wang,* and in 1936 married Tang Na, a romantic theater
critic who held the leftist political views that were de rigueur in
Bohemian circles at the time.

After Japan's attack on Shanghai broke up the city's film industry,
Jiang took the bold step of journeying to the Communist headquarters in remote Yan'an. Her beauty and personality won Mao, who
divorced his existing wife to marry her in 1938. The union—effectively the fourth for Jiang and Mao alike—was controversial because
the woman he divorced was a Long March heroine and some senior
party stalwarts felt Jiang was pushy. Mao's colleagues—in those
days his near-equals—gave their blessing to his divorce and remar-
riage only on condition that his new wife, Jiang, should remain a
housewife, keeping her pretty face and acid tongue out of affairs of
state.

By the mid-1960s all that was history. Jiang Qing was eager for a
role on the political stage, and a beleaguered Mao needed her rough-
hewn talents more than at any time since the first years of their
twenty-seven-year-long relationship. Within the hothouse of Mao's
court, Jiang came to make an identification between the revived
Maoist cause and the impulses of her own personality. Her rebellious
temperament she transmogrified into an expression of "class revolt"

by "workers" against "capitalists." Mao and Jiang were about to become one of the most arbitrarily powerful husband-and-wife ruling teams any major nation has ever known.

The first task was to attack "old" and "bourgeois" cultural manifestations, and it was a sign of the link in Mao's mind between the army and the cultural realm that Jiang in 1966 was named adviser on the arts to the PLA. Soon Chinese theatrical stages were thick with warriors, and Chinese operas resembled a *Liberation Army Daily* editorial set to the music of Tchaikovsky. The purpose of Mao's attack on *Hai Rui Dismissed from Office* was political. Its author was not only a playwright but vice-mayor of Peking, and a secondary object of attacking the play was to unhorse the mayor of Peking, Peng Zhen, one of many senior officials who in Mao's view had come to regard the winning of political power as an end in itself. Such Communists, who had strayed from the revolutionary values of the Yan'an era, were the Cultural Revolution's first human target. Once a senior official was criticized, a green light was on for a witch hunt against middle-level officials, and a ripple-down effect eventually hit junior officials and ordinary folk. Willy-nilly, the green light to lambast someone as "capitalist" allowed people at all levels to express pent-up grievances about work situations, neighborhood affairs, or even tangled love affairs.

Distrusting much in the adult world, Mao turned to youth as "pure." He closed the schools and told young people to become "Red Guards" and roam the land and "rebel." Just at this time, young people in the West were also rebelling and I found myself in the midst of the anti–Vietnam War movement at Harvard. It was a time of wrenching feuds over East Asia policies, quickly sprouting student politicians, proliferating committee meetings, tense demonstrations almost every week, and occasional riots and bombs. Out of fury with Washington's policies in Vietnam and other parts of East Asia, liberal professors and students gave China the benefit of any doubt.* For young people in revolt against the authorities above them, the entrenched hostility within America to Communist China was itself enough to make them want to hear only good things about

---

* In eighteen months during 1967–68 a single firm, China Books and Periodicals in San Francisco, sold 250,000 copies within the United States of Mao's *Quotations* (Henry Noyes, *China Born: Memoirs of a Westerner,* London: Peter Owen, 1989, p. 82).

China. And it was a tendency of the time, at least in Cambridge, for people in search of alternative forms of society to look hopefully to China's unique socialism.

There seemed to be a symbiosis—with Vietnam as a common ingredient—between the mood of the 1960s in the United States, Western Europe, and China. Dimly I wondered if there could be a similarity of impulse between the idealism of the newly established Peace Corps and the apparent idealism and zeal to learn from the grass roots of the Chinese Red Guards and professors who were "going to the countryside."

But it was hardly so, for in China a political pathology made puppets of the citizenry. A collective emotion descended upon society, and buses moving along Chang An Avenue, on reaching the gates to the Zhongnanhai compound where Mao lived and worked, stopped and passengers rose to their feet and sang the political anthem, "The East Is Red." In the lanes beyond Tiananmen Square, artists, infected with the unispeak of the time, signed their paintings, not with their own names, or any name, but with the phrase, "Ten Thousand Years to Chairman Mao." Everyone had to be ideologically "remolded." Even the horses from a Shanghai circus were sent to a commune to be remolded. The commune was next to a military barracks, and each time the PLA trumpets sounded, the horses stopped ploughing and performed a few steps of a waltz, mindful of their former profession.[7]

Gao Yuan, a high school student in Hebei Province who became a Red Guard, recalled in *Born Red,* a memoir written after he had left China for the United States, the sudden pressure to "revolutionize daily life," and the trivialization it produced. "When you got out of bed in the morning," he said, "instead of saying, 'Let's get up,' you said, 'Carry the revolution through to the end.' When you went to bed, you said, 'Never forget class struggle.' People greeted each other with 'Serve the people.' If you bought anything, be it a movie ticket, pencil, or bottle of soy sauce, you had to initiate the transaction with a quotation [from Mao]."[8] Mere words to a high school pupil turned into terror for anyone who became a target of the Cultural Revolution's drive to root out the "bourgeoisie."

Tang Mingzhao, a veteran journalist who had worked for a Chinese newspaper in New York in the 1940s, and returned to Peking after Liberation in high hopes for the new China, recalled to me a few years later in Peking what it was like to be on the receiving end of criticism from Red Guards for links with America and a "humanistic" outlook. "Being criticized was like having mirrors held all around you," said this lively Cantonese who later became undersecretary of the United Nations. "You had an image of what your face was like, but you didn't know what you looked like from odd angles. Then, when Red Guards grilled you, you learned."

Occasionally, some of the madness seemed a shade less mad when viewed through the lens of the Chinese language. The Red Guards' incessant cry, "Long Live Chairman Mao," was a little more interesting when one knew that the phrase used for "long live," *wan sui* (literally "ten thousand years"), was an ancient one, used by citizens in saluting the emperor. The Japanese used the same two characters, pronouncing them *banzai,* in saluting Emperor Hirohito during World War II.

Most of the few foreign journalists who remained in China during the Cultural Revolution were from the Communist bloc or from Japan, and one of the most interesting of them was Branko Bogunovic of the Yugoslav agency Tanjug. He was a bright, doctrineless man, cheerful in his acceptance that little can be done about the follies of the powerful. Near the lane where he lived in Peking, Bogunovic watched a Russian military attaché besieged by Red Guards for four hours. They insulted him, jostled him, and held a picture of Mao within inches of his face the whole time. "Afterward," Bogunovic told me over dinner in Cambridge, "this man, a hero of Stalingrad, wept like a child."

"Parents were afraid of their children," he went on, recalling the case of his own elderly servant whose three daughters became militant Red Guards and reviled their mother. From a Communist country where the police were powerful, Bogunovic found the ne plus ultra of rebellion in a scene at the police ministry building in Peking. "There was a banner with the minister's name, Xie Fuzhi, followed by an X," he recalled. "When I saw that, I began to doubt if mankind had a future." The X was written by Red Guards as a kind of "pointing of the bone," a threatening attack meant to signal Xie's doom. The police minister survived that immediate death wish, but died in mysterious circumstances a few years later.

How far out on a limb Mao put himself in relation to his colleagues by stirring up this political frenzy was revealed when the Japanese Communist chief Kenji Miyamoto came to China early in 1966. The Japanese Communists, along with Liu and Deng, feared a large America-provoked war in East Asia, and they came to China to argue for "joint action" (a concept espoused by Liu) between Russia and China—and other Communists—to support Vietnam and deter America. In Peking, Miyamoto worked out a communiqué with Deng and other Chinese leaders that went part of the way toward the "joint action" position. Meanwhile Mao was resting and brooding at a hot spring resort enclosed by bamboo groves near Canton.

Unexpectedly, Mao sent word to Peking that he wanted to see Miyamoto, and Deng and other Chinese leaders dutifully came south with the Japanese for the audience. In front of Miyamoto, Mao blazed at his top colleagues: "You weak-kneed people in Peking!"[9] The Japanese Communists cringed in astonishment at the scene. Mao said the communiqué must call for a united front against both American imperialism and Soviet revisionism. Miyamoto would not agree, so the Peking draft communiqué was torn up and no communiqué was issued. Before Miyamoto and his colleagues left Canton, Mao went on to amaze and distress them by urging the Japanese Communist party to put arms directly into the hands of the Japanese people and prepare for "people's war."

The Vietnam War was indeed tearing apart the political fabric of a number of nations. Before leaving Australia for Harvard in September 1965, I found out how tense Chinese-American relations had become when the American consulate in Melbourne denied me a United States visa, on the grounds that I opposed the Vietnam War and favored recognition of the Peking government. "Your views are incompatible with the American national purpose," wrote consul Lin Roork in rejecting my application, as precise as a doctor telling me I belonged to the wrong blood group. I eventually obtained an American visa, thanks to an intervention by the leader of the Australian Labor party with the American ambassador in Canberra, but Consul Roork's political moralizing made me wonder if China and the United States were not similar in being highly ideological civilizations; at least America sounded that way whenever the topics of Vietnam or Communist China were in the air.

As arguments over the Vietnam War raged in the West, two issues stood out. Was the National Liberation Front, the Communist force in South Vietnam, a mere arm of Hanoi, or was it an indigenous southern movement that would, upon military victory, build a separate regime in Saigon? And was Hanoi, in turn, part of an "Oriental red chain of command" (a phrase used by Vice-President Hubert Humphrey)[10] that stemmed from Peking? On the answers to these questions hinged one's view of American policy in East Asia, and one's view of the impact of the Chinese Revolution on Asia. In 1965 I went to Saigon to find my own answers.

Saigon was still a leafy, stylish place, despite an ominous and decaying air, a stronger candidate for the impossible accolade "Paris of the East" than the usual choice, Shanghai. But I sensed a regime near the end of its span. "Saigon is like China must have been before the Communists took over," I wrote in a letter to Bob Holt, a Melbourne friend who was president of the Labor party in the state of Victoria, "demoralized, without a purpose any bigger than anti-communism, corrupt beyond description, dominated by generals squabbling for power, a school of idleness and vice." American diplomat Peter Tarnoff, later president of the Council on Foreign Relations in New York, said of his ambassador over a French lunch: "When [Henry Cabot] Lodge came back to Saigon, I met him at the airport, and he said it was good to be back because here he would have power. In America, he said, he had missed out on power, but in Saigon he will effectively be vice-president of South Vietnam." The remark called to mind the presumptions of such American envoys to China during the 1940s as General Albert Wedemeyer and Ambassador Patrick Hurley, and I felt Washington was making the same mistakes in Vietnam that had lead to the "loss" of China.

Over the next few weeks I arrived at answers to the two questions that had enticed me to Saigon. "The VC [National Liberation Front] are not independent of North Vietnam," diplomat Peter Tarnoff told me. "That issue is now dead; anyone who wants to raise it is refusing to discuss Vietnam seriously." I concluded that Tarnoff was right. The war was Hanoi's war, and if Hanoi won it, Vietnam would be a single entity ruled from Hanoi. My second conclusion surprised me more than the first. There was no Oriental red chain of command from Peking to Hanoi, I realized, and no link existed between the Vietnam War and the prospects of "people's war" in Japan or virtually anywhere else. Hearing the Chinese froth about solidarity with Vietnam in Mao's China had in no way prepared me to hear in Saigon of deep Vietnamese resentment at one thousand years of Chinese bullying of Vietnam, or to hear Vietnamese criticism of Chinese as materialistic and antiforeign. It seemed that Mao was wrong to see the war as a clue to the prospects for social revolution all over Asia and beyond.

Although I saw that Hanoi and the National Liberation Front were essentially one, I remained critical of Western actions in Vietnam on broader grounds. "Having once been isolationist," I said of the Americans in a letter to Tony Staley, an Australian classmate who was later a conservative cabinet minister, "they now have sprung to the opposite extreme, and think they ought to control much of the world. It involves them in a very vulgar replacement of other nations' wishes and interests by their own. They cannot seem to break through to mutuality in their international relations." I felt the point applied both to Vietnam policy and to China policy. I feared the war could one day involve China and once more produce, as in the Chinese civil war of the 1940s, and again in Korea in the 1950s, a confrontation between Washington and Mao's Communists.

The anticolonial syndrome still had immense power over my mind. I saw the Americans "trampling" on Saigon, just as the British had trampled upon Canton at the time of the Opium Wars, and such a syndrome impelled me to give the benefit of the doubt to the society being trampled upon. Saigon and Canton even had some visual traits in common, each surrounded by lush fields of brilliant green under the glare of a tropical sun, each hunched upon a muddy river alive with a hundred kinds of boats. "The Saigon River has more motorized craft than the Pearl River," I noted in my diary, "and the street scenes of Saigon are more modernized than those of Canton. It is the difference between an Asia prospering in the arms of the West [Saigon], and an Asia poor and independent [Canton]."

I felt the South Vietnam regime would lose as the Chinese Nationalists had lost, because of an involuntary forfeiting of the nationalism issue to the Communists, and because of a lack of a social purpose that could match communism in its appeal as a faith. Saigon seemed a "heap of loose sand," as prerevolutionary China was described by Sun Yat-sen, and I did not think such an incoherent social order would last.

In Peking, Mao linked Vietnam with his Cultural Revolution by the discovery of an alleged common international and domestic "class enemy." He extolled warrior virtues, made of politics a branch of warfare, and held up "bourgeois culture" as a target for political attack. In the process, by the end of 1966 the "Great Helmsman," as Mao was often called during the Cultural Revolution, had set in motion the purge of half the Chinese Politburo.

"He is China's Khrushchev!" cried a Red Guard with gleaming eyes and a sweating face at a Peking rally in 1966. "Down with the revisionist, down with China's Khrushchev!" The beleaguered Liu Shaoqi stood gray and bent before an angry crowd. Mao had been obsessed for a decade by the turbulence inside the Communist bloc, in particular by Khrushchev's criticism of Stalin in 1956, the ensuing eruptions in Poland and Hungary, and the danger to his own rule in China of these European precedents. By the mid-1960s, an enemy of Mao's was almost by definition a Khrushchevite. "In launching the Cultural Revolution," the dissident essayist Wang Ruoshui later said to me, "Mao had the shadow of Khrushchev in his mind." It was true.

The word "revisionism" was the linguistic whore of Communist history; it meant everything and it meant nothing. For Mao, revisionism originated as the term for Khrushchev's unacceptable departure from Stalinism, but later became a label for any political idea that at a given moment he did not agree with. "Mao was worried that after his death he'd be dethroned," explained Wang Ruoshui, who as a senior editor of People's Daily was privy to such inside information. "He felt Stalin's biggest mistake was not having forestalled Khrushchev. In China, revisionism had only to do with this fear of Mao's about his personal image." A "revisionist" simply was anyone who dared to criticize Mao, or could be accused of doing so.

Mao did not esteem the post-Stalin Soviet leaders, and in a post-Stalin world he felt that he, not Stalin's successors in Moscow, was the paramount Communist figure. When the "little red book" of Quotations from Chairman Mao appeared in 1966, the foreword by Defense Minister Lin Biao began tellingly: "Comrade Mao Zedong is the greatest Marxist-Leninist of our era."[11] At the same time Mao believed deeply in the Soviet Revolution of 1917 as a foundation stone of socialism, and he kept a shrewd eye on his future prestige as a revolutionary. If Stalin could be rudely cast down from greatness by upstart Khrushchev, Mao, who was China's Stalin as well as China's Lenin, might face a similar downgrading at the hands of Liu, Deng, and other colleagues. In particular, Mao feared Liu and Deng could do a "de-Stalinization" on him for the folly of his Great Leap Forward.

Thus, Mao developed a distrust for anyone who became an obvious number two figure, especially if the deputy began to imagine himself one day becoming number one. Liu Shaoqi did think Mao should consider retiring, and in the 1960s Liu was next in line to become chairman of the Communist party. The Cultural Revolution was in part Mao's reassertion of his claim to indefinite continuance as number one in the face of Liu's ambition and growing prestige. Against the charges of being a "capitalist roader" and a "revisionist," the dignified Liu made only modest resistance, seeking, in line with his fidelity to the Communist party's organizational procedures, to summon a meeting of the Central Committee to review the Cultural Revolution! In 1967 he was dismissed from all his posts and put under detention; two years later he died of pneumonia, heartbreak, and ill-treatment.

At first Deng Xiaoping, the secretary general of the party, sought to go along with Mao's wildly leftist line, distancing himself from President Liu. This tactic worked only for a while and soon he, too, came under criticism as "that other top party person in authority taking the capitalist road." [12] Although in private Deng contemptuously called the Red Guards "babies," in public he tried to save himself with an abject confession. "I have shown myself to be an unregenerate, middle-class bourgeois," he croaked in a closed-doors speech of October 1966, "a man whose world view is not yet transformed, who has not yet scaled the heights of socialism." Deng's twisting and turning did not save him, and at a Red Guard rally in August 1967, he was finally denounced ("Cook the dog's head in boiling oil," the crowd cried), and soon afterward dispatched to do manual labor in Jiangxi Province. [13]

The sharp change from the apparent political calm of Peking in 1964 to the political ructions of 1966–67 taught me a lesson about the false facade of stability of a Communist state. The messy and very public way in which democracies aired and corrected their problems could give the appearance of instability, but in reality that process made for stability. The real instability lay in dictatorship's rigidity, secrecy, and repression of opinion, for without freedom, change could only come through bullet, coup, or dictator's whim.

There was pathos as well as political infighting in the events of the late 1960s. Liu said he simply did not understand what the Cultural Revolution was all about, and Foreign Minister Chen Yi, also a longtime associate of Mao's, said: "I have always told comrades who were close to me that if I were to lead the Cultural Revolution, there would be no Cultural Revolution." [14] The foreign minister, who had given fiery speeches against "American aggression" in Vietnam during my 1964 visit to Peking, was locked up by Red Guards and lost twenty-seven pounds in weight. The most Mao did to defend Chen Yi was to murmur, "I cannot show him to foreign guests in this condition." [15]

Zhou Enlai went along with Mao and his Cultural Revolution and weathered the storm. Born in 1898 to a prosperous family rooted in

Zhejiang Province on the southeast coast, Zhou had studied and agitated for the leftist cause in Japan and France and joined the Communist party in 1924. The choirboylike portraits of Zhou that I found on sale in bookshops in 1964 had seascape backdrops, while those of Mao had backdrops of hills and fields. The variation correctly hinted at the difference between a cosmopolitan and a nativist. A specialist on military strategy during the turbulent early 1930s, Zhou was at that time a coequal of Mao's. But after 1935, when Mao during the Long March emerged as philosophical and organizational leader of the rustic Communist movement, Zhou never mounted a frontal challenge to his authority.

Zhou became premier when the PRC was founded in 1949 and had remained so ever since (foreign minister as well until 1958). He stuck to the role of stage manager for whatever production Mao sought to mount in any given season. When the turmoil of the Cultural Revolution hit, Zhou was well placed to orchestrate, moderate, and survive. Generally avoiding intrigue, not getting too deeply into questions of theory, he allowed himself to denounce Liu and Deng as "capitalist roaders" and swallowed the apparent rise of Defense Minister Lin Biao to be the new number two to Mao.

In the spring of the tumultuous year of 1968, I found myself in Prague to write about Alexander Dubcek's "New Course" reforms for *The New Republic*. Prague exhibited a cynicism about Marxism that did not yet exist in China, and the Czechs considered Mao's China distant and strange. When I heard China dismissed as a far-off curiosity, naive in its socialist extremism, I actually felt my sympathy for China rise a notch. Czechs spoke darkly of "Eurasian" Marxism. They felt that the farther east you went, the less progress and culture you would find. "Remember Stalin was not a European," sniffed a Prague editor in a reference to the dictator's Georgian origin. How could "Eurasian" socialism sit smoothly on Czechoslovakia, a pretty brooch on Europe's bosom? As for the Chinese Communists, in Czech eyes they were worse than Stalin.

The dictatorship of the proletariat was as ill-fitting in Czechoslovakia, with its strong middle class and democratic traditions, as was Mao's "down-with-all" Cultural Revolution in China, with its respect for tradition and the family. In Prague I saw an attempt at "political reform" in a Marxist state (as it would later be talked about in the China of Deng Xiaoping, but never implemented). Dubcek felt Lenin and even Marx had thrown little light on the problem of the political system in a post–class struggle society. What kind of political system would follow the dictatorship of the proletariat? According to Marx and Lenin, the state would begin to "wither away," but no one expected that, so Dubcek was treading on virgin soil.

In an authoritarian state, you cannot do much to change your government, but the government does not do much to change you either—unlike a totalitarian state, where no realm of life is truly private. Under Dubcek, totalitarianism at least was replaced by authoritarianism; he cut back the scope of the Communist party's dominance. Visiting a magazine's offices, I looked into the censors' room and saw them with their feet on their desks reading comics. "They have nothing to do," an editor said with a smile. The press began to reflect the real life of society. The Czechoslovakian Boy Scouts, long forbidden, reappeared. "We begin to see that socialism as interpreted here in the past," said an editor of *Literarny Listy,* the magazine of the writers' union, "is not an aim in itself. Freedom is the more ultimate aim."

"The Czechoslovakian progressives," I wrote in my diary of Dubcek's circle, "are in the process of qualifying Lenin's communism as much as John Stuart Mill and William Beveridge qualified Adam Smith's capitalism." A real opposition party had not yet emerged (as it would in Poland twenty years later), but I believed that would happen, for Dubcek was taking the first steps toward a democratic political system while trying to cling to a Marxist economy. Visiting a Czechoslovakia that the Chinese Communists called "revisionist" suggested to me that the Cultural Revolution in China was not about the flowers of socialism and could only be about power and personality.

The sculptor Auguste Rodin called Prague the "Rome of the north" for its seven hills, and on an April afternoon in 1968, I climbed the one topped by Hradcany Castle, on a path winding by churches and courtyards, the Vltava River flowing silently behind me. I was overwhelmed by the beauty of peach and pear blossoms in the sunshine. Moments later, having descended, I was in a gloomy alley and the blossoms were gone and the chill of still-damp stone walls made spring seem like winter again. Four months later in August 1968, against my expectation, Moscow invaded Prague and put an end to Dubcek's New Course. Soon it was as if the blossoms of the Prague spring had never been.

The Czechoslovakian crisis of 1968 affected Mao's view of Russia in a way momentous for ties between China and the West. If "the

new czars" in Moscow could invade Prague to "rescue" Czech socialism, Mao reasoned, maybe they would again fish in the troubled
waters of China and seek out a "pro-Soviet" faction in Peking to
support with Soviet forces. Mao's chosen adversary of the late
1960s, Liu Shaoqi, had felt "joint action" between China and Russia
should be mounted to counter America in Vietnam. But Mao was
already looking beyond Vietnam, and he saw the Russian intervention in Czechoslovakia as a signpost to a future in which Moscow
would be his biggest headache.

Mao, although irrationally anti-Dubcek, made one acute observation on the Czechoslovakian crisis when he pointed out that
American-Soviet relations were not damaged by Moscow's invasion. So the world learned that an issue of peace and war could
produce one alignment of international forces, and an issue of justice
within societies could produce a quite different alignment.

China's problems were Gargantuan, and the Chinese Communists
as yet had spent less than two decades tackling them, compared with
five decades of Communist rule in Russia. Perhaps Mao in his Cultural Revolution was being more honest about the unsolved problems of socialism than were the stability-minded Russians? At the
time I felt it was possible. From afar, in the face of bizarre events, I
tended to give China some benefit of the doubt because it was a
great civilization that could be expected to conduct itself with at least
a minimum of wisdom and rationality, and because the Vietnam
War and Peking's exclusion from the international community
seemed to put China in an aggrieved position.

But we students of China at Harvard saw the Cultural Revolution
through a glass darkly, as the Vietnam War preoccupied us and
access to China was minimal. There were virtually no Americans on
the spot in China to observe the telling local detail. Few non–Communist bloc journalists other than the Japanese got inside the issues
of the Cultural Revolution. My letters to clergyman Zhao Fusan and
other acquaintances from 1964 sank into China without a trace.

I learned much about China at Harvard, from John King Fairbank,
who stressed the wrongness of assuming the Chinese were just like
us and interpreted modern Chinese history in terms of the impact
on China of superior Western power, and also from the former
China diplomat John Carter Vincent (in whose house I rented a
room). After Washington "lost China" to Mao's Communists, Vincent had been dismissed from the foreign service by Secretary of
State John Foster Dulles in 1953. In the 1960s, the Vietnam War and

the international problem of China's isolation were, in Vincent's view, the urgent features of the China issue. And I learned from Samuel Huntington, who said of Mao's Communists: "Surely one of the most outstanding achievements of the mid–twentieth century was the establishment in China in 1949 for the first time in a hundred years of a government really able to govern China."[16]

Yet at Harvard I did not learn to understand the Cultural Revolution. I focused mainly on China's international position and was not open to accept the pathology of Mao's actions. China's upheaval in 1966–67 could not be explained by the "impact of the West" approach of Professor Fairbank, by China's reaction to the Vietnam War, which preoccupied Vincent, or by the "political order" theories of Professor Huntington—nor yet from any comparison between Chinese utopianism and my own Christian quest for a "new man." All of these approaches underestimated the role of the personal drama of Mao and Jiang Qing in the Cultural Revolution, as well as taking insufficient account of Chinese stoicism, fatalism, and collectivism. The key to the upheaval was to be found in the age-old ways of Chinese culture, in harness with the ways of Communist dictatorship, and in Mao's personal quest for untrammeled power and the phantom of perfect socialism—all far removed from Western experience and from our agony over Vietnam.

CHAPTER FOUR

■

FROM MARXIST TO MONKEY KING

FOR lean, tall, bespectacled Yang Bingzhang, who came from Shandong Province to study at Peking University in 1964, the Cultural Revolution was an exciting opportunity to express the Marxism he had been studying in class. It became Yang's task as a Red Guard to write periodic reports to the central authorities on the turbulent situation at the university, where a series of witch hunts fueled by "class struggle" was uncovering "enemies" behind every bush. Yang felt himself to be in an epic battle between darkness and light and saw communism drawing closer each day. In his enthusiasm, he wrote a report in July 1966 addressed to Mao that among other things criticized Jiang Qing for failing to understand socialist theory. He took a bus to the reception office of the headquarters of the Communist party and told the desk clerk he had a six-page letter for Chairman Mao.

To Yang's surprise Jiang Qing, who had visited Peking University the previous day and addressed a small group of which he was a member, hearing of his arrival with a letter for Mao, said she would see him. "I hadn't asked to see Jiang Qing," Yang lamely told a friend later. Within a week after Jiang read Yang's letter, her largesse in receiving an ardent young Red Guard turned to fury. Yang was put in prison.

"It was lonely," he told me years later, as we traveled by train in southwest China, of his fifteen months of incarceration. "I was the only person in a room meant for four people. I learned to play chess with myself, using dirt and soap to make a black and white chess board on the floor of the cell." Later Yang was given a cellmate. "He was a high school senior from Hubei Province," Yang said, "and his crime had been to put up a poster in Xidan [a section of Peking] saying that Lin Biao, despite appearances, was not a loyal supporter of Mao. This young man played chess with me." Yang also advanced his knowledge of Russian while in prison. "I had only one book in my cell," he said, "Mao's *Works*. With my knowledge of Russian from two years of courses at Peking University, I roughly translated Mao's writings from Chinese into Russian, using a cut open toothpaste tube as a pencil."

The leftism that Mao promoted in 1966 had broken itself on the rock of factionalism, and during 1967 he appealed to the army to restore law and order, turning the sword against rebellious youth whose innocent passion had so recently inspired him. Soon leftists were being arrested as a gardener might pluck away withered blooms. Yang Bingzhang and millions of others experienced a souring of idealism, a puzzlement at doctrinal hair splitting, and an ensuing uphill struggle to align private values with a public realm that no longer seemed appealing or even rational.

One day early in 1967 Yang was taken from his cell "to meet the masses" at his campus, Peking University. In a reception room, he was pushed down in the painful, bending "jet plane" position, arms yanked high behind him, head thrust forward toward the floor, as students and teachers and staff built up political credit for themselves by denouncing him. "It was agonizing," he recalled as he puffed on a cigarette, "and I was on the verge of fainting. I begged them to let me straighten up, or lie on the floor. I said I would listen to all the attacks, but I couldn't bear this 'jet plane.' " His fellow members of China's premier university, formerly intelligent and friendly folk but now behaving like zealots, did not agree, and after hours of "jet plane" treatment, the crowd trampled upon Yang and he lost consciousness. "The guards from the prison truck rescued me," he said softly, "put me on the back of the vehicle, and drove me home to prison. I was so glad to be back in my cell!"

Around this same time, three female students from Yang's campus, indignant at the news that an ex-landlord was living in their neighborhood, rushed off to confront him. They burst through the front door of the old man's home, in the lawless manner sanctioned by the Cultural Revolution, and screeched that the landlord had been a bad element since birth, and that he was opposing Chairman Mao.

This particular old man had seen enough, and he had had enough. He came out of his kitchen bearing a carving knife, and mustering a strength almost beyond his capacity, he lunged at the first student and stabbed her to death. He had time also to kill a second before he was captured. Two days later the old man was stood against a wall and shot.

Such was the atmosphere of fear and despair that suicide vied with murder as the chief cause of death in the summer of 1967, and the capital's crematoria could not cope with the corpses. Some people who were too poor to buy poison sprang in front of trains to end their lives. It was just as bad in many other cities of China. Photos from the southern province of Guangdong showed female Red Guards carrying baskets filled with the cut-off ears and noses of men from factions opposed to their own. In Tibet, boiling water was poured on "class enemies" to make them confess, some were crucified, and "feudal" Buddhist monks were forced to copulate publicly with nuns.[1]

Coping with loss of faith in the Communist party was not a simple matter for Yang Bingzhang. "After I came out of prison I had lost much hope," he said. "I decided to write a critical book about the party and the arrogant authorities, and to send it to Chairman Mao. A strange thing!" he said of his own action. "It seems like what a mad person would do." Yang in general now adopted the opposite view to that put out on any topic by the Chinese government. Yet he made a sharp distinction between "the authorities" and Mao. "Still at that time Mao was my idol," he said. "I felt he had weight, he would analyze things, and if something was wrong, he would change his mind—that is why I wrote a letter to him, and a whole book for him." From the village where he had been dispatched after leaving prison, Yang made a package of his six-hundred-page work entitled *Chinese Politics* and posted it to Mao in Peking. "The postage cost me ten yuan," he said, "which was a quarter of the annual allowance I was getting in the village. There was no reply," Yang went on with a laugh. "But after writing the book, I felt I didn't owe the damned authorities anything any more."

Not long afterward, Yang's method of coping took a bizarre turn when he resolved to escape from China and try life in North Korea. "A friend of mine went to the China-Korea border to look at the landscape," he recalled of his one year of preparation. "Then I went, and later my friend went again. I bought clothes, did research on Korea, and planned what to say if I was caught creeping across the border." When the day of escape came and Yang proceeded beyond the frontier, he indeed was captured and put into prison by the North Koreans. "Kim Il Sung's prison was worse than Mao's prison," he said without rancor. When the Koreans arrested him, relations between Peking and Pyongyang were strained, but later they improved and within a year Yang was released and sent back to China. Years afterward, he could laugh at the two huge slogans that had been erected on either side of the border he furtively crossed. On the Chinese side, the slogan was Mao's slap at North Korea's friendship with Russia: TO COMBAT IMPERIALISM, YOU MUST COMBAT REVISIONISM. On the Korean side the slogan was a defense of North Korea's own agenda in the face of its giant neighbor's obsessions: NATIONAL INDEPENDENCE!

One reason why the Cultural Revolution was bewildering to those of us outside Chinese culture was that it combined fascism and communism. The mob hysteria was in the fascist mold, while the manipulative politics from on high, making use of the mob, which had its own agenda of grievances, was classic Leninism. In the Confucian tradition of selecting a label to make a reality, a form of words hilariously at variance with the reality of maneuver above and terror below was devised to describe the struggle: "proletarian" versus "capitalist," and "revolutionary" against "counterrevolutionary." Qiu Yehuang, a young intellectual, was riding a bus in Peking when he heard yells of "Capitalist! capitalist!" and he turned round to see passengers on the bus beating a middle-aged man. "He was very frightened and didn't know what to do," Qiu recalled in an interview with the American scholar Anne Thurston.[2] "No one did anything to stop the beating, because if you tried to help, you could be called a capitalist and be beaten too. They beat this man until he died, and then they just threw him off the bus onto the ground."

One of the female classmates of Gao Yuan, the high school Red Guard in Hebei Province, was beaten purple in a holy war between factions at Gao's school. Gao went to see her in hospital. "Our generation," she said to him, "growing up in peace and happiness, never experienced torture. When I read *Red Crag*," she went on, in a reference to a harrowing account in novel form of Nationalist torture of Communists in the city of Chongqing in the 1940s, "I could not imagine how human beings could be such brutes. Now I know."[3] Now people knew. The glow of moral exceptionalism left the Communist party, and political tricks above and spineless "going along" at the grass roots ate away at hope.

During the Cultural Revolution family life became a helpless adjunct to political life. As Liu Shaoqi lost out to Mao and the battle lines of left and not-quite-so-left were drawn, Liu's student son, Yunruo, saw his star fall at the Peking Aeronautics Institute. The easy stick with which to beat him was Russian "revisionism," for Yunruo was in love with a Russian girl whom he had met in Moscow while studying there in the late 1950s. The head of state and his wife, Wang Guangmei, had resisted Yunruo's plan to marry the Russian girl. "Relations between China and Russia are going to get bad," Liu said to his son. "It is not wise to marry a Russian girl." In vain the son insisted that his only intellectual interest was science, and his girlfriend's was literature, and that the two of them wished to steer clear of politics. "Once she enters my house," Liu Shaoqi reasoned, "she has entered politics."

In November 1966 Jiang Qing tipped off her forces at the Aeronautics Institute to watch out for a "foreign spy" lurking on the campus. Soon Yunruo was under fire for his links with the Russian girl; his love letters to her in Moscow were condemned as "illicit relations with a foreign country." Yunruo was sent to prison. Upon his release eight years later he was mentally ill, and soon afterward he died of lung disease, still unmarried, at age forty-four.[4] Being from an elite family did not mean that Liu Yunruo could escape the tyranny of associations and live as an autonomous individual.

I spent the hot, tumultuous summer of 1967 in Hong Kong and what I saw did not reflect well on Chinese communism. Hong Kong, a corner of the world where politics usually counted for little, was at political fever pitch and Mao's moon-faced portrait smiled down from shops, banks, and offices. The Cultural Revolution had spilled out upon this last jewel of the British empire, and the people of Hong Kong were "rebelling" against their British overlords—or were they? I saw leftist demonstrators, neat and well-groomed bank clerk types, arrive at the scene of a protest against a British company or government office with bandages ready in their pockets and cans of red paint under their arms. Within an hour they were lying "bloody" and bandaged on the sidewalk, "beaten" by the "oppressive imperialist authorities of Hong Kong."

There were no local roots to the Hong Kong crisis of 1967. The Hong Kong leftists had their eyes on Peking and were trying to be more Maoist than Mao for political safety's sake. Moderate Hong

Kong businessmen who had spoken well of China to me in 1964 and 1965 had fallen silent. A third of Hong Kong's nearly 4 million people were refugees from Chinese communism; in their view Mao's China was a dismal place, but they had tried not to think about it as they toiled to better themselves under a low-key British administration. The Chinese Communists, their own worst enemy when it came to dealing with Hong Kong, had reminded the Hong Kong people of communism's oppressiveness and Peking's proximity. "Peking has lost Hong Kong public opinion for five years," a businessman friend told me.

Meanwhile, four hundred GIs were arriving each day at Kai Tak airport from Vietnam for R & R (Rest and Recreation—irreverently known to the locals as I & I, Intercourse and Intoxication), and the Chinese Communists were warning that if America interfered in Hong Kong, China would fight America.

The political adviser to the British governor of Hong Kong did not feel Peking was trying to reshape the future of Hong Kong. "If they wanted it back," he said to me, "they would write a letter to London and ask for it." That Peking was not trying to take back Hong Kong, but rather encouraging it to "Maoize" under Britain's trembling gaze, suggested to me that the Cultural Revolution was more political indoctrination than a drive for institutionalized political change.

The summer of 1967 was unhappy and damaging for Hong Kong, and during it (as again during the summer of 1989) it became clear that when Peking was in the grip of one of its power struggles or political dramas, events outside China (sometimes events anywhere outside Peking) were a very dim consideration for the tenacious monks of the Chinese Communist party. I felt more admiration for British rule in Hong Kong after the summer of 1967 than I had in 1964, when, after some weeks amidst the single-minded political purposefulness of Peking and Canton, I had been struck mostly by Hong Kong's gaudy commercialism. "The main hope for Hong Kong," my businessman friend said, "is that China itself will settle down." Yet Communist China had not settled down, and perhaps never would.

Was the entire Cultural Revolution no more than politics as personal spite, furthered by politics as theater? Not quite. When Mao tore the lid off the caldron of Chinese society, there did bubble up (until he used the army to jam the lid back on) morsels of Chinese social and intellectual vitality. Some serious-minded Red Guards embraced utopian elements of Marx's thought. With the Paris Commune as their model and quotations from Marx's *The Eighteenth Brumaire of Louis Bonaparte* on their lips, they proposed for China a government whose members could be recalled from below if they failed in their duties. One Red Guard said to the American journalist Anna Louise Strong: "Our generation is given by history the task of eliminating imperialism from the world." Another expressed to Strong the idealism that the danger in Vietnam evoked in youth who took revolution as a claim on their own moral responsibility. "If the Americans invade China," he said to the leftist American, "we shall help make revolution in America by the way we handle their troops."[5]

Yet despite the existence of some idealism, the acquiescence of many millions of Chinese in weird and unjust instructions from on high was striking. The unappetizing point must be made: millions of Chinese people were participants in, as well as victims of, the Cultural Revolution.

Gao Yuan, the high school Red Guard in Hebei Province, related in his memoir *Born Red* how Chinese within the same family treated each other in the town of Yizhong. One of Gao's teachers hung himself after being criticized for his family's landlord background. "His wife and children refused to come to the funeral," Gao recalled, "saying they wanted to cut off all relations with this antiparty element. Many children of teachers under criticism had publicly disowned their parents, and a few were even helping to expose their parents' crimes. It was only practical."[6] Only practical indeed! A friend in Canton later remarked to me that the "most resented point" about the left-wing zealots of the Cultural Revolution was blaming a whole family for one person's error. An even more revolting phenomenon was members of a family, in the face of political pressure, turning upon each other in an attempt to save their own skins.

Why did not head of state Liu Shaoqi resist Mao more forthrightly? Perhaps because he could not quite believe, until too late, that Mao intended to get rid of him as well as much of the rest of the Politburo. But the question immediately led to a second: when Liu was attacked, why did almost none of his colleagues stand with him against Mao? Zhu De, the military leader, and Chen Yi, the foreign minister, defended Liu with some courage, but they and Liu did not make common political cause against Mao. Deng Xiaoping did not come to Liu's defense, and no sooner was Liu isolated than

Deng became Mao's next target. The eventual absurd indictment of Liu as a "capitalist roader" was read out to the nation by none other than Premier Zhou Enlai. Throughout the Cultural Revolution, at Peking's scores of embassies around the world only two Chinese diplomats defected, a commercial officer in Damascus and a chargé d'affaires at The Hague. "Did you know it was wrong?" I later asked the party chief of Chongqing, Xiao Yang, of the Cultural Revolution. "I was enthusiastic for it," he replied as he thought back on his youthful years in Peking. "In the early part of the Cultural Revolution, only two types of people were not happy with it: those quite ignorant of politics, and the mentally ill."

There were several reasons why millions of Chinese went along with arrant nonsense in the late 1960s. Mao's stature was so high among many people that you could only compare him to the father of a family. It simply did not occur to most people to doubt Mao, and the Cultural Revolution was Mao's. The Chinese Revolution still had some moral momentum, especially among people of low family status, who had benefited from it, and among people of high family status who out of guilt at prior privilege remolded themselves in a socialist direction. And there still was a deep underlying patriotism in the China of the 1960s, by the light of which the very sense of being Chinese was inseparable for most people from going along with the public mood of the moment.

"Going along" for many older Chinese meant a resignation to the status quo out of a long-evolved skepticism that any given political order had permanence or meaning. For young people, a tremendous excitement stirred when Mao, flattering youth as the pearl of great price in Chinese society, pulled the lid off what had been a tightly controlled polity, threw away the rule book (for a season), and told the Red Guards to follow their impulses and inherit the future. In a society where life was rather boring, the Cultural Revolution had initial appeal simply as entertainment.

Years later I asked the dissident essayist Liu Binyan about the balance of responsibility between government and people for the Cultural Revolution. "The leftist line brought out something bad in the people," he replied. "The Chinese people abandoned their conscience. People were prepared to see the whole world destroyed," Liu went on, "just so they could preserve themselves." Liu Binyan's observation—and Gao Yuan's remark that turning in kith and kin was "only practical"—pointed back to the simple, fundamental struggle to survive that lay at the heart of Chinese daily life.

What did Chongqing party chief Xiao Yang think, as he sat in prison, of the charges of being on the "capitalist road" that had been made against him? He thought the charges were probably correct! The Cultural Revolution was unleashed by Mao, yet it could only become a violent storm because the people were sufficiently "Maoist" after two decades of Communist indoctrination to respond to some of his calls.[7]

Private values were so held back as to be a virtually nonexistent force against wayward public policy. Most Chinese believed that to take an individualistic stand was either wrong or foolish. Many indeed were Maoist enough to accept the idea that the thoughts in their minds determined their daily actions, and they shared Mao's vision that society could be a moral family if geared to correct values. Others had simply learned from experience, or it had been drilled into them, that the only way to survive was to move with the tide.

The Red Guards and we Western students of the 1960s all were taught to consider public affairs to be of high importance, we all came into adulthood in a Cold War atmosphere, we all carried in our souls the impact of nuclear weapons as a fact of life, and we all were surrounded by the viewpoint that technology would heavily shape the future. Anti–Vietnam War students at Harvard could have seemed Maoists of a sort, for we felt torn by a disjunction of values, we were disenchanted with the United States government (and other authorities affecting our lives), we felt society had to change if we were to be happy, and we thought our ideas could change the realities around us. Our struggles and the Cultural Revolution seemed to intersect at a hope for moral renovation. The anti–Vietnam War movement was based on a political analysis of the world around us. But we also made a cultural analysis: outmoded authorities were preventing the self-realization of the individual in a diverse world.

Like the Red Guards, we protesters in the West railed against the rigidity of established institutions. As a New Left, we were unhappy with aspects of the Old Left, and likewise, Red Guards felt their elders had slipped back from socialist values. The family suffered great blows both in China and the West during the 1960s. In our New Left and Christian documents we made statements like: "We do not wish to consider children as property," and in China the fluid Cultural Revolution years brought a parallel loosening of family values and a reduction in family authority.

Yet the differences between us were basic. We radicals in America often found that our attachment to causes changed our career plans, and even our thinking about the meaning of a career. The Red Guard experience was not a path to an alternative vocation, but a brief diversion from a life of regimentation. We in the West had more freedom than we knew how to use, whereas the Red Guards were being manipulated from on high. Feeling that many institutions "no longer served the needs of man," as a manifesto from a group of us in the Christian Peace Conference and the World Student Christian Federation declared, we could have formed new institutions, but in the end we mostly did not. Our scattered "communes," international student groupings, and urgent ad hoc committees did not endure into the 1970s; we resumed life in a fairly conventional mold. The Red Guards were not at liberty to fashion new institutions to replace the old. In America we looked at the political options and sometimes turned aside from them all. Chinese youth never had any real political options. Behind our complaints about our "powerlessness" there probably lay a confusion about goals. The Chinese did not have the luxury of confusion; in the Cultural Revolution Mao gave them some power, then he whipped it away.

The call by Mao and some utopian Red Guards for a "new man," and my own Christian idealist quest for a "transformation" of human relationships through a richer community both failed. It was not surprising that a Christian idealist at Harvard would miss some of the flaws in the utopian notions cast about in Peking. I was groping to clarify the relationships between interests, ideology, and values. The ideologies involved—Christianity and Maoism—tended to obscure the interests and enduring values. Mao and Nixon were soon to demonstrate that realpolitik could contribute more than ideology or moral values to the "return of China" to international society that I so earnestly sought.

Politics in China was mostly personal, and never more so than during the psychodrama that Mao launched in 1966. Into his seventies, disappointed by much he saw around him yet still vaultingly ambitious on behalf of his dream of socialism, Mao, who now looked like a calm, well-fed Buddha, went against many people's expectations of him and made a very personal shift of gears. He returned to a number of Chinese traditions: interest in Buddhism, a cyclical way of viewing history, the leader's "imperial" sense of himself as part of a long cultural tradition, and a political partnership between the "emperor" and his wife, the would-be empress. Ironically, as we observers in the West viewed the China issue in terms of international relationships, Mao was at the other extreme of viewing China's condition in acutely personal terms.

The personal meaning of the Cultural Revolution seemed proved by its almost total lack of a political agenda. I asked myself how China would be different after the therapy of leftist renewal was over. Perhaps the rectification of the people's thinking amounted to a policy goal, but exactly what did it mean to rectify the people's thinking? Would the Tibetans be rectified into believing in Chinese socialism? Would a faith in Mao as "the Red Sun of our hearts" make industry efficient, reduce the burden of overpopulation, or help China deal more effectively with America's superior power?

Mao's quest for a "new man" as the product of his own "thoughts" was the quest for a phantom. Mao's ideal vision of socialism had obstinately declined to come into being despite two decades of "liberation." He came up with a notion of ever-sharpening class struggle, and multiplying class enemies, to explain the failure and fuel further pursuit of the elusive new man. If socialism had not fulfilled its promise, at least Mao would offer a good Marxist reason why not (a *new* bourgeoisie had sprung up!). Far from aiming at a realizable political goal, Mao in his lunge after this phantom was doing battle with the suprapolitical enemy of his own mortality.*

Two more ingredients connected the drama of Mao the man to the concrete events of the Cultural Revolution. In a dictatorship the personality of the leader was magnified a thousandfold. If Mao liked a certain Peking opera, the resources of a leading theater were marshaled for its production, and Chinese audiences got a season of that opera whether they wanted it or not. It was as if all Broadway theaters were instructed to prepare shows that the president and first lady would like for that winter's private performances in the East Wing of the White House.

In America we shied away from acknowledging the endemic ways of dictatorship. Seldom in awe of a leader, we did not know what it was to treat a politician as a god. We were so free we could not understand unfreedom. "The absolute monarch," wrote a biogra-

---

* Among the few people who in the 1960s saw Mao's personal drama as the root of the Cultural Revolution was the psychiatrist Robert J. Lifton. In his *Revolutionary Immortality* (New York: Vintage, 1968) he perceived the Cultural Revolution as a "last stand against death itself—of the leader, and of the revolution" (p. 151).

pher of the tyrannical Empress Wu of the Tang dynasty (618–907), "is like an actor posturing before a gigantic distorting mirror, which projects his or her every movement to colossal dimensions."[8] Mao's frown could mean the purge of a hundred bureaucrats. His enigmatic citation from a misty ancient poem could freeze the Chinese government in indecision over a major policy for months. His enchantment with a lowly female secretary could result in the reshuffling of an entire bureau. His early morning irritation with the Russians could by evening bring the renaming of a famous Peking street as "Anti-Revisionism Street."

It was not that the democracies lacked human beings as singular as Mao—or Hitler or Saddam Hussein or Idi Amin—but that in the democracies such men were unlikely to become head of the government. And in a dictatorship, unlike in a democracy, when the imperiously willful or vengeful person became leader, there were few checks upon him; his whim became the law, his hunch turned into a Five-Year Plan, his fart polluted the empire.

Discussing the cult of personality with Edgar Snow, Mao contrasted Stalin and Khrushchev. "One reason Khrushchev fell," he said to the American journalist, "was that he had no cult of personality [as Stalin had]."[9] By this remark Mao made it clear that he was conscious of the cult of personality that had built up around him in China. He did nothing of consequence to stop Lin Biao and Jiang Qing adding to his godlike image. Whether he enjoyed the cult was not the point, for he knew very well that in China dictatorship, to be effective, must be personal dictatorship, with the people in thrall to a leader who embodied virtue and monopolized truth. Building up Mao was both a method and a goal of the Cultural Revolution.*

Time after time, the events and philosophy of the Cultural Revolution reflected Mao's and Jiang's personal concerns. The play about Hai Rui that Mao ordered attacked as the first shot in the Cultural Revolution had come out in 1961. Strikingly, the playwright's earlier writing on the Ming dynasty official whom an emperor dismissed was directly inspired by Mao's having singled out Hai Rui for *emulation*. Why then did Mao in 1965 turn against *Hai Rui Dismissed from Office?* Because in the political context of the time, Mao and Jiang felt that he, Mao, was being hinted at as the play's target;

---

* Snow observed aptly after his trip to China in 1965 that all the interest in building Mao up suggested that someone wanted to bring him down—*The Long Revolution* (New York: Random House, 1972), p. 69.

Mao's dismissal of his defense minister, Peng Dehuai, in 1959 was being criticized by analogy with the emperor Jia Jing's unjustified dismissal of Hai Rui during the Ming dynasty.

The mayor of Peking, Peng Zhen, thought Jiang Qing's politicized ballets and operas were a silly hobby. She approached him at a banquet one evening and asked him to allocate a theater troupe in Peking as a base for her work. "She wants this, she wants that," Mayor Peng subsequently complained to a friend. "Doesn't she realize the mayor of Peking has other things to do besides help her with her games?" But they were not games; Jiang Qing's artistic concoctions were deadly political grenades. She was not a bored housewife inventing activities to pass her time, but the second-most-powerful person in China, whose idiosyncrasies were reflected in twists of high policy.

Soon after Mao and Jiang returned to Peking from their lengthy stay in Shanghai, Hangzhou, and elsewhere in 1966, Jiang gave a speech at Peking University. Accompanied by security chief Kang Sheng and ideologist Chen Boda, two of China's half-dozen top leaders, she climbed onto a platform beside a Ming-style pavilion under lights set in trees. "She has never been a proper daughter-in-law," cried Jiang, and the students of China's premier university could hardly believe their ears. At the height of the Cultural Revolution, Jiang was devoting a speech to an attack on Zhang Shaohua, the young wife of Mao's troubled son, Mao Anqing, by his early wife Yang Kaihui. "Her mother is a political swindler," Jiang went on of her hated daughter-in-law. "Shaohua took advantage of Mao Anqing's mental illness to have sex with him—and so snare him into marriage." [10] A grievance within the Mao household was being dressed up by Jiang as a Cultural Revolution issue!

At length the owl-like Chen Boda rose from his seat and went across to Jiang, and students in the front heard him whisper, "I think you should stop now." Jiang stared at Chen and confessed her fury. "It's true, I *am* upset," she said. "For ten years I have suffered from this woman and her family. Thanks to her, my heart problem has flared up again." One female student in the audience, the daughter of an associate of Liu Shaoqi's who was being forced out of office, was bold enough to cry out to Jiang the pathetic words: "You are not taking a revolutionary position."

Jiang Qing blew up her personal prejudices into a metaphysic. The Cultural Revolution leader who insisted that every time an official was purged his wife also be felled ("Wang Guangmei [Liu's wife] is a spy") was the housewife who quarreled with the wives of both Mao's two sons by his early wife Yang, and stored up resentment at her inability to distance Mao from these daughters-in-law. In an extra twist to the case against Liu Shaoqi, Jiang tracked down a daughter from an earlier marriage of Liu's that ended in divorce in 1947. After fantastic inducements had been offered to this young woman, Liu Tao, she rose at a public meeting and declared: "My father really is the number one party person walking on the capitalist road." Jiang felt the speech was halfhearted, so she arranged a meeting between Liu Tao and her mother, Liu's former wife, who naturally did not esteem Liu's current wife, the cosmopolitan Wang Guangmei. A second, tougher text from Liu Tao not only vilified her father but added a hair-raising portrait of his wife's "spying."[11]

Wondering why factionalism was so prominent in Chinese politics, I found myself focusing on the Chinese way of defining themselves less by their individual traits than by their membership in a group. Such stress on a person's function in a collective put a premium on connections and loyalty. Since the family was the group that most defined a Chinese, and the family was very much a social entity, the factionalism of society at large interacted with family and marriage links. A common phrase for "public" or "state" is *gong jia;* *gong* means public and *jia* means family. And in truth in China the connections and loyalty that mark family life also mark political life, making the state a "public family." At the top, family members are like fingers on the hand of the Politburo.

Tang Na, the former husband of Jiang Qing in Shanghai during the 1930s, learned during four tempestuous years—when he three times tried to kill himself—about her strong will and vengefulness. Years later in Paris, where he was the proprietor of a Chinese restaurant, Tang broke his long silence about his marriage with Jiang in four long evenings of conversation with me. A suave and romantic theater critic, Tang had given a warm reception to Jiang's performance as Nora in Ibsen's *A Doll's House* in 1935, and one day soon afterward the pair met in the street and almost the first thing Jiang said to the man-about-town of Shanghai's cultural left wing was, "I'm a revolutionary!" Tang Na said: "It was enormously exciting to me that this new actress from Shandong [Province], very seductive, said to me right there on Huaihai Boulevard that she was a committed revolutionary." In that disordered and ardent epoch the term "revolutionary" had the power even to spur a seduction, but three decades later it was a mere talisman, like a ring worn to bring good luck.

Tang Na explained Jiang's hold over Mao and by extension the basis for the marriage whose political flowering in the 1960s was so fateful for the Chinese people. "I think Jiang Qing did to Mao what she did to me," he said of the encounter of the two in Yan'an in the late 1930s after the Japanese attack had broken up the Shanghai film industry. "She was attractive and she presented herself as a revolutionary—the combination hooked Mao." Jiang left Tang because she was a hundred times more attached to power than to love. She never walked out on Mao, but she transcended her role of housewife within the marriage at every opportunity in a manner foreshadowed by her rejection of a commitment to Tang, and she eventually used Mao's power to build a political career for herself. As Jiang mounted the political stage in the 1960s, the masses waving the little red book became audiences for her performances of left-wing politics as theater. The humble actress of the Shanghai years got even with her detractors by labeling them "bourgeois" and proved at last that she could do what men did.

The convulsion of the late 1960s began from above, and to the degree that it came to include "rebellion," this mostly was the fake variety of rebellion-on-instructions. The idealism of the Red Guards was terribly misplaced. They were puppets, wiggled this way or that by Mao and Jiang and other leftists. Supreme power did not change hands during the Cultural Revolution; it had been Mao's beforehand, and still it was Mao's when the storm subsided, so there was no "revolution."

The Cultural Revolution reflected Mao's evolution from a Marxist to the "Monkey King" of one of his favorite novels, *Journey to the West*. The novel's hero is a monkey with a red behind called Sun who performs fantastic feats. He steals and eats peaches of immortality in gardens of paradise, he storms the gates of hell in order to remove his name from a cosmic blacklist, he covers thousands of miles in one leap, and reaching the world's outer boundary, pisses on the base of a pillar to show his disrespectful spirit.

Sun the Monkey King copes with adversity by plucking hair from his body—the character *mao* for "hair" happens also to be Mao's name—and then biting it into pieces and shouting "Change!" Each fragment turns into a small monkey, and he has at his command an army of supporters. Mao during the mid-1960s often referred to

Sun, whose impish irreverence and infinite aspirations fitted his own mood. Mao said rebellion was the essence of Marxism, learning was no doorway to truth, and young people were preferable to older people because they lacked knowledge and experience.

"We've been the Monkey King upsetting heaven," Mao candidly said to Anna Louise Strong on the eve of the Cultural Revolution as they talked of the Russia-China split. "We've thrown away the heavenly rule book. Remember this, never take a heavenly rule book too seriously—one must go by one's own revolutionary rules."[12] He actually declared in 1966 that the true revolutionary and the Monkey King were one and the same type of character![13] I often wondered why Mao chose to harry and remove Liu, Deng, and others by the use of Red Guards, rather than have them voted out by the central committee, or simply nabbed by the security police. I later asked the opinion of Wang Ruoshui, one of the shrewdest political analysts I knew in China. "He did it that way to escape responsibility," said People's Daily deputy editor Wang. That was the way of Sun the Monkey King.

At the eightieth birthday luncheon for Anna Louise Strong in Shanghai, Mao asked half a dozen of the guests their views on the current world scene. The answers did not impress him. All six people had the same view, he complained; the group must have met together beforehand to orchestrate a point of view. It would be more interesting, Mao felt, if someone had a divergent view. Yet over the next year this same man received the tearful, mindless adoration of 11 million Red Guards at rallies in Tiananmen Square. He made no speech, but merely appeared before the throng with an upraised arm and a glassy smile, as the young zealots chanted slogans of praise and solidarity with his Thought.

Contradictions no less sharp marked Jiang Qing's behavior. Her left-wing views and denunciation of art for art's sake made her sound like a citizen of Sparta. Yet she indulged in the luxuries of an empress, flying in melons from the far west of China for dinner parties and ordering her toilet seats covered with fur. She was a lover of the performing arts, yet she brought about the deaths of scores of brilliant artists. To understand such contradictions in Mao and Jiang is to understand the Cultural Revolution.

My explanation combines traits of dictatorship, traits of Chinese political culture, and the cumulative effect of Communist organization and propaganda on the Chinese people from 1949. The dictator lacks knowledge of many things in his realm, and he is constantly being flattered. Cut and thrust of opinion coming up from the grass roots may have been an impressive idea to Mao, but as supreme leader after 1949 he almost never experienced it. No free press or parliament or independent political groups existed to toss up disagreeable opinions that he actually had to reckon with. Mao at Anna Louise Strong's birthday party was in a novel situation. He was not accustomed to hearing the views of people from the grass roots on world affairs, or any other affairs. Those half-dozen birthday guests (presumably mostly foreigners) were not "the people" as Mao thought of the people. They were six individuals, and he wanted to hear from them as individuals, but such a discussion had little to do, in Mao's mind, with the processes of Chinese politics.

When Mao turned against a left wing spiraling into factionalism in 1967, two leaders of the Cultural Revolution in Shanghai flew up to see him in Peking. They reported to him that Red Guards in the port city had been quoting a statement of Mao's from the May Fourth period four decades earlier: "The world is ours, the nation is ours, society is ours." Mao ordered the Shanghai Red Guards to stop quoting the statement, snapping that he didn't "altogether recall" using those exact words.[14] A text had existed; it went out of existence.

Between the supreme leader's views and the grass roots, there was no intermediate level on which ideas were tested and debated. Debate might be good if it gave the citizens a keener sense of the public good, in Mao's view, but it was not meant as a process with an open-ended outcome; it was not a quest for truth. As a dictator of the Communist brand, Mao felt he knew the destination to which society was evolving. The last act of the drama of the unfolding of communism had been written well in advance by Marx and Engels and Lenin.

And as a dictator in the tradition of the Chinese emperors, Mao in his later years tended to view the Chinese masses, whom he once called "blank" as well as poor, as actors with a fixed role in the political drama, not as participants with thoughts of their own. Part of these masses, the Red Guards, he needed in 1966 to help topple Liu and Deng, but only as an orchestrated force, not as public opinion in all its variousness and unpredictability. When the Red Guards had done this job and started to give "rebellion" their own shade of meaning and develop a taste for guns and spears, Mao turned them off as a fireman might turn off a hose.

So Mao, pursuing a phantom, smashed his enemies, but not his

Enemies, which were time and the very forces of history. He reasserted his power, although he did not seem clear about the sociopolitical uses this power would be devoted to. He was wrestling with his own self-doubts, battling against the mortality of his revolution and against his own mortality. The convulsion did not produce a new type of rule for China, only a new and not improved team to assist the supreme ruler during his final years.

The really amazing features of the Cultural Revolution were the way so many millions of people acquiesced, even enthused, in the distortions involved in carrying on political struggle in the mode of theater, and how personal politics in China was revealed to be, as wives were made to pay the price for their husbands' mistakes, merit meant little compared with connections in gaining or losing an appointment, and Mao and his wife dealt with the whole realm of China as if it was their own household; personal prejudice became the kernel of public policy.

The violence and theatrics of the Cultural Revolution put a stop to Liu's and Deng's early 1960s stress on the economics of results and the politics of order, yet an enduring effect of the Cultural Revolution was to disillusion many thinking Chinese with the whole box and dice of Marxism. In that respect "Monkey King" Mao gave pragmatist Deng Xiaoping a delayed second opportunity. A decade and more later, after Mao's death, Deng would pick up the threads of the pragmatic authoritarianism that Mao had so rudely knocked out of his hands in 1966.

CHAPTER FIVE

■

AFTER THE STORM

AS the 1970s began Mao still bestrode the stage in Peking, a King Lear who kept everyone around him guessing. The supporting cast lacked the familiar faces of Liu Shaoqi and Deng Xiaoping, and now featured Lin Biao and Jiang Qing, together with the cosmopolitan survivor Zhou Enlai. The Western world tried to understand what the Cultural Revolution had been about, but usually set aside its bafflement in favor of a hope that at least the madness of it was over.

A stirring occurred in most Western countries' policy toward Peking, because it was widely felt that when the torment of Indochina ended, the West would have to share the future in Asia with China. That torment had cut short Lyndon Johnson's presidency in 1968 and was a major preoccupation for his successor, Richard Nixon. Mao, for his part, helped by Zhou Enlai, seemed ready to ease China's isolation and reduce the risks of the Cultural Revolution period's simultaneous hostility to Russia and America.

From Harvard during the Cultural Revolution, I had several times tried to obtain a visa to return to China, but no Peking bureaucrat was willing to risk the allegation of being "soft on imperialism" by approving a visa for a "foreign devil" (an old term for a foreigner that came back into use during the Cultural Revolution) who might or might not write "the truth" after his visit. I had finished my courses in history and political science with professors John Fairbank, Samuel Beer, Adam Ulam, Henry Kissinger, and others, gained my Ph.D. with a doctoral thesis on the socialist philosophy of R. H. Tawney, and been appointed to the Harvard faculty in the Government Department. One of my tasks would be to teach Chinese politics.

The Chinese embassy in Ottawa phoned my apartment at Harvard's Kirkland House on the sunny afternoon of Memorial Day in 1971, as students played Frisbee on the grass outside my window, and an official in Ambassador Huang Hua's office said: "You should come to China immediately. We think it would be a good idea for you to arrive two weeks before Mr. Whitlam." The chain of events leading to this beckoning finger—very exciting to me after the closed door of the Cultural Revolution period—had begun with an earlier phone call from the office of Gough Whitlam, leader of the Australian Labor party.

Whitlam, as opposition leader in Australia, like Senator Edward Kennedy and other Democratic senators in America, wanted to go to Peking in order to move relations with China off dead center and broach a new post-Vietnam era in Asia-Pacific politics. But Peking was giving mixed signals to the Kennedys and Whitlams of the Western political scene.

The Australian Labor party's opportunity came from a Chinese decision earlier in the year to cancel wheat purchases from Australia —giving the order instead to Canada—while complaining of the "anti-China" statements of the Australian government, which had an embassy in Taipei. "If you go into a shop to buy toys," a Chinese official later said to me in likening the conservative Australian prime minister, William McMahon, to a rude salesman, "and the man behind the counter curses you, after a while you buy your toys somewhere else."

Whitlam had no contacts in China, and when he asked me to help him make the trip there, I approached two acquaintances, the French ambassador in Peking and a Chinese Communist magazine editor in Hong Kong, in an effort to persuade Premier Zhou Enlai to receive Whitlam for a discussion of China-Australia relations. "We see an opportunity," I wrote to French envoy Etienne Manac'h on April 28, 1971, "to push Australia toward the kind of realistic policy on China that France seven years ago adopted." I had talked with Manac'h about Indochina in Paris a few years before, in the course of preparing articles on the Vietnam Peace Talks for *The New Republic* and *The Atlantic Monthly,* when he was head of the Asian desk in the French foreign ministry. Knowing of his opposition to the policy of the United States and its allies in East Asia, I said in my letter: "If

Whitlam wins the next election, there will be a stark change in Australia's China policy, as well as her Indochinese policy. . . ."

The Manac'h link bore swift fruit as the Frenchman acted boldly and skillfully in a "personal capacity." On May 7 he received my letter and on the next day he cabled me (in French) to say, "I have made an approach . . . in the direction you propose." Manac'h worked through foreign ministry official Han Xu, later ambassador in Washington, who put the request before Zhou Enlai on May 9, and the next day Whitlam in Canberra was jubilant to receive an invitation to come to China and discuss China-Australia relations. I received a cable from Whitlam on May 11 that read: "Eureka. We won." [1] The Australian government of William McMahon was furious and made a big fuss about Manac'h's role, and my own, and poured scorn on Whitlam for knocking on the door of the Chinese Communist dictators.* But Whitlam had the opportunity he wanted, and he enthusiastically made plans to fly to Peking.

The Chinese Communists, anxious to revive a foreign policy that was paralyzed during the late 1960s, sought to replace Taiwan in the China seat at the United Nations and gain extra diplomatic recognition from Western countries, especially the United States, which still had its embassy to China in Taipei. During that spring of 1971, the Chinese were trying to decide how much of what they wanted from America could be won directly from the Nixon administration, and how much they would secure only from Nixon's opponents. In the usual way of Communists who have drunk deep at the well of "united front" doctrine, they were bestowing winks on liberal Democratic party senators, while at the same time communicating in an increasingly businesslike way with Henry Kissinger in Nixon's White House. Should they coax Nixon further, they asked themselves, or focus on cultivating the Democratic party alternative?

In April 1971, I met with Senator Edward Kennedy to talk about China policy at the Cambridge home of Jerome Alan Cohen, the specialist on Chinese law. The small group of Harvard sinologists in Cohen's leafy back garden included Edwin Reischauer, who had been President Kennedy's ambassador to Japan, and James Thom-

---

* Manac'h's memoirs, *La Chine* (p. 421), contain this Delphic diary note on his intervention (I translate from the French): "I only hope that my discreet mediation, which risks being discovered, will not provoke too much brouhaha on the Australian domestic scene, or within my own prudent department."

son, who had worked in the White House under presidents Kennedy and Johnson. Senator Kennedy was soon afterward going to Canada for meetings connected with health policy issues and he planned to see Ambassador Huang Hua while in Ottawa. Reischauer urged Kennedy to put together a bipartisan group of senators for his hoped-for China trip. As a political supporter of Kennedy at that time, I could not see the point of Reischauer's idea and said I hoped Kennedy would go to China alone. I wrote in my diary that evening: "Kennedy ought to just get himself to China. He ought to go all out to embarrass the [Nixon] government, taking this China initiative himself, staking a claim to the presidency in which he would be an infinite improvement over Nixon and Johnson." That was how Whitlam was playing the China card in Australia.

The Chinese invitation to Whitlam in May was among other things a test case to help Zhou Enlai make up his mind on policy toward America. I realized from later talks with Chinese officials that if Prime Minister McMahon had at any time shifted his policy to accord with Whitlam's ("one China, capital in Peking"), China would have been quite happy to play the "McMahon card," and forget about the Whitlam card. As it turned out, the American and Australian cases evolved in opposite ways. The Chinese invited the American Ping-Pong team to Peking, and the Nixon administration was in the mood to respond favorably to the gesture. Nixon himself was soon to take some of the steps toward diplomatic recognition that Peking sought and the Democrats were left standing empty-handed. In Australia, by contrast, McMahon folded his hands and the opposition Labor party essentially took over China diplomacy from the government.

Henry Kissinger, who as national security adviser was handling the Nixon administration's approach to the Chinese, talked to me from time to time about Vietnam and China, and I found him concerned with structures of international relations, rather than with moral postures in international relations. If equilibrium could be achieved, he felt, nations would behave better—they would have to —than when disequilibrium prevailed. I admired Kissinger and found that his realism fitted in with my views about the distorting effect in Asia of the ideological hostility between America and China, and with the opportunities presented to the West by the Moscow-Peking split. For someone like myself coming from left of center, the striking virtue of Kissinger was his open mind about

China. "What should we talk to the Chinese about?" he would ask, a totally different approach from the more usual, "When are the Chinese going to become worthy of our recognizing them?"

It was a feel for balance of power politics that made Kissinger a refreshing force in American policy toward Asia. He saw that China and America had a mutual interest in drawing closer to each other as a way of countering Soviet power, and he correctly scoffed at the widespread view that the problems pertaining to the bilateral China-America relationship—blocked financial assets, Washington's opposition to Peking's seating in the United Nations, the competing diplomatic and property claims of "Two Chinas"—had to be tackled first and directly. He felt the breakthrough with the Chinese would come on broader grounds and he was absolutely right. Just as Kissinger's (and Nixon's) approach to China was geopolitical, rather than ideological, it happened that Mao's approach to America had become similar. It astonished Kissinger that Mao could see, when most of his former Harvard students and colleagues could not, that Nixon really was on the way out of Vietnam. As he drily put it in his memoirs: "Understanding of the direction of our Vietnam policy seems to have been greater in Tiananmen Square than in Harvard Square."[2]

China's "Ping-Pong diplomacy" signaled a new openness to America and the resumption of an active Chinese foreign policy around the globe. The Chinese had decided to end the boxed-in situation that the simultaneous frostiness of their relations with Moscow and Washington had put them in for more than a decade. Peking wanted very much to get seated in the United Nations and speak there on behalf of the Third World, and it intended to become more involved in international economic relationships.

The shift in China's policy was an easy step in a way, because after years of shuttered isolation, there was much slack to take up and the world was eager to find out anything it could about China. Yet the step was effected with a clever mix of utter secrecy and eye-catching theatrics. Mao and Zhou Enlai shrewdly encouraged opposition groups in the United States, Australia, Japan, and other countries, just enough to stimulate the governments concerned to move on China policy, but not to the point of frightening those governments into an anti-China posture. Viewing United States policies in Indochina, the Chinese leaders read the mixture of frustration, sense of failure, and desire to "wind down the war" that existed in Washington, and calibrated their responses to Nixon's

gestures toward China with his steps to limit his Vietnam commit-
ments. And Mao and Zhou, in order to dramatize their reborn foreign policy, chose tools like Ping-Pong and relaxed banquets with
shark's fin soup and crab legs, which caught the world's imagination
and made the Chinese seem very human and civilized, quite unlike
their fist-clenching image of the 1960s.

From opium to Ping-Pong was for the Chinese nation an overdue
and heart-warming advance. Opium in the nineteenth century had
been a symbol of Western influence on a China too weak to resist
Britain's transfer of the lethal poppy from India to the China coast,
whereas Ping-Pong, at which the Chinese were world cham-
pions, was a symbol of regained Chinese initiative. China chose the
mode, knew the West would accept its invitations to come and play
table tennis in Peking, and grandly offered to send coaches to the
West to improve the game's standards there.

At Harvard as the academic year wound down in May 1971, I
prepared for the trip to China that the phone call from the Chinese
embassy in Ottawa had conjured into existence by dusting down
Chinese language cassette tapes. Studying Chinese in daily classes
while working on my doctoral thesis, I had written each new ideo-
graph on a "flash card" and carried the pack of square white cards
with me around the campus like a thief bearing the secret code of a
safe he was hoping to crack. Although my mind had become quite
well stocked with Chinese characters, my tongue was far from
fluent. Before leaving on my trip I listened to recordings in a shrill
woman's voice of articles by Mao, including "Serve the People,"
"In Memory of Norman Bethune," and "The Foolish Old Man
Who Removed the Mountains." I wondered how a China capable
of such ideological zealotry could grasp the outstretched hand of the
West. So much had happened to the Chinese and ourselves in the
years since my previous visit that I could hardly wait to see post–
Cultural Revolution China. One half of my mind thought Whitlam
would succeed with his mission, and the other half that in the face
of Chinese ideological rigidity he would fall flat on his face.

The editor of The Atlantic Monthly had been spurring me on to
return to China and now commissioned a series of articles on the
"new China" I was traveling to see. I looked forward also to firsthand observation of China's reactivated foreign policy as a step toward starting a course on the subject at Harvard. "How long will I
stay?" I asked the Chinese official on the phone to Ottawa. "As long
as you wish," he replied. I said I would stay six or seven weeks, and

divide my time between investigation of China's domestic condition in the wake of the Cultural Revolution and interviews on China's outlook on the world. I devised a plan to visit eight cities and cover about seven thousand miles. So in June of 1971, I took the train from Hong Kong and walked across the wooden bridge at Lo Wu that separated Britain's commercial jewel from Mao's sterner realm.

Back in China after seven years, I reversed the direction of my previous journey and entered the country from the south. But the foreign ministry insisted that I come at once to the capital for "discussions." On the flight to Peking from Canton, a hostess of the Chinese airline CAAC recited a quotation from Mao as part of the preparation for take-off. During the trip north I took a nap, and as we descended toward Peking the hostess cried solicitously into my ear: "We're here. Stop sleeping." Foreigners were few, and each one was treated with an individual touch. The Chinese people still knew little of the outside world.

Yet China was a different land from what it had been in 1964. On the road from Peking airport to the city, the trees that in 1964 had been three feet high now formed a green canopy that turned a rural road into a boulevard. I felt on familiar ground but could see that a storm had shaken the earth. Soldiers on duty in factories and schools showed that Mao had jammed a new lid of military authority on a chaotic Red Guard–riven society that had not "rebelled" quite according to his formula. I would find that a certain recovery from the Cultural Revolution had occurred and observe a substantial degree of normalcy and order in the nation. But I also found that the Cultural Revolution had interrupted economic progress and knocked the stuffing out of intellectuals, and I knew that China had lost much goodwill in Asia and Africa. After observing the Cultural Revolution from distant Harvard, I was most struck by China's partial recovery from the chaos of the 1960s, and less disturbed than I should have been by the ongoing grotesqueries of totalitarianism.

At times I felt I was being shown around a house that was being renovated, and ushered only into selected rooms. The owner pointed out fancy areas, but I did not know how much of the whole they represented, or how serious were the problems that lay behind the large curtained-off sections. The mystery in part sprang from the deceptive nature of "normalcy" in Communist China. Yang Bingzhang, the Peking University student who was imprisoned in

1966 for criticizing Jiang Qing, was sent to rural Shandong Province after his release. "Were your rights curtailed during this period?" I asked him when we were traveling together in Sichuan Province years later. "Were you supervised as an ex-prisoner?" Yang burst out laughing. "Rights in the countryside?" he cried. "There are no rights in the Chinese countryside. What rights could be curtailed?"

In a remote Chinese village, Yang was reminding me, you were so much out of touch with urban life that you might as well be forbidden to make contact with the city. A commune was likely to be as bereft of comforts and gadgets as a labor camp, and the pressure to conform in a gossipy village supervised by party officials was hardly less than under detention. In the West, the line between being imprisoned and being free was unambiguous, but in China there were many gradations between the two conditions; the "normal" state of a citizen living in his home and going to work in field or factory each day could be highly misleading. The Chinese Communists had myriad ways of chipping away at a citizen's freedom without arresting him and making his unfreedom obvious. In the early 1970s, a tableau of normalcy and Chinese skill at keeping up appearances hid a police state's constant intrusion into mental and private life.

From Peking I went to the dusty northwestern town of Yan'an, where after the Long March the Communists had fashioned a unique Chinese socialism, and a sixty-six-year-old resident named Wang told me life in Yan'an was far better than in prerevolutionary days. "Every house now has a thermos flask," said the grizzled, leathery farmer, who wore two Mao badges on his shirt. "Thanks to the communes, we also have planned manpower to bring about production increases and buy new tools. People say Mao must be good because our ancestors didn't have these things." I wondered if collectivism and poverty went together. Were Yan'an households each to have an automobile, rather than a thermos flask, would the Maoist ethic, "Serve the people," have as much appeal? If the citizens of Yan'an learned that families in parts of East Asia had their own cars, would they turn against collectivism for its inability to move the Chinese people beyond thermos flasks to cars? I asked the farmer if he had one great wish for China. "That Chairman Mao should live for one hundred years," replied this old man who knew nothing of life outside China.

Another sign that the Cultural Revolution was not entirely over was the absence of Zhao Fusan, the pastor at Rice Market Church whom I had met in 1964. "He is not in Peking," I was told by a Chinese official. "He is ill, he had a heart attack," whispered a frightened mouse of a man at Rice Market Church. In fact, Zhao still was in a labor camp as a result of the Cultural Revolution.

Despite the stratospheric communication between Kissinger and Zhou Enlai, American and Chinese societies were terribly cut off from each other. No airline flew between the two countries, in Peking there were no American diplomats, resident journalists, students, or businessmen, and articles about America in the Chinese press were politically biased. Nearly all of the scattering of American residents in China were "three hundred percenters," fellow travelers who had years before made their way to Peking out of attraction to the Chinese Revolution or dissatisfaction with their own land. In aggregate they were in no way representative of the United States, and their eager support for each twist and turn of the Chinese Communist line sometimes hid an alienation from the Chineseness of the world they had chosen to share.

Chinese society was contradictory, like a terrain drenched from a storm, yet lit by the rays of a healing sun. Airplanes still were inscribed only with the slogan TEN THOUSAND YEARS TO CHAIRMAN MAO, yet people were once again visiting ancestors' graves with offerings of food and paper money in Buddhist fashion. A professor of physics told me he learned more truth ("socialist truth") while feeding pigs for two years in a village than during decades in his laboratory. Yet he also mentioned that he was relying for world news not on his own socialist government's news outlets, but on the BBC from London. "American imperialism" was a swear word on hundreds of millions of Chinese lips, even as the secretive Chinese government was beginning a close tie based on geopolitics with the Nixon administration.

Because my view of the Cultural Revolution still was opaque, I was unsure of the distinction between the receding past and an approaching future. Had Mao set his ship of state on a post–Cultural Revolution course, with fresh supplies on board and a newly trained crew, or were the criss-crossing patterns of the terrain simply a sign of the twilight that marks the close of a dynasty? The Cultural Revolution had failed to revivify revolutionary values, and the retreat from the Cultural Revolution looked like an admission that revolutionary values were of little use for the urgent tasks of economic development. Yet as long as Mao lived, the logic of the revolution's winding down would be denied.

For some thirty days and evenings my constant companion, assigned by the foreign ministry to supervise much of this 1971 visit, was a quintessential neo-Mandarin named Zhou Nan, later China's deputy foreign minister and later still China's chief representative in Hong Kong. Zhou was a tall, commanding man with a square open face, a scholar-official in the Chinese tradition. He joined the Communist party as a student at Yenching University in the passionate 1940s, and as a diplomat he had served in Pakistan and Tanzania. He had been sent to a village during the Cultural Revolution.

I liked Zhou Nan for his calmness even in the most maddening situations, his delight in citing poetry of the Tang dynasty (618–907), and his carefulness in not telling a lie when he could not give me the truth. Under pressure, he would obscure a piece of information by employing allegory, citing ancient verse, or using other devices of Chinese indirection. Zhou Nan liked ritual, protection from crowds, and applause from waiting bystanders, although all these baubles of privilege made me writhe. He felt such conduct showed there was order in the realm and confirmed his status as a Mandarin.

One day Zhou recalled with approval Engels's remark at Marx's funeral that Marx had done for history what Darwin did for biology. I told Zhou I did not think there could be laws of history and that he had swallowed too readily the Marxist view of history as an escalator, moving upward regardless of any movement by the people riding on the steps. I said both democracy and individualism depended on a view of history as open to human will, and that as long as men were free, history was open, and that history could never become a science in a free country. "Yours is a social democratic point of view," Zhou Nan said with a certain amount of friendly distaste.

It was standard for Chinese officials, when speaking of foreigners coming to China, to use the words "invitation" and "guest" and "friend." Zhou Nan would remind me, if he thought I was probing too much, that I was a guest in China. It was inaccurate because, with the exception of a side trip from Peking to Xian and Yan'an hosted by the foreign ministry, I was paying for my trip (although not for Zhou Nan and my guides). But like many of the ways of the Mandarins, the usage "guest" had a point to it. It was a Confucian tradition to choose a label that created its own reality. A guest could be controlled as a colleague could not be. A guest could be isolated from locations not to be penetrated in a way a neighbor dropping by could not be.

Virtually everyone who came to China throughout the Mao period was referred to as a guest. I felt it implied that China was not fully part of the world of nations, not one nation among others, but some realm apart. In the case of all other nations I knew, you could make a visit as an individual with a particular purpose. But in China a wrapping of "foreign guest" had to be provided for any non-Chinese, whatever he might be doing in China.

Formal dining was an important buttress for the "guest" syndrome. Over millennia, Chinese officials have used the banquet to charm, soften, or overwhelm guests. One was really helpless at a banquet. The dishes were so excellent that you felt inadequate before them. They arrived when the kitchen wanted to present them, not necessarily when you were ready for a fresh offering. And during all this, your host proposed toasts that gave him the chance to edify or rebuke you.

The term "friend" was used as a suction pump designed to draw off from the visitor all juices of objectivity. A friend could be expected to make automatic, laudatory responses to all that he heard and saw. In truth, a friend ceased to be an individual. He became a category, and he could be fed the prefabricated food that nourished the simple kind of hunger his category experienced. There was ethnocentric condescension in this usage. Edgar Snow was irritated to be welcomed as "an old friend of Mao Zedong" when he visited Peking University in 1970. The appellation made it seem he "could not exist without Mao's imprimatur," and at times he felt "guested to death."[3]

One of the first foreign writers the Chinese "invited" to "come back to China" was Jack Belden, author of *China Shakes the World,* a marvelous portrait of China just before the Communist triumph. He never returned, but I have no doubt that he would have been uncomfortable indeed in the pigeon-hole of "guest." The China he investigated in the mid-1940s had its tragic aspects, but it was not a regimented land. Belden wandered freely (if not always safely), relying on himself, beholden to no one, without entanglement in ritual or waiting for invitations. Virtually none of the leading Western China journalists of the 1930s and 1940s could have been happy with the PRC's "guest" and "friend" categorizations designed to minimize freedom.

Guo Moruo, the highest-ranking scholar in Mao's government,

told me in 1971 that the "exchange of scholars" was going ahead vigorously. But the list of names he offered did not exhaust the fingers of two hands. Additional American scholars "have asked to come," Guo said with a touch of pride. It all seemed far removed from normal intellectual exchanges in the modern world. Not only was Guo upholding a "you come to us" mentality, but he implied that the visitor was either "invited" or forbidden. No intermediate category existed, no private ebb and flow of individuals moving across frontiers for diverse purposes.

The grand gesture of "invitation" was a dictatorship's technique to mask the colossal lack of freedom of movement to and within China. And because Western scholars of Chinese affairs were forbidden unless invited, there was always the danger—no doubt it was the Chinese hope—that they would strain to be pro-China in order to be invited a second time. An invitation suggested a stamp of approval.

I soon found out why the Chinese embassy in Ottawa had summoned me to Peking two weeks in advance of Whitlam; I was to be a resource. The small narrow world of the Chinese foreign policy establishment knew little of Australian politics, and a Harvard faculty member could also answer some questions about former professor Kissinger. "Are the policies of the Australian Labor party public?" Zhou Nan asked me, and he seemed mildly surprised to hear they were. "Which members of Whitlam's delegation are left, and which right?" he inquired unblushingly. He asked my suggestions for Australian journalists China might "invite" to cover Whitlam's trip.

Zhou Nan was riveted by the Pentagon Papers case that was unfolding by the day in this summer of 1971. "Who will benefit, the Republicans or the Democrats?" he asked, and he was quite unable to believe that Daniel Ellsberg might have acted alone in divulging the Pentagon Papers. "Is it the Morgans who are behind him?" he probed. "Or the Rockefellers?"

Across a coffee table laden with cakes and nuts and beer at the old International Club in the Legation Quarter on a stiflingly hot morning, Peng Hua of the foreign ministry sought information on Kissinger. "Just how much power does he have in Nixon's White House? Is he still Germanic and anti-Russian? Is it true that he is nonchalant about the use of nuclear weapons? What does he think of Japan?" In his memoirs Kissinger said of Zhou Enlai, whom he was soon to meet for the first time: "His command of facts, in particular his knowledge of American events and, for that matter, of my own background, was stunning."[4] Some of that knowledge had been quite recently garnered.

Early in July 1971, Nixon gave an interesting but little-noticed speech in Kansas City that praised the Chinese people and predicted a world of "five great economic superpowers" (U.S.A., U.S.S.R., Japan, Western Europe, and China). I mentioned the Kansas City speech several times to Peng Hua, Zhou Nan, and other Chinese officials in Peking over the next week. Kissinger wrote in his memoirs: "Zhou [Enlai] spent some time in our first meeting [in July 1971] . . . expressing his general agreement with the concepts outlined by Nixon in a speech in Kansas City on July 6. This put me at a disadvantage since I was unaware of either the fact or the content of the speech."[5]

Whitlam arrived at Peking airport from Australia one steamy evening early in July 1971, and in the ensuing weeks he explored China with energy and curiosity, determined to see every monument, taste every dish, and talk to every child. I admired the way Whitlam, a lawyer six feet seven inches tall who was trying to reform his own Labor party and woo the Australian electorate at the same time, enjoyed himself despite the big political risk he was taking. Not only did the Australian government scoff at Whitlam's trip, but Ted Hill, chief of the "Australian Communist Party (Marxist-Leninist)," a teeth-gritting pro-China group, tried to prevent him from reaching Peking. Hill saw Labor party people as "social fascist hyenas," worse than right-wingers. As the veteran journalist Richard Hughes reported in the London *Sunday Times,* Hill urged Peking in a cable from Melbourne not to give Whitlam or me a visa, but the Chinese government rejected Hill's advice, and Chinese officials leaked news of the rejection to Hughes in Hong Kong.[6] In line with China's twilight condition in 1971, Peking welcomed Whitlam, but in public continued to champion Hill and his remnant, quoting him in *People's Daily* and stocking airports and hotel lobbies with free, unread copies of his overheated newspaper *Vanguard.* In Australia Hill was nothing, but he knew Mao and the other top Chinese leaders and in China he passed for a world leader, being one of those red gargoyles on the edifice of China's idea of itself that helped convince the Middle Kingdom of its middleness.

While we were in Peking, Whitlam asked Foreign Minister Ji

Pengfei what the Chinese government's attitude to Hill would be in the event of a Whitlam government. "Noninterference," replied Ji. "We do not know what is best for Australia." The Chinese press talked of Australia in Marxist terms—"sharpening of class struggle" —but in practice the Chinese Communists seemed to have no interest in "making revolution" Down Under. This dual behavior intrigued me and I felt I was watching China in the act of shedding revolutionary values while pretending not to.

Shen Chunyi was a Peking schoolboy during the Whitlam mission, and years later when we had become friends, he brought out of memory a scene from that time. "I was learning English and always eager to practice with anyone," he recalled. "One day in the summer of 1971, I saw some foreigners in Wang Fu Jing Street, surrounded by a crowd. I knew at once who it was. *People's Daily* had said Australians were in Peking. There were rather few foreigners, so I realized these were Australians. I went up to them, trying to speak to them, but the Australian accent was difficult to understand." Shen laughed at the memory of those days. "You see, in political meetings," he explained, "the government told us, through our teachers, that we must not pay attention to the foreign guests. But we couldn't resist—it was exciting. The officials told us not to act stupidly when foreigners were around. We had to be careful about that."

Although I still was an Australian citizen, I had been influenced to a degree by American idealism even as I still possessed Australian skepticism. At a factory or commune, the first American journalists who came in to cover the American Ping-Pong team trip and its aftermath tended to ask questions about freedom of choice in work and living arrangements. We Australians tended to ask about the absence of trade unions and to raise our eyebrows at workers having to put up with military men beside them on the workshop floor. After dining one evening at the old International Club with Seymour Topping of *The New York Times* and William Attwood of *Newsday,* I wrote in my diary: "Wherever in the world these Americans go, they remain mentally in their own country, adopting their managerial approach to things. They talk about wage scales in a commune as if it were the Chrysler Corporation. There is an ethnocentrism in this. Yet there is also an openness to any demonstration of practical achievement by the Chinese."

Back in 1964, the watershed between vice and virtue had been Liberation, and for all the exaggeration about Chiang Kai-shek's failures, the myth of Liberation did have some truth to it. Moreover, exaggerations often could be detected because the record of pre-1949 China was fairly open to the foreigner. By contrast, the before-and-after mythology of the Cultural Revolution that I heard each day in 1971 was seldom believable, certainly not to one who had been in China in 1964. One day during a visit with Whitlam to Qinghua University, an official droned on about the disasters from which the university had recently been delivered. A long catalogue of evils—all canceled by the glorious Cultural Revolution—were put down to the account of Liu Shaoqi, the former Chinese president, and Whitlam's colleague Tom Burns, a politician from the state of Queensland, listening keenly, interrupted with a question: "Did President Liu live in this part of Peking?"

A startled look came over the face of the official, for Burns had been taking his remarks at face value as facts, but the man had been speaking theology. It did not matter in this theology where Liu had lived, or even whether he had set foot on the Qinghua campus; he had become a suprarational source of evil. A degradation of morality occurred after the 1960s. In earlier years, people who spoke of the bitterness of pre-Liberation life often believed their own words, but the Qinghua University official probably knew that blaming Liu for alleged flaws on the campus was farfetched at best.

I was exhilarated by the chance to use my knowledge of Chinese, but vulnerable because of my inadequate grasp of it. Awe for the special world of the Chinese characters put me into a receptive posture toward what I read and heard. Straining to catch words spoken faster than in the classroom, eager to understand each nuance of Chinese culture, I was hardly prepared for lies. Yet there were lies, and beyond the lies often there was a cunning determination to keep truth in short supply.

In Changsha, a hot city in south central China where Mao had spent his student years, I saw a building in a compound with high walls topped with broken glass, and I asked my Hunan Province hosts what it was. "A gymnasium" came the reply, but five minutes later I found out it was a prison. "It used to take one hundred men ten days to produce those crates of machine tools," a spokesman intoned at a plant in Xian, the graceful treasure trove of China's past that was the capital during the Tang dynasty. "Now it takes ten men two days." I could not verify the pronouncement with interviews among the workers. Probably the factory authorities, under fantastic pressure to portray the present as being as rosy as the past was dismal, overstated the improvement in productivity. In a park in the silk city of Wuxi, a woman holding a tiny child smiled to catch my attention, then she nudged her child and it said, "Long live Chairman Mao." The woman paraded up and down in front of me and the child continued to gurgle, "Long live Chairman Mao."

I tried to understand how Chinese individuals could lie and play-act like this and in some cases I felt there was a simple fear of the consequences of telling the truth to a foreign writer. But the most insidious reason was the collective zeal that had descended on China. In all societies there exists a balance between individual truth and collective truth. In America most of our truths are individually held, although some collective truths are strong (such as belief in the Constitution), but Communist China has always been the opposite, and with the Cultural Revolution it became dramatically so.

"We must become religious again," wrote Ludwig Feuerbach a century and a half ago, "politics must become our religion."[7] This was actually experienced by the Chinese. Collective meanings designed on high were clamped upon the people, eclipsing personal ethics. As the balance tipped heavily away from individual satisfactions and toward society's imperatives, many people flew helter-skelter into the treacherous cave of politics as religion and sincerely made of the wider social world their own personal world. Such super citizens were prepared to put Mao before their family or even their own material interest. The collective zeal produced, in addition to lies and play-acting, a great deal of altruism.

Maoist behavior at times reminded me of evangelical Christian behavior, as one day in northwest China when I happened to leave a face cloth behind in a hotel room in Xian. Staff members found it and laundered it, and by plane and car it was sent to the northern Shaanxi Province village where I was staying. A young man on a bicycle rushed up one afternoon as I was visiting the tomb of the Yellow Emperor, bearing my face cloth in a neatly wrapped package, and presented it to me with a triumphant smile and a quotation from Mao.

People could be honest about other people's personal property, yet dishonest about things of the mind. In Peking a cabdriver told me with a straight face that the reason he chose his girlfriend was that she had "beautiful Mao-thoughts"; a moment later he declined my tip. Whereas in the West, an evangelical Christian preacher might agonize sincerely over biblical doctrines from the pulpit, and an hour later put his hand in the church's till for funds to landscape the garden of his villa, the Chinese citizen of the early 1970s would not steal a dime, but on any matter touching public policy he may not have believed a word he was saying.

Most people obey the law, and many behave courteously toward strangers, for a variety of reasons of which fear of punishment is one. A sense of common interest can also spur the citizen: he behaves well because he does not want others to behave badly toward him. And there are factors that go beyond the prudential: doctrine can evoke altruism, and people lift their standards of behavior as others around them lift theirs. All these motivations I found in the China of the early 1970s. At the same time there were signs that collective zeal had passed its peak. The theory of class struggle was still loudly mouthed, but in people's minds it had been invalidated by the subjectivism of the Cultural Revolution. The use of unbelievable class labels in the 1960s had undermined the whole notion of class analysis, and during the 1970s Mao paid a heavy price for such manipulation: the Communist party lost the mental allegiance of many of the Chinese people.

During a visit I made to Peking University, the eminent philosopher Feng Youlan, author of *A History of Chinese Philosophy,* met me in a traditional-style reception building by a lotus pond. Professor Feng remarked that "extreme leftists were responsible for the violence" of the Cultural Revolution, and a young political guardian broke in to correct him. "No, they were reactionaries," he said, the words coming at me like a pistol shot, carrying a "truth" that had been manufactured out of plain cloth in the latter phase of the Cultural Revolution. The term "reactionary" had become little more than a swear word, and many people in addition to Professor Feng knew it. Having heard the Communist party label black as white so insistently, and turn "left" into "reactionary" with the stroke of an ideological wand, millions of people step by step became deaf to anything from the party's lips, a loss of credibility that was working itself out during the early 1970s.

Problems and changes were discussed as a morality play, as when factory officials told me Soviet help to China in the 1950s was marginal, and in the next breath denounced the withdrawal of that aid in 1960 as a terrible blow from which China had not yet recovered. Rarely was a problem seen as other than totally solvable by applying Chairman Mao's line. Any shortcoming was viewed as a leftover from the mistakes of evil men, now exposed and overthrown. One drawback of such morality-play treatment was the constant twists and turns of line, for if the past was any guide, today's "correct" policy by tomorrow might well be called "the capitalist road," and today's "wise" leaders rejected as "traitorous." Chinese politics still was a Peking opera. Good and evil were never less than crystal clear; heroes were flawless and villains were grotesque. The lively music and gaudy costumes were arresting and the audience—so the leaders hoped—was not inclined to worry too much about the twists of the plot.

As for those of us who were observers of the Peking opera from a greater distance, why did our fascination with China and our eagerness to go there continue undiminished after the Cultural Revolution? Children of the 1960s, some of us felt a residual guilt and irritation at the West's contribution to China's isolation since 1949. Watching the war in Indochina grow ever fiercer, we insisted that Mao's concern about the war on his doorstep be understood lest, as in Korea, an American-Chinese confrontation should occur without warning. And my generation of students of the Orient was simply keen to gain firsthand experience of China. The Cultural Revolution, rightly or wrongly, did not lead us to favor a continued isolation of China.

A more remarkable continuity was to be found on the Chinese side. Why were many of the middle-aged and older Chinese I interviewed during the early 1970s still so patriotic and such believers in the basic values of the revolution? One day in 1971, driving through the millet fields of Shaanxi Province, I overheard Zhou Nan and two Chinese companions in the backseat of the car talk about China's condition. The insistent theme of their conversation was backwardness, and the need to wrench the country out of it. Economic development was a topic that brought excitement to their voices; these three men, I felt, were modernizers as well as patriots.

As I continued to sit silent in the front seat with the driver, Zhou Nan asked one of his companions, a Shaanxi official, where he had been during the Cultural Revolution.★ The mood of the conversation in the backseat of the car changed abruptly. Bubbling talk about steel and cotton and computers gave way to terse, grunted remarks. These men had awful memories of the Cultural Revolution, but

---

★ Although the Chinese government would later say the Cultural Revolution lasted a full decade, from 1966 until Mao's death in 1976, and many Westerners would fall in with this usage, all the Chinese I met in the early 1970s referred to the Cultural Revolution in the past tense.

usually they were well bottled up. Although Zhou Nan felt in his heart that the Cultural Revolution had been a disaster, over a month as we together traced thousands of miles and ate three meals a day he never denounced it. He still saw the Communist party as the guiding force for China's long-delayed modernization and he hoped Mao was now on a new track. He believed that after economic modernization was achieved, some political freedom would follow, and he felt that the Communist party's success in making China a force in the world offset some of its failures at home.

CHAPTER SIX

■

THE OPENING

BEHIND a curtain of secrecy, China inched toward America during the spring of 1971, and it was ironic that this historic shift was the work of a tiny elite at the top, which bore no evident relation to the views of the masses. Mao and Zhou handled it in the manner of a monarchical court of eighteenth-century Europe, a style that suited Kissinger and Nixon and helped inspire their own secretive diplomatic ways. Foreign ambassadors in Peking—I talked with eight in the summer of 1971 as I probed China's new foreign policy—nearly all held a relatively high opinion of Chinese competence, for the foreign policy realm they closely observed was more professionally handled than many realms of domestic policy.

One day in a talk with Peng Hua, the foreign ministry official, I suggested (based on my knowledge of Senator Edward Kennedy's thinking) that it would help Americans appreciate the Chinese position on Taiwan if Peking could clarify its likely future treatment of Taiwan after "liberation" of the island. I complained that Zhou Enlai had never addressed this question and said it was unrealistic to keep saying China's future treatment of Taiwan was a matter of internal Chinese policy. I knew that Zhou would soon meet three American journalists and speak to them about United States–China relations, and I urged Peng Hua to try to arrange a response.

Two days later Zhou Enlai gave such a clarification on Taiwan in a talk with Seymour Topping of *The New York Times*, William Attwood of *Newsday,* and Robert Keatley of *The Wall Street Journal.*[1]

There would be no reprisals against the people of Taiwan after its "liberation," the Chinese premier said. Taiwan people would be able to go back to their home provinces in China, should they wish, and the leaders in Taipei would be offered a dignified retirement. Moreover, the economic well-being of the Taiwan people would improve as income tax was abolished while wage scales remained the same. Zhou Enlai's response raised as many questions as it answered, but the premier had recognized for the first time the reality, if not the right, of American concern with the concrete fate of Taiwan. That I seemed to have prompted this gave me an impression of Chinese foreign policy making as tight and rational.

One day my link with Edgar Snow brought a glimpse of the bureaucratic divide-and-rule ways of the Chinese monarchical court. The veteran journalist had encouraged me in a number of ways and written a preface to *China and Ourselves,* a book of essays I coedited while a graduate student. With a letter of introduction from Snow to the journalist Tang Mingzhao in my pocket, I walked down the steps of the Xin Qiao Hotel to take a taxi to Tang's office. Taxi drivers were under the thumb of the state, and my driver, shown the name and address on the envelope of Snow's letter, brazenly said he didn't know where Tang's unit, the very well-known Association for Friendship with Foreign Countries, was located and disappeared into the staff booth. Twenty minutes later a travel official came out of the Xin Qiao Hotel and said I was wanted urgently on the phone. It was the foreign ministry; I was required there immediately. Postponing the delivery of Snow's letter to Tang, I went in quiet fury with my driver to the foreign ministry, where Zhou Nan and his colleague Ma Yuzhen were waiting for me. The meeting about my program seemed routine, and then out of the blue Ma raised Snow's letter. Just what was in it? I explained it was merely a letter of introduction from a "good friend of China." "We will deliver it for you," said Ma, and when Tang Mingzhao gave me a luncheon three days later, Zhou Nan was present throughout. Any sign that I might slip out of my allotted role in the Whitlam diplomatic project and walk a path of my own choosing was treated with swift corrective action.

When Zhou Enlai summoned Whitlam to a late night dialogue on a hot rainy July evening, the Labor party leader arrived at the Great Hall of the People to find that the session was to be an open one in front of half a dozen Australian journalists. By this means Zhou put Whitlam under considerable pressure; the Australian's promises about future Australia-China ties would be written in stone, and Zhou's rather imperious handling of him would be reported back to every household in Australia.

This was my first sight of Zhou Enlai. He was slim and handsome, with a penetrating gaze and hands that flew at the service of his rhetoric. Sitting back in a wicker armchair, he seemed a loose-limbed willow of a person, at one with his chair as people are with the scenic backdrop in old Chinese paintings. At times he whispered, at other times he projected his streaky voice across the Fujian Province Room of the Great Hall like an actor in a large theater. Born into a rich family of Zhejiang Province, Zhou had stepped into the revolution as a matter of choice, and he talked with the grace and balance of an aristocrat even as his words laid out Communist principles.

Zhou chose this dialogue in the Great Hall of the People to reveal —whether Whitlam desired it or not—my role in the background of Whitlam's presence in Peking. Zhou had been talking to Whitlam about the Chinese military (a hint to us of a budding crisis over Defense Minister Lin Biao), and in particular about a press editorial celebrating the fiftieth anniversary of the founding of the Chinese Communist party. Then the premier turned to me. "This can also serve as reference material for you, Mr. Terrill," he said a little inaccurately, "for you are a professor both in America and in Australia." Zhou Enlai turned back toward Whitlam. "He's your adviser, eh?" Whitlam looked startled. "Yes," the Australian opposition leader said. "I suppose I can be indiscreet enough to say that when we were hoping you would receive a delegation from the Australian Labor party, we phoned him at Harvard." Zhou tossed back his head and laughed. "And he came first as your vanguard officer!" the premier said, making sure his point was clear to the listening Australian journalists.

I was in China as a Harvard professor gathering material for my courses and for articles in *The Atlantic Monthly,* yet I was also there, as Zhou put it, as "vanguard officer" for Whitlam. It was the Chinese, not Whitlam or I, who saw matters that way, and to a degree set matters up that way. There were other occasions, too, on which the Chinese drew me, an independent observer, out of the stalls and onto the stage to become part of the performance. The Chinese were very effective at this manipulation, in part because the foreigner could not in China discern as easily as he could back home the boundary line between the stalls and the stage.

Hugh Dunn, who would at different times be Australian ambassador in Taipei and Peking, told me something his tutor at Oxford said about the Chinese language. "Studying Chinese has a tendency to make you think you've got hold of the key to something no one has ever had before," the tutor remarked. "If you get that feeling, put your Chinese books away for a week and play golf." During my study of Chinese at Harvard, at moments when I felt the Chinese characters made my mind soar too much, I turned back to the political philosophy of Tawney, which pinned me to my identity as a citizen of the West. But my mind did soar for a moment when Zhou Enlai asked me where I had learned Chinese. "In America," I replied. The premier beamed and said: "That is a fine thing, for an Australian to learn Chinese in America!"

On July 16, 1971, I was driving through the streets of Wuxi, a lakeside city of silk mills in the Yangzi Valley, when over the car radio came an announcement from Peking that changed the history of the last quarter of the twentieth century. Henry Kissinger had just finished successful talks with Mao and Zhou Enlai, and Richard Nixon soon would be visiting China. Whitlam had hardly taken his leave of Zhou when Kissinger arrived at Zhou's door, and nothing would be the same in the Asian region or quite the same in the contours of world politics. Winston Lord, who traveled with Kissinger on the secret flight from Pakistan (and was later ambassador in Peking) told me the mission was "The most exciting event of my life—except my marriage."

I admired the skillfulness of the maneuver Nixon and Kissinger had effected, but as a student of Chinese affairs who had been in Peking in the desperately anti-American atmosphere of 1964, and at Harvard during the Vietnam War, I also realized what a price the United States and China, and their friends in the Asian region, had paid for twenty years of mutual isolation.

A few days after the stunning news from the car radio, I left Wuxi for Mao's home province of Hunan. In the oppressive heat of a Changsha hotel room, I sat down to handwrite an article for *The Washington Post* on what I knew from the Chinese side of the Kissinger breakthrough.[2] Zhou Nan as my attending Mandarin seemed a little uneasy that I was devoting time to this article, which drew discreetly on some of our conversations as we traveled, and I think he felt I should be away from my desk inspecting newborn socialist wonders in Changsha. He kept coming to my room to remind me that the hour for a farewell banquet in my honor was fast approaching. At length I finished the piece and took it to the post office for cabling to Washington. I had to write it out again in block letters so that the Changsha post office, where no one knew English, could consult its alphabet book, identify each letter, and ensure correct transmission by that ponderous means.

During the farewell banquet with our Changsha hosts, Zhou Nan excused himself with a murmured remark that he had to settle some administrative matters. He was away half an hour. Later that evening, as our train chugged south from Changsha toward Canton, Zhou drawled: "Your article was interesting. Just two strange things in it." During his half-hour's absence from the banquet, the wily Zhou had been down to the post office. I was more awestruck than appalled by this surveillance, and more concerned about my relation with Zhou Nan, I must confess, than with the probable implication that the Chinese people were being shepherded and monitored by their government in the same way. Looking back on the incident, I was struck by Zhou's having divulged to me that he had gone to the post office to read the article. Perhaps we had established a relationship that made him think I would not interpret his act in too bad a way. Or perhaps he was reminding me that I was in China and that he, Zhou Nan, was in charge of me.

Kissinger, who phoned me in Cambridge a couple of months later to say the piece cabled to *The Washington Post* from Changsha was the most interesting newspaper article he had read from China, was especially struck, and pleased, to read in it that Chinese officials said they preferred to deal with Republicans rather than Democrats in attempting to establish ties with America, because it had been Democrats (Truman and Acheson) who backed Chiang Kai-shek to the hilt and fought China in Korea, and because "Democrats have been very keen on collusion with Moscow." Kissinger also was intrigued that I had reported that the Chinese appreciated his skepticism about Russia's "peaceful" intentions, and took the view that his past non-involvement with American policy toward East Asia was a point in his favor. When two articles I wrote about the 1971 trip to China came out in *The Atlantic Monthly,* they won the National Magazine Award and the George Polk Memorial Award for Outstanding Magazine Reporting, and at a dinner of the Washington Press Club in January 1972, Kissinger came over to me after his speech and said of the pieces: "They were the first thing I gave the president to read in preparation for the trip next month." At the time, I felt I had succeeded in conveying the rudiments of Mao's China to President Nixon, although later I would regret some omissions.

I had been surprised that Nixon in his first years in office had been so much calmer about communism in Europe than about communism in Asia. Yet Nixon changed. Edgar Snow had been pleased when Kennedy defeated Nixon in 1960, and he told the Chinese that Kennedy, unlike Nixon, was prepared to move on China policy.[3] It didn't turn out that way, and while still in China in the summer of 1971, I wrote in my diary at Wuxi: "Nixon's acts [in relation to China] seem less out of step with his words than some of those of previous Democratic administrations."

An incident related by Edwin Reischauer, my senior colleague at Harvard's East Asian Center, brought home to me Nixon's change of views on China. Early in 1969 Nixon had met with Reischauer, George Taylor, a conservative specialist on China, and three other sinologists who like Reischauer tended to the side of the "doves." In the Oval Office, the four doves all criticized the existing policy of nonrecognition of Peking and keeping China out of world forums, and then Taylor spoke in favor of the existing policy, saying the United States should wait until China came around to a less anti-American position before holding out a hand. President Nixon broke his silence. "You know, I used to think that way once, too, Mr. Taylor," he said.

As for the evolution of the China issue in Australian politics, the rug was simply pulled from under the feet of the pro-American Australian prime minister McMahon. He had denounced Whitlam for sitting down with the leaders of an evil regime in Peking, and he was engaged in a protest to the French government at the role of Ambassador Manac'h in assisting this unworthy coupling. But his outrage at Whitlam froze on his lips, for Nixon himself was about to climb into the ring to deal with the red tigers of Peking. Paris shrugged off Canberra's complaint about Manac'h's role, and the next year the voters of Australia, swayed in part by the China issue, voted McMahon out and Whitlam in as prime minister.

It was the event of the decade in Washington, if not quite in Peking, when Nixon flew off to China in February 1972. His eight-day stay in China was the longest visit to any foreign country by a U.S. president, and the first time a U.S. president had ever negotiated on the soil of a nation that had no diplomatic relations with Washington. When Mao and Nixon met in Mao's study, less than a day after Nixon's arrival in Peking, Mao joked, "Our common old friend, Generalissimo Chiang Kai-shek, doesn't approve of this."[4]

With Zhou Enlai in Shanghai, Nixon signed a communiqué that put American-Chinese relations into an entirely fresh phase. Battered by Vietnam and seeking leverage against a threatening Soviet Union, Nixon and Kissinger gave the Chinese side guarantees against the use of force, interference, or any bid for hegemony in Asia. Zhou Enlai, also apprehensive about the Russians ("John Foster Dulles's successors," as he described them to Whitlam, objecting to their "interference"), agreed to take steps toward "normalizing" relations with the United States even while Washington retained full diplomatic ties with Taipei. To his great credit, Nixon accepted that a cooperative world was not a luxury but a necessity. He wanted an "overall structure of peace" in East Asia to help America get beyond the Indochina tragedy.

The Atlantic Monthly had wished to send me to China to cover the Nixon-Mao summit, but as I was not an American citizen I was declared by the White House ineligible for the press party, so as Nixon reached Peking, I was sitting before a camera in the CBS studios in New York with anchorman Charles Collingwood. Each morning and evening for nearly a week, as Collingwood presided, I chatted fairly inconsequentially with Walter Cronkite and Bernard Kalb broadcasting from the Great Wall or the Forbidden City, making comments on a China that now held Americans in thrall. As Nixon drove into Peking from the airport, the veteran Collingwood in his rich theatrical cadences made a slip of the tongue that rolled back the decades: "We are now watching President Truman enter the capital city of Chinese communism," he declared.

The evening Zhou gave a banquet for Nixon in the Great Hall of the People, Cronkite from his chair on a balcony above the head table asked me to comment on why the Chinese had served the Nixons Jell-O for dessert, but when I looked into the screen beside me in the New York studio, I saw before each dinner guest a white plate holding a brilliantly colored tangerine. "Is it Jell-O, Walter?" I inquired, "Or are those tangerines?" Such were the wonders of television technology and the trivialities that made up the actual moments of a historic event.

What struck me during Nixon's trip was the American capacity for renewal and enthusiasm in dealing with China, for it was as if the years of fear and hostility between the United States and Mao's China had never existed. Just after finishing my first commentary with Collingwood, on Nixon's arrival day in Peking, I wrote in my diary: "I felt excited as Nixon's plane drew up at the Peking airport with the American flag fluttering in the north China sky and the music of the Stars and Stripes echoing across a wintry morning scene. I tried to keep my commentary sober and balanced, but I am not sure I succeeded."

Nixon was even less sober. On leaving Washington, he compared his trip to China with his countrymen's voyage to the moon, while in Peking he quoted Mao's poems as if they were Holy Scripture, and upon his return he said his trip was "a week that changed the world."[5] Yet as summit meetings go, it was indeed a great event and it did change the world. China had emerged with a flourish from the Cultural Revolution, triangular diplomacy was born, the Russians were like ants on a hot stove, and most of the domestic critics of both Mao and Nixon had for the moment been silenced.

Kissinger had told me during a visit he made to Harvard in January 1971 that there were two groups opposed to a relationship with Peking: those who did not want to abandon Chiang Kai-shek's Nationalists, and those who did not want to upset the Russians. Kissinger was perfectly suited to handle Nixon's China move, for he had never been one of those Republicans whose experience of the "loss" of China to Mao left in them an unshakable sentimental loyalty to the Nationalists on Taiwan, and in a sense Kissinger wanted to "upset the Russians." Once he began dealing with the Chinese, Kissinger was aided in his goals by a continental European's respect for Chinese culture. He thought Zhou Enlai was a refined, subtle man, and about few other political figures around the world did he feel the same. He appreciated in Mao and Zhou a sense of humor that he missed among the Japanese and many others, and he found the concentration of power at the top in Peking congenial to his diplomatic method. Liking to act alone, to hold all the strings in his own hand, to employ the tools of surprise and flexibility, he found to his pleasure that the Chinese Communist leaders operated the same way.

All this made Kissinger rather pro-China for a season. For America and the world that was a good thing, I felt. As I told Kissinger in his office at the White House after Nixon's China trip, I thought he had brilliantly enabled America to ease out of its messianic posture toward Asia. "Well, we've done it with China," he said, "but not yet with Vietnam." I saw Kissinger again just after Whitlam was elected prime minister of Australia at the end of 1972, and expecting to talk with him about China, I was surprised on entering his office to find him waving a cable from Whitlam over Vietnam, protesting Nixon's "Christmas bombing" of Hanoi. The Vietnam War issue still dogged the China issue, and although Kissinger now had a Voltaire-like awe for the Chinese, he saw the North Vietnamese as stubborn obstacles to his grand strategic plans in Asia. "The Vietnamese, south and north, are all the same, and impossible to deal with," he complained. "It's a case of French Cartesianism without French skepticism."

I asked Kissinger if the Chinese had ever hinted agreement with his complaints about the North Vietnamese. "Yes, they have," he replied. "They know how difficult the Vietnamese are." Later events would suggest that Kissinger was correct.

Around the time of the Nixon-Mao summit, I found many American commentators more pro-China than I was.★ One exception was William F. Buckley, who in a debate on his show Firing Line treated me with the curled lip of ideological distaste, pronouncing "Mr. Terrill" like a prosecutor spitting out the name of a felon. Buckley's first question set the tone: "In China, what kind of thing did they hide from you and why?" Despite his addiction to contentiousness, Buckley was correct in criticizing the "celebration" of Mao's China that the Nixon visit became in some quarters, and he was correct to say that I was not as outraged at the tragedy of higher education in China as I should have been.

His narrowed eye whipping up from his clipboard to fix me in an icy gaze, Buckley suggested to the viewers of Firing Line that I was "making excuses" for China. To a degree I was. I was eager to make the points that Communist China was a going concern, not about to return to Nationalist rule, and that detente with Mao was in America's interest. Thus focused, I tended to gloss over the repression of freedom within China. As Buckley put it to me in his rolling-thunder way: "The assault on the spirit [perpetrated by the Communists on Chinese cultural life] is something that you take

★ When my 800,000,000: The Real China, a book that stemmed from my 1971 trip, was reviewed in China Quarterly, the leading journal of Chinese affairs, the reviewer spoke of my "essential personal repudiation of the Chinese Revolution" (China Quarterly, Number 52, p. 741).

rather more casually than I would judge to be useful for the metabolism of mankind." *

A serious difference between us was summed up in our respective parting remarks. "It is not a small thing," I said, "that Mr. Nixon has agreed on a live-and-let-live policy with China." Buckley swept this aside with the comment: "I desire the liberation of the Chinese people from their current slave masters." For the time being these two statements came from opposite political poles and made no contact with each other, but in a later era they would not seem so contradictory.

There were others who behaved as if China were still the fire-eating enemy of the first two decades of Mao's rule. In Washington after my December 1972 visit to Kissinger's office, I left the White House to take a plane to New York, and while making a phone call in a booth at National Airport, I noticed a bespectacled man with an intense expression in the next booth. On the Eastern Shuttle I looked up and saw this same man. As I entered the Chinese mission on Manhattan's West Side, to visit Ambassador Huang Hua, I glimpsed him once again. With the unwelcome eye of American officialdom watching over my China contacts and travels, there were times when I still compared Washington and Peking as the hearts of two highly ideological civilizations. †

As an alien living in the United States, I was required to seek Washington's permission each time I visited a Communist country, there was occasional surveillance of my phone calls and letters and movements, and although I was on the faculty at Harvard, an extension to my visa was denied in 1970. When I was given three months' notice to leave the United States, I felt not only an alien but alienated. Yet once Harvard had put me on the faculty, it felt an investment in me and colleagues wrote letters to the Immigration and Naturalization Service of the Department of Justice on my behalf.

* Since the *Firing Line* debate dwelt on censorship in China, I was amused to find on consulting the published transcript of the program that Buckley had done a little sanitizing of his remarks. At one point the televised discussion was about the way applause is manufactured in China. A studio question arose, from the editor of the *Harvard Crimson:* Would Mao be applauded if he appeared at Carnegie Hall? Mr. Buckley took the opportunity to sneer: "Mr. Terrill, you are just the kind of person who would leap to his feet and give Chairman Mao a standing ovation." The printed transcript omits this fairly silly remark.

†In 1991 I obtained under the Freedom of Information Act my FBI file for these years. It totals 172 pages.

Senator Edward Kennedy, who had sought my advice on China, also supported my appeal with an impact that in Boston belonged only to him. Soon I was given an extension of time on my F-1 student visa for a period of "practical training." The first activity I undertook for my "practical training" was a new course in the Government Department at Harvard on Chinese foreign policy.

In the period of Peking's opening to the world, I had learned that China was like a mirror, and much that was seen depended on the observer's own stance. Nixon's starting point was his quest for peace in Asia, Kissinger's was leverage against the Russians, and Whitlam's was a lawyer's belief in the need for and possibility of a rational world. Businessmen saw China as a market, conservatives saw it as an exemplar of law and order, and my mentor Professor Fairbank saw the opening of China as a golden opportunity for renewed access to documents and field reports that would boost China studies.

In his dialogue with Whitlam in 1971, Zhou Enlai had burst out: "Why is there such a lack of ability in East Europe?" The premier, who was skilled in rhetoric, gave his own answer: "Because the minds of the Eastern Europeans are not their own. They're not independent, they're controlled by Russia." Zhou had a point, but why did not part of it at least apply to China? Certainly China was independent, but the same political system Russia had imposed on Eastern Europe had been imposed by the Chinese Communist party on the Chinese people. The mind of an intellectual in Peking was "not his own" any more than was the mind of an intellectual in Budapest or Prague or Warsaw.

For my own part, I did not focus sufficiently on China's authoritarian political system as a hindrance to the nation's economic and social and cultural progress. One reason may have been that in person Zhou Enlai seemed not at all a driven authoritarian, but a charming and fairly reasonable man, and it was also true that I knew less about conditions within China than I would come to know in later years. Moreover, the prior image in my mind of the Cultural Revolution had been bleak, and in 1971 I found enough that was placid and workmanlike to make me feel an instinctive relief at the passing of what had existed before.

But the most important reason for glossing over China's authoritarian political system was that in my mind during the early 1970s, the China issue was one not of social philosophy, but of peace and war. Fighting still raged in Indochina, the PRC had not been recognized by the United States or Australia or dozens of other countries, and Peking was not present at the United Nations. Some hawks in the United States still spoke of "taking China out" with a nuclear strike, and perhaps this made me bend over backward to see as much recovery from the Cultural Revolution as I could, in the hope that China's condition would not provoke a draconian step by the West. Rightly or wrongly a safe landing from the Vietnam nightmare concerned me more than a probe into the human rights abuses of the Chinese government. The Whitlam mission as the context for my 1971 trip had shaped my impressions more perhaps than I realized at the time.

By the mid-1970s, progress was great on nearly all of the international challenges that had concerned me for years, including the Vietnam War, China-Australia ties, Peking-Washington relations, and the Taiwan issue. Only now would I cast a steady eye on the relation between the world's biggest population, more than 800 million by now, mostly stoic and silent, and the world's most idiosyncratic Communist government, as in Mao's final years it increasingly became a jungle of ambition and vanity.

■

CHAPTER SEVEN

MAO'S BORROWED
TIME

A strong role for the military was integral to the post–Cultural Revolution political settlement that had come out into the open at the Ninth Congress of the Communist party held in the Great Hall of the People in April 1969. Defense Minister Lin Biao's PLA had in the mid-1960s been Mao's ally in leftism, and from the late 1960s it was also Mao's ally in clipping the wings of "ultraleftism." When I visited communes and factories and universities in 1971, unarmed military sat in the reception rooms as cohosts. Within the foreign ministry, PLA men filled unlabeled senior posts, and expressions of the moral values that suffused Chinese public policy ("serve the people") often came from the lips of military figures. At the Ninth Party Congress, half of the 279 members of the new central committee were military people, fourteen of the twenty-five Politburo members were military, and Defense Minister Lin was named in the very party constitution as Mao's successor.

Yet the army's prominence did not signify a solution to the divisions that stemmed from the Cultural Revolution, but rather set in motion a new struggle at the top of the Communist party. The military, having tasted the sweetness of a broad political role from 1967, was reluctant to disappear back into the barracks, as many powerful people expected it to. And Defense Minister Lin, whose ears were filled daily with praise for himself as Mao's "closest comrade in arms" and successor, grew impatient to fill Mao's shoes. Unlike Jiang Qing, who was also beginning to see herself as Mao's successor and had entered the Politburo at the Ninth Party Congress, Lin could not bide his time. Jiang needed a few extra years to build support, but for Lin more time might only bring further criticism of the dominance of the PLA.

Lin Biao was born in 1907 in a village of Hubei Province, the second of four sons of a landowner and proprietor of a handicraft factory. He was trained at the famous Whampoa Military Academy in Canton, during a period of cooperation between the Communists and the Nationalists, when the academy's head was Chiang Kaishek. A member of the Communist Red Army from its founding in 1927, he was made commander of the First Army Corps in 1931 at the age of twenty-four. He was a slight, taciturn man with a high-pitched voice, whose uniform hung on him as from a hook.

Lin made the Long March and during the civil war of the 1940s the Fourth Field Army under his command won brilliant victories in northeast and central China. Already balding—which led him to leave his military cap on at all times in public—Lin benefited from the falling out between Mao and Defense Minister Peng Dehuai in the late 1950s, eventually replacing Peng. His second wife was the formidable Ye Qun, a schemer like her husband, originally an assistant in the Central Research Academy, who rose in step with her husband. Now Lin was the official successor, although his status bestowed no extra confidence upon him.

Mao had already begun privately to attack his defense minister for maneuvering to become head of state (an office vacant since the fall of Liu Shaoqi) and flaunting military power in the political realm. Mao was displeased also that Lin resisted the developing rapprochement with America. If not pro-Soviet, the defense minister at least wanted China to be evenhanded toward America and Russia, and not drop China's guard altogether against the United States. "If you can ask Nixon to China," he evidently said to Mao, "why can't I ask Brezhnev?"[1]

Mao had once put out the slogan, "Let the People of the Whole Country Learn from the PLA," yet as he and Lin battled each other during 1970 and 1971, Mao drily told the nation the slogan was "incomplete," and he added a second part, logically a cancellation of the first part and heavy with political implication: "Let the PLA Learn from the People of the Whole Country."[2] I received a hint of the struggle going on at the top when in July 1971 Premier Zhou Enlai, who was feeling the growing tension between Mao and Lin (and also shaping up as Mao's chief instrument in containing Lin), had urged me to study carefully an editorial published in *People's Daily* to mark the fiftieth anniversary of the founding of the Communist party. The editorial warned against those who "become conceited at the moment of success" and stressed Mao's point that "the gun must never be allowed to command the party."[3]

In September 1971, a Trident of the Chinese air force crashed in Mongolia, some 150 kilometers beyond the Chinese frontier, and Lin Biao, his wife, Ye Qun, and three other senior pro-Lin PLA colleagues were found dead amidst the wreckage. Almost no one knew whether the five boarded the Trident at the seaside town of Beidaihe, its place of departure, or whether they were killed in Peking and put onto the plane, nor whether the plane crashed through lack of fuel or a mechanical failure, as the Chinese government said, or because it was sabotaged.[4] This shocking event followed several alleged attempts by Lin and his son to murder Mao by blowing up his train, bombing his home, and poisoning his food. Even years later, all that could be said of the violent drama with reasonable certainty was that Mao began to move against Lin in 1970, Lin moved against Mao during 1971, and by September of that year Mao won.

It was a story of two men's pride and ambition, with Mao unwilling to see full power move into Lin Biao's hands and Lin too insecure to simply wait. It was one more instance, too, of the dialectic of order and disorder in the PRC, for by the time Lin Biao's name was inscribed in the party constitution of 1969 as Mao's successor, Mao already doubted Lin's suitability to succeed him. The fall of Lin Biao proved, just like the fall of Liu Shaoqi, that rising to high office beside Mao had its perils; as Mao himself once said, citing a maxim of the Han dynasty (205 B.C. to A.D. 220): "A tall thing is easy to break, a white thing is easy to stain."

Years later Charles Elliot, a senior editor at Alfred A. Knopf, phoned to ask if I would write an introduction to an "explosive" manuscript on the true facts of how Lin died that had made its way from within military circles in China to Knopf's publishing offices in New York. A Chinese who cloaked himself in utter secrecy had put the account in English translation into Elliot's hands. I read the manuscript, which leaned heavily on a diary written by an official close to the secret investigation of Lin's death, and found that although much of the story fitted in with known facts, there were spectacular additions. Mao was said to have lured Lin and his wife to dinner at a guest house in the hills west of Peking, and then had the arriving Lin limousine blown to smithereens by rockets fired at point-blank range.

I asked Charles Elliot if I could see the original Chinese manuscript, but Knopf did not have it and had never set eyes on it. I had some doubts about the authenticity of the book, although I felt I might still write an introduction if I saw at least part of the Chinese manuscript. Elliot managed to obtain from the Chinese middleman a portion of the manuscript, and after reading it I declined to write an introduction. The book's diary form betrayed it, for in the Chinese manuscript (the handwritten original) the diary extracts themselves had been extensively changed and revised, and the manuscript was written on a type of notepaper never seen inside the PRC. Perhaps some audacious offspring of Chinese military officers, knowing from family talk quite a bit about the Lin-Mao showdown, while studying abroad concocted the "diary," and then the book.

In 1983 Knopf published *The Conspiracy and Death of Lin Biao* with a useful introduction written by the journalist and historian Stanley Karnow. I told Charles Elliot, who agonized over this publishing decision, that one good thing about doing the book was that it might challenge Peking to answer the string of unanswered questions about Lin's final days, but alas, it did not have that effect. The case of Lin Biao was a reminder of just how secret and bitter high politics were in Mao's China. Decades afterward, the Chinese government continued to keep its own people and the world from knowing how the top two leaders of China had sought to deceive and probably murder each other.

Mao's repulsion of Lin was the last phase of the Cultural Revolution, and Lin became the third great target of the political destruction that began in 1966. Liu Shaoqi and the orthodox cadres around him who had "settled down" too much were the first. The utopians who arose during the crusade against Liu became the second target when they spiraled into factionalism and violence. Lin Biao, whose armies had come into politics to rout the utopian left, encountered Mao's disapproval for his ambition and became the third target; he found out, like Liu and the Red Guard heroes before him, how impermanent fame was in the PRC.

The end of Lin Biao was not the end of the power struggle. Zhou Enlai, who had never been enthusiastic about the leftist policies of the 1960s upon which Lin rose to power, in helping Mao turn back Lin's challenge reached the pinnacle of his influence within the Chinese government.[5] Mao needed Zhou's help in exploiting divisions within the military created by Lin's political maneuvers. It happened that the new opening toward America began as the Mao-Lin crisis rose to its climax, and Zhou's central role in this foreign policy shift reinforced his alliance with regional military commanders who wanted to see Lin (together with his leftist and anti-American line) brought low. But Zhou was battling cancer of the bladder and his illness was known to members of the Politburo.

One day in 1973 at a reception in the Great Hall of the People for Prince Sihanouk of Cambodia, Wang Hairong, a relative of Mao's who was assistant foreign minister, walked into a room of foreign press with Deng Xiaoping on her arm. "I have been at a reform school in Jiangxi Province," Deng said by way of explaining his six years on the scrapheap. "He is now a vice-premier," Ms. Wang chimed in sweetly.[6] Such was the Chinese Communist way of signaling a resurrection. Deng was back because Mao needed a replacement ready in the wings for the ailing Zhou Enlai.

I went to China just at this time to gather material for a book on five diverse Chinese cities, with a contract in hand from Atlantic Monthly Press, the publisher of my *800,000,000: The Real China,* a book that grew out of *The Atlantic Monthly* articles from my 1971 trip. I focused my research on Shanghai and Peking, and also on Hangzhou, a serene city that Marco Polo fell in love with in the thirteenth century, Dalian in Manchuria, where the stamp of Russia and Japan still was visible in the architecture and well-laid-out streets, and Wuhan, a raw industrial bastion seven hundred miles inland yet capable of receiving oceangoing ships.

One evening at a cinema in Hangzhou, a few months after Deng Xiaoping's reappearance at the Great Hall of the People, I glimpsed how intriguing this obstinate, flinty victim of the Cultural Revolution was to the Chinese people. In a documentary film about the May Day festivities of 1973, Deng appeared clumping toward the camera, smiling cautiously, and the packed cinema erupted in "oohs" and "ahs." Not for years had people seen Deng's face or heard his name mentioned in a favorable way. Peking had last spoken of him as "the number two person taking the capitalist road" (after Liu Shaoqi). Now presumably he was back on the socialist road, or at least he was needed by Mao on whatever road the restless, maverick chairman was treading by 1973, and the Hangzhou audience greeted the sight with a mixture of pleasure and embarrassment. They did not cheer him—the habit of six years was not cast aside in one moment—but the excitement at his return was palpable.

Under the orange tiles of Peking's palaces a new power struggle began, heightened by the knowledge that Zhou's disease put a sharp limit on his remaining days, between Mao's Cultural Revolution victim, Deng Xiaoping, and his own wife, Jiang Qing, who was a beneficiary of the Cultural Revolution. Jiang did not like Deng's law-and-order politics any more than Deng liked her ideological ballets and operas. Both had their eyes set upon the post-Mao era, while Chinese society continued to stagger under the hit-and-miss influences of Maoism, and the Communist party exemplified the endemic tendency of the Chinese state to elevate power above policy.

The issue of Mao hovered over nearly everything. Did this official quote Mao much this afternoon, were there hints in the remarks by that official of criticism of the Mao cult, why were some people still wearing a Mao badge and others not? "Whether [Foreign Minister] Qiao Guanhua quotes Mao or not," Bryce Harland, the New Zealand ambassador, said to me, "depends on who is in the room with him. When he's alone, or with low-level officials, he doesn't refer to Mao at all. On the other hand, when Wang Hairong is there," Ambassador Harland went on in a reference to Mao's leftist relative who was assistant foreign minister, "Qiao scatters his remarks with quotations from Mao." If there was a sense that people did not always mean what they said about Mao, the reason lay in the realization that his vast span would soon draw to its end. The Mao issue was eerie because Mao was a colossus, but a sinking colossus.

Gough Whitlam, now prime minister of Australia, visited Mao on the eve of the chairman's eightieth birthday in November 1973 and found his walk a stiff shuffle and his hearing poor. Mao told Whitlam his body was "riddled with diseases," and during the conversation he picked at rough patches of skin on his cheeks. When Whitlam countered pessimistic remarks by Mao on China's problems by saying that China's sturdy youth would guarantee the "future of the revolution," Mao deflated him and with a gesture toward his premier across the room, added, "Neither Zhou nor I will be around for the conclusion of the Chinese Revolution."[7]

In the Chinese political system, and perhaps in all dictatorships, the view held of the aging dictator in his final phase has little in common with the view that will be held of him the morning after his death. Unlike in the West, no mediating force of public opinion exists through elections to validate or undo leaders, and the mechanics of the rise and fall of a top leader is utterly secret. A resentment against Mao, a doubt about the wisdom of his policies over recent years, a suffocation at his monopolization of China's mental space—all were building up, but none was openly expressed.

China before the industrial revolution in Europe was a land of great cities—around the year 1800, six of the world's ten largest cities were Chinese—but a century later it possessed the image of a peasant land. It seemed an interesting aspect of Communist rule that China was on the way to a new urbanization, seeking to catch up with a West it once surpassed. China's old cities had been of a peculiar kind, more bureaucratic than commercial, and I wondered whether the emerging Chinese urban life under Communist rule would be different, and perhaps converge with urban life in the capitalist West and Japan; this was the question I had in mind in writing my new book, *Flowers on an Iron Tree*.

I took the view that Marxism was an agent of modernization, its script being played out, not in the most advanced societies, as Marx expected, but in the more backward societies and often in the crucible of war. I expected Marxism to break down China's particularity, to narrow the gap between urban life in China and elsewhere. At the same time I expected, as I had argued to the bespectacled young ideologue, Shi, in Canton in 1964, that modernization would eventually undermine communism in China. "Communism probably obviates itself by the self-moving nature of the change it sets in motion," I wrote in my diary in 1974, holding fast to the same theme. "It does not matter, for isms cannot be as important as the minds that invent them for a purpose."

But I was too optimistic. The Chinese Communist party was behaving like a violinist engaged to perform at a party and arriving at the salon without his violin. He served drinks, he told beguiling stories, he was willing to wash dishes, but he did not make music—the reason for which he had been summoned. There could be no other point to the Chinese Revolution than to restore China's independence and develop China economically. The Communists achieved the former goal promptly after their victory over the Nationalists in the late 1940s, but they failed in the latter goal, because they put "Redness" above "Expertise" (in Mao's phrase); they put political struggle over economic rationality. Especially from the

1960s onward, the Communist party was like the violinist who for-
got his violin, doing everything but "make the music" of economic
advance that alone could give ordinary people a measure of the
"victory of socialism."

Chinese urban life failed to manifest the traits that in the West and
Japan have been associated with modernization—individual autonomy, cosmopolitanism, hedonism, and cultural freedom. This was
still "Chairman Mao's realm," a China in the grip of primitive collectivism, yet secure in its own view of itself as unique and morally
superior to other nations despite its backwardness. In the summer of
1973 tiny children at a Shanghai school in innocence and ignorance
sang for me a song, "We Miss Our Little Friends in Taiwan Province," and in Peking I was shown underground bomb shelters built
to protect China against evil imperialists about whom the Chinese
people knew little. There was much ritual and politicization, which
led me in Dalian, after a visit to a theater and a middle school, to
write wryly in my diary: "One goes to the theater for political
education, and one goes to a school for song and dance performances."

Some foreigners liked the ringing certainties and Spartan hearti-
ness that still could be found in Mao's China. "I shall miss Peking,"
a French woman said to Angela Terzani on the eve of returning to
Paris after some years in the Chinese capital. "You feel protected
here."[8] When I visited an Australian friend of mine, Rachel Faggetter, who was teaching English in Peking, I found her looking fit and
tanned. "I have never felt as much peace in my life as in Peking,"
she told me.

Rachel had edged toward an acceptance of the Chinese way of
putting collective considerations first. At her language institute there
was a practice called "Teachers and students in mutual criticism" *(pi
jiao ping xue),* under which matters were resolved by group sessions
in which each person criticized himself and bared his soul. Rachel
was impressed by this process and felt Australian education was the
poorer for having nothing like it. She valued friendship above enterprise and had always approached politics with a certain naiveté. She
did not care (did not know!) whether her Chinese students held left
or right political views. She liked their ordered ways. Rachel was
happy in China (as I have always felt she would have been happy in
eighteenth-century England) because forms pleased her. I could
never esteem the forms in China, the way Rachel did. To me they

were ropes trussing up the individual. Too much was swept under the carpet in order to achieve that seductive peace, I felt.

The China of the mid-1970s was not a country making rapid economic progress or one that had clarified its political path. It was a society so strident about what it was against that no clear message came through about what it favored. There was much talk of economic development, but it was abstract and pertained to long-range plans, such as "reaching the level of the advanced countries within twenty-five years." The underground train in Peking was a symbol of how form outstripped content in China's economic development. "The gulf narrows," I wrote in my diary after my first ride in the Chinese-made, beige-colored carriages, "between life in Peking and life in the cities of the West and Japan." But Peking went nowhere with its underground as for many years it consisted only of two short lines, the army had control over it, and foreigners were generally not allowed to use it. (Even twenty years later it covered only a fraction of Peking and had frequent operational problems.)

In the early to mid-1970s, I think some of us Westerners tended to condescend to China because of its backwardness, and in our fascination with the exotic—because China's modernization promised to be different from our own, or Japan's—we indulged its repeated failure to produce economic results. I saw a China where you could buy a single sock or glove in a department store, and a China of falling birth rates, and I took these to be signs of good organization, whereas I might have seen them as signs of poverty and Chinese parents' lack of freedom to choose the size of their family.

On the airplanes of the mid-1970s, as Maoism began to fray around the edges, travelers were addressed no longer as "Comrades" (as during the Cultural Revolution), or as "Comrades and Passengers" (as in 1971), but simply as "Passengers." I wasn't always ushered to the front of the line in shops, as had once been routine, and Mao badges were uncommon. The Red Guards of the Cultural Revolution period had not been denounced, but they had been tucked safely into mythology, and as an organization they existed only as a social club in middle schools. One day in Wuhan I heard on the radio a program of songs commemorating the Red Guards, and it reminded me of Paris around the mid-1970s, when Daniel Cohn-Bendit and other giants of the 1968 student movement were being perpetuated in books and films. In Shanghai, when the Communist Youth League re-emerged with a big congress in 1973, a single Red

Guard was elected to the ruling committee of 103 persons. This young man had been sent to a village after the Cultural Revolution and in 1973 he still was in the village; he did not attend the Youth League congress, but as a token he was named in absentia to the league's ruling body.

In 1975 I returned to China as a member of the Committee For Australia China Relations, a group that had fought for ties between Australia and China and now contented itself with the more tranquil activity of spurring Australia-China cultural exchanges. As we traveled to Peking, Shandong Province, Changsha, Guilin, and other places, I had the impression, in these last years of Mao's life, of a Chinese Communist party painstakingly trying to stretch a net of ideology over a reality that didn't fit it, yet of a populace that was rather tame even as its adherence to Maoism sagged. Near Changsha I took a bus that had on the front, "Drive for the Sake of Revolution," and in Shandong another labeled "Going Down to the Villages Is Glorious," and I wondered if these slogans had any meaning for ordinary people.

A leftist mythology prevailed, as Peking handed down frames of reference and local folk had to fit all social and cultural phenomena into those rigid frames. Often the result was people talking ardently about things they did not fully grasp, let alone believe. At one primary school in Jinan, the city in Shandong Province where Jiang Qing had studied piano and drama, our Australian delegation was harangued by a cloud of political lackeys about the evil influence on the school and education in general of "class enemy" Lin Biao, who had died four years before. I found a chance to ask one child directly in Chinese: "Is there class struggle in your school?" The boy was silent, but the headmistress hissed "yes" across the room. At length the poor pupil squeezed out the Delphic sort of reply Chinese under supervision learned to devise: "It's difficult to say there is class struggle in our school, but it's also difficult to say there is not."

Also in Jinan, at a theatrical performance in the municipal hall, I watched a magician do a trick with a magic wand and a rosette on his lapel. With each wave of the wand, the rosette would come and go, or change color or shape or size. The audience, dressed in the lace T-shirts and six-sided hats of Shandong Province, roared with laughter, reliving from a fairly safe distance its 1960s experience with Mao badges worn as talisman, insurance policy, boast, or protection. In the rest room of the municipal hall the toilet tissue consisted of recent issues of *Red Flag,* the Communist party's monthly journal. It was one of the few places I ever saw the magazine actually in use.

When our Australian delegation reached Guilin in Guangxi Province, its mountains so precociously sharp-sided that to be on top of one of them was like being high up in the Empire State Building, I wondered at its social and political remoteness from Peking. Like the people of many quite large Chinese cities, the people of Guilin almost never saw in the flesh a top Peking leader. "If TV were a big force in the lives of the people," I noted in my diary, "maybe this lack of firsthand contact with leaders would be less acute." But TV was hardly known in 1975 and the government in Peking had no human face for Guilin folk.

Many an observer of Mao's China returned home and reported a blanketing blandness, which was appealing if the observer was inclined to like the safety and good order of China, and distressing if he was inclined to judge the health of a society by the presence of sparks of creativity. I had not yet learned that the sea of blandness hid much, virtues as well as banality and cruelty, and that beneath the clichés of "socialism" lay plotting and begging, revenge and murder, stoicism and cunning. "In China, people are always smiling," said the writer Liu Fusheng of this bland exterior in an interview with Anne Thurston, "and you don't know why they are smiling. They smile when it is not appropriate to smile. . . . Outwardly, people are smiling, nodding. But inwardly, everyone is throwing stones."[9]

The political line still was aggressively Maoist, as Mao declared that to avoid the emergence of "another traitor like Lin Biao," it was necessary to mount yet one more campaign for the study of Marxism. But an absurd attempt jointly to denigrate Lin Biao and Confucius as "feudalists" strained ideological credibility to breaking point. "Do the people believe anymore?" I inquired in my diary while in Hunan Province toward the end of the 1975 trip. "Do they know the difference between left and right? These people are not terribly interested in politics," I went on. "I doubt that communism as a political ideology has been internalized. China is probably more like Mussolini's Italy—in the relation between official ideology and the minds and hearts of the people—than like Hitler's Germany."

Back in the United States, where the main concern about China was how much longer Mao would live and whether America-China relations would be affected by his death, I had an experience that taught me that the new view of China held by Nixon and Kissinger was not as firmly rooted as I had thought. As a participant in public debate about American policy toward China in the early 1970s, I had felt I should put an end to the precariousness of my immigration situation by seeking resident status within the United States. After my application for a "green card" went into the bureaucratic thicket, a Ms. McKeon of the Justice Department's Immigration and Naturalization Service gave me a political examination in the federal building in Boston in April 1972. She put me under oath and asked questions based on notes, clippings, and letters from a file in front of her about my opinions and travels and contacts.

Visible in her file was a clipping from *The Boston Globe,* an interview by reporter Timothy Leland with Edwin Reischauer, James Thomson, and myself about the outcome of the Nixon trip to China two months before. I was peering closer to try to see which passages of my answers to Leland she had marked with a blue pen when she barked, "What do you think of the Vietnam War?" I replied that it was a terrible thing and the sooner it was over the better. This being an interrogation, not a conversation, Ms. McKeon simply looked at me as I answered and then moved on to her next question.

"Have you been to Russia?" "Yes." "What did you do in Poland in February of 1969?" This part of the questioning was very detailed. Ms. McKeon asked when I had last been in Australia and I said the previous August. "I thought you were in Red China last August," she shot back grimly, and the term "Red China" speared me like an arrow from the past. At the end of a long segment on my views about China, Ms. McKeon said: "If we allowed you to stay on in the United States, would you still want to visit Red China again?" I replied that probably I would, and she handed me a pamphlet about rules on resident aliens visiting China.

After all these distasteful topics, it was a relief to get on to some wholesome ground. "Are you insane?" Ms. McKeon inquired. "Did you come to the United States for the purpose of prostitution?" "Are you a polygamist?" Bruised but intact, I got my green card and felt enormously happy. But one frosty evening in 1975, on my way back to Boston from China via Canada, after the trip with the Committee For Australia China Relations, I was hit by a bombshell. American officials, handling formalities for entry into Boston before departure from Montreal, as was usual, asked where I had been on this trip. When I said "China," they nodded knowingly and I was led into a side room and told I had broken the laws of the United

States and forfeited my right to reside there. I had forgotten Ms. McKeon's pamphlet!

As a resident alien—not yet a United States citizen—I was technically required to seek Washington's permission before visiting "hostile" countries. The exact phrase in the rules was "the Communist portions of China, Vietnam, and Korea." It had been my assumption, after the Nixon visit to "the Communist portion of China" and three years of a thickening China-U.S.A. relationship, that China would no longer be on that blacklist with North Korea and North Vietnam. But I was wrong and I learned that some things had not changed. I had indeed visited China without seeking permission and my green card was taken away from me. I was allowed to fly from Montreal to Boston "on parole," and I had four weeks in which to appeal. The appeal was successful, thanks in part to Senator Edward Kennedy, but I learned that the China issue still retained a power to unhinge some Americans, and I wondered if ghosts from the past era of Peking-Washington hostility might one day stalk back to center stage.*

The year 1976 in China was dark with disasters and portents, which put further on edge a nation made restless by the knowledge of Mao's imminent death. Mao began the year in a typically paradoxical manner. He received Julie Nixon Eisenhower and her husband, David, and spoke warmly of America and what he and Nixon had achieved for the peace of the world ("How is Mr. Nixon's leg?" he inquired of Nixon's daughter, referring to the former president's phlebitis).[10] Yet the same week he published two militant poems that expressed his undiminished yearning to remake everything around him. "We can clasp the moon in the Ninth Heaven," ran one of them, "And seize turtles deep down in the Five Seas," and the second poem ended: "Look, the world is being turned upside down."[11]

When the Eisenhowers reached Shanghai, the pastry chef at the Peace Hotel baked a fancy cake for the couple to take back to San Clemente for Richard Nixon's sixty-third birthday, but as they

* My FBI file, obtained under the Freedom of Information Act, indicates that observation of me effectively ceased about this time. A memo dated November 7, 1974, from the Boston office of the FBI to the director in Washington, said: "Boston believes that any FBI contact with subject might result in public embarrassment to the Bureau, based on information in his file. Boston is, therefore, closing this case."

waited for the cake to be brought up to their room, a messenger arrived at the door to say Zhou Enlai had died of cancer. Mao's inclination to lurch to the left was strengthened by this loss. Moreover, Zhou could have smoothed the consequences of Mao's death, but now, instead, the death of Zhou while Mao was still alive ensured an intensified, one-on-one battle for the succession between Deng Xiaoping and Jiang Qing.

Mao did not attend Zhou's funeral in January 1976, which some Chinese friends later told me they found shocking, and during the next months he frowned upon Deng's stress on economic development and revived the unsettling, ardent themes of the Cultural Revolution. "Class struggle is the key link and everything else hinges on it," he remarked, again like the violinist proud of his lack of a violin. And he downgraded the twin concepts on which Deng had been building his post–Cultural Revolution career. "Stability and unity do not mean writing off class struggle,"[12] he said.

Mao was sinking physically yet the government did not cease to revolve around him, and that was a recipe for intrigue, rumor, and manipulation. The two chief factions bidding to inherit Mao's power, headed by the disparate figures of Deng and Jiang, prized any scribbled words of Mao's that could be construed as support for their views or plans. But Mao could no longer reciprocate the attention of his court. "His words were unintelligible," Prime Minister Lee Kuan Yew of Singapore (who spoke Mandarin) told me after spending a painful few minutes with Mao in May 1976.[13]

Mao wavered back and forth between Jiang's views and the less ideological views of Deng and his widening group of supporters. One reason for Mao's indecisiveness was that both sides were trying to twist his arm for a blessing, and nothing makes an eighty-two-year-old man more contrary-minded than an awareness that he is being used for plans in which he will not figure. The struggle was as petty as it was momentous. "The chairman has been criticizing both sides," Jiang Qing wrote in a letter of self-criticism that Mao evidently required her to pen. "But [Deng] never alludes to the criticism of him and his friends and goes on overstating the chairman's criticisms of us, particularly of me."[14]

The greatest of Chinese festivals, Qing Ming in the spring, is a time when the dead are honored as families clean the graves of their ancestors and leave offerings of food. At Qing Ming, which is a sort of Chinese Memorial Day, the dead and the living are joined, each needing the other, the one already returned to nature and the other reminded of its destiny to return to nature. During the 1976 festival, in the month of April, wreaths and poems recalling Zhou Enlai were placed by ordinary citizens on the steps of the Monument to the People's Heroes at the center of Tiananmen Square. Tension arose as it became clear that the poems and spontaneous orations from among members of the crowd that built up were not only in praise of Zhou, dead three months before, but critical of Mao ("The day of Qin Shi Huang is done" ran a verse evoking a tyrannical early emperor whom Mao admired), and also of Jiang Qing ("Lady X, indeed you are insane, To be empress is your ambition," began another poem). The spirit of the demonstration was that the wrong man had died (Zhou) and the wrong man was still living (Mao).

Many Chinese felt that Mao as well as Jiang Qing had treated Zhou poorly in his last years, and one of them was a Shanghai friend of mine, Dr. Dong Fengchong, who was part of the team of physicians that attended the premier during 1975 and 1976. "I was the only nonparty doctor," Dong recalled, "so when they had a [Communist] party meeting I had to withdraw. Zhou heard about this and criticized it—afterward I joined in the meetings." According to Dong, an operation on Zhou for cancer of the bladder was unfortunately delayed. "Mao had to sign the approval for it," he said in a reference to a surprising but true rule of life among members of the Politburo, "and the paperwork dragged on and on—Zhou was furious."

At Tiananmen Square the government removed the wreaths and poems and an orderly if excited memorial turned into an angry demonstration that involved one hundred thousand people and lasted fourteen hours. To the Communist party, and not least to Mao, "the people" had been like a tapestry hanging as a backdrop to the Communist party's all-important struggles and deliberations. It was quite another thing to behold the people as a tide of original opinions reflecting varied interests. The militia dispersed the demonstrators, and there was some violence and scores of injuries, but few if any fatalities. In the aftermath Mao dismissed Deng Xiaoping from his posts, blaming him for the Tiananmen Square demonstrations and saying, "That man has never been a Marxist!" He then elevated the fairly obscure Hua Guofeng of Hunan Province to the number two position in the regime. "Victory rallies" were cooked up to celebrate the government changes, but in a classic Chinese tactic of evasion many people said they were sick and stayed away. The leftists assailed Deng for a saying that they felt proved his lack of socialist conviction. "It doesn't matter whether the cat is black or white," he had said in a speech on agricultural policy in July 1962, "as long as it catches the mouse."[15]

Deng Xiaoping had been heavily involved in China's foreign relations, coming to the United Nations in 1974 to deliver a speech on Mao's new idea of "three worlds," which put America and Russia together as a "world," bunched Western Europe, Japan, and Eastern Europe into another "world," and tucked China righteously into the "third world." So the period after Deng's fall was a worrying time for the American and other governments that judged China important.

The United States had withdrawn from Vietnam, the foreign policy of Mao and Zhou had made broad strides since the Cultural Revolution, and a tacit strategic partnership had come into existence between Washington and Peking. But the approaching end of the Mao era robbed Chinese policy toward Washington and all of the West of consistency and initiative, and within the United States, the Watergate crisis and the resignation of President Nixon had brought new questions about the American end of the China-America tie. Under President Gerald Ford, George Bush was sent to Peking to head the American Liaison Office, as the semidiplomatic mission each nation had set up in the other's capital was called, but it was still Kissinger, now secretary of state, who ran China policy.

Kissinger was not as pleased with United States–China relations as he had been a few years earlier. On a visit to Harvard in the spring of 1976, he surprised me by saying: "The Cultural Revolution should be no more puzzling to us in America than the internal American political events of 1972–76 [read Watergate] are to the Chinese." I realized that domestic politics both in China and the United States could still make a plaything of the foreign policies of the two countries, and I wondered just how fruitful the relationship would be when Nixon and Mao were no longer there to nurture it. At about this time, I came across a pair of poems about Kissinger and Nixon, written by a man in the city of Xian and widely circulated in China. They reflected some suspicion of the American leaders' motives in drawing close to China. "A visit to China is the only way out," one poem said, "For a brief respite from blazing fires that singe the eyebrows." Said the other, "With painted face-mask, disguised as a beauty, he comes to negotiate / But the demons-demasking-mirror in the city of Peking is truly inexorable." I sent a translation of the poems to Kissinger and in his reply he drily remarked: "It is always gratifying to see that one's efforts inspire verse, even when it includes some poetic license."[16]

In this tense period I felt a yawning gap between official China's honeyed words and the legerdemain and distrust I was observing within China. "Everything Deng did in foreign relations was laid down by Chairman Mao," chirped a Chinese diplomat to me in Washington in the summer of 1976. "It is hard to believe," I wrote skeptically in my diary that evening, "that a 'class enemy' could correctly conduct China's foreign policy."

A few weeks later I had a sharp exchange with officials of the Chinese Office over a speech I had given in Philadelphia in which I said it was nonsense to call Deng a "counterrevolutionary," and that the notion of Deng "walking the capitalist road" could have no meaning within China's socioeconomic system. Xie Qimei, a senior Chinese diplomat and later a United Nations undersecretary, said to me tersely: "If you don't understand that Deng is a counterrevolutionary, you don't understand anything about China."

I wondered what young people in China thought about the case against Deng as a counterrevolutionary, and later I asked the opinion of a teacher at a Peking institute. "We were pressured to write essays criticizing Deng," he said. "People were divided. I felt the case against Deng was ridiculous and, like some others, I refused to write these pointless essays."

"But could you just refuse?" I asked.

"We said we were too busy preparing our lessons," the teacher told me, "and we pointed out there was nothing new to say about Deng. If necessary we started an article, then kept saying it wasn't quite finished yet." The foot dragging caught the mood of Mao's China at its eleventh hour; the husk was intact but the core had no life.

At the Washington end of the valued but ambiguous America-China tie, many congressmen took the view that nothing would be lost by the United States' standing pat on Taiwan, keeping an American embassy in Taipei while developing relations with Peking. This attitude brought furious denunciations from Peking, yet at other times Chinese officials and media gave the impression that the Soviet threat was the alpha and omega of international life and that the Taiwan issue by comparison was a bagatelle. "The danger," Lin Ping, head of the America-Australia desk in the Chinese foreign ministry had said to me in Peking in 1975, "is that the tiger [United

States] will go out the front door, and the wolf [Russia] will come in the back door."

Did Peking still believe in "imperialism" as the key to world politics? It no longer wanted American troops out of Europe or Diego Garcia in the Indian Ocean, yet it continued to assert the principle that foreign military bases were a threat to peace. Chinese officials referred to the Third World as an entity, and when I pointed out that most international conflicts were among Third World lands, they said "imperialism" caused them all, apparently by some mysterious remote control. Chinese diplomats often merely folded their hands and smiled, afraid to commit themselves to a candid opinion, ultimately waiting for Mao's death to clarify which of his ideas would endure and which would go the way of Mao.

Mao's leftist impulses, for which Jiang Qing and her associates were a useful outlet, at times threw shadows on Sino-American relations. These were the days when American Express traveler's checks were rejected within China on the ground that the American Express Company had started to do business with Taiwan, and when Peking told *The New York Times* it could not have a bureau in Peking so long as the newspaper accepted advertising from Taiwan.

It fell to my friend Zhou Nan, who had escorted me around China in 1971, to deal with *The New York Times* over the Peking bureau issue, and even his sophistication could not hide the stupidity of Chinese policy. Zhou was now a diplomat in the Chinese mission at the United Nations, established when Peking replaced Taipei in the China seat of the United Nations in October 1971. Negotiations over a *New York Times* bureau in China reached the point where Zhou, who had been dealing with Seymour Topping, a senior journalist experienced in China, demanded to see the top editor, A. M. Rosenthal. According to Rosenthal's story, which he related at a Nieman Foundation dinner at Harvard in April 1976, Zhou Nan's streak of pomposity well matched the policy itself. "I went around to West Sixty-sixth Street," Rosenthal said of his visit to the Chinese mission to the United Nations, "and Mr. Zhou [Nan] pulled out from his pocket a piece of paper that began, 'I am instructed by my government,' and proceeded to address me as if I were a foreign minister." The editor went on: "What Zhou Nan said boiled down to an intimation that *The New York Times* would have to cut out all advertising from the KMT [Nationalists]. I said I could not agree, and I walked out."

China and the Western nations not only wanted different things, they saw the world in different hues, and they had different modes of action. The Chinese were used to stating an ideal, Westerners to dealing with the facts as they saw them. In the summer of 1976 the British foreign secretary went to Peking and at a banquet to welcome him the Chinese foreign minister said: "The Chinese and British peoples have always been friends."[17] That was not true, but the Chinese minister's assertion was less a simple lie than a piece of Confucian formalism. Reiterating a norm was meant to have a power in and of itself, a call to take the long view and see the sunshine through the clouds.

There was little sunshine during the remainder of 1976. In midsummer the military hero of the Chinese Revolution, Marshal Zhu De, died, a terrible earthquake killed hundreds of thousands of people in the city of Tangshan, and a decision was made that Mao would no longer receive any foreign visitors. One evening Mao scratched out on a piece of paper the highly ambiguous words, "With you in charge, I am at ease,"[18] and gave it to Hua Guofeng, the beneficiary of Deng's fall, who took himself to be anointed as the supreme leader's successor.

China was living on borrowed time, and the Chinese people were jumpy. Mao possessed enormous power, but it did not include the power to stop people from realizing he was dying, and looking beyond him to a post-Mao era. Political change in China usually had to do with jockeying for place, dished up in terms of "class struggle," but even the man in the street understood that political change was soon to come simply as a result of the uncompromising law of human mortality.

"Chairman Mao has left this world," began a Communist party announcement in September 1976. It was a stunning, if not highly emotional moment, because many hundreds of millions of Chinese had no memory of a China without Mao. He had led the Communist party for four decades and his name had become synonymous with the "new China" of post-1949. Everyone wondered if Mao's revolution could go on without Mao.

The day Mao died, I was on a beach in Morocco south of Casablanca with a friend from Thailand, enjoying a short holiday before the fall term began at Harvard. A swarthy young man dressed in a jeliba strode across the sand, made a short bow to my Thai friend, and said to him in French: "I am terribly sorry that your president has died." For Africans, Mao was a symbol of the entire Orient, and his death was momentous news around Casablanca.

Within China it was widely felt that the post-Mao years could only be an improvement on the final Mao years, yet there was a deep uncertainty, for authority in the PRC had been epitomized by Mao's sayings and his upraised arm. You could breathe easier without a dictator, but the day after he died, how did you look at your neighbor and what did you say to the person riding beside you in the bus? I felt Mao's revolution could not go on without Mao. Yet my Chinese friends knew no other road than that of revolutionary campaigns, arbitrarily defined class struggles, and devious efforts to survive amidst such political storms. Many of these Chinese didn't believe in Maoism any more, but they were inured to conformity, and I wondered if they would know how to live effectively in an environment that required initiative and contained risk.

Citizens filed past the bier to view Mao's body and a student named Li later described to me his moment beside Mao's glass coffin. "Many people cried as they shuffled by," Li said, "but I *didn't cry!*" His eyes bulged as he recalled the fear that had gripped him. "Guards were staring at me—why wasn't I crying like all the rest! Panicky, I riveted my eyes on Mao's body. I felt Mao was about to leap up from his coffin and ask me why I wasn't crying. I almost believed his lips were going to shout out: 'Li, you're a counterrevolutionary!' "

At the funeral held in the open air at Tiananmen Square, the bland Hua Guofeng gave the oration, dividing it between passages on the greatness of Mao and passages on the treachery of Deng. In ancient China before the Qin dynasty of the pre-Christian era, when emperors were entombed, a certain number of warriors and servants had to be killed and buried together with the Son of Heaven (from the Qin onward the imperial tombs contained the terra-cotta substitutes that so delight modern tourists). And there was the cosmological issue of whether the wooden coffin should face north or east or west or south. During the 1970s I did not think about the problem of burying Mao in terms of these imperial traditions, although I might well have done so. Many Chinese thought Mao should be cremated, the norm in urban China, and Mao himself had years before selected a site for the ashes of himself and Jiang Qing in Babaoshan Cemetery in western Peking. But the demands of politics brought a swing back to tradition. Hua, as Mao's chosen successor, could not afford to squander the physical Mao and could not agree to a grave site that Mao would share with his opponent Jiang. Hua needed an awesome Mao presence to remind the nation of his mandate to succeed Mao, so embalmers were summoned from Vietnam, where they had prepared the body of Ho Chi Minh. Mao was mummified, and in due course put on display in a glass sarcophagus within a new edifice on Tiananmen Square.

Flying back from Casablanca to Boston, I began to think about China's next phase. Mao had been the last of the titans of World War II struggles. Britain hardly missed a step in doing without Churchill after the war's end, and likewise France suffered no clear retrogression in the years after de Gaulle's death in 1970. But in China leadership had a special mystique, and I wondered if the Chinese after Mao could really throw off the "way of the emperors," or whether a people used to gazing upward would find themselves supplied by the Communist truth-makers with an ersatz Mao. China would be better off without the Mao of recent years, I felt, but only if it resisted the temptation to thrust another Mao into his shoes.

CHAPTER EIGHT

■

CHANGE

AS the Chinese people mourned Mao, two issues overrode all others in the public life of the nation. Could the political credibility of the Communists, low after the suppression of the Tiananmen Square demonstration at Qing Ming in April 1976 and the ensuing purge of Deng Xiaoping, improve without Mao? And was there still time for a Communist party government to meet effectively the huge challenges of economic development?

Before leaving for my holiday in Morocco at the end of the summer of 1976, I had written an article for *The New Republic* about the political outlook in Peking, and in it I expressed the view that when Mao died, his wife, Jiang Qing, and her leftist circle, called the "Gang of Four" by their enemies, would soon fall and "Deng Xiaopingism," if not Deng himself, would prevail. The Gang of Four consisted of the sixty-two-year-old Jiang Qing and three Shanghai men: political journalist Zhang Chunqiao, young former cotton mill worker Wang Hongwen, and pamphleteer Yao Wenyuan. My article came out in *The New Republic*'s September 25, 1976, issue, and the Gang of Four was arrested October 6, a month after Mao's death. Hua Guofeng, the man now in charge, whom Mao apparently had chosen as successor,* took a step Mao might

---

* Mao's scribbled words to Hua, "With you in charge, I am at ease," were ambiguous. Did he mean with Hua in charge of China, of irrigation in Hunan, of the agenda for the next day's Politburo meeting, or what? Zhang Hanzhi, Mao's

not have approved of and threw in his weight with the military and the pro–Deng forces in a decisive move against the leading leftists.

Hua was as smooth and inscrutable as an eggshell, offering no clue to what lay inside. Like Mao, he had much experience in Hunan Province and he looked a bit like Mao in middle age, but he was no blazing star. Born to a peasant family in 1921 in Shanxi Province, he worked as a teenager in the guerrilla resistance to the Japanese invaders in north China. After Liberation, he was sent to Hunan, married a Hunanese woman, and built a career as an official in Mao's home county of Xiang Tan. When Mao revisited his birthplace in 1959, Hua was host and soon afterward he became a senior party official of Hunan Province. He was enthusiastic in his praise for the disastrous Great Leap Forward and he rose like a helicopter during the Cultural Revolution. Mao's enemies each step of the way became his enemies.

At the Ninth Party Congress of 1969, Hua became a central committee member, and he helped Mao in the struggle against Defense Minister Lin Biao. Meanwhile he did not neglect Mao's home village; he linked it by rail to Changsha, a boon for tiny Shaoshan, and set up in the village a color TV plant. In 1973 Hua was named to the Politburo and in 1975 he became minister of public security.

A couple of weeks after Mao's death, late in September 1976, China moved toward a coup d'état after a Politburo meeting at which the two opposing forces waved pieces of paper purporting to be words of Mao giving them his blessing. The Gang of Four nominated Jiang Qing as chairman of the Communist party and Zhang Chunqiao as premier, but this proposal created a deadlock. The anti–Gang of Four forces decided to forget about debates and votes and turned to the gun. Within twenty-four hours of the Politburo session, Hua's security forces lured Zhang, Wang, and Yao to a further meeting and as they arrived, knocked them to the floor, handcuffed them, and imprisoned them. Soon afterward Jiang Qing was arrested in her bedroom at her villa near the Peking zoo. "The chairman's body is hardly cold," she cried as she was led away, "and yet you have the gall to mount a coup!"[1]

---

interpreter for a meeting with the New Zealand prime minister on the evening he wrote the words for Hua, and a trusted aide to Mao, told me at Harvard in March 1991, "No one knew what the chairman meant by those scribbled words. Myself, I did not think he was appointing his successor."

Never had so many top Chinese Communist party leaders fallen at one stroke. Of the twenty-two persons elected to the Politburo at the Tenth Party Congress of 1973, five had been purged as 1977 began and five more were dead, and these ten casualties included eight of the eleven-member core Standing Committee of the Politburo set up at that last congress of the Mao era. It was a dizzy burst of the Communist game of musical chairs, and it left the enigmatic Hua as the chairman of the Communist party and Mao's putative successor.

In a little-known conversation with American journalist Anna Louise Strong, Mao had remarked of the problem that his nemesis Nikita Khrushchev had with Stalin: "It's hard to be the son of a patriarchal father."[2] In those words lay—as well as a view of Stalin —an echo from Mao's own childhood and perhaps a glance ahead of how China would handle the succession to Mao himself. The gap Mao left initially was filled by Hua, and yet it remained even as Hua took the helm. The PRC as if by instinct began to invent a new supreme leader, but Mao's shadow was so long that no one—certainly not the pedestrian Hua—could move beyond its reach and become his own Mao. The structure of personal rule from Mao's day was pretty much intact, as Hua was called a "wise leader" the way Mao had been, and railroad station halls displayed the two portraits of Hua and Mao side by side. But the issue of who was to rule (that is to say, which Communist would rule) did not seem settled for long.

In 1978 I returned to China on a trip with Australian friends to visit the Buddhist art at Yungang, northwest of Peking, and the newly displayed terra-cotta figures from the tomb of the emperor Qin Shi Huang in the ancient city of Xian. In Peking, at a concert to celebrate the National Day of October 1 in the Capital Stadium, we observed Hua Guofeng. He sat on a dais with most of the rest of the Politburo above a stage as music and dance extolled him. When children of kindergarten age sang of Hua's wisdom, a slight smile crept across the supreme leader's broad pale face. I wondered how he could sit there and listen to political adulation from five-year-olds. A few days later at a primary school at Datong, an industrial city near the caves of Buddhist art at Yungang, I looked over the shoulders of second-graders and noticed in each lesson book the characters of an identical phrase: "Heed the Words of Chairman

Hua." At a concert in the People's Theater in Xian, a steely hen of a contralto roared out a song about the beauty of Hua's birthplace in Shanxi Province. Hua was being built up as a poor man's Mao by a system whose repertoire contained no other mode of governance but semimonarchical ideological paternalism.

Hua's contribution was to represent some continuity with the Mao era, yet within a year of Mao's death, Deng Xiaoping, twice dismissed from office by the Great Helmsman, and denounced by Hua at Mao's funeral, was not only back in the government as a vice-premier, but breathing hard down Hua's neck at all moments of decision. On paper Hua and Deng were cooperating, with Hua as Deng's superior, but appointments to high posts during 1977 and 1978 were more often associates of Deng's than of Hua's, documents about economic development that Deng had authored in 1975 (and been assailed for by Mao) were again quoted, and it was less often Hua than Deng who handled key negotiations with foreign leaders.

Deng was far senior to Hua, having made the Long March and met Mao a quarter-century earlier than Hua did. Despite his fall in the Cultural Revolution, Jiang Qing's disparaging description of him as "bullet-headed"[3] and Mao's calling him a "dwarf,"[4] it may have been that Deng never totally lost the respect of Mao. At any rate he enjoyed the quiet support of most of those who suffered—while Hua prospered politically—in the years of the Cultural Revolution.

When Prime Minister Whitlam talked with Mao back in 1973, the Chinese leader had made the stunning remark, "There is one good thing about China's poverty—it makes people want to make revolution."[5] It was that kind of nostalgic ideological militancy that the Hua-Deng policies of the late 1970s set aside in order to tackle China's economic development more modestly and scientifically. A huge task lay ahead of them, especially in the villages. Agricultural productivity in 1978 was below the level it had been in 1952, and rural per capita income increased by an average rate of only 1.6 percent between 1957 and 1979.[6] In the late 1970s material incentives were set in place, foreign investment was invited, political shackles were removed from some areas of economic decision making, and Chinese intellectuals were told they were needed even if their political views were heterodox.

As Deng and Hua surveyed the wreckage of the late Mao era and gave priority to economic development, they began to commercialize the countryside by breaking up the communes and allowing families to make their own production decisions and marketing plans (but no land reverted to private ownership). A diversity of decentralized economic activities arose in the villages, and the hierarchy of political guardians, called "cadres" by the Communists, which formerly directed rural life, lost some of its power. As Mao's principle of self-reliance was let slide, trade between counties and between provinces rose sharply; people within their own neighborhoods soon could buy clothes from Shanghai, cassette recorders from Canton, and furs from the far west.

In the wake of the retreat from Mao's policies, traditional Chinese social and commercial life—private markets, lively magazines, a less inhibited popular culture, a modest sartorial flair—bubbled back into view. At the same time, Stalinist urban economic development with its central planning and its functional edifices continued to shape Chinese life as before. The banal apartment blocs, belching chimneys, and darting Japanese vans of Peking increasingly gave the capital the nondescript character of suburban East Berlin or a city in Siberia. The new before long looked shabby, and not very Chinese, and in many places neither old China nor Maoist China seemed much in evidence; a socioeconomic order of artifice and compromise was coming into existence, its ultimate shape unknown. Yet most Chinese felt life was improving, and the farmers especially were happy to leave long-range and philosophical questions to one side and welcome Deng's refreshing maxim tossed down condescendingly from on high: "To get rich is glorious."

One day during 1978 in Peking, I saw something amidst the bushes and rockeries of Sun Yat-sen Park that would have made Mao turn over in his glass sarcophagus. With a Toyota car in place as a backdrop, groomed and smiling people were lining up beneath their sunshades to be photographed. A display board nearby suggested a variety of poses in front of this trophy of non-Chinese modernization. Each click of the camera seemed like a step away from Maoism. A few days later "shopping opportunities" were offered during our Australian group's trip outside Peking and our Chinese hosts said, "Come back to China and bring your friends too." The reasons for receiving foreigners had become more commercial than political.

Guo Moruo, the eminent writer and longtime friend of Mao, had told me in 1971 that the Cultural Revolution had "blocked all channels for the restoration of capitalism." Perhaps Guo believed this. Yet the Chinese people's impulse toward individual freedom and material accumulation revived rapidly in the years after Guo's and Mao's deaths. Deng would soon privately tell several foreign heads of government that he realized Marxism had failed in China.[7] And indeed, the Communist party had not changed the basic conservatism, materialism, and family-mindedness of Chinese culture. The effort to block "capitalist restoration" seemed as futile as an effort to block the east wind by editorials in the Communist party newspaper *People's Daily*.

China now was a society departing step by step from Marxist ways in an effort to be efficient that often did not succeed. A headline in *People's Daily* cried, "Sackings in Tianjin," but the story beneath was of the firing of just two people—in that city of nearly 8 million —and these two had failed to report for work for eighteen months. Job security—the Chinese called it the "iron rice bowl"—was a sacred right not easily denied.

A China in change was a magnet to me and I went back twice in 1980, in January to stay with the Australian ambassador in Peking, and later in the year on a research trip hosted by the Academy of Social Science to visit people and places that were sources of information on Mao's career. I returned again in the summer of 1982 with an Australian television company to make programs on the new economic policies in Shanghai, life in the PLA, and Chinese food, and twice more in the fall of 1982 and the fall of 1983, both times aboard a cruise ship that stopped at various Chinese ports, giving lectures to passengers who were being offered China without discomfort.

The expanding Chinese tourist industry of the early 1980s reminded me of a handsome new building whose interior is filled with garbage. Ambitious plans at the top lost their way as implementation descended to a middle management system in which incentive and innovation were rare. In Beijing in 1982 I stayed at a shiny new hotel called the Yanjing on the western part of Chang An Avenue and when I went into the café no one greeted me or showed me to a table. As I sat down I saw a dozen members of the staff clustered around a service counter, but none came to take my order. When I walked over to the counter and asked for fried noodles and a beer, a blank face returned my look without a word or a smile, and the voice inside it transmitted the order over the shoulder to a colleague, who in turn shouted it over his shoulder to the kitchen. The noodles were dumped before me by a silent, grim-looking man in a white jacket stained on its every square inch with food and drink, and when I had finished the noodles, a warm beer arrived. The café gave the impression of lassitude and unconcern for customers; no one took responsibility and no one seemed to take pride in his work. The hotel was new but the management system was not.

China still was a land of secrets and closed doors, if no longer of red flags and Mao badges and loudspeakers, but the faces and words of the people suggested a desire for change in the direction of what was coming to be known as "reform." I knew China was changing when I tried to ask a question of some tiny children in a park in the industrial bastion of Chongqing high up on the Yangzi River. ONE ONLY IS GOOD, said a notice in the park, and it referred not to beer but to children, for birth control was a high priority as the post-Mao leaders for economic reasons sought to reverse Mao's policy of the more babies the better. I thought it would be interesting to ask the kindergarten kids if they would like to have a brother or sister, and when I spoke with the teacher in charge of the children she waved me ahead to ask what I wished.

To my surprise, the children proved so unruly and preoccupied with their games that I could get no sense out of them. They screamed, ran about fighting each other, and declined all suggestions and admonitions from the teacher and myself. In the Mao years, the teacher would immediately have hauled her charges into line, they would have answered my questions and probably each child would have said the same thing. "They are nearly all 'only' children," said the teacher, managing a smile. "People are starting to call them 'little emperors' because they can be a bit spoiled." It was a far cry from the world of Chinese childhood that Fox Butterfield accurately captured not long before in his book *Alive in the Bitter Sea*. "I was constantly struck by the almost universal good behavior of Chinese children," the *New York Times* journalist had written of the China of just a few years earlier.

In Canton's Cultural Park I came upon a tableau whose blend of elements captured the eclecticism of Hua's China as it turned into Deng's China. A young woman was depicted against a painting on canvas of a vaulting heaven in a rendition of Mao's 1957 poem "The Immortals," written in memory of his wife in the early Hunan years, the martyr Yang Kaihui. Yang was dressed in a black skirt and white blouse in the career girl style of the passionate May Fourth period when "democracy" and "science" seduced urban youth. Of course the tableau was a swipe at Jiang Qing, the later wife, but there were also goddesses and hobgoblins, for Mao's poem linked the memory of Yang with a mystical vision, employing the old Chinese legend of Wu Gang.* The tableau contained no "class enemies," and offered no political theme other than the personal jab at the jailed Jiang Qing. The Canton citizens in front of me, eating ice creams and clutching plastic purses and holding children aloft to see the pretty display, were agog at the colored lights and costumes and the romanticism of the spectacle. The memory and poetry of Mao had been reduced to a cross between a Macy's Christmas window display and a Buddhist temple's depiction of nirvana. That night in a Canton hotel room I wrote in my diary: "It's bread and circuses— what happens now to politics?"

In my research, I focused more and more on the systemic problems of Chinese politics. I started to probe how aspects of Chinese culture reinforced Communist authoritarianism, how power and personality interacted at the top of Chinese politics, and how the mystique of leadership won special acceptance in China. Chinese officials were cool to a project I began in 1977 on the life of Mao, claiming that the "personal lives of our leaders are of no interest," and "policy is what counts." When I talked with Li Rui, a distinguished scholar-official who wrote a biography of Mao's early years but never dared to carry the story on through Mao's career in power, the historian said: "The present political situation in China does not require a full biography, but history will require it."

Later, in 1980, after finishing my biography of Mao, I went to China as part of a small group of sinologists who specialized in the life and thought of Mao, hosted by the Chinese Academy of Social Science and organized by Edward Friedman of the University of Wisconsin. Often in the seminars of our delegation, the dialogue with our Chinese academic and think-tank hosts was like talking with priests. Numerous questions produced a pained smile instead of an answer and I wrote in my diary in Peking: "Never before have I heard so often the remarks, 'We haven't researched that yet,' or, 'More work has to be done on that issue.' " Yet it was an improvement on the false response one often got in the Mao years.

Semiofficial intellectuals twisted themselves in knots trying to make a distinction between "true" Marxism and "false" Marxism, while in the streets and offices and homes beyond the academy win-

---

* Wu Gang searched persistently for immortality and the gods responded by having him chop down a cassia tree on the moon. But as fast as Wu cut down the tree, it grew back to its full shape, so he had to chop on for eternity.

dows, Marxism was unraveling from the core. I tried to discuss the substantial Marxist theories of Zhang Chunqiao, the imprisoned Gang of Four member, but any specific point was swept aside with the merely political comment that Zhang lacked a "deep understanding" of Marxism. "Feudal fascism" was the verbally ingenious but intellectually barren formula offered up to describe the ideas of the various close colleagues of Mao who had recently fallen.

"The essence of Marxism is theory's unity with practice," Mao biographer Li Rui told us as he sought to remain a Marxist by suggesting that Mao's theories had departed from reality. It was only partly convincing, about as much so as a Catholic insisting he need take no notice of the pope. A leading historian, Li Xin, summed up for our Mao delegation the limits of the new post-Mao mental freedom. "To oppose the Communist party's thought is not a crime," he said in a relatively candid moment. "But no one can propose some other organization to replace the Communist party." Professor Maurice Meisner of the University of Wisconsin raised with Yu Guangyuan, an avant-garde social thinker, the issue of democracy. Putting the question tactfully, Meisner asked Yu how China could avoid the Russian way and promote more democracy. Yu offered a "retirement system" and an end to "automatic seniority" for cadres; a vision of democracy that added up only to antibureaucratism.

People's Daily journalist Wang Ruoshui went no further in our discussion with him about democracy than to speak of the necessity of reforming the Communist party itself; he made no mention of a change of system that would undercut the leading role of the party. "You can't have a dictatorship over ideas," Wang remarked, but he knew all too well that a dictatorship over people existed. Even this courageous journalist talked with obfuscation of "class struggle against feudal ideology," as if China's chief political problem lay elsewhere than with the Communist party's monopoly of power. Wang quoted Lord Acton's words: "Power corrupts, and absolute power corrupts absolutely," which made me guess that he understood the systemic problem of Leninism, but felt he could go no further toward articulating it than by alluding to Acton's dictum.

A middle-aged friend of mine was more free to say exactly what he thought over dinner in a relative's home, and he told me he had become a passionate advocate of a greater role for law in China, to which I objected that under a Leninist system law can mean nothing. "Look," my friend said, "we're not going to be able to rid ourselves of the party dictatorship directly. That would mean civil war." His

idea was to pressure the Communists to grant as much constitution-
ality as possible and to focus on economic development. "In the
longer future," he said, "a higher level of economic development
will bring new possibilities of political change." It was a typical view
of democratically minded Chinese of mature age in the early 1980s.

Our Mao delegation at times fumed at the breakdowns in transportation arrangements that were common in China. One day at the
end of a stay in Tianjin to attend seminars at Nankai University, we
trundled out to Tianjin airport at 5:00 A.M. for an Iluyshin 28 flight
to Changsha with an intermediate stop in Peking and were greeted
with the news of a four-hour delay because fog enveloped Peking.
We waited like caged lions in an adjoining guest house, anxious to
get to Changsha for a seminar and the pursuit of documents about
Mao's early life, and then toward noon we were summoned to the
plane, but did not board. At 4:00 P.M. the flight was canceled. Professor Stuart Schram of the University of London paced the terminal
in quiet fury, Professor Tang Tsou of the University of Chicago
muttered curses in Chinese, and Professor Jerome Chen of the University of Toronto mounted a protest with a Mr. Guo of the airport
authority. Edward Friedman and Maurice Meisner played bridge,
and sitting beside them, I wrote postcards home.

Mysteriously, the flight was announced for 5:00 P.M. and we took
off. During the stop in Peking we ate a pleasant meal, but no sooner
were we in the air headed south for Changsha than the pilot announced a problem with the radar and said we would land at Tianjin
for repairs. The professors were not thrilled to go back to that bare
little airport, with its terminal building the size of a small American
house (serving a city of 8 million people). About 10:00 P.M. we took
off, but another mechanical problem developed and we returned yet
again to Tianjin! Airport official Guo was not to be seen, and had he
been there I think Jerome Chen would have torn him to pieces. One
of our delegation slumped on a chair in tight-lipped silence, another
shouted at anyone near him, a third was drinking, a fourth wanted
back his money for the entire trip, and the two bridge players continued to play bridge. At this point another plane was substituted
and we boarded it and arrived in Changsha at 2:00 A.M., hot and
tired and bothered. Such could be the experience of travel in China.

At Mao's first home in Shaoshan, not far from Changsha, a local
official, showing us around the quiet village, murmured almost in-
audibly: "You could catch sparrows in front of these buildings."
Mao had gone out of view and out of fashion, yet it was the issue of

Mao that still inhibited open inquiry into Chinese contemporary history. Mao's absence was a heavy presence, and there was a nervousness associated with any comment on him that resembled the attitude to Stalin in Russia between Stalin's death in 1953 and Khrushchev's critique of him in 1956. The Communist party was getting ready to re-evaluate Mao, and until a document was handed down to the nation, the topic of Mao was an uncomfortable one.

As we drove around Hunan Province, I argued with Tang Tsou about the theory of the Gang of Four as an explanation of China's various shortcomings. "The Mao problem is solved," Tang said one afternoon in Changsha. "The material that is emerging about the Gang of Four will clarify Mao's role and the Mao problem." I did not believe that the theory of the Gang of Four provided a resting place for political debate and infighting within the Communist party. "One way to solve the Mao problem," I rejoined, "would be to let talk of the Gang of Four die away, dropping the whole style of discussing politics as a morality play and acknowledging conflict as a normal part of political life." But although China was changing, it hadn't changed enough to view Mao historically and demythologize politics. The system could not tolerate an open search for truth; and the system, now once again as much Liu Shaoqi-ist as Maoist, was unshaken.

One night at a dinner in Peking given by the Academy of Social Science for our delegation, the theorist Yu Guangyuan talked about a forthcoming encyclopedia being produced at the academy and Edward Friedman inquired about the publication timetable. "One thing is sure," Yu said with a grin, "the volume that contains the letter 'M' will not appear for the time being, not until something happens."

"The issue will inexorably move," I predicted in a diary note that evening, "from the Gang of Four, to Mao, and then to the system itself—pushing the lid right off Pandora's Box." Indeed this was the direction Hua and Deng involuntarily took by their decision to put the Gang of Four on trial, an event scheduled for several months after our Mao delegation's visit.

Thirty-five judges and six hundred selected citizens invited to be "the public" gathered in the Ceremonial Hall of the Public Security compound on the Street of Righteousness just east of Tiananmen Square. It was November 1980, and the long-awaited trial of the

Gang of Four, accused together with Chen Boda, the ideologist, and five military associates of the dead and disgraced defense minister Lin Biao. I watched videotape of the Gang of Four trial in Taipei, where it had been acquired by Taiwan intelligence.

It had been Hua who arrested the Gang of Four a month after Mao's death—the four political leaders had been in prison without charges being laid ever since—but by the time of the trial it was Deng who called most of the shots. His purpose was to make the "Lin Biao and Jiang Qing Counterrevolutionary Cliques" the scapegoats for errors of Mao that it was not yet convenient to pin on Mao himself, and to elbow aside the half-Maoist Hua and himself become supreme leader.

In the Ceremonial Hall the ten defendants were accused of "persecuting" fellow leaders, intellectuals, and ordinary citizens, and of trying to "usurp" the power of party and state. It was all a prepared political script in which "crimes" and political miscalculations were indistinguishable, and the first charge against Jiang gave the flavor: "The accused, Jiang Qing, conspired to prevent Deng Xiaoping's appointment as vice-premier in the fall of 1974."[8]

The three male members of the Gang of Four either confessed or said nothing, and the former head of the air force said, "Jiang Qing is the chief culprit, I'm her accomplice, I hate myself." But Jiang defied the court from beginning to end, shouting that one woman judge was a "bitch" and Deng was a "fascist." She made the point that all her actions had followed from the policies of the Ninth and Tenth Communist Party Congresses in 1969 and 1973, at both of which she was duly elected to the Politburo. As passions rose she shifted her ground a little and summed up her defense in a shouted remark to the cowed judges that got to the heart of why she was on trial: "I was Mao's dog; what he said to bite, I bit!"

When Jiang was accused of persecuting former head of state Liu Shaoqi and his wife, Wang Guangmei, she replied: "Most members of the present central committee of the party and most of our government leaders *competed* with each other in those days to criticize Liu Shaoqi." Jiang's right arm chopped up and down in a steady beat of emphasis as she went on: "If I am guilty, *how about you all?*" A judge cried, "Shut up, Jiang Qing," and six more judges chimed in, "Shut up, Jiang Qing." No evidence was offered by the court that Mao at any time opposed Jiang's attacks on Liu and his wife, or most other activities of the Gang of Four and the Lin Biao military associates.

A climactic moment came over the issue of Mao's view of Jiang. The judges sought to answer Jiang's point that she did what Mao and the party wished by quoting examples of his undoubted periodic irritation with Jiang's ways. "You're fascists, you're Chiang Kai-shek Nationalists," she shouted back at the court, calling into service the classic Communist swearwords. "I despise you, Jiang Wen," she went on, addressing the chief judge. "You are selling your strength so desperately to Deng Xiaoping. Oh, he'll certainly promote you!" As pandemonium broke out in the courtroom, Jiang was frog-marched out. "It is right to rebel," she screeched as she moved gracefully down the aisle, reviving Mao's now-forgotten slogan of Cultural Revolution days.

It was the Deng era that saw TV become a force in Chinese life as TV sets appeared like mushrooms after spring rain, and each evening, ironically, Jiang offered a refreshing thirty-minute entertainment in Chinese living rooms. Her willfulness was for many younger Chinese a breath of fresh air in a social and political system in which conformity was the norm and to fail to confess in the face of party accusations was almost unknown. "You know I have long hated Jiang," a young teacher friend from Shanghai wrote to me after watching the trial, "but now I hate her a bit less." To savor her insults against the Communist party was perhaps to take an ounce of revenge against its oppression.

"How was I on TV?" Jiang asked her prison guards after a torrid session in which the former actress clashed with witnesses accusing her of "counterrevolution" back in the 1930s, and vengeful acts during the Cultural Revolution against her detractors from the Shanghai of those years. The female guards were afraid and said nothing. "What do you *mean* you didn't watch?" Jiang blazed. "Guarding me is your job. How could you *not* watch?" Small wonder the Chinese government cut back the TV coverage of the trial as the weeks progressed.

While the verdict was being weighed the judges dispersed to their usual occupations, and during this time I met one of them, the sociologist Fei Xiaotong, in the living room of Professor John and Wilma Fairbank in Cambridge, Massachusetts! Of course it was the Politburo, not the legal organs, which decided the fate of the "Lin Biao and Jiang Qing Counterrevolutionary Cliques." Two members of the Gang of Four, Jiang and the Shanghai theorist Zhang Chunqiao, received the death sentence, suspended for two years "to see how they behave," and the others received various terms of imprisonment. The ten of them together were convicted of framing and persecuting 729,511 people, of whom 34,800 died.

Meanwhile, during 1980 the archenemy of Cultural Revolution days, Liu Shaoqi, was rehabilitated and the Communist party again called him "a great Marxist revolutionary." More important than the redressing of an injustice was the assertion of the continuing authority of a Communist party that haughtily rewrote history to suit the imperatives of power. "China, our new friend," I wrote in a *New York Times* op-ed article in May 1980, "is in the grip of a more orderly, predictable authoritarianism—but it is still authoritarianism. Communism as an idea may be dying in Beijing; the Communist party is growing stronger."

That same year, I again found myself in India after an absence of twenty years and throughout my weeks there I weighed comparisons of China and India. "Being in India," I wrote in my diary, "is like living each day with a sack of wheat on your back, as the burden of India's size, heat, noise, and poverty weighs down the spirit." Yet India impressed me far more than in 1960, when I had arrived by boat as a wide-eyed Australian student, and I now compared it favorably with China for its political freedom. Indians were obsessed with religion, just as Chinese were obsessed with issues of social order. But the sanctions upon the individual in India sprang from tradition; in China they sprang from current politics. In social modernization, India seemed behind China in some respects; routinely in the big Indian cities, for example, marriage was arranged, whereas urban Chinese mostly chose their own spouses.

"Calcutta is a city of words," I wrote in a letter to a British friend, Endymion Wilkinson. "People say sentences at you even when they don't seem to have a thought, or an intention of listening for a response. Marxist phrases fly around—the state government is Communist—as no longer in Peking." For Indian intellectuals words were cheap, whereas for Chinese intellectuals words were dangerous.

I found the economic record a mixed one. Indian industry had done better than Chinese, while Indian agriculture, despite a huge advantage over Chinese agriculture in cultivable land (30 percent of the total land in India, 11 percent in China), was less successful than Chinese in the basic task of feeding a huge population. Yet nothing seemed more important than India's political freedom and China's lack of it. Indians would talk (their heads off!) to me about anything and would approach me for conversation or companionship without any fear. By comparison China was mentally a virtual prison. It had gained clout as a nation on the world scene, but the Chinese individual as yet had little to boast about.

On October 1, 1949, atop the Gate of Heavenly Peace, overlooking Tiananmen Square, Mao declared Liberation and proclaimed the founding of the People's Republic of China.

In Shanghai, Liberation was celebrated with red stars and banners attacking feudalism, imperialism, Japanese invaders, and Chinese businessmen who had cooperated with foreigners. In the decade that followed, Mao would pursue close ties with the USSR and instant communism in the Great Leap Forward.

Anti-American feeling ran high when the Korean War erupted. In August 1950, in a tableau in Peking, actors mock the United States military, personified by a character adorned with a dollar sign, as South Korea abases itself before Uncle Sam.

3

4

In its calculated anti-Westernism, China sought ties among nations of the Third World. In May 1955, Premier Zhou Enlai was welcomed home to Peking airport from the Afro-Asian conference in Bandung, Indonesia, by Liu Shaoqi, number two to Mao in the regime.

The two Red chieftains, Mao and Nikita Khrushchev, genial but wary, met in Peking in 1958 to discuss nuclear weapons, danger in the Taiwan Strait, and how to deal with America.

5

6

In January 1960, when the Great Leap Forward had essentially failed and Peking–Moscow relations were fast deteriorating, Mao met with his colleagues in Canton (Guangzhou). On his right is Premier Zhou Enlai, and on his left, with a stick, is Deng Xiaoping. Lin Biao, holding documents, has just been named defense minister.

7

In September 1962, Mao with his wife, Jiang Qing—making one of her first prominent public appearances—greet Madame Sukarno, wife of the Indonesian president, in Peking.

The Monument to the People's Heroes, built in 1958, at the center of Tiananmen Square. The key acts in the drama of Communist China, from the founding of the regime in 1949 to the massacre of 1989, were played out at Tiananmen Square.

By 1966, Mao's astonishing Cultural Revolution was under way. As he returns
the applause of Red Guards, Lin Biao, the rising new number-two figure in the
regime, is at his left. Farther away is the doomed head of state, Liu Shaoqi, and
two beyond him another target of the Cultural Revolution, Deng Xiaoping.

(OPPOSITE) Mao and his deputy, Liu Shaoqi, conferred at Zhongnanhai, the
leadership compound adjacent to the Forbidden City, in October 1965. It was
the eve of the Cultural Revolution, which was to see Mao become a god and Liu
fall from power and die of beatings, pneumonia, and lack of medical care.

A parade past Tiananmen during the Cultural Revolution. A statue of Mao is borne aloft amid red flags. The characters behind Mao say, "Long Live the Thought of Mao Zedong."

CHAPTER NINE

■

CHINA, AMERICA, AND FRIENDSHIP

UP until the late 1970s, China and America still did not have full diplomatic relations because the Taiwan issue obstructed that step, and debate went on in different ways in both countries about when "normalization" of ties between Peking and Washington would be possible, and how the Taiwan issue would be "solved." Just before the Gerald Ford–Jimmy Carter presidential contest of 1976, Jerome Alan Cohen of the Harvard Law School gave a pessimistic talk at Harvard's East Asian Center on the incomplete state of United States–China relations. "I don't agree with Jerry a bit," I wrote in my diary that evening. "If Ford is elected I think normalization will come within six months (longer under Carter)."[1] I did not share the widespread view that Washington's insistence on keeping an office in Taipei and supplying arms to Taiwan would indefinitely prevent normalization. "I doubt that Peking will make a fuss over weapons supplies to Taipei," I wrote to my friend Rachel Faggetter, now back in Australia from Peking, during 1977. "So what will happen is that Taiwan will lose its major diplomatic links, yet go on with an essentially separate life for many years to come."

It did not help efforts to predict the timing of normalization that the words uttered by Chinese officials on the Taiwan issue frequently were mystifying. Xie Qimei of the Chinese embassy in Washington, who would later become undersecretary of the United Nations, during the late 1970s came to my office at Harvard—an unusual step then for a Chinese diplomat—and declared: "We do

not think there can be a peaceful solution to the Taiwan question."
He and other Chinese officials repeatedly told me that a resolution
of the Taiwan issue was a condition of normalization. Yet the apex
of the Chinese government was so obsessed with the danger from
Russia that it hinted to the White House China's "understanding" if
the United States could not take any steps on Taiwan "just now."

This was why Kissinger was able to remark, when as secretary of
state he came to Harvard in 1976, "It's impossible for Peking to
respond to our fancy legalistic formulations. China and America did
not come together to solve the Taiwan problem," he went on, "but
to contain Russia. When Peking and Washington want to settle Taiwan, it certainly can be settled."

Behind the mystery of Peking's words lay a peculiar Chinese tendency to talk nearly always about labels and seldom about realities,
even while acting with due respect for realities. While Peking and
Taipei railed against each other and bemoaned their "divided" country, the Taiwan Strait had, in fact, been tranquil for years and the
coexistence of the two territories, following a bloody civil war, was
one of the great success stories of international relations in the late
twentieth century. Mystifying too, at least to one not born and
brought up in America, was Congress's jealous guarding of its turf
on China policy over and against the claims of the executive branch.
"How can you sit there," the chairman of the Asia-Pacific subcom-
mittee, Clement Zablocki, inquired of me when I testified, along
with the University of Michigan sinologist Michel Oksenberg, before his group in March 1976, "and urge recognizing Peking and
breaking with Taipei?"—a step which still had not been taken. I
thought the Wisconsin Democrat was about to enlarge on the evils
of communism, but he went on: "You urge, in other words, that
the Shanghai Communiqué [Nixon's agreement with Zhou Enlai in
1972], signed only by the executive branch, be placed *above* the 1954
treaty with the Republic of China [Taiwan], which was ratified by
Congress!"

I took the Kissinger view that Peking cared about relations with
America in a way that transcended its obsessive complaints about
the Taiwan issue, and I had become certain that "normalization"
was imminent after a talk in Peking with Assistant Foreign Minister
Wang Hairong in the summer of 1978 and a subsequent talk with
Carter's assistant secretary of state for East Asian and Pacific Affairs,
Richard Holbrooke, at an Asia Society conference in Thailand.
Wang's remarks showed that the Chinese wanted normalization for

strategic reasons that extended well beyond Taiwan, and Hol-brooke's that the American side believed it could normalize without sacrificing anything in Taiwan's concrete situation. Thereafter, I was convinced that full United States–China diplomatic relations were imminent, and that the Taiwan issue would be finessed.

In my new book *The Future of China,* written in 1977, I had predicted that China and America would establish full diplomatic relations before the end of 1978, and for the time being agree to disagree on Taiwan. Prediction became reality when President Carter and Deng Xiaoping in simultaneous announcements in December 1978 established full diplomatic relations between the United States and China, pinning down what Nixon and Mao had staked out six years before. It had long been an American assumption, especially in Congress, that steps ahead in Sino-American relations would take something away from Taiwan. It was an achievement of Carter's—later strengthened by President Ronald Reagan—that ties with Peking brought no damage to Taiwan.

Deng came to dine at the White House and wear a cowboy hat at a Texas barbecue in an atmosphere of anxiety on both the Chinese and American sides about Soviet expansionism. When I saw him in Washington at a dinner at the Hilton Hotel, he looked subdued and was sniffling with a cold, but his words against Moscow were vigorous to the point of being warlike. During the state dinner at the White House, the actress Shirley MacLaine told Deng with awe that a scientist in Peking said to her his years of caring for pigs during the Cultural Revolution were "the best years of my life." The Chinese leader buried the Mao era with the deflating response: "The man was lying."[2]

After the quaintly misnamed "normalization" occurred, China policy began to take its place as one part of overall American foreign policy, and to lose the volatility and overlay of passion that years of isolation and an excess of ideology on both sides had given it. Within the Western alliance, Carter's step gave the United States the initiative—lost in the late 1940s to Europe—on policy toward China. Gone were the years of America trying to make a China in its own image and of China "exporting revolution."

Gone, too, was "Peking," for the State Department made the bizarre decision to heed China's demand that foreigners spell and pronounce the name of its capital city in a new fashion. It was not that the Chinese or anyone else changed the name of the city from Peking to Beijing, for the two words in Roman letters are variant ways of pronouncing the unchanged two Chinese characters that mean "Northern Capital." "Beijing" is the way the two characters are pronounced in Chinese, while "Peking" (or slight variants upon it) was the way the non-Chinese world had long pronounced these characters.

It was a bizarre decision because Americans do not say "Paree" but Paris, or "Moskva" but Moscow, or "Roma" but Rome; in no other case known to me do we in English adopt the non–English-speaking foreign capital's language's own pronunciation of its name. The episode revealed the China-centeredness of the Peking government, the deference to it of an American government pleased at normalization, and the cultural gulf between China and an American populace with no way of knowing that by saying "Beijing" they were speaking Chinese in the middle of an English sentence.

While trying to hold on to Mao's idea of twin evil "superpowers," Deng and the other post-Mao leaders in reality tilted heavily against Russia at the end of the 1970s, and with a wink and a shuffle moved close strategically to the United States. Frequently I talked about China's policies with a neat, slim Mandarin named Zhang Wenjin. A veteran diplomat who could soften even a harsh pronouncement by his grandfatherly air, Zhang, China's assistant foreign minister, had an architect brother living in the United States and knew the West quite well. Kissinger had been escorted by Zhang into Beijing from Pakistan on his first trip to China and afterward said the assistant foreign minister "looked like a Spanish cardinal in an El Greco painting" and referred to his "austere elegance and understated intelligence."[3] Over lunch in Beijing in the winter of 1979–80, I asked Zhang Wenjin to explain the difference between the presence of fifty thousand American troops in Korea, which China no longer criticized, and the presence of fifty thousand Russian troops in Afghanistan, which China was vociferously criticizing. The dapper minister replied: "Really, the American role in Korea is an isolated phenomenon, while the Russian role in Afghanistan is part of something larger, and expanding." In Chinese eyes, America was no longer expansionist, while Russia was.

In January 1980, Carter's secretary of defense, Harold Brown, came to Beijing, on a historic first visit by a defense secretary to Mao's China, to discuss the Russian threat with the Chinese leaders. During his visit I went into the "Friendship Store" to buy a pair of gloves and ran into two members of Brown's party. "When I came here with [Carter's national security adviser Zbigniew] Brzezinski in the spring of 1978," said Michael Armacost, an aide to Brown who would later become ambassador to Japan, "I certainly did not expect that the secretary of defense would come to Beijing within eighteen months. Without the Beijing-Washington relation," Armacost went on, "Vietnam troops may well have been in Thailand by now." Moscow's move into Kabul had put new life into Sino-American relations. The United States and China became tacit allies in supporting the precarious position of Pakistan, Thailand, and other countries against threats whose ultimate source was Soviet power. By the time Carter's presidency drew to a close in the winter of 1980–81, the bilateral relationship between Beijing and Washington was thickening, although beset with arguments over textile imports from China, civil aviation, and other specifics. The relationship as a deterrent to Russian global adventurism and a force for stability in Asia was already of great importance.

It happened that just as Deng came to visit Carter and solidify ties with America, a bloody conflict broke out on China's 650-mile southern border with Vietnam. It was the culmination of a dramatic shift from amity to rancor between Beijing and Hanoi, as two socialist nations that had long been "as close as lips and teeth" began shooting at each other; two haughty nationalistic dictatorships had found compromise more distasteful than a bout of violence. The angry conflict tore a veil off some strains afflicting China after thirty years of communism and gave a clue to Deng's short fuse and how he reacted boldly to provocation. "We are going to teach Vietnam a lesson," he said revealingly. "Vietnam won't listen to us," Assistant Foreign Minister Wang Hairong complained to me like a headmistress speaking of a fourth-grader. But the performance of China's armies did not match China's high pride; the military outcome was not clear-cut, China lost thousands dead and tens of thousands wounded, and Vietnam's spirited resistance to China's views did not cease.

For Deng no less than for Mao, war had been the crucible of politics, as uprisings against warlords, civil war against Chiang Kai-shek, and defense against the Japanese invaders provided the key experiences and case studies of decision making in his career. Definitions of courage and cowardice, skill in timing, clues to the choice between compromise and absolute resolve—all had been learned by Deng in those armed conflicts. If Deng sounded like a warrior when he discussed China's disagreements with Vietnam, and when in Washington he urged Carter to resist Russia more vigorously, indeed he had come into politics through war, and the older he got, the more this atavism would guide his response to any provocation. The guns of anger crackled on the China-Vietnam border early in the Deng era, and they would crackle at Tiananmen Square late in the Deng era.

During the 1980 American presidential election campaign and for a period after Reagan's victory over Carter, a battle of opinions occurred within Reagan's circle between an ideological approach toward China and a national interest approach. In congressional testimony and several newspaper columns I spoke out for a national interest policy, which I took to be a true conservative policy. During my visit to Beijing in 1980, when Assistant Foreign Minister Zhang Wenjin expressed alarm about Reagan, I said to him: "If Reagan is elected, his strategic anti-Russian point of view will prevail, when it comes to China policy, over his moral pro-Taiwan point of view." So it proved. Reagan soon pursued the policy of national interest toward China, continuing the approach that essentially had been common to Nixon and Ford and Carter. This meant leaning toward China (despite its dictatorial government) as a counterweight to Russia, and viewing a good relationship with China as the key to peace in Asia.

China's foreign policy had departed from some Maoist principles and was growing more modest and cost-conscious. "We won't be able to donate military assistance as in the past," Zhang Wenjin told me. "You know, lots of countries didn't pay the bill to China and other countries for foreign aid." The minister laughed. "Egypt didn't pay Russia, and we actually encouraged Cairo not to pay Moscow. In the future," Zhang went on, "all our military and economic assistance will be approached like tailoring a suit. We'll take the measurements, look at the stature of the one seeking the suit, consider the price, and come up with the garment if it's worth it." During the mid-1970s, Zhang Wenjin had praised turmoil and talked about "international class struggle," but after the lunch with him in 1980 I noted in my dairy: "He sounded today like a blend of Bismarck and an overseas Chinese businessman."

The days of Mao's China "punishing" American Express because it also did business in Taiwan, and laying down to *The New York*

Times that it could have a bureau in Beijing only if it didn't publish advertisements from Taiwan, gave way to the more comfortable days of Deng's China weighing the balance of power, counting its foreign aid pennies, and worrying about the unmodernized condition of its once-vaunted armies. It was a foreign policy that was essentially negative; China was buying time, coping as best it could with the gap between its ambitions and its capacity.

At the same time Chinese foreign policy became ever more nationalistic, and one day in 1982 I found Zhang Wenjin a little snappy on policy toward America. "China suffered from the 1950s to the 1970s when there was no link with America," he said over lunch in a favorite dining room of his at the Xin Qiao Hotel, "but America suffered more." I was dubious about this, but the minister swept on with a couple of Chinese proverbs for my edification. "The best shopkeeper doesn't hang all his fine goods outside the window," he remarked when I mentioned some doubts within the United States about China's real weight in world affairs, "but keeps them stored behind the counter." He delivered another swipe at America: "It's better not to have a big name, and be able to live up to it, than the other way round."

By the time Premier Zhao Ziyang, one of Deng's chief aides in the drive for reform, arrived in Washington in his gray Western suit and red tie to visit Reagan in 1984, the smoke and mirrors and ideological arias of past United States–China relations were not in evidence. Zhao was born to a landlord family in 1919 and joined the Communist party in Henan Province on the eve of World War II at the age of nineteen. A specialist on economic policy, he made his career in Guangzhou★ and there, during the Cultural Revolution, after unsuccessfully trying to survive by denouncing Deng as a capitalist roader, he was himself paraded through the streets in a dunce cap as a class enemy.

In the 1970s he reappeared, first as party chief in Inner Mongolia and then once more in Guangzhou. In the later 1970s he was party chief in the important province of Sichuan, where he pioneered a number of reforms, and after Deng won supreme power in 1978, he was brought to Beijing and made a Politburo member. Zhao enjoyed golf and was more likely to quote Alvin Toffler's *Future Shock* (which he had read in translation) than Marx's *Das Kapital*. When I saw him in Washington at a Chinese embassy party during his visit

★ Canton's new name.

to Reagan, he still looked like a landlord's son, with his prosperous mien and receding hairline. "The danger and the glamor have both gone from the China issue," remarked Donald Anderson, a State Department official who had been consul-general in Shanghai, as we chatted at the Chinese party. "Zhao's main purpose is to sell China economically to the United States government and the private sector."

Peace or war was no longer an issue between the United States and Communist China, which had fought each other in the Chinese civil war of the 1940s and soon after in Korea, and almost did so in the Taiwan Strait in the 1950s and again over Indochina in the 1960s. The two countries were now "friends." My long-standing approach to China primarily as an international issue came to an end. But to what purpose had China and the United States become friends? I did not expect that China with its bicycles and America with its automobiles would see life from similar angles, and I was not sure whether China and America could find a common mode of opposing the Soviet expansionism that both denounced. "I *hope* we'll grow closer together," a middle-aged journalist friend, Li Yanning, said reflectively of China and America when I lunched with him during Defense Secretary Brown's visit to Beijing, "but I don't know how close it can be." In fact, despite the strategic convergence, Chinese and Americans had hardly begun to assess each other morally and philosophically.

For Americans, China was like a suitcase that had been quickly opened, its contents that had previously seemed a tightly bound unity falling out in a tumble on the rug. China turned out to be a variety of things: a market huge in potential, but difficult to crack; a place of historical and natural wonders, but of social constrictions that left the traveler feeling he had been at a theatrical performance; a welcome counterweight to Russia, but a firm supporter of the murderous Khmer Rouge in Cambodia. The Chinese themselves opened the "suitcase" by being more candid than before about failures and unfinished tasks within their society.

About this time, I effected a change in my own immigration status. Had I been a sculptor or a taxi driver, I might have remained an Australian citizen even after living in Boston for many years, but being an occasional commentator on American policy toward China, I felt uncomfortable at times with my outsider's classification. At congressional hearings I did not feel able to say "you Americans" should do this or that, and yet I was not at ease with saying "we Americans." Five years had elapsed since Ms. McKeon had examined me and granted me a green card, and at a ceremony in historical Faneuil Hall in Boston in 1979, I took the next step and became an American citizen. I was no longer a guest who made suggestions when asked, but a voter and taxpayer and participant in American public policy discussion. I think the step reduced a tendency I had to dwell on the Chinese point of view on any question. I no longer had to strive to fulfill the function of "Mr. China," for I now belonged in America just like everyone else.

One summer morning in Shanghai back in 1975, while on the trip with the Committee For Australia China Relations, I had come upon a large crowd intently reading four large sheets of paper on a building wall in Sichuan Road. The text of two thousand characters in black ink on white paper was a citizen's complaint at the trampling of his constitutional rights, the boldest thing of its kind I had ever seen in China. Worker Zhai felt he had been victimized in an incident at his Shanghai Machine Repair Plant, and a previous big-character poster he put up to air his grievance had been removed "by some influential and privileged man," who sent militia "with brooms and buckets" to wash it off the wall. "Even in Ethiopia," the neat black characters said, "revolutionaries made use of wall posters. Yet the wall poster has met with deep distress in its homeland."

Surprised at this cry for rights, I glanced around nervously at the sea of faces, but no one was looking at me and all eyes were riveted to the text on the wall. The next day I crept back before dawn to photograph Zhai's poster, realizing I had seen an early shoot of a growing demand in China for human rights.

After Mao died in 1976, an assertive urban stratum of educated and individualistic people pushed in quiet ways for a more predictable environment. They were reacting against the patriarchal, arbitrary ways of the late Mao period, and they felt China needed less political talk and more economic progress. Frequently they appealed, as Zhai did in Shanghai, to China's own constitution. "The Communist party is supposed to guarantee the weapon of the wall poster to the Chinese people," Zhai wrote, "but it does not." In those demands for observance of human rights of the late 1970s, petitioners disavowed any utopian or anti-Communist sentiments and stuck to modest requests. Typically, posters were respectful of Mao and the Communist party's leading role in politics.

At Harvard during 1978, invited to give a lecture in a series of New England China Seminars, I spoke about the start of a demand for democracy in China. Some people thought I was looking for mushrooms in a desert, but I felt "constitutionalism," as I called these first shoots, was the natural beginning within the Chinese system for an attempt to make the Marxists do in practice what they proclaimed in theory. "Democracy within Marxism" was probably an impossibility, but I felt the urban stratum calling for human rights might one day go on to ask for democracy without Marxism. In the late 1970s the roots of this stirring were almost totally internal, but within a few years the new America-China relationship's contribution to social restiveness within China became clear.

A year after I spoke of the rise of a new public opinion in China and published the text of Zhai's poster in my book *The Future of China,* a "Democracy Wall" made a dramatic appearance in Beijing. A few hundred meters of gray wall by a bus depot on Chang An Avenue was plastered during late 1978 and 1979 with bold political and literary expression from the grass roots.

The best-known talent behind Democracy Wall was Wei Jingsheng, the editor of a lively unauthorized magazine called *Exploration.* Entirely a product of the PRC, Wei was born in 1950 into an army family and later worked as an electrician at the Beijing zoo. In *Exploration* he and his friends, some of them from campuses but most of them workers, argued that Deng's vaunted "four modernizations" of agriculture, industry, defense, and science and technology would not work without a fifth modernization—democracy.

Many of the essays, epistles, and petitions on Democracy Wall and in similar outpourings in other cities were written from within an acceptance of the Communist system, asking for "more democracy," but others probed the Communist system's fundamental flaw of concentration of unaccountable power. In his earlier poster in Sichuan Road in Shanghai, Zhai had raised the technical argument that rights guaranteed in China's constitution were not being respected. At Democracy Wall a more basic starting point was adopted —why does China lag?—and the influence from outside on the Chinese cry for democracy began to be seen. "Why is it that the Chinese people show so few achievements inside China itself," one Beijing wall-poster writer inquired, "yet win Nobel Prizes once they go abroad?" An answer was supplied that got to the heart of the contradiction in Deng's agenda for modernizing China: "Because the production and development of science requires a particular kind of soil—and that soil is democracy."[4]

One reason why Deng allowed Democracy Wall to come into existence was that the prodemocracy forces' call for more freedom helped him in his power struggle against Hua Guofeng and other semi-Maoist colleagues in the Politburo. By the fall of 1979, however, Deng's supremacy over Hua was not so much in question, and meanwhile he had grown tired of the sniping at his own heels in the wall posters by Wei and others at the bus depot on Chang An Avenue. A squad of workers arrived at Democracy Wall with brooms and scrapers and hoses and removed all the essays and letters and petitions. Like a lazy old man reaching for the nearest familiar battered pair of shoes and worn-out cardigan, Deng plucked modes and concepts from the Maoist past. Wei Jingsheng was tried and put in prison for fifteen years for twin offenses from the classic canon of xenophobic and class-obsessed Chinese communism: "passing military secrets to a foreigner" and "counterrevolutionary activities." Other activists of Democracy Wall were also imprisoned, most of them workers like Wei. Deng established a pattern he would stick to in later years of dealing more harshly with prodemocracy activists from industry or the army than with those from the campuses.

The flowering of friendships with individual Chinese was not the least of the benefits of Deng's reforms and "normalization" between China and Western countries. By 1982 there were more than ten thousand Chinese students on campuses in the West, and an array of American and other Western academic, research, and commercial connections had been established with Beijing, Shanghai, Nanjing, Chengdu, Dalian, Xian, and other Chinese cities. American publications like *Time* and *Newsweek* were available in the hotels, Chinese TV offered a window on the real life of America, Japan, Taiwan, and other lands, and gradually some Chinese officials and many intellectuals developed a commitment to and vested interest in the nexus with the West. Young urban Chinese found in the West and its people and ideas a force that changed their lives.

I began to make close friends in China for the first time and one of them was Shen Chunyi, who had been a student at a lecture I gave at the Australian National University in Canberra back in 1978. A sturdy twenty-eight-year-old with short-cropped hair, square hands, and bright eyes, Shen lingered in the seminar room after the audience left and asked many questions about my talk on "Chinese Politics Since the Death of Mao." Especially he took up eagerly my view that the Tiananmen Square demonstration of April 1976 marked the beginning of public opinion in PRC politics. Shen had been two years in Australia, studying English, and was about to return home to Beijing. "I doubt that capitalism will collapse in Australia," he said as if entertaining a new idea. "The capitalists are too strong."[5]

A few months later at Harvard I received from Shen in Beijing a letter that showed how dizzying for a person brought up in Mao's China was the combination of two years' study in the West followed by a return to his original unit in China. "I am teaching beginners [in my language institute]," he wrote, "and it is very tedious and boring. What I learned in Australia seems to be of little use." Shen came back to Beijing just as Deng put an end to Democracy Wall and arrested Wei Jingsheng. "China cannot afford to allow the kind of democracy you have in the West," his letter went on. "With the bulk of the population backward, there can be no genuine democracy for all. It is always for the few (I mean the ruling elite)."

In this 1979 letter Shen had come to understand the Chinese Communist political system, but not yet to see beyond it. "I don't reject the introduction of democracy," he wrote. "I am merely stating that any authoritarian government can't and won't allow it." I could hardly wait to see Shen again in Beijing, for the state of his mind seemed to reflect the strains China was experiencing as it sought to modernize and open itself to the West.

On a wintry day in January 1980, during my stay in Beijing as a guest of the Australian ambassador, I paced anxiously up and down the lobby of the Xin Qiao Hotel in the old Legation Quarter, waiting for an overdue Shen. Then through the glass of the revolving door I caught a glimpse of him standing on the sidewalk outside. "I don't want to come inside the hotel," he muttered as he pulled off a glove to shake my hand on the front steps of the hotel, "because I don't like having to answer the questions of the plainclothesmen at the door."

Shen Chunyi, whose father was a factory worker, smiled with pleasure at our reunion as we sat down on unstable chairs in a nearby café whose little tables were adorned with plastic flowers. Yet I could see from the way he twisted his napkin that he was nervous. "We Chinese experienced the trial of Wei Jingsheng since I last wrote to you," he said, "so we have to be careful." I wanted to ask about Wei's trial, but wondered whether Shen, even in an out-of-the-way café, would feel at ease with this depressing topic. In fact he moved to it like a cat to a saucer of milk. "We are not bold like Wei, but we sympathize with him," he said of his own circle of semidissidents. I asked why Wei had conducted his own defense and Shen replied: "Because lawyers in China are mostly playthings of the party. The problem with the legal system," he went on of Deng's recent introduction of new civil and criminal codes, "is that it doesn't apply to everyone—party cadres can influence the outcome." Like many Chinese, Shen found Wei's offenses of spilling secrets and conducting "counterrevolutionary activity" a concoction. Could a dissident really possess military secrets about China's border war with Vietnam to offer a British journalist; does democracy run "counter" to the revolution; is a publicly expressed thought an "activity"?

Shen summed up the measure of freedom in Deng's China by a reference to two books by George Orwell that he had read while in Australia. "It's the difference between *Animal Farm* and *1984*," he said: "*1984* is about the stupidities and deceptions of dictatorship. It's more or less admitted now that we have had these things. But the character of the pig in *Animal Farm* is totally unacceptable within China. You can't personally insult the leader!" Later, as my stay in Beijing that winter of 1980 came to an end, Shen made a farewell remark: "We are like birds in a cage. We can fly, but there are limits on all sides. It's not the same as being trussed up and unable to fly. Nor is it like being outside the cage."

During the early 1980s, on my visit with the delegation of professors studying Mao, and the trips on board the *Pearl of Scandinavia* and the *Royal Viking Star,* I saw Shen in Beijing a number of times and watched his views evolve. The distress on returning from Australia gave way gradually to a more stable period in his life and thinking, but I doubted he would ever regain the faith in the system that his upbringing had planted in him. One evening in 1982 Shen and I arranged to dine at the fancy "imperial" Fangshan restaurant in Beihai Park, but when we met at the front door he said he had been too busy to make a reservation, as he had undertaken to do, and we were turned away. I suggested the restaurant at the Nationalities Hotel, where the guards at the front door seemed rather relaxed by hotel standards about local Chinese coming in and out; Shen agreed and we fought our way onto a creaking, low-slung bus. But halfway to the Nationalities Hotel Shen changed his mind and said he just didn't want to go into any hotel. As we settled at a table in the Mongolian Hotpot restaurant near Wang Fu Jing Street and sipped a cold beer, Shen looked me in the eye and said: "I wasn't too busy to phone for a reservation at the Fangshan—I didn't want to. Did you notice there were many empty tables at the Fangshan?" he continued. "Reservations are just a means of control. Had I phoned, I would have had to give my name and phone number. That leads to questions at the institute—and I have to explain what business I had dealing with you. All this I hate."

I apologized to Shen for suggesting a meal at the Nationalities Hotel, and he asked me, in turn, if I was upset over the foul-up at the Fangshan. Not really, I said, but why hadn't he told me when the idea of eating at the Fangshan first arose that he did not care to make a reservation? "I felt ashamed," he said. "I hoped we just might get in without a reservation. I didn't want you to have the impression that China, even after the fall of the Gang of Four, is just about as bad as Russia."

One day I told Shen Chunyi how I had asked Hu Sheng, a senior party intellectual who had suffered in the Cultural Revolution, about the leftist slogan, "The moon is not rounder abroad," a weapon used by the Communist party against cosmopolitan Chinese in the 1970s. "The slogan is not false," Hu Sheng had replied in our 1973 conversation, having to tread very carefully in the atmosphere of the last years of Mao. "But it is also true that the moon is not rounder in China." Shen lit a cigarette and made his own younger person's commentary on the slogan. "After all," he said, "there is only one moon." I wondered if through the 1980s young Chinese, ruled by an elite so little able to handle the gulf between Chinese communism and values in much of the rest of the world, would really be able to live as if there were only one moon.

As the state presumed less in the ideological realm, civil society came to the fore, and forces and expressions of civil society such as religion, private business, personal attachments, and varied modes of dress became more prominent. In urban China especially, the individual seemed to be pushing out from behind the barriers of political and cultural collectivism. This incipient individualism was linked with Western influence, the new materialism, a freed aesthetic sense, and heightened sexual awareness.

"I was shocked," Shen Chunyi recalled of having read *Playboy* while studying in Australia. "In Australia I learned the theory of sex, but certainly I never touched an Australian girl." When he returned to Beijing, however, Shen found himself becoming sexually active for the first time in his life, and he told me of courting a girl named Chen Aiqing. One evening at dusk in sprawling Coal Hill Park, as they sat on a bench by the lake, Shen touched her breasts, then kissed her. "It was the first time I had touched a girl like that," he said. "I was terribly excited. I said to myself, 'How successful! So the Western way works in China!' " Remembering our previous conversation about whether the moon was brighter in China, or abroad, I quipped: "There is only one moon!"

"We knew that in the West a hug leads on to sex," Shen said of the assumptions of his upbringing. "But we always regarded it as a capitalist activity." Two years in Australia had shaken his view of capitalism, especially his moral judgments against it. Shen told me that he and Aiqing had spent the night in a room that belonged to a teacher friend who hardly used it because his wife lived away from Beijing and he was often out of town visiting her. The next morning Shen said to himself: "Is it really so easy?"

In sexual behavior as in politics, Shen had passed outside the boundary of the orthodox. I saw his new freedom as part of his quiet protest against a system that, as he put it in a letter to me, "asks the blind obedience of the masses." Often I got the impression that he used the word "democracy" as a synonym for "happiness."

Although the individual began to push through the frames of collectivism in Deng's China, actual sexual behavior showed how far removed from Western individualism most Chinese still were. The majority Chinese approach was to think of sex within the rubric of reproduction; a person fulfilled a role, rather than gave expression to impulses, and morality pertained to that role, not to the intrinsic act. In this sense the sexual conservatism of the Chinese was not at all Puritan; no gap existed between the realm of the spirit and the realm of the flesh, as in the Greek thought that influenced the West. At times it was hard to tell how much it was the lack of freedom under Communist rule that thwarted the individual self-expression the Shen Chunyis of China were reaching for, and how much it was Chinese cultural conservatism. Often I felt one reinforced the other.

Visiting Shen Chunyi again in 1983, when I was traveling on board the *Royal Viking Star,* I found that teachers and students at his institute no longer had to write essays celebrating the fall of the Gang of Four. "All that's gone," Shen said with a grin as he reflected on the shift away from ideology. "That doesn't mean, by the way, that we could write an essay attacking Deng Xiaoping." The edge had gone off Shen's political dissent, and he felt Deng in particular had improved the food situation in China. "If we try to get rid of communism we'll make matters worse," he summed up. "I think we have to hope for an evolution toward the liberalized situation in Yugoslavia." He railed against "bureaucrats," but not against the Communist political system itself, and he spoke of "limits" to what the Chinese could hope for. "You know I didn't agree with the prison sentence given to Wei Jingsheng," he said. "Yet his ringing appeal for democracy probably wasn't helpful. If China voted today, Wei would lose, Deng would win."

The Shen of 1982 and 1983 was a symbol of the initial success of Deng's reforms in bringing some improvement in standards of life while damping down the ardor for political change. He was a by-product of an urban China in transition. "Whether he hardens into a dissident or gravitates toward a new-style Chinese establishment," I noted in my diary in November 1983, "depends on where China goes in the next decade. If China fails badly in achieving its goals for modernization, Shen might be found at the barricades, or feeding pigs in a village, or in exile. If China goes forward with Deng's policies and enjoys solid economic success, it will need its Shen Chunyis and perhaps value them." Which direction would China take and what would happen to Shen? Only later would I find answers to those questions.

CHAPTER TEN

■

IN SEARCH OF
WEALTH AND
POWER

IN what way and to what degree had the credibility of the Communist party advanced since the departure of Mao? Deng's stress on modernization was bringing a period of common purpose between government and people, and his sincerity in giving a high priority to economic development was widely acknowledged. But the monopoly of the Communist party over public life continued, so power and "truth" remained fused. In that sense, political credibility was hardly greater under Deng than under Mao, and it remained to be seen whether a focus on economic development had truly stilled the storms of political struggle. The trial of the Gang of Four helped Deng politically for a few years after 1980, but it also perpetuated the old Maoist evils of guilt by association and politics as a morality play.

Especially in Shanghai, home to most of the Gang of Four, the concept of "deeds of the Gang of Four" was the unfailing explanation for every flaw and failure. "But for the Gang of Four," a Shanghai economist told me in 1980, "China's GNP would now be three times what it is." He said Jiang Qing and her friends "chopped down forests" and "worsened China's traffic problems."

A Mrs. Wu, my escort on a visit to the Shanghai Academy of Social Science, came up with a piece of news about an editor whom I had asked to see. I first met Wang Zhenglong in 1973 at Harvard, where he arrived as the youngest member of the first journalists' delegation from the PRC to visit the United States, and later in

Shanghai he had been helpful to me with contacts and advice. He
was a son of the Cultural Revolution, propelled to the editor's chair
of the Shanghai newspaper *Wen Hui Bao* by the churning politics of
the 1960s while he was still in his twenties. A leftist, Wang nonetheless admired America and was fascinated by technology.

"You cannot see Mr. Wang—he has disappeared," Mrs. Wu said
in a conspiratorial tone. I said that "disappeared" was a vague and
chilling term, which I disliked, and that if Wang had been sent away
from Shanghai, I would like to have his current address and write to
him; even should he be in prison, I said in an attempt both to praise
and make use of post-Mao reforms, China's new civil code would
give him the right to receive a visitor. "You should realize, Mr.
Terrill," said Mrs. Wu as her agitation pushed her to say more than
she intended, "that Wang was very deeply involved with the Gang
of Four in Shanghai."

Only on my last day in Shanghai did I get beyond the word
"disappeared" when a senior literary journalist who had been tossed
out of *Wen Hui Bao* upon Wang's elevation there was sent to speak
with me. "When the Gang of Four was arrested," said this victim of
the Cultural Revolution, "editor Wang took full responsibility for
the disastrous drop in standards at *Wen Hui Bao*. One night he went
home from the office, climbed to the top of the apartment building
where he lived, and jumped down to his death."

Silently I figured out that Wang had been thirty-five when he
committed suicide, but it was a harder task to calculate how much
China lost by the habit of guilt by association and by treating politics
as a Peking opera. I had welcomed the fall of the ultraleftists, but I
was beginning to feel that I did not believe what Deng said about
the Gang of Four any more than I had believed what Jiang had said
about Deng ("He sold all our crude oil at deflated prices," she
frothed of Deng during the raucous polemics of 1976.) [1]

In Beijing a few days later I raised with New Zealand–born veteran "300 percenter" Rewi Alley my concern at the fate of Wang
Zhenglong and other followers of the Gang of Four, but he became
angry, banged his arms on the side of the armchair, and said they all
were "anarchists." "Don't you understand the terrible danger to
China of anarchism?" he cried.

It became fashionable to beat the breast and catalogue China's
every shortcoming, but since the shortcomings were blamed on the
Gang of Four—never on Hua, or Deng, or any other current office-
holder—the breast beating became a political ritual. The exaggera-

tion, for a purpose, made a sensational battle between good and evil out of what in the political process of democratic countries would be an institutionalized balancing of jostling opinions and interests. Deng's Communist party led the way in this reverse egotism, for to blacken the reputation of the Gang of Four was to build up the legitimacy of a government promising to rescue China from the horrible days when leftists were in power.

All this explained my own paradoxical response to the early post-Mao years. Just as a rising standard of living would not necessarily make for greater contentment among the Chinese people, so my own attitude toward economic change unaccompanied by political change was less than euphoric. Even as China loosened up, I found that the issue of the entrenched Leninist political system transcended both the ideological errors of Mao and the economic achievements of Deng.

In society at large, the mask of ideology was being pulled back from the face of China, and humor and irony and anger jumped out from daily life as they had not done under Mao. The buoyancy of this loosened-up China suggested to me that if the people's energies were unleashed by a politically free environment, China indeed could attain the superior performance that Chinese communities outside the PRC displayed. Yet I felt that the immediate spectacle behind the mask of ideology would prove exceedingly mixed, and that negative passions and conflicts of interest would increase as the Maoist grip on China's body and mind weakened.

Occasionally I glimpsed the toughness of Chinese social relations. The daughter of Frank and Ruth Coe, American expatriates who lived in a courtyard home in central Beijing, was born in China and spoke Chinese with a precise Beijing twirl, so the family had learned how rude Chinese often are to other Chinese. "My daughter called the airport the other evening to find out the time of arrival of a plane her friend was coming in on," Ruth related, "and the voice at the other end of the line snarled at her and said, 'What do you want to know that for?' " Miss Coe asked if this wasn't supposed to be an international airport. What did the man mean by speaking to her like that, and did he know to whom he was talking? Dramatically, she declared that she was a foreigner. "The man's tone changed," Ruth said. "He backed down. Politely he gave my daughter the flight information."

In Beijing one morning in October 1983, I went shopping with a young factory worker, Sun Muzhi, and we had trouble with taxis as one driver declined to take us to Wang Fu Jing Street because it was too close to lunchtime, another would not wait half an hour for us to browse in a bookstore, and a third refused to go to the Liu Li Chang art shops simply because he wished to head in a different direction. Sun did most of the talking with the drivers, and I became irritated at the supplicant's posture he assumed. "Taxi drivers are China's 'presidents,' " he explained, "and very well paid. You can't do anything with them! They get behind the wheel and think they're God!"

By 1983 the streets of Beijing, once sparse, could be clogged with vehicles. After a long slow afternoon excursion to western Beijing, Sun and I went into a crowded "masses" restaurant for dinner and found ourselves sharing a large round table with dark-skinned farmers taking a few days off to spend surplus cash. Opposite me were two men and a woman with wild staring eyes, who all silently shoveled food into their mouths and between gulps guzzled beer from opaque plastic cups. One man grew dissatisfied at the speed of his beer intake and took the jug of beer, poked the spout into his mouth, and upturned it. A tiny beggar boy appeared at my elbow and a waiter came and shooed him out of the room. "There's more and more of them," Sun said. "They are from the countryside. They come to Beijing because of some misfortune or to try their luck. Often they will shout if you don't give them money," Sun went on. "And they will announce how much they want." I wrote in my diary: "The Cultural Revolution turned into a free-for-all, with grudges and opportunism masquerading under labels of political principle. Now China has entered an age of economics. I only hope the political free-for-all of the Cultural Revolution is not replaced by an economic free-for-all, with people kicking each other aside to get ahead."

The Chinese people wished to *try* an economy as open as possible because they were fed up with the alternative of a bureaucratic economy. In Beijing in 1983 I lunched with a young foreign ministry friend at the tall luxurious new Great Wall Hotel, which was like a Boeing 747 parked in a village, a glossy slab of modernity amidst the low dusty desolation of a part of the city without urban graces. The young diplomat, who had recently returned from study at Tufts University in Boston, spoke of his enthusiasm for the new materialism in the countryside, and of the need for an equivalent unleashing of incentive in the cities. To my surprise he praised tipping. "There will never be good service in this country," he said as we finished our meal and I signed the check, "until we adopt your system of tipping."

The early 1980s were uneven politically, and within the general trend of liberalization, every now and then a crackdown occurred against a vague evil like "spiritual pollution" or "bourgeois influence." These campaigns came and went like rainstorms without warning, leaving many urban people wary. It seemed that China was half free and half open to the world, and that rear-guard forces tugged from beneath the surface to sabotage any steps toward freedom and cosmopolitanism.

The ritual of receiving "foreign guests" and presenting political ideas to them in Peking opera terms was fraying at the edges, but still it existed. On a visit to the Guangxi Art Institute in Nanning, I found that musicians had been deployed around the campus to play for my pleasure as I moved among the buildings. Like security guards on duty at all points of the grounds, students bearing *pipa, er hu,* and other instruments kept an eye on my movements to ensure a flow of music to my ears at every moment of my stay. After I left, a companion observed that the musicians stopped playing, packed up their instruments, and departed. "When the acting is good," Angela Terzani said aptly in *Chinese Days* in a summation of both the appeal and the grotesqueness of the ritual of receiving foreigners, "you have the fascinating feeling of having been to the theater; when it is second-rate, you are just angry."[2]

Although the Chinese were opening their mouths and ears before the foreigner, the Communist party still tried to keep foreigners from easy communication with ordinary Chinese citizens. While I was on a visit to the industrial bastion of Chongqing on the Yangzi River, my assistant Yang Bingzhang, the former Red Guard who now was a graduate student at Harvard, suggested I meet a medical couple he knew who belonged to an army unit. It wasn't "convenient" for a foreigner to be received in a military barracks, so Yang invited them to the People's Hotel where he and I were staying. But these Chongqing folk didn't quite see the People's Hotel as a hotel for the people. "They won't come here," Yang reported. "They said they know it's a fine place, but they don't feel it's for them. As army people, they are nervous about registering their names at the front gate." Yang strode up and down my room puffing on a cigarette. "My goodness, they seem to think of the hotel as non-Chinese territory. I mean, isn't this part of China?"

Often when I traveled around China in the company of a PRC

citizen who was unconnected with the government, I hit my head against this wall between Chinese society and the realm in which the Communists sought to contain foreigners. A tourist hotel, like the imperial palace of an earlier epoch, was a forbidden place evoking awe and speculation from ordinary folk. One day in the lobby of the Great Wall Hotel in Beijing, I overheard an argument at the entrance to the hotel's Cosmos Club disco. A Hong Kong visitor who was accompanied by a local Chinese friend was in heated debate with the doorkeeper of this classy new disco, who refused to admit a local Chinese. "You may come in," said the doorkeeper to the Hong Kong visitor, "but not your companion." The Hong Kong businessman patiently sought to elicit a reason for this discrimination, and meeting only a stone wall varnished with a smile, he raised his voice. "If there is something unhealthy on Chinese soil," he called out across the lobby, "you should get rid of it." But the policy against locals entering the Cosmos Club stood and the pair of would-be customers stalked away.

If, in the cities, there were "walls" between Chinese society and the niche created for foreigners, the life of the distant countryside was so much a closed book to the non-Chinese world that the Communists hardly needed to make special quarantine arrangements. I often reminded myself of one staggering fact: 80 percent of the Chinese (some 700 million people) lived in villages, and it was generally illegal for a foreigner to drive out and spend a night in most of these villages.[3]

In Shanghai, in particular, I came upon political unevenness and frustration on the part of some people with the strains and limits of the changes of the early Deng era. In 1983 as I traveled along the China coast on board the *Royal Viking Star,* giving lectures to the passengers on recent Chinese history, I arrived at Shanghai and looked up a young construction worker friend in the former French quarter. Although Jiang Shengde and I had met several times, I had never before gone to his home, and at the appropriate neighborhood committee booth in Huaihai Boulevard, I asked the woman in charge which door was that of Shengde's family. "I don't know him," she replied with a brick wall of an expression that could not hide her lie.

I found the right door myself, and when I entered the Jiang family living room, Shengde looked at me with bulging eyes, then his face turned the color of the green sweater his mother was knitting in her armchair and he signaled me to leave and wait for him downstairs.

"The situation is tense," he said as he pushed me into a shop door-way with my face turned away from the sidewalk so no one could see I was a foreigner. "No, not in the family, the national political situation," he went on as I stared at a display of silk scarves. "Two of my friends have been arrested for vague offenses probably related to contact with foreigners." The police had summoned Shengde for questioning and said, "You have a foreign friend, don't you?" in a wheedling tone that veiled a threat. After that interrogation, Shengde had taken out my letters to him, burned them with a match, and thrown the ashes into the Huangpu River. The drive against "spiritual pollution" had cast its shadow over the life of Jiang Shengde.

"I want to leave China," Shengde said in English, surprising me with the first words I had ever heard from him in that tongue. Nor had I thought of him as a likely candidate to go abroad, for attending college was not a high priority for him. But he was utterly deter-mined to leave China and his painstaking self-study of English proved it. "I think marriage is the best route for me," he said. "Can you introduce me to a foreign woman who might make an arrange-ment to marry me?" Shengde gave me a new phone number to pass any message to him, but this time he wrote it backward. "Remem-ber that," he said as he wrote a horizontal arrow on another part of the paper to signal that the phone number should be read from right to left.

I turned over in my mind all aspects of my contact with Shengde and recalled that in an article in *The Atlantic Monthly* a few months previously I had quoted him. Although I had not used his real name, it seemed possible the critical tone of the quotations had led the Shanghai police to investigate my sources. Shengde later told me he doubted his contact with me was the main reason for his being questioned, but the unpleasant thing was that one never knew. My close association with him had not prepared me to anticipate his fear or his unshakable resolve to emigrate to the West. His feelings about his country seemed to me bewilderingly absolute; the half-free and half-open condition of China had brought him anguish and made him restless.

Shengde, by leaving the country, would not have been missing much, for Deng had not improved the condition of industry the way he had improved that of agriculture. The young man's con-struction job in nine years had brought him no advance in pay or position and he had no paid vacation beyond the handful of public holidays. The year before, in 1982, when I arrived in Shanghai on board the *Pearl of Scandinavia,* Shengde decided to take a day off to spend with me. I thought this would mean phoning in sick or asking his boss the previous day for the next day off, but it was not so easy. The day we were to meet, Shengde had to rise at 5:00 A.M., take the ninety-minute bus trip to his work site and spend an hour applying for that day off! After another ninety-minute bus ride back home, he joined me just in time for lunch on his "day" off.

During my 1983 stay in Shanghai, after visiting Shengde, I went to see my surgeon friend, Dr. Dong, who had been one of Zhou Enlai's doctors. An energetic, calculating man, Dong sat on official committees and was linked by marriage with a high official in Beijing. But he was edging his family toward a life in America, and his wife, also a surgeon, was already working in New Jersey. At Dong's spacious apartment in Fuxing Street in the former French quarter, I found him dressing for a banquet that evening to welcome a delegation of cardiovascular surgeons from San Francisco. "I have waited a long time for China to change and improve," he said as he rummaged in a closet for a tie. "In some ways things were better in Shanghai when I returned from my medical studies in America in 1947 than today. Yet the last couple of years have been more encouraging than anything since Liberation."

"But, you know, some things irritate me," Dong went on. "I just came back from New Jersey last week, and the party secretary at my hospital asked me for a list of the gifts I was given while away. They never asked for a list of gifts I myself gave!" Just the day before, the San Francisco surgeons had presented Dong with a quartz alarm clock. "I was hardly home from the meeting with them," he said, "when the official at my hospital phoned to say I must hand the clock over to the foreign affairs office of Shanghai City."

Dong was ready for his outing with the visiting Americans and we prepared to leave the apartment. "Tonight I am taking the Americans to dinner at the Red House," he said, referring to a French restaurant nearby. "I bet the party officials won't ask me how much of my own money I spent on the hospitality!" We went downstairs to the hubbub of Huaihai Boulevard where above us by the sidewalk was a slogan in huge characters: CONTROL THE POPULATION, DEVELOP THE ECONOMY. Dong mentioned that both his son and daughter were in America and he reckoned that all of his four children lost ten years of their lives through the political campaigns of the late Mao era. "My daughter cleaned windows for a decade and her hands were terribly frostbitten," he said. When I asked Dong if his son and daughter would remain in the United States, the surgeon gave me a blunt look. "I hope so," he grunted. We bade farewells and I strolled toward the Bund, marveling at the frustrations and bitterness about an unfair environment felt even by a privileged doctor in the era of reform.

In the summer of 1984 I began a project for *National Geographic* on Sichuan, Deng Xiaoping's home province, and saw how the rural economic changes outstripped the urban ones. On a plane trip from Canton (now called Guangzhou) to the Sichuan capital, Chengdu, I picked up the glossy new CAAC inflight magazine and read boastful articles about CAAC's revamped service. As the plane took off, two large bags of oranges fell from the overhead compartment and began to roll toward the back of the Boeing 727. Although the plane was still moving at a steep angle and the seatbelt sign was on, the men who owned the errant oranges scrambled along the floor trying to retrieve them one by one, and the hostesses, chatting among themselves, took no notice.

Chengdu is a handsome, lively, two-thousand-year-old city, laid out in a geometric pattern with boulevards and a palace compound (now largely destroyed) as Beijing is. At its leading hotel, the Jin Jiang, I found all the horrors of a prereform Chinese hostelry without any of the prereform innocent sincerity. A rat ran across the floor of the room of my assistant, Yang Bingzhang, as he entered with his suitcase, and in my own room half-empty teacups sat on the coffee table, a sign of staff having used an empty guest room for a leisure time rendezvous. In the dining room, tables remained piled high with dirty dishes while waitresses stood about in clusters chatting among themselves about boyfriends, movies, and ways to wangle more days off.

Half the staff at the Jin Jiang Hotel had arrived through what the Chinese called the "back door"—connections rather than merit—and they were sons and daughters of officials for whom a job in the hospitality industry was not a professional step but a sinecure. This big hotel, the center of foreign-Chinese contact in Chengdu, was a place for gilded youth to have fun and gossip and meet people. As sons and daughters of privilege, the youths were not the least bit oriented to serving anyone, nor did the wage structure offer them much incentive to excel.

For all of the political tensions and managerial nightmares in urban China, many rural areas made a great advance in the early 1980s, and few more than parts of Sichuan, home to 102 million people (were it a nation, Sichuan would in population terms rank number eleven in the world). From Chengdu, I drove one autumn day under misty clouds on a road crowded with vehicles of commerce into Wen Jiang County, on the Chengdu Plain, one of the densest belts of rural humanity in the world. I entered a new home, a two-story concrete villa with a flat roof and brightly colored window frames, huge and flamboyant by Chinese standards, and inside I met Wang Yongdi, a genial man in his forties who had taken up growing flowers and potted plants as a private rural business on ten mu (one and a half acres) of flat, damp land. It was piquant that potted plants, which Mao could not abide and forbade in his presence, had become the rage for home decoration after he died. Wang had shrewdly cashed in on the trend and become one of the richest men in Sichuan. He paid thirty-two hundred yuan a year to a collective (team) for the use of his land, and the house he built at a cost of ten thousand yuan sat on the team's land, but otherwise he was on his own and in most respects he had become the post-Mao king of the village by virtue of his wealth. "At first, the contract with the team was for three years," Wang explained as we inspected his azaleas, "but things have gone well for everyone, so now the contract has been renewed for fifteen years."

During a lull in the conversation, while Wang Yongdi was out of the room, Mr. Yu, the Communist party secretary of Wen Jiang County, who was accompanying me, asked Mrs. Wang quietly how much the family's net income had been the previous year. This was a moment of high drama, for Secretary Yu was a cadre of sinking power and the Wangs were a family of rising wealth, and Mrs. Wang, looking as if she wished her husband would come back, avoided an answer. As we sipped tea and the mugs and lids clinked in the silence, I noticed on the wall a crimson banner headed with gold characters: PAPER OF HONOR. "The Government and Party of Wen Jiang," it read, "Warmly Congratulate the Wang Household for Encouraging the Schools of the County with a Donation of 10,000 Yuan." Philanthropy had returned to China! So, too, had begging, for as I strolled alone behind the house, I saw a group of villagers standing mournfully at one of the gates of the Wang property, and on top of the walls around the nursery compound, broken glass was arrayed. In fact the Wangs were hauling in an annual gross income of some eighty thousand yuan, more than thirty times the average for a rural Sichuan household.

My travels through the Sichuan countryside brought home to me the irrelevance of Marxism to its economic life. Houses and farm buildings typically sat in a cluster, with tall thin bamboos rising over them and lush green fields of corn and rice and wheat all around. The small clusters did not lend themselves to collective work, whereby masses are summoned by bugle to work in a team under a flag. Ironically, the backward poorer areas of China were more suited to collectivist agricultural organization than were richer areas like Sichuan, which, according to Marx, should have been "ripe" for a "higher stage" of economic organization.

At the Temple for Capturing the Tiger on Mount Emei, one of Sichuan's illustrious sanctuaries, I watched farmers bow before a huge bronze Buddha surrounded by forty-seven hundred statuettes and realized that as the ideology of Maoism left the villages, Buddhism and Taoism were coming back. The acts of obeisance reminded me of photographs of the bowing before Mao's image in Beijing in the 1960s, and when I mentioned the similarity to an artist friend in Chengdu a few days later, he surprised me with the remark, "Religion is a strange thing. I was amazed recently that so many people in modern and sophisticated New York turned out to see the pope." At the twelve-hundred-year-old Bright and Prosperous Temple by Qiong Hai Lake in Xichang, a day's train ride south of Chengdu, an old curator told me: "Two years ago, the resort [lake and temple] took in 60,000 yuan tourist income. Last year, 120,000 yuan. It's the farmers," the curator explained. "Since the economic reforms began, the farmers have lots of money. They want to travel and see some culture." Inside a nearby pavilion, children were playing checkers, adults were playing cards, and young people danced to a Strauss waltz, their cassette recorder standing beneath an elegantly written Buddhist motto: SUPREMELY HAPPY WORLD (ji le shi jie). I felt the commercialization of the countryside and the return of religion fitted well together. The post-Mao leaders were buying off the bodies of the Chinese people, and as for their minds, the leaders cared only that they not be anti-Communist.

Although Chinese urbanites remained more hard-nosed about religion than villagers, a revival of religion occurred to a degree in the cities too. In Chengdu, a Pastor Li, who graduated from Drew Theological Seminary in New Jersey in the 1930s, escorted me into a service at the city's main Protestant church. A congregation of six hundred, about one-quarter of them young, huddled in overcoats in black-lacquered pews. "Formerly, many people, especially youth, called themselves atheists," the old pastor said, "but lately we hear less such talk." One of the new members at Pastor Li's church was a young man who during the Cultural Revolution saw a pile of confiscated books ready to be burned. A Bible and some other Christian books were among them and he scooped these up and read them. "The young man came to the conclusion," Pastor Li said, "that the great achievements of the West, which everyone in China from Deng Xiaoping down now acknowledges, are linked with Christianity." The recruit, then thirty-three years old, had singled out three seminal Western concepts: individual autonomy, compassion for the welfare of others, and respect for personality.

Taking the political shackles off the villages and towns was just like taking a cage away from around the birds within it. In these initial post-Mao years, the result in many parts of China was new energy, productiveness, and a modest prosperity. The gross value of agricultural output in China grew as much in the years 1978 through 1986 as it had in the twenty-one-year period from 1957 to 1978.[4]

Yet potted plant grower Wang Yongdi's type of enterprise was far easier in the villages than in the cities because the family was a natural farming unit, whereas the factory lent itself more to socialist planning. Land could be divided and essentially rented, but industrial assets could not be divided and rented to workers. City folk soon envied the new buoyancy and materialism and opportunity for advancement in the countryside, and all of China took the money-making spirit of the farmers as a positive ethos for the age.

Millions of urban families used slowly improving earnings to buy a TV set, and although the early programs were so much like government press releases that the TV set seemed little more than an addition to the living room furniture, TV for a time was a point of sharp envy for rural Chinese when eying the cities. I felt Deng may have been opening Pandora's Box with the lightning growth of TV (from 1978 to 1984 the number of TV sets grew twenty-two-fold),[5] for even the government-sponsored programs provided extra information about the world and contributed to the mood of rising expectations. The American diplomat Stapleton Roy mentioned to me over lunch in his Beijing apartment in the summer of 1980 that he had just seen a TV documentary showing the living quarters of some of China's high officials. "Very opulent," commented Roy, who would later become United States ambassador to China, "comparing favorably with foreign ambassadors' homes. Millions of Chinese saw the program. I feel this kind of image will sink into people's minds and one day there will be resentment, and trouble."

People had accepted privation as long as all were deprived together, but toward the mid-1980s unease grew at the unfairnesses of progress. A neighbor was envied for his success in private business, bureaucrats were resented for using office to line their pockets, and the foreign world provided an unsettling measure of how backward China was. On a visit to Japan, Deng was given a deluxe car by the president of the Nissan company. In Beijing one day I noticed a snazzy Nissan car outside the Friendship Store, and who should come out of the shop and climb into its backseat but Deng's daughter. "She uses the Nissan all the time," a Japanese diplomat said of Ms. Deng, who is an artist, "for shopping and going out to dinner." Frank Ching, who wrote from Beijing for *The Wall Street Journal,* told me he one day ran into Ms. Deng as she entered the Beijing Hotel. "Did you sign in at the front door?" Ching asked her. "Oh, no," Deng's daughter replied, touching her fancy clothes. "Not necessary. I mean, I'm not dressed like ordinary people."

While I was in the Sichuan capital in 1984, I met a young man who was on top of the world because he had begun to build up a store of foreign exchange that one day would help him leave China. I asked how he did it. "I began by sending a joke to the Chinese edition of *Reader's Digest* in Hong Kong," he replied. "They accepted it for publication and I got thirty-five U.S. dollars in payment." I wrote in my diary: "The Chinese once more are going overboard clutching a single key to happiness. It was true during the May Fourth period just after World War I, when the ideas of science and democracy from the West were grasped as a panacea. For Chiang Kai-shek in the 1940s, American support was his simplified solution to all challenges. Mao in the 1950s saw the Soviet way as the pearl of great price ('The Soviet Union's today is China's tomorrow'). Now money making and Western things are all that counts, all that China is thought to need for a glorious future—and the Communist party no longer offers much by way of addition or alternative to cash and the West."

"Today is March 8," said Yang, a twenty-five-year-old factory worker whom I met one night in a Chengdu coffeehouse, "and do you know what's on?" March 8, International Women's Day, was usually a fairly heavy occasion that centered upon themes of protecting females from discrimination at work, unsafe abortion, and other abuses. But Yang took my arm and said he had a surprise in store. The red-and-white banner across the front of the ballroom on the ninth floor of the Jin Jiang Hotel read: SEVENTY-FIFTH ANNIVERSARY OF INTERNATIONAL WOMEN'S DAY. Beneath it a fashion parade began with a roll of drums just as we took our seats. A pretty girl in a crimson *qipao,* her alabaster face made up to the gills, minced from behind a curtain as a cassette recorder played 1950s dance music. Next came a young man in a purple blouse and lemon walk shorts, his lipstick glinting in the rays of a spring sunshine, cast into the ballroom through windows from a veranda where an overflow crowd stared in fascination. Then a wedding couple, she in a decorative white satin frock and lace veil, he in an ivory linen suit with a red tie and a red carnation at the lapel, his shoes like mirrors. Not a single garment was Chinese. All were Western, most were gaudy, and few looked inexpensive. Several middle-aged women from the Chengdu Women's Federation—the fragile thread linking the fashion parade with March 8—had orchestrated the afternoon. That big red-and-white banner was a fig leaf for a splurge of vanity, pro-Westernism, and sexiness.

In military circles, the shift from the collective glories of the Mao era to the money making and admiration for Western things of the Deng era was difficult to adjust to. In Chongqing one evening a young woman named Chen from a PLA family complained to me about her situation. "I've been in this damned army for ten years, and got nowhere," she said, explaining that she had enlisted, in Beijing, during an era when it was noble to do so. "The alternative, then, was feeding pigs in the countryside," she went on, flicking the ash from her cigarette. "Now everyone's getting educated and making money. We're left behind. You know, for the first six years in the PLA my pay was only six yuan a month [plus board]."

She now wished she had not left Beijing, when her father, a middle-level PLA officer, was transferred to Sichuan. It came as no surprise to me that between Chen and her father there was a generation gap as deep as the Yangzi Gorges. To Chen, her father seemed out-of-date and meek about the PLA's sagging fortunes. "Those ungrateful Communists!" she had recently said to her father, "you served forty years in their army, and yet they treat you no better than an ex–Chiang Kai-shek Nationalist!"

Her father was shocked. "What, then, do you believe in?" he asked his daughter, hardly daring to conclude that she was now against communism.

"Father, I believe in myself," she said to him.

"If you young people go much further," the military veteran rejoined, "there'll be trouble."

My assistant Yang Bingzhang arrived in Chengdu by train after two weeks in Beijing. "Since I got to Beijing from Boston," he told me over dinner in the cavernous catch-as-catch-can dining room of the Jin Jiang Hotel, "I haven't met anyone who says they're happy. Young people express it openly," he went on. "Older people probably wouldn't say it to a foreigner like you, but they say it to me. Two things really make people discontented. Urban wages are not rising to catch up with prices. And the social pressure to *have something foreign* is terrible."

As a former Red Guard in his late 30s, Yang had mixed feelings about the bread and circuses and extreme pro-Westernism of the reform era. When we shopped in Chengdu's excellent clothing markets for a T-shirt with Chinese characters on it for a Boston friend of mine, and found only T-shirts with English messages (LA OLYMPICS was a favorite at the time), Yang clucked his tongue in disgust. In the hotel after dinner he said: "I've been talking to some waitresses. They hate Chinese things. All they think about is foreign countries." Yang, who had been for several years a graduate student at Harvard, went on with agitation: "They're naive about the West. They think it's all flowers and free sex. My generation was interested to go to the West for a purpose. These kids just think of getting there—of leaving China. The first great invasion of China by the West was with guns," Yang went on, in a reference to the Opium War of 1839–42, "and now the second is with money."

"Wasn't there a middle one by Marxism, Bingzhang?" I suggested.

"You would hardly know," Yang said with a laugh.

While in Sichuan, I went to the charming town of Leshan, south of Chengdu, to write about a huge Buddha carved from a cliff overlooking the confluence of the Min, Dadu, and Qingyi rivers for *The New York Times*. After work one night at the Leshan Hotel, a crowd of staff and their friends were watching on TV a badminton match between China and Indonesia. "Do you want China to win?" I asked a pretty waitress, and she replied, "Of course I do," looking at me as if I were an idiot. Yet just a few years before, the slogan everywhere in China was "Friendship First, Competition Second," and Chinese sports lovers were hesitant to express partisanship toward their nation's athletes.

In the northeastern city of Dalian on a warm October morning during the 1983 *Royal Viking Star* trip, I strolled down Stalin Street and came upon a billboard that read: CHERISH THE FLOWERS AND GRASS AND TREES TO BEAUTIFY THE CITY. A little farther down the sidewalk, which had been nicely designed and constructed by the Japanese when Manchuria was under Tokyo's control, I saw a second: DISCUSS CLEANLINESS, DISCUSS PUBLIC MORALITY, DISCUSS COURTESY. I was wondering what had happened to Communist ideas in all these Boy Scout–type messages when a sterner slogan caught my eye: FOR THE FOUR MODERNIZATIONS, TRAIN THE BODY. FOR THE MOTHERLAND, WIN GLORY.

A dismantling of Maoism was occurring, despite official denials, and because de-Maoization was less a goal than a process, no one could be too sure how much of communism would be left after it ran its course. Into the vacuum left by the evaporation of Maoism, the post-Mao leaders quietly inserted two very un-Marxist ideas: Confucianism to undergird law and order, and nationalism, one card that is always safe to play in China, to provide a direction for policy that Marxism had ceased to provide.

Most of my friends became tinged with nationalism in these years, despite their cynicism about the Communist party. Frequently I saw eye to eye with them on democracy, human rights, and many other issues, but where China's national emotions were involved, we disagreed sharply. Typically they felt Hong Kong's future would be quite rosy under Beijing's rule after 1997, which I did not. Many of them felt Japan was cheating and exploiting China, and I saw no evidence of this. Some puzzled me by saying the United States had been "insincere" toward China in continuing to sell weapons to Taiwan.

Nationalism served Hua and Deng well in many ways, for to be nationalistic was to save face after the failure of Maoism. The concept of "modernization" came down from on high to cement the people's solidarity with the Communist party's version of nationalism; it offered a vision of a strong China and a better way of life for the citizenry. Blurring the differences between the goals of the state and the goals of the individual, the government told the people that under its leadership they could be a match for anyone in the world.

For a while in the 1950s nationalism had meant love of country,

as many Chinese felt about the new post-Liberation China the way
a person feels about the great love of his life. Such pristine patriotism
did not survive into the 1980s and the nationalism of the early Deng
period was more negative and less altruistic. People felt strongly for
their country because they didn't like the spectacle of its being left
behind by Japan and Taiwan and Hong Kong, and they wanted
progress for China in order to enjoy a better life as individuals.

"Comparison is the source of all unhappiness," the philosopher
Sören Kierkegaard wrote, and indeed there was a strain of unhappiness in the negative nationalism that came upon China in the 1980s.
I felt that nationalism, valuable as it was to the Communist leaders,
carried a political danger because its root was a comparison between
China and the non-Chinese world. At a crossroads in his life, my
young friend Shen Chunyi had decided he wanted to leave China
again, yet he still felt a bristling pride in China, and in illustration of
the dualism he told me the story of a demonstration in Beijing the
night the Chinese women's volleyball team defeated the United
States team in New Jersey in April 1982. After the game was over,
young people left their TV sets for the streets, where they lit brooms
to make torches, and paraded across the city, chanting in delight.
Foreigners were insulted, even hit, and when a large mob reached
the gates of the American embassy, the young demonstrators cried:
"We shall certainly beat the Yankees!"

Two things struck Shen about the demonstration, which he
watched but did not join. "Nearly everyone in that mob would leave
China tomorrow if they got the chance," he said. "Yet they were
gripped by a frenzied patriotism." They were jeering at what they
admired but felt was beyond their reach. "And I noticed," Shen
added, "that whereas people who mix too much with foreigners are
punished, these antiforeign hooligans were not touched." One
thinks of a remark that Bo Yang, the Taiwan writer, would later
make: "You could say that the Chinese are the most patriotic people
in the world, but also the most anxious to become foreigners."[6]

Into the 1980s, on China's National Day, October 1, a portrait of
Sun Yat-sen appeared in Tiananmen Square, and indeed there was a
strain of Sun Yat-sen's philosophy in the Communist party's groping approach to China's modernization after Mao had gone. The
pragmatic modernizing zeal of the Honolulu-educated activist of
China's revolution against a moribund Confucian monarchy seemed
reflected in Deng's efforts to find a better way than Maoism. Sun's
occasional unrealistic blending of incompatible policies also found

an echo in the "market plus planning" policies of the post-Mao period.

"As Maoism recedes," I wrote in my diary as I tried to discern China's direction in the 1980s, "the historical goals of the Chinese Revolution in its broad form, first stated by Sun, are reasserting themselves: to lift the Chinese masses out of backwardness, to catch up with the West, and to make China a great world power as befits a great civilization." But I wondered how Deng would reconcile his Marxism with the broader aim of seeking wealth and power for China, and whether the hopes of the individual for self-realization would be accommodated by the drive for national strength. Would more liberal economic policies triumph, or lose out to centralized Communist politics? Was there such a thing as "Deng Xiaoping-ism," with a positive vision for a reformed communism, or was the old schemer just scrambling to dismantle Maoism as far as he could while still clinging to the Leninist political system? In Deng's China as in Mao's, change always seemed to bring as many questions as answers.

CHAPTER ELEVEN

■

CATS AND MICE

AS the PRC turned thirty-five in 1984, a widespread view held that it was better governed than at any time since the early 1950s, and Deng Xiaoping as an anti-Mao was popular in the way that anyone who pulls the veil off a myth becomes popular. The new Deng policies had produced the varied fruits of economic progress, rising expectations, fresh inequalities, new social and economic forces such as small businesses, anger at corruption, increased personal mobility, recurrent cries for more political freedom, and an aching desire on the part of many young people to leave China.

Even as I welcomed most of the changes of the reform era, the more Deng pulled back the veil, the more I could see flaws, not just in Maoism, but deep in the bones of the Chinese Communist political system. The trial of the Gang of Four in 1980, a key event in Deng's consolidation of power, had showed Chinese Communist dictatorship to be mendacious and oppressive. Half a decade later, despite departures from Maoism—the new official candor, the priority on economics, a more open debate about history and culture, the general assertiveness of Chinese society before the demands and controls of the Chinese state—the Communist political and military organizational system was intact.

Certainly there was no indication that Communist rule plus reform in the Deng style would add up to democracy. The unleashing of family farming in the countryside was a substantial change with possible systemic implications. But the changes in the cities—a retirement system, less red tape, more scope for technical and managerial experts when faced with political generalists—were only a dictator's refinements, not reforms that acknowledged the fundamental rights of the people.

Democracy was far away and one reason hinged on the distinction between Marxism and Leninism. Marxism (a view of history's movement and a doctrine of class struggle) was fading in the smoke-filled rooms of Beijing, but Leninism (an organizational theory by which the Communist party monopolized power) was at least as robust under Deng as under Mao. There still was no competition for the Communist party, and no freedom even to propose an alternative to its rule. If you expressed doubts that the party embodied the will of the people, you were a subversive. Were plans to reform the Communist system good news to democrats, or only to the Leninists who led it? Short of an end to the Communist party's monopoly of power, might reform merely help authoritarianism survive, and perhaps streamline it?

During the spring of the PRC's thirty-fifth anniversary year, I was walking into the building of the Carnegie Endowment in Washington, D.C., when a familiar voice called out my name and beckoned me across the lobby. "The Chinese keep asking me," said Richard Solomon, a China scholar with the Rand Corporation who would later become President George Bush's assistant secretary of state for East Asian and Pacific Affairs, "why has Ross Terrill turned from a friend of China into a critic?" It seemed strange to Beijing officials, Solomon related, that as Deng's reforms flowered I should be so grudging about acknowledging the improvements.

I had recently written an article on the bleak outlook for Hong Kong after Britain's decision to return the flourishing colony to China in 1997. Entitled "Deng Xiaoping City?" in an allusion to the fate of Saigon as it became Ho Chi Minh City, the piece may have helped prompt the question to Solomon from the Chinese diplomats and researchers with whom he spoke.[1] But the most important reason for my skepticism about Communist China's prospects lay in a folder of notes I held in my hand as I went into the Carnegie Endowment building. I was to give a speech there in the "Face to Face" series and my topic was "Jiang Qing and the Chinese Political System." I had completed a biography of Mao's widow called *The White-Boned Demon* (the phrase was an epithet offered up by her detractors), and the experience of researching it had made me cautious about the longer-term future of Deng's reforms.

Chinese officials in Beijing and Chinese ambassadors abroad had tried to dissuade me from writing about Mao's fallen widow, and in the process revealed an authoritarian cast of mind that blended Confucianism and Stalinism. "We have explained that she is a bad woman," one official said. "Why are you interested in a bad woman? Write about a good woman!" Another official offered as an objection to my biography as big an untruth as I have ever heard about China. "Personalities don't count in our political life," he said, "only policies." Actually, in studying the careers of Mao and Jiang Qing, I found that in Beijing family feuds, informal networks of influence, and personal grudges time and again made playthings of policy issues.

"It is all water under the bridge," objected Assistant Foreign Minister Zhang Wenjin when I broached my Jiang Qing project over lunch at one of his favorite haunts, the Xin Qiao Hotel in Beijing. "Now all we're interested in is economic development." But I did not think Deng had solved all of China's political problems by the trial of the Gang of Four, or that his admonition to the Chinese people to "get rich" would keep off the agenda the cry for political freedom. It seemed to me unlikely that the "truth" as pronounced by the judges at the trial of the Gang of Four would fully satisfy a populace that still could recognize truth for itself. "I can't encourage you," diplomat Zhang Wenjin said to me. "But I won't discourage you. Knowing you, I suppose you'll go ahead anyway."

Three editors from Beijing publishing circles, all alumni of the same labor camp in the later stages of the Cultural Revolution, invited me to lunch at the Fangshan restaurant and expressed an ambivalence about my work on Jiang Qing that was predictable for intellectuals in their shoes. "Western writers are too interested in the personal aspect of politics," said editor Percy Fang, who wrote a biography of Zhou Enlai, "and Chinese writers are too little interested." I said I felt the latter would change as the reform era progressed. All three of these relatively open-minded literati agreed that Jiang had been central to the Cultural Revolution and that the Mao-Jiang marriage was inseparable from the issue of the Gang of Four. Yet none of them was able to help me in my search for materials because of their fear of meddling in an issue that the Communist guardians on high had declared settled ("She was a bad woman").

My friend Li Yanning of the official news agency put the most persuasive case against the project. "Deng and the others suffered terribly in the late Mao period," he said, "and any suggestion that

they are rather similar to the ultraleftists upsets them enormously."
I told Li I realized official Beijing would be irritated by an objective
reconstruction of Jiang's rise and fall and that I was prepared for
such irritation. "I just don't believe political struggle is a past issue,"
I said to Li. "Indeed I think Deng is still obsessed with the past
because the legitimacy of the present regime depends upon an inter-
pretation of the past, including the trial of the Gang of Four." Li
surprised me by lighting a cigarette and saying quietly, "I agree with
you." I saw Jiang's rise and fall as a mirror to the Communist political system, especially the interaction between personality and dictatorial politics.

In Chinese affairs the wheel always turns full circle if you wait
long enough, and I did not doubt that an objective study of Jiang
Qing would in the long run prove worthwhile and be acknowledged
as such. Even before I finished the book, some of the cooked-up
charges against Jiang had been undermined. For example, Xu
Yiyong, a Communist Youth League staff member whose association with Jiang in Shanghai in the 1930s had been a basis for saying
Jiang was a "traitor," was in the early Deng era suddenly declared
not to have been a traitor after all! Was Jiang then still a traitor?
Although Assistant Foreign Minister Zhang Wenjin had advised me
not to tackle the Jiang project, a few years later, toward the end of
his term as ambassador in Washington, he drew me aside at a lunch
in the Colonnade Hotel in Boston and amazed me by saying, "By
the way, I'm glad you wrote that book about Jiang Qing."

As the "Spanish cardinal" Zhang Wenjin knew very well, the
personal factor still was of supreme importance in Chinese politics.
With Deng rising to the stature of a real successor to Mao, it seemed
inevitable that China would once again face the political problems
of one man's, or one family's, will being the law, of the supreme
leader arbitrarily purging ambitious deputies, of talk about "class
struggle" being used to hide and dress up naked power struggle, and
of the inability to replace the supreme leader without resort to dog-
eat-dog struggle. Indeed it would take only until 1986 for Deng to
clash with the first of his chosen successors.

There were spectacular economic gains in China during the mid-
1980s. Between 1983 and 1986 the gross value of both agricultural
and industrial output increased by a total of some 50 percent, a far
better rate of growth than during the 1960s or 1970s.[2] Deng had

been accused by the leftists of pragmatism for saying, "It doesn't matter whether the cat is black or white, as long as it catches the mouse." One of his responses in 1975 had been characteristically crude: "They sit on the toilet," he said of the Gang of Four, "but do not manage a shit."[3] As the Deng era peaked, no one could deny that his cats of variegated color had caught many mice.

Yet controversy swirled about the side effects of rapid growth and the relation of economic change to pressures for political liberalization. Chen Yun, second only to Deng in seniority, attacked "capitalism" for producing the evils of crime and corruption, while the party general secretary Hu Yaobang (supported by Hu Qili, a younger Politburo member) blamed "feudalism" for the same evils.

Hu Yaobang was born in 1913 in Hunan Province to a poor farmer and ran away from home and joined the Communist party at an early age. He completed the Long March as a youth tagging along with the Red Army, doing odd jobs. Almost without education, he became a devourer of books and for many years led the Communist Youth League. "Hu Yaobang was that rarity among Chinese leaders —he was himself," Bette Bao Lord wrote in her memoir *Legacies*. "He departed from the text. He succumbed to emotions."[4] An incident in 1984 after Hu had become party general secretary suggested his boldness and highlighted the perils of trying to change communism from within. "Marx and Lenin can't solve our problems," *People's Daily* said in an article based on a speech by Hu. Two days later the newspaper published a correction: Party Secretary Hu had meant to say, "Marx and Lenin can't solve *all* our problems."[5]

As usual in China, the arguments within high Communist party circles in 1986 produced a moment of opportunity for restless pens in the press to express themselves, and for students to raise their voices both in support of political reform and in anger at educational grievances. On the campuses, first in Wuhan and Hefei (where astrophysicist Fang Lizhi was a professor) and soon on 150 campuses in seventeen cities, December 1986 saw the largest demonstrations in China since the Tiananmen Square riots of 1976. For several weeks the government response was a rather nervous stop-go effort to contain the burst of street politics, without simply crushing it. The press assailed the students, but did not pretend the demonstrations had not occurred.

Deng blamed Hu Yaobang for the rash of student demonstrations and the government's hesitation ended in vintage fashion as Hu resigned, saying he had "made mistakes." The students had taken "reform" seriously and pressed the point of its connection with democracy by marching in the streets. This startled most of the old revolutionaries who wanted only to tinker with reform. Deng had stabilized the situation by defining reform as a streamlining of socialism, not as some kind of transition into the unknown realm of democracy. "Democracy is far away," I wrote in *The Boston Globe* in January 1987, "yet we will hear more from the Chinese students because a little reform is a dangerous thing."[6]

Deng brought in Zhao Ziyang, who had led the reform effort in Sichuan Province and as premier visited Reagan in Washington in 1984, to replace Hu as general secretary of the party. In the showdown between Hu and Deng, Zhao, despite his progressive views, did not defend Hu any more than Deng, in the showdown between Mao and Liu Shaoqi just twenty years before, had defended his close colleague Liu.

Deng tried to limit the consequences of his open policy so that authority within China would not be affected, but a connection between the two existed in the experiences of young people. Yuan Weigong, a tall well-built man of pale complexion with a round face, told me how his mental horizon had been broadened by joining a foreign company in Beijing. After college, Yuan, who was the son of a diplomat and part of the technically educated middle class that the reform era enlarged, took a job at World Knowledge Publishers. "My first boss was warm-hearted and treated me like a kid," he said, "and my second boss was awful. He treated me neither as a man nor as a kid." Yuan left the publishing house to work at the Sheraton Great Wall Hotel, a fruit of the reform era. "It was like coming out of a cave," he said of his transfer to the foreign-owned hotel. "I admired Sheraton because although they were in the red [at that time], they treated us young Chinese well." A cheerful and gregarious man, Yuan befriended executives from a European communications company, who soon snapped him up for their newly opened Beijing office. "I could never go back into a Chinese firm now," Yuan said after four years with the European company.

During 1985 a phone call came from Florida to Boston, and it was Shen Chunyi, the Beijing teacher who had spent two years studying in Australia, announcing his arrival in America. In Beijing, his life had improved under the reform policies, but not enough, and the gap between the frameworks within which he was contained and the horizon that his knowledge of the West had opened to him had become too great to bear. In America, Shen at first lacked the masterfulness that I had observed in him in Beijing, as he battled to balance study with part-time jobs and found American girls more assertive than Chinese. But he advanced, leaving Florida for Dominican College in California, where he gravitated to the topic of international business. We kept in touch and one day he phoned me with exciting news: he had fallen in love with a Japanese classmate and they were off to Nevada to get married. Neither of them had ever met the parents of the other (hers lived in Tokyo). Later, both found jobs with a corporation in Minnesota, although still not American citizens or even green card holders, and Shen Chunyi began a life that the semidissident from the time of Democracy Wall could never have imagined. America gradually ceased to be an abstraction for him, and as he became a self-confident individual, the China-America dichotomy lost its bewitching power over him (so, probably, did the China-Japan dichotomy). In their hearts, many Chinese oscillate between extremes of disdain for the Westerner and near-worship of him. As Shen settled down in the United States, he found himself taking a more realistic middle position.

One day in Cambridge, Yang Bingzhang, the former Red Guard who had been imprisoned during the Cultural Revolution and later traveled with me in Sichuan, came into my office at Harvard's East Asian Center to talk about a CBS News program on China he had just watched. "In the film Chinese people stared at foreigners just as animals stare," he said. "And intellectuals gave answers to the American journalist that simply were false. I don't see how modernization can succeed in China. My goodness, what was our Chairman Mao doing for thirty years!" Yang had spent three years as a graduate student at Harvard, an experience that changed him and allowed him to look back on the politics and culture of his own country with a fresh eye. He went on to speak of a Chinese girl he had met in the apartment of friends. "She has just arrived from Beijing and has no money, but she wants to study," he related. "I told her to get a job. She said she thought it would be better to marry an American, because that way everything would be paid for. I pointed out she may not like or be liked by the American man for long. She said, 'In America it's easy to divorce someone'!"

I realized the power of Western society to recast the ideas of a student from Communist China, but I resisted to a degree Yang's notion that Chinese behavior in general was at a low ebb. "I tell you," Yang went on adamantly, "most of those who came to Boston from China are interested basically in money. In that CBS documentary you could see what I know to be true: when Chinese in China confront the foreign world, their main thought is that those damned Westerners are far richer than Chinese are! I can tell the people from the PRC in the streets," Yang added bleakly. "Compared with people from Taiwan, they lack creativity, their gestures are all alike, they are part of a pack.

"Even your views on China have changed," Yang commented. "I think a lot of American specialists on China begin with curiosity, go through various stages of being interested in this or that feature of China, and end up looking down on the Chinese."

"I hate the Communist dictatorship," I rejoined, "and I think what is disturbing you about the Chinese people is not something inherent in Chinese culture, but a conformism and an envy that are the results of decades of the Communist system." It was not China itself that weighed me down, but the games and rituals and subterfuges of Chinese Communist officials. At the same time, the combination of conformism and materialism in the era of Deng disturbed me as it did Yang.

I reflected in my diary on why I had tired of dealing with Beijing bureaucrats. "It is hard to have an interesting discussion with an unfree person," I wrote. "I do not want to hear X say again that China will never become a superpower, or Y that all will be rosy in Hong Kong under Communist rule after 1997, or Z that there is no contradiction between the logic of the economic reforms and the monopoly of political power enjoyed by the Communist party; for I doubt any of them believe what they say."

Just at this time my continued interest in Sichuan Province salvaged my affection for China, brought home to me how much liveliness existed under the clamped-down lid of Communist power, and taught me that Beijing politics was very far from being the totality of life in the Chinese realm. Sichuan was a sort of Texas of China far from the nation's capital, pragmatic and good-humored and commercially minded, and it had been the cradle of many of the post-Mao reforms. I found in the Sichuan character a certain independence of spirit that in the context of the reform era translated into a refreshing apoliticism and bluntness about the shortcomings of socialism.

As Deng's reforms changed Sichuan, which in the late 1970s had been the base of Premier Zhao Ziyang, Hu's successor as party chief and now heir apparent to Deng, I saw a quite new set of issues arise from their fruits and side effects. In the villages the release of new energy by a return to family farming produced a huge one-shot benefit, but I wondered how future investment and technological innovation were to be ensured. For years Deng had been laying down a plethora of new policies, but one result of his pulling the lid off parts of the economy was the bubbling up of disparate, potentially divisive forces. As localities began to think for themselves, a new policy from Beijing could unravel before it was implemented in the farflung counties. In some respects coast and hinterland were going down different roads. Parts of the far west of China, poor in capital and cultivable land, were becoming a "fourth world" zone for which "modernization" was a fancy Beijing-cum-foreign concept to be met only in the movies.

In 1984 and 1985 while working on the *National Geographic* project on Sichuan, I enjoyed evenings at a lively basement café in Chengdu called West China Coffeehouse. "After the economic reforms," explained Li Pingfen, its founder and mastermind, "people's lives got richer and they needed more things to do." Early in 1984 Li raised 130,000 yuan capital, 80,000 of it from friends and organizations and a hefty 50,000 yuan from his own funds, mainly profits from a soft drink business he had started on the side, and "West China" opened. By 1985 the takings had risen to fifteen hundred yuan each day and 10 percent of that was profit. The coffeehouse, a completely private outfit, a child of the reform era, was employing thirty-eight people.

I found that the conversation over cakes and coffee or Sichuan beer on the café's soft couches was generally about culture or private life, seldom about politics. When I mentioned this impression to Li, he looked pleased and said, "You're right. This is a pleasant, relaxing place. Who'd want to talk about politics here?" The coffeehouse had caught the spirit of the times.

Li had never set foot outside China and knew no foreign tongue, but growing up in his party official father's circle gave him curiosity and open-mindedness. When he lost the job he held in a factory, after his father died and the influence of the family declined, he studied economics by himself and then started the coffeehouse. "For thirty years," he remarked sadly, "our government ignored serious economics. In your country the entrepreneur is given his proper place in society, a high place. But in China, although the Communist party talked Marxism, which says economics is the base, it put politics at the base. In the West you've proved that economics really is the base."

Back in Beijing I watched a crazed elderly lady rummage deep into a green porcelain trash bin in a busy street. She picked pieces from the bin and stuffed them into her mouth without looking at them, while pedestrians nearby hardly cast her a glance. The spectacle seemed a symbol of the seamy side of the loosened-up China of the later 1980s. Theft and armed robbery and rape increased, as did embezzlement and extortion and spectacular crimes like highjacking and ingenious bank robberies. Trials of rapists and robbers were held before fifteen thousand spectators and TV cameras at the Capital Stadium, and at the end of the evening the criminals were shot on the spot. It was not that deviant, disordered, or frightening phenomena in China exceeded those of most other countries, but that in the 1980s they multiplied and the Maoist China of tight discipline and few loose ends was stood dramatically upon its head.*

A young Chinese man, a French literature specialist, lost his camera while moonlighting as an interpreter on a trip with a group of Belgian tourists. To replace it he raided a jewelry store and was disturbed in the act by an elderly janitor, whom he killed with a hammer. "Crimes like that shocked us all," a former classmate of the culprit told me, "we weren't used to it." Loss of face, a growing materialism, and a less secure work environment motivated the additional crime. In Beijing a woman taxi driver had an argument with her boss, whom she felt was giving her unfavorable shifts and an inadequate bonus. Losing the argument and gaining no redress, she sprang into someone else's taxi and careened along Chang An Avenue. Reaching Tiananmen Square, she zigzagged across its broad expanse, killing eight people and injuring many more, before coming to rest beside the portrait of Mao near the vermilion Gate of Heavenly Peace.

Confidence tricksters arose to take advantage of the new social fluidity, presenting themselves as the relative of some high official, obtaining permits, carrying off products for their own use, giving instructions that reflected orders "from above." Effortlessly they ripped off a society whose habit of responding with alacrity to the demands of connections made it laughably vulnerable to an imposter. During a couple of days in the northeastern port of Dalian, while

---

* To be sure, there were swaths of a medieval China that the Maoists did not change much. High in the mountains of southern Sichuan, I visited a stronghold of the Yi people, China's fourth-largest ethnic minority, and found little knowledge of the Chinese language, people sleeping with goats and pigs, and a shrug of the shoulders at much of the political doctrine emanating from Beijing.

traveling on the *Royal Viking Star,* I came upon five fights in the street and found a Deng-style "social discipline" notice at a cinema near the international seamen's club. "Do not fight in the theater," ran one of the regulations, "and do not knock people over as you enter and leave the theater." There were no appeals to proletarian or socialist values, but a simple law-and-order line with a whiff of Confucianism to deter rambunctious behavior.

Down in Sichuan, the provincial authorities mounted a campaign to educate people in the law to try to stem the crime wave. "Everyone Has a Responsibility" cried notices about respecting traffic rules posted on city walls and by country roads. "Line up in queues instead of elbowing in," said other notices, "Give precedence to old people." It was as if thirty years of socialism had accomplished nothing in the direction of a public ethic, and the Chinese government was having to approach its people as moral raw material, finding new ways to induce the individual to treat others worthily. At dusk in a park on the banks of the Jin River in Chengdu, a young man reached to take the wallet from the back pocket of my trousers. Watching his outstretched hand with fascination, I suddenly rasped in Chinese, "Don't be silly." He stopped and looked embarrassed, and it seemed he had little experience at picking pockets.

In the Jin Niu (Golden Ox) district court of Chengdu, I sat huddled in an overcoat and gloves as Judge Tan Changhua, resplendent in a blue uniform with red epaulets the size of dinner plates, cried, "Bring in the defendant." Xiang Jiachuan, aged twenty-five, a thin, loose-limbed farmer in khaki pants, blue jacket, and cloth shoes, slouched across the concrete floor of the court to hear charges against him of stabbing and robbery. Some two hundred spectators jammed the gallery and in the center of the court chamber sat a grisly pile of exhibits from Xiang's crimes. A jacket with stab holes in it, a shattered wristwatch, a blood-stained shirt, and a pork butcher's chopper.

Expectantly I glanced around the chamber, with its varnished wooden tables and spindly folding chairs, as if in a hope that I would see some clue to whether China's legal reforms were basic or just cosmetic. Judge Tan, whose career before the Deng era was entirely within the police force, boomed out rules and instructions. If Xiang didn't like the attorney he could find another (as provided in article 27 of the Criminal Code of 1979) . . . If Xiang thought any member of the court was prejudiced against him, he was free to bring forth proof of that prejudice (article 24) . . . The defense attorney had the

right to challenge any of the prosecutor's accusations (article
114). . . .[7]

Xiang was no novice in the demimonde of criminality in rural
Sichuan. Back in 1981 he stole, was arrested, and went to prison for
nearly three years. Only a few weeks after his release from prison,
and before he had been able to resume his work as a farmer, he had
a fateful encounter with a pork peddler in his home village of Gaojia.
After drinking *xiang bin,* a cheap, fiery liquor that became ever more
popular in the reform era, he stumbled down a riverbank and
dropped his bicycle into the shallow water. "I said to Yan the pork
peddler," Xiang testified matter-of-factly in a thick Sichuan accent,
"get my bike and I'll sell the pork for you while you do it." Yan
said it was too cold to go into the river to fetch the bike.

"I killed a pig that day," began the pork peddler Yan when he
was called to the witness stand, "and took the meat to my usual
selling spot by a bamboo grove. Xiang asked me to fetch his bike.
When I refused he stabbed me in the back and in the hand."

The court learned as the prosecutor's case and the testimonies
went on that the day after Xiang's attack on the pork peddler, a
policeman arrived and accused him of the assault. "I offered to pay
for Yan's medical costs," Xiang told the court. "I was afraid. Being
just out of prison, I thought I'd get extra punishment for this thing
with Yan. So I bought a knife."

"Why?" asked Judge Tan, not unkindly.

"To kill myself." A muffled collective gasp rose from the hard
folding chairs on which the spectators crouched in their coats and
scarves and caps.

"Why didn't you do so?"

After a pause Defendant Xiang replied softly: "I didn't want to
die. And I thought, I want to kill Yan before I kill myself."

A few weeks later a Ms. Liao and a Mr. Zhou, two members of
an entourage around Xiang that seemed half to like him and half to
fear him, sat down with Xiang to talk in a teahouse on the outskirts
of Gaojia. "They advised me to hide in the house of a friend," Xiang
related.

The judge interrupted: "Why didn't you?"

"I told Liao and Zhou, all my friends that I could stay with were
in jail. There was no one left to go to." After much drinking, Xiang
ended up "borrowing" the watch of his companion Zhou. Soon an
argument flared and Xiang became angry and took out a knife. Zhou

ran away, leaving his bike, which Xiang took possession of. Judge Tan broke in. "Did you ask for Zhou's watch, or did you borrow it, or did you steal it?"

From the defendant came a flash of the candor that gave him some appeal to the gallery. "Asking, borrowing, taking—it's more or less the same." Laughter erupted across the room. With the watch, it turned out from testimony by Zhou and Liao that Xiang had also taken Zhou's green bag, which contained sunglasses and playing cards. These items were all laid out before us on the floor of the courtroom, as incongruous as stuffed toys in a refrigerator.

"I was annoyed with Zhou," Xiang went on. "I lost my temper. I felt he was a nuisance so I took my knife to him." More loud laughter broke the tension. Then Judge Tan asked Xiang where Zhou's watch was now, and the reply was that he had sold it in the county town of Xindu, the main town of the area in which Gaojia and the other villages lay. The wretched Xiang redeemed himself a little with another flash of candor. "I'd stolen the bike—that was going to be reported to the police," he said. "I felt I might as well be killed for a sheep as a lamb and have a watch as well."

"My plan was to kill [pork peddler] Yan," Xiang continued, "but on the way to Yan's I changed my mind. My heart softened. I thought, it can't have been easy for Yan's mother to bring him up . . ." As Xiang broke off a muffled murmur rose in the gallery.

Xiang said he went to a teahouse, where he drank stronger things than tea, and then he mounted Zhou's bike and headed for a nearby village. He soon collided with another cyclist, Yang, who was on his way home from shift work at a cement factory. Both Yang and Xiang fell to the ground. Xiang asked Yang to pick up his bike, holding a flashlight to his face with one hand and a long knife in the other. According to the prosecutor, Yang, in tears, picked up Xiang's bike. According to Xiang, Yang refused, saying, "You knocked me over, you pick it up yourself." Xiang soon took out a knife and stabbed Yang in the head.

The defense attorney, He Chunyi, whose salary, like Tan's, came from the law department of Golden Ox district, in no essentials differed from the judge, who in turn followed the line of the prosecutor. "Xiang was guilty of everything," Attorney He told me with a shrug after the court adjourned for Judge Tan to consider his verdict. He added that in China there never was any conflict between a person's defense and the general interest, the client did not enjoy confidentiality in talking with his lawyer, and a defense attorney who believed a client to be guilty had a duty to make that person confess.

When the court reassembled a smiling Judge Tan pulled out from his stiff uniform a prepared statement and announced that the defendant was guilty of various charges of robbery and assault. Xiang was sentenced to ten years in prison, and there could be no appeal. I sent a note to Judge Tan asking to interview the convicted man, and soon Xiang was brought before me and guards took off his handcuffs. "Do you regret what you have done?" I asked. "Yes I do," Xiang replied sadly. His father died when he was eleven, he told me. He had five brothers and two sisters, a family riotously larger than the size permitted by Deng's one-child family planning policies. None of the family members were present for his trial.

Over spicy Sichuan dishes at the Chengdu Hotel, I asked Judge Tan why Xiang went off the rails. "Many reasons," the judge replied. "He was brought up in the Gang of Four period when the schools were in bad shape. He is the kind of character who couldn't learn a lesson from his first imprisonment. And when he got out and went back to Gaojia, some people discriminated against him as an ex-prisoner, which made him bitter." Xiang Jiachuan's trial was an open one, attended by a foreigner, and that didn't happen in the Mao era, and there was a certain dogged adherence to minor legal rules. But the prosecutor, judge, and defense attorney acted in unison as guardians of the Chinese state. Perhaps justice was done in this sad case, but without an independent, professional judge, and a lawyer responsible only to his client, I could not be sure.

It belonged to the mood of the mid-1980s that everyone knew much had changed, and yet also that certain basics had not changed. On the eve of a departure from Sichuan, I was sitting with my notebook at the People's Hotel in Chongqing, making a list of what was different from the Mao period and what was not. There was a distant noise of shouting or singing outside the window, but I ignored it. "CHANGED," I wrote: "People less afraid to speak up; UNCHANGED: State manipulation of all news." My assistant, Keith Wong, a student from Hong Kong, called my attention to the noise. I thought it might be a wedding or a retirement celebration, but Wong said it sounded too disordered, so we went downstairs to look. A man at the hotel reception tried to stop us and I said we were just going for a walk. The man looked stern and declared, "It is too dark for walking," but we brushed past him.

A huge chanting and swaying crowd covered an expanse of hill-side steps opposite the hotel. Like a magnet it was drawing onlook-ers, and we joined them and found ourselves near the gate of the Chongqing city government offices. "Give us back our lives!" came the cry rolling down the hill. As a foreigner, I could not go through the gate, but Wong as a Chinese could slip in unnoticed. The three hundred to four hundred demonstrators were students from the chemistry department of Chongqing University and their banners stated that four days earlier an explosion had rocked chemistry lab-oratories at the university and cobalt was released. No satisfactory analysis of the degree of danger came from the university authorities and no preventive measures for the future were taken. The students were bringing their view of the matter to the higher level of the city government.

"It was a purely student demonstration," one young chemistry major in spectacles said to Wong. "To our disappointment no teach-ers would join us." *"Give us back our lives,"* the cry went up more loudly into the cool, damp night. Students with arms locked surged toward the building's front door, where a Jeep was parked at an angle in an apparent attempt to bar the way. Turning around to observe the crowd of older onlookers, I saw faces that were wary, anxious, even fearful. I returned to the hotel and for an hour the demonstrators chanted and surged as I looked across to the hill from my balcony. The students, as far as I could see, still had not entered the city government building, nor had the military or police who were present attacked them or driven them away.

Next day Chongqing newspapers and radio offered no news about the chemistry students' demonstration opposite the People's Hotel. I felt I understood why there was some fear on the faces of the onlookers at the midnight protest, for the dictatorship was a given and could not be mocked. Yet I also understood why the chemistry students were rather fearless, for the dictatorship, still powerful as a Leninist force, had nevertheless run dry as a Marxist fount of truth; it could be looked in the face, even contradicted, when the court of appeal was the rationality required for economic development. To the two-column list I had been working on in the People's Hotel when the demonstration flared, I added a line: "CHANGED: A real protest was allowed to continue; UNCHANGED: The protest will never be read about in the Chinese press."

. . .

A couple of years later, in the fall of 1988, I went back to China to revisit Sichuan and to discuss in Beijing welcome new queries about publication in China of some of my books. Among my old haunts in Chengdu, I decided to check on the progress of Li Pingfen and his coffeehouse. At West China I was surprised to find chicken bones on the floor and candles sitting in mugs to help out the dim electric bulbs. "We met heavy competition," Li said with a wry smile. "Other new coffeehouses put in more beautiful fittings, offered live music, and also kept their prices down." And Chengdu's big tourist hotel, the Jin Jiang, had tried to put West China out of business by having it incorporated into the hotel. "How petty," said Li. "A vast hotel worrying about a small café! Jin Jiang Hotel just relies on the state; we rely on ourselves."

Income at West China had plummeted from a peak of two thousand yuan a month to six hundred yuan, and staff was down from thirty-eight to twenty-six. In a declining situation, Li in 1987 had turned his attention from the coffeehouse to a beverage and candy enterprise owned by Guanghan County, not far from Chengdu, that was near bankruptcy. Li and his associates stepped in on the basis of a contract with Guanghan County to try to turn the business around, and in their first year gross output approached 3 million yuan, and 10 percent of that was profit for Li and his couple of helpers. He walked off with nearly three hundred thousand yuan for his planning and management efforts.

On China's economic experience in the later 1980s Li Pingfen had mixed views. "Yes, priority has at last been given to economic development," he said, "but the methods are often flawed. The environment still is not favorable to business activity. China is not yet giving full play to individual talents." Li reached for a comparison with the United States. "In your country, fairness of the laws is very important," he said. "In the New Deal, Roosevelt stressed that competition must be equal competition." But in China, businessman Li saw tax dodging, backdoor deals, and undue influence. I did not believe that Li himself would lack ability at backdoor deals and using networks of influence if he really had to employ these methods, and he shrugged his shoulders as he addressed the issue. "I just don't like it," he said. "One reason for not setting up any more shops or cafés [like West China] is that to make a profit you have to break two laws—price laws and tax laws. That's why I went to Guanghan."

At his coffeehouse Li Pingfen had scored initial success in a starved market. Later he felt the chill winds of competition and made a striking move from penny capitalism to a substantial business operation, owned by a county government, but operated by him in return for no guaranteed income, just the possibility of rich reward. Did Li still believe in the market and competition? "Yes, I do," he replied, "as long as the market is open and the competition is fair." This was a big challenge for the further progress of Deng's reforms.

One day during my fall 1988 journey through Sichuan, on the road from Jiang An to Chongqing, my car reached a market town and as it slowed almost to a halt a policeman put his head in the window. "Can I have a ride to Chongqing?" he quickly asked Ms. Deng Yiming, a Sichuan Province official who was traveling with my guide Zhang Ling and myself. "No," said Deng and rolled up the window. "The police think they can use their office to do that," commented Zhang offhandedly. In addressing Deng the policeman was neither authoritative nor supplicatory, but something hesitantly composed of both. When the refusal came he accepted it without word or gesture. The sleeves of his smart green uniform receded from the car window ledge. He turned away in silence and merged with the crowd.

The episode seemed to confirm that state authority had lost its moral gloss in China, and the reason was the collapse of the state ideology of Marxism as a belief system. The policeman did his job but there was no special aura about him. Nor did the citizens respond to him as if his uniform connoted irresistible authority. Behind this welcome change there loomed a large question: could a civilization like China's, which had always lived by ideas, survive without a widely believed public philosophy? The recent growth of materialism, violent crime, corruption high and low, and a nihilist strain in cultural life all suggested the lack of an effective public philosophy.

One crisp November day I attended mass at the Catholic cathedral in Chengdu. Buried among four hundred worshipers, I found myself moved by the grandeur of the ritual and the slow quiet singing, an emotion that seemed different from emotions I recalled as a Protestant churchgoer years before. Now, in China, I saw religion not merely as a massage for the individual soul, but as a social need following the all-round failure of Marxism as a faith. I looked across at the fine pale faces of two young women as they knelt. Gleaming black tresses slanted across each high forehead. The eyes were closed and the brows were knitted in concentration. No doubt for these

citizens any alternative center of philosophical authority was entic-
ing. The church's system of belief made no contact with the official
system of belief of Communist China. For years that gulf put an
intolerable strain on Chinese Christians, but now that the official
system of belief had lost credibility, the Catholic faith—like the
Protestant—appealed to more Chinese people than at any time since
the Communists came to power.

At the turn of the century Mao Zedong used to go with his
mother to chant hymns and appease the gods at a Buddhist temple
near the family farm in Hunan Province. At the age of nine, he had
discussed with his mother the problem of his father's impiety. "We
made many attempts then and later to convert him [to Buddhism],"
Mao later said, "but without success. He only cursed us."[8] Mao
considered his father an avaricious man. His narrow focus on money
making seemed an obstacle to his conversion to Buddhism, as well
as to his understanding his son's desire to become educated and
improve the world. Beholding his father, Mao came to feel self-
interest was not enough if China were to progress. For him and
millions of others, communism soon became an altruistic faith
promising a better tomorrow. But as Mao aged and died, the wheel
turned again and communism lost its power as a faith for most
Chinese. What would take its place, I wondered, in rural China, in
the cities, in the minds of youth, for the elderly?

One day in Beijing toward the end of 1988, I talked with Zhao
Fusan about the decline of Marxist faith. I had known Zhao for
twenty-five years, since his days as a pastor at Beijing's Rice Market
Church in the early 1960s, when the Chinese Revolution still had
some moral clout and Pastor Zhao claimed the West was running
out of moral steam. Zhao, now a social science researcher, saw the
balance between the individual and society in China in danger of
tipping too far away from collective moral values. "Consumerism
is galloping along too much," he told me. "I'm glad there's a
new consciousness of individualism, but that, too, could swing to
an extreme." Zhao went on to criticize Western individualism as
"selfishness," and we sharply disagreed on this issue. He seemed to
feel a great gulf between Chinese and Western ideas of freedom and
morality. "In the West," he said, "it is thought children should have
the freedom even to make mistakes. In China, it is thought that
parents have a responsibility to make young people good."

I asked Zhao if religion could help to provide a new public philosophy for a China running out of moral steam, and in replying he

measured his words. "Given China's culture," he said, "religion has never had the role it has in Europe, with Christianity, or in Southeast Asia, with Buddhism. Religion can raise the issues, it can challenge people to answer the question of values. It can't direct the course of moral development in China, but it can be a conscience." Reflecting on his words, I wondered where the Chinese conscience was to be found at the height of the Deng era.

CHAPTER TWELVE

■

REFORM AFTER REVOLUTION?

BY the late 1980s, some Communist officials knew China was no longer in a pristine world where choices were black and white, words were invoked to try to change realities, and political life was a puppet show of friends and enemies. They spoke of problems candidly and in a tone recognizable to non-Communists and non-Chinese. "We just don't know what a 'planned commodity economy' will look like!" confessed Xiao Yang, the chief of China's most populous municipality, Chongqing, when I dined with him in October 1988. He pronounced the words "planned" and "commodity" with an emphasis suggesting an awareness that contradictory ideas were being thrust together.

In the land where Mao made a revolution, shareholding came back as some workers were given their bonus payment in the form of shares in the capital stock of their factory. "An ownership system of shareholding is just right for our situation now," said Sichuan Vice-Governor Pan Haiqing in Chengdu during that same visit to Sichuan in the fall of 1988. "It reduces interference in industry by the state. It's better for the initiative of the workers in an enterprise." Pan, a former engineer, added a startling tribute to the role of shareholding —evidently meant as a first step toward some private ownership of large industry—in breaking down equality. "Though we've been trying to 'break the iron rice bowl' [cast-iron job security], in fact distribution has remained very egalitarian. The share system will bring a welcome change in distribution."

"In the countryside people build huge houses, but put little in them," remarked Xiao Yang in Chongqing, which had 13 million people in 1988, "whereas in our cities people snap up appliances but no expenditure goes on a house and rents are derisory." But under China's planned system, how could urban housing be made a commodity, instead of a highly subsidized, state-owned virtual freebie? Mayor Xiao was also bothered by an inflation rate above 20 percent, a shock for a people used to prices as flat as the Gobi Desert. Orthodox Communists—and Xiao didn't sound like that any more—pointed to such an inflation rate as a reason to leave the reforms in their half-baked state. Xiao acknowledged with regret that dealing with inflation, with all its economic, moral, and historical ramifications, required a further delay in the deregulation of prices and a cutting back of investment. "We just have to solve the present problem, then later we'll move forward again," he said.

A China that four decades before "revolutionized" itself in the Liberation of 1949 had through the 1980s been trying to "reform" itself. Reform-after-revolution was an odd idea, for reform and revolution were supposed to be alternative goals and methods, and revolutionaries for a century scoffed at "reformism" as mere fiddling with the system rather than changing the system.

Deng's reform coming after Mao's revolution was like grafting half a banana onto half an apple. The revolution brought to power a Communist party that monopolized political power, and reform opened the economy to market forces. But political paternalism and economic autonomy did not mix; at minimum, reform-after-revolution suggested that something had gone wrong with the revolution, and indeed this was the near-universal view in China. The big question remained of what the goal of reform-after-revolution was supposed to be. *Could* the goal be clear if modernization had edged aside socialism as the prized value?

Nearly everyone in China I asked about the matter said the goal of reform was prosperity, and that was understandable in a country with a per capita income one-twentieth that of Taiwan. But the goal of *revolution* was also supposed to be prosperity (as well as independence from foreign bullying). At times I thought of reform simply as retreat, as if the aim of the Deng era was to unravel the Mao era —prudently, without admitting the fact, and taking into account what the rest of the world, Asia in particular, had achieved during the Mao era. This made it less puzzling that the Chinese leaders spoke only of the road, never of the destination.

After Deng commercialized the countryside, households leased land by contract from a collective entity and operated it just like private land. "If the contract system is working so well in the country-side," I asked Wang Gaolong, an official in Jin Ma (Golden Horse) County not far from Chengdu, "why lay down that a contract can last only for twenty years?" Wang looked at once vehement and confused and he replied, "We won't stop at twenty years . . . not necessarily!" He was expressing his enthusiasm for a system—private enterprise under state or collective license—that had brought prosperity to Golden Horse County and much of rural China. He was also spontaneously questioning the party's line that contracts are good enough for today and tomorrow but not for the day after that.

The pressure of events had forced the Communist party virtually to stand on its head ideologically at its Thirteenth Congress in 1987. Party General Secretary Zhao Ziyang stated that China was only at the "preliminary stage of socialism," a term that justified small business, family farming, shareholding, and all the other unsocialist phenomena (including Zhao's son's sharp business dealings) that engaged the energies of the Chinese government and people.[1] I felt the "preliminary stage of socialism" was simply a delaying device to satisfy orthodox Communists who insisted that the words of Marxism still had a meaning—somewhat akin to saying the preliminary stage of sleeping is being wide awake.

"Marxism isn't suitable for China," Lin Ling of the Sichuan Academy of Social Science said with agitation one day in Chengdu in late 1988. But as if wary of his own conviction, he climbed back to political safety: "Of course, one day it will be." I thought of the famous prayer, "Lord make me chaste, but not yet." Communism was pushed well into the future, and indeed it seemed as far off as prosperity, but no one knew any longer which was supposed to come first, and many probably believed neither would come.

China was not alone in this predicament. "Reform" was offered in most of the Marxist countries during the 1980s to meet various dissatisfactions with Stalinism that came to be expressed in the liberal words of the American Declaration of Independence and the French Revolution. But such liberal words were inapplicable within a Leninist political system; no one had ever reformed a Leninist political system and thereby produced a genus recognizable as "democratic Leninism," although as early as 1968 Dubcek of Czechoslovakia had tried.

To be fair to the Chinese Communist attempt to rescue the future following the failures of Maoism, modernization had everywhere proved a deceptive beast, which changed its skin as the seasons passed. It always surprised those in its embrace because the comprehensive change it involved altered values, terms of reference, and even language. It changed the very ground under a society's feet and forced, in honest minds, a frequent redefinition of goals. In a number of realms this discontinuity was becoming evident in China.

"An agricultural nation just cannot be a modern nation," burst out Xiao Yang, the mayor of Chongqing, in a candid moment during our dinner. The modernization of Chinese agriculture (as distinct from its highly successful de facto privatization) mostly meant the *shrinking* of agriculture as farmers entered rural industry or left village for city. In a decade of reform, 80 million Chinese farmers left the land and another 100 million were expected to do so in the following decade.

"I almost prefer the Mao period," said a Beijing woman as she lamented rising prices for pork and her children's school expenses. "In economic things, you knew where you stood under Mao." The paradox in China, as all over the world, was that rising material levels and increased opportunities produced not contentment but anxiety and ever-growing appetite. Xiao in Chongqing made a striking complaint: "People are silent when things go backward, and they're not happy when things move forward!" Today's achievement was tomorrow's crisis.

Modernization was also breaking up the solidarity of the generations as change put the young in a different mental and material position from their parents. A China that offered more to its youth found that as a result it was losing the spiritual adherence of its youth. Those who never knew a hungry past did not show gratitude for half a loaf; those who had not experienced tragedy were not inclined to prudence. When the young heard Deng speak of "democracy," in their naiveté they grasped the word, infusing it with a real meaning, and they drew the conclusion that the bitter old struggle between capitalism and socialism had receded.

Late in 1988, I was driving around Beijing with two young companions and we were chatting about music. Mr. Zhang, a government official from Chengdu, and Miss Song, a student of journalism and international politics from Beijing, both liked romantic Chinese songs as well as Western disco. "It's amazing, now, to remember how we used to have to hide Deng's cassettes," said Zhang in a reference not to Deng Xiaoping but to the recordings of the Taiwan chanteuse Deng Lijun. "Today few care what we listen to," he added.

"The fuss used to be all about what was good for China and what was not good for China," explained Song with a little smile. "And these songs are capitalist songs, you see."

We drove on past gray apartment blocks through rays of a winter sun refracted through smog. Zhang turned toward me with a broad smile. "But the whole world is capitalist!" he said. "It seems so stupid for us Chinese to be hung up over the issue of capitalism versus socialism!"

Song sighed. Silence reigned as we all felt, I think, a sense of a generation passing and perhaps of the era of communism passing as well. For Song and Zhang the individual was the meaningful unit. Anything that obstructed individual expression, be it socialist ideology or the collectivism and hierarchy of traditional Chinese ethics, was to them a tiresome, incomprehensible enemy.

During the 1980s, the muscle-power of society and the economy grew at the expense of the muscle-power of the Communist party and the state. The party lost some of its authority not only over the world of ideas, but over individual enterprises and other vanguard forces of the economy. The party reminded people of failure and yesterday, while the new economic forces suggested success and tomorrow. The world of individual enterprises (interestingly called "individual household," *ge ti hu*) was so removed from Maoist values that in Chongqing, for example, half of these small businessmen were former criminals or former labor camp inmates, the core outcasts and victims of the Mao era.

The threefold strength of the Chinese economy under Deng lay in the decollectivized countryside, small business, and industrial enterprises that enjoyed injections of foreign money. All three realms were distant from the official values of Communist China. The urban small business people were as apolitical as it was possible to be, the dollar and the yen represented imperialism, which it was the mission of the Chinese Revolution to sweep away, and Communist bureaucrats were disdainful of farmers because of Marx's bias toward urban workers as the true revolutionary class. Yet "individual households" and foreign money and family farming were the reasons for such dynamism as the Chinese economy possessed.

Through the early 1980s Beijing neither banned small business nor publicized it; there was no niche in Marxist theory for it. Three decades before, it had been declared superseded by the grand wave of state enterprise. Only in 1987 did the Communist party officially state that the "existence [of individual enterprise] was allowed."[2] Beyond the obvious problem of the need for a secure environment for a small business's future development, this Communist furtiveness about capitalism posed a second problem: private enterprise's success could be embarrassing because it showed up the failures of *public* enterprise.

A regional airline arose to give the state company, CAAC, a taste of competition, but it remained so hamstrung that CAAC was not challenged. Small business was encouraged to provide needed services and mop up unemployment, but the small was forbidden to grow into the large. Shareholding was designed to give workers an incentive to excel, but the workers were not permitted to sell their shares. Reform was always under pressure to remain a token. As a token, it could not produce great results, yet if reform went beyond the token stage it would challenge the Communist system. So it was that economics and politics collided, the goals of reform remained unclear, and half-baked reform became a recipe for accelerating crisis.

"Deng didn't intend economic reform to lead to political reform," a Beijing intellectual remarked to me. "If he thought that would happen, he wouldn't have launched economic reform." The tension over this interrelationship was constant. From Democracy Wall in 1979, to the student demonstrations in 1986–87 that brought Hu Yaobang down, some people got the "wrong idea" that political reform (as distinct from administrative streamlining) would be part of the retreat from Maoism. Deng and also Zhao Ziyang used the word "democracy," but invariably Deng, and most of the time Zhao too, pulled back from any engagement with its meaning. At times of fear, they added a prefix—*bourgeois* democracy—which put the whole topic out of bounds. So "democracy" went on and off the agenda of Chinese public life as fresh fish might go on and off the menu of a desert café.

Either economic reform would lead on to political change, I thought, or political nonchange would dilute the economic reform. "The aborting of reform is almost certain," I wrote in a diary note as 1989 began. "In the short term at least, politics is likely to win out over economic rationality, and the new economic forces will not win political victories. Long term may be different," I went on.

"The Communist party's moral authority is steadily declining. The rise of a middle class based on the new economic policies will eventually produce a politics of individualism."

The glaring inconsistency between political and economic thinking was evident in the words of Vice-Governor Pan in Chengdu. Pan had warmly praised shareholding as "good for the initiative of the people," yet when I asked him if in current conditions the Communist party still was able to represent the interests of all the Chinese people, his answer was straight from Mao at his narrowest. "The Communist party represents the interests of all the Chinese people," Pan said, "because the people include those who support the socialist system; there is another handful we call the enemy." But if people needed to express themselves, economically, in ways more complex than an imposed collective design allowed, why not in political ways as well? That was the swelling issue of the late 1980s.

China's rulers knew that communism had run dry as a fount for future policy, but, liking their own power, they were not about to step aside for any non-Communist alternative rulers. They wished to be reformers, but also to remain revolutionaries, and the contradiction was a guarantee of trouble.

Beyond the Gobi Desert, the Soviet Union under Mikhail Gorbachev also began in the mid-1980s to reform an errant revolution. Like Deng, Gorbachev opened the windows of his nation to the West and declared the need to reject past failed Communist dogma. But from the start the Soviet rescue effort differed sharply from that in post-Mao China. Whereas Deng's most radical acts were in the villages, Gorbachev left the Soviet countryside largely untouched and strangled in a bureaucratic grip. And while Deng tried to push economic reform without political reform or individual freedom, Gorbachev began to shake the Soviet Union's political institutions to their foundations. Even more so in Poland, Hungary, and Czechoslovakia, the ruling Communist parties edged away from insistence on a monopoly of power for their organizations, and non-Communists put their feet in the door of the halls of state. In Moscow, Gorbachev began to open the archives and allow a fairly free look at the Soviet past, but Deng did not think economic progress had much connection with freedom of the mind and did not permit such a second look at the Chinese Communist past.

Gorbachev hoped the Soviet people would put freedom ahead of the pocketbook, while Deng hoped the Chinese people would put the pocketbook ahead of freedom. But both of the giant red nations were juggling words, mixing oil and water, and allowing the short term to obscure the shape of the long term. The quip in Gorbachev's Moscow as *perestroika* unfolded would have had its point also in Beijing: "We are shifting from driving on the left side of the road to the right side—gradually."

In world affairs during the 1980s, Deng took most of the claims to moral exceptionalism out of China's foreign policy and yanked it in the direction of unabashed national aggrandizement. At Harvard in the mid-1970s I had established a course on China's foreign policy that spelled out Mao's theories of "imperialism' and "three worlds" and "contradictions" and "united front" and "hegemony," and one of my students was an Australian foreign service officer, Richard Broinowski, who was spending a year in Cambridge in search of the flesh of theory to cover the bare bones of diplomatic practice. Early in the Deng era Broinowski became Australia's ambassador in Hanoi and in the autumn of 1984 we had lunch together in Melbourne. "I still consult the notes from your lectures on China's foreign policy," he said, "especially when facing a visit from a journalist. Yet I must tell you they make less and less sense to me in terms of today's realities."

I was glad to hear Ambassador Broinowski say that, for I myself could no longer accept all I had said in those lectures on China's foreign relations in the early and mid-1970s. It was partly because Mao's grand ideological view of the world was being replaced by Deng's nationalism and his *commis voyageur* mentality, and partly because I tended to take any words coming out of official Beijing less at face value than I used to.

In the days of a revolutionary Chinese foreign policy, I had listened to Premier Zhou Enlai talk in apocalyptic terms about Japan, not quite aware that he was playing a card against Washington. Later, after Nixon visited Mao, Beijing stopped attacking Japanese "militarism" and tried to use improved relations with Japan as a card against Russia. This was the old Communist "united front" strategy of separating out the major enemy and building an opportunistic front against that enemy from any available forces. The policy was really a manifestation of Mao's idea of "turning weakness into strength."

By the time Deng fashioned a reform-era foreign policy, China was more involved in the world by virtue of its new stress on economic development, and the world had become more complex than a pageant of "imperialist superpowers" lording it over a poor and righteous "Third World." Most of the world's disputes in fact were among the Third World nations. And to Burma and Vietnam—not to speak of Tibet—China, under Deng as under Mao, seemed an "imperialist superpower" rather like the United States and the U.S.S.R. "Never seek hegemony," Mao had preached as he positioned China against the evils of Russia and America. Yet to the Vietnamese, Deng's China seemed to be seeking hegemony in Indochina.

As for British colonialism, Japanese imperialism, and American hegemonism, the three targets of Mao's value-laden world view, their years of influence upon the Chinese territories of Hong Kong, Taiwan, and Singapore, among other places, had helped produce brilliant results that served only to show up the failure of the PRC to progress. Of all the parts of the old Chinese imperial realm, none had reached economic levels like those in Hong Kong and Taiwan. Ironically, the distinguishing mark of Deng's foreign policy came to be a drive to complete China's "reunification" by pulling the flourishing entities of Hong Kong and Taiwan back into the musty temple of the PRC. Here was a task Mao had not managed to fulfill and if Deng could see it through he would go beyond Mao. A second distinguishing trait of Deng's foreign policy was the sale of armaments to whomever would buy them—including both Iran and Iraq as they tore each other to pieces—for the purpose of earning hard currency needed for investment in China's internal modernization.

China's foreign policy continued to lack any flavoring of human values or positive ideas about the future of international society. Beijing had replaced "revolution" with "nation" as the policy's central value; neither interacted much with the rights and welfare of the individual. To "recover" Taiwan, for example, might add some shine to the collective glory of China, but it could not be expected to do much for the freedom and standard of living of people in Taiwan.

As the theory fell away from Chinese foreign policy like the wilted outer leaves from a lettuce left in the sun, China's own "imperial" problem stood revealed. It was seldom mentioned, but it was true, that the Chinese Communists had inherited the Qing dynasty's imperial mantle. The Han domination of Tibet, Xinjiang, part of Mongolia, and other parts of western China had been handed from the Qing dynasty to Mao's Communists with scarcely a blink. (In between times, Chiang Kai-shek's Nationalists had ruled Xinjiang and Inner Mongolia, and would have liked to have ruled Tibet, which to this day the Taiwan government considers a part of China.) Wouldn't a true "liberation" of Tibet have relieved it not only of feudal hierarchy but of Han colonialism? Like the Russian Communists, the Chinese Communists in the name of Marxism were sitting astride an empire even as they shouted the verities of anti-imperialism. Beijing chose to call the Tibetans, Uighurs, and Mongolians "minority peoples," but in many parts of the world they would have been called subjugated nations, standing in need of some of the "independence" that Beijing loudly championed in other regions.

In 1988 I went to discuss the Deng era with Zhou Yiliang, a friend of twenty years who taught Buddhist and Japanese history at Beijing University. Over tea and candy covered with sesame seeds in the musty study of Professor Zhou's home, we talked of the changes of the 1980s. Professor Zhou had a gloomy view. "Today it's just like pre-1949," he said vehemently. "Rotten politics and bribery everywhere. You can't get a license, a certificate, you can't do anything, without first presenting a gift. Provincial officials, to get anything done in Beijing, have to bring carloads of gifts for the families of officials in Beijing." I asked if the remolding of thought during the Mao years had not been thorough after all. "In some ways," replied Zhou, "I over-remolded myself!" Out of guilt at coming from an upper-class family in the face of communism's bristling new morality, the professor had rejected—he now thought—too many pre-Communist values.

Zhou Yiliang regretted that Confucian ways were no longer honored. "There is no sense of justice [zheng yi] in the China of Deng," he said. "All the old ethics were destroyed, but nothing new has come." Whether or not Confucianism was a solution for China's crisis of values, I could see that the lack of an effective, believed public philosophy was a chronic issue.

"The power of the party lay just with one leader," Professor Zhou conceded of the late Mao period, during which he had played a role as a political adviser to Jiang Qing and other leftists. "It wasn't a reflection of the interests of the working class." I felt much the same was true of the Deng era. Yet by the late 1980s there had been one change: few people believed any more that Deng (or any leader) "could do no wrong," as Zhou used to believe of Mao. Said Professor Zhou: "When I first met you in 1971, I was a firm believer in Mao's doctrine. Later I came to see words and deeds diverge. I don't believe anymore."

From Professor Zhou's home at Beijing University, I went to visit Mao's mausoleum on the bare vastness of Tiananmen Square. As a line of people shuffled ahead, waiting to enter the beige and terra-cotta hall, a leaflet about the mausoleum was offered for purchase at half a yuan by hoarse-voiced vendors. Inside the lofty marble chamber, ushers called out *"Qing jing"* ("Please observe silence"), and the crowd of mostly out-of-town, rural visitors, including quite a few military, fell silent. Never in China had I been amidst so many people who were so quiet. Inside the glass sarcophagus the body of Mao lay on its back, bathed in soft lights within the gloomy hall, the face bright pink and the corpse clad in a loose-fitting green army uniform.

I walked out the south door of the mausoleum, past a sculpture of revolutionary figures clutching guns and books—illustrating Mao's twin themes of war and ideology—to face commerce and carnival. On sale were toy pandas propelled by an inner motor, and earrings that could be pierced through the ear on the spot. Near the vendors' stalls was a notice in neat black characters on a white board: MAO ZEDONG, ZHOU ENLAI, LIU SHAOQI, ZHU DE MEMORIAL HALL. In the era of Deng, Mao's victim of the 1960s, Mao was required to share the honor of his mausoleum with three other eminent friends (and sometime enemies) of the revolutionary generation. Beside me stood a young man who said he was from an army family in Hubei Province and on his first trip to Beijing. I asked him if he admired Mao. "Yes, of course I admire him. He was our leader," the young man replied crisply.

Over the years the Mao mausoleum was often open and closed on alternate days, and that seemed a symbol of the dual nature of Mao's reputation among the Chinese. He was admired as a strong leader, but he was criticized because in the end he did not bestow on citizens the prosperity they had come to expect as they began to compare China with other countries. The majority of ordinary Chinese by the late 1980s wanted more than anything else a normal life with steady material progress, it seemed to me, and they would accept any leader who could smooth the path to such a life.

The "scar literature" of the 1970s by now seemed distant, because the almost religious political vision that gripped millions in the

The Cultural Revolution brought the repression of individual thought and
the mass mobilization of labor in the countryside. Here, farmers, soldiers, and
Communist party officials work together on an irrigation project linking the
Jinshui and Manghe rivers in Henan Province.

12

热烈欢呼毛主席的最新指示发表！

13

14

At the height of the Cultural Revolution in Shanghai, students and teachers from Tong Ji University march to support Mao's latest instruction calling for a "proletarian revolution in education." Their posters were called "spears and daggers" aimed at the heart of backsliding "revisionists."

In a surprise move that would end China's isolation from the West, Gough Whitlam, the leader of the Australian Labor Party, and other Western politicians were invited to Peking. Whitlam is seen here with the author on a commune near Shanghai in July 1971.

15

Western visitors were welcomed cautiously and with much ritual in Mao's last years. Zhou Nan, a foreign ministry official who was the author's guide for a month in 1971, later became deputy foreign minister and later still, in 1990, chief Communist representative in Hong Kong.

In February 1972, after finishing historic talks with Mao in Peking, President Richard Nixon took a stroll in Hangzhou with Premier Zhou Enlai. The next day in Shanghai, Nixon and Zhou signed a communiqué that established a new era in Sino-American relations.

16

Mao makes a point to Henry Kissinger, as Zhou Enlai looks on, in February 1973. China and the United States were struggling to consolidate the gains of Nixon's 1972 trip, even as Washington continued to recognize Taipei as the capital of China.

18 Jiang Qing, at the height of her power as Mao's health failed, hosts Imelda Marcos of the Philippines in 1974 at a performance of a "revolutionary opera" brimming with political propaganda.

19a

The entire Communist leadership assembled at Tiananmen Square for Mao's funeral in September 1976 (ABOVE), among them Jiang Qing and the other members of the "Gang of Four." Within a month they had been arrested and, thereafter, in the same photo of the funeral (BELOW), China and the world saw only blank spaces where the four top Maoists had stood.

19b

20

Deng Xiaoping, exiled during the Cultural Revolution, returned to public life in 1977 and began his climb toward the summit of power. Here, in March 1978, he listens to sustained applause from the Chinese People's Political Consultative Conference, of which he was elected chairman.

In December 1978 full diplomatic relations were announced between the United States and the PRC, leaving Washington with only an unofficial presence in Taiwan. President Jimmy Carter welcomed Deng to the White House in January 1979.

21

22

In the new atmosphere of intellectual freedom in the Deng era, a group of Western sinologists researching the life of Mao visited China in the summer of 1980. They met with Chinese companions in front of the house in Shaoshan, near Changsha, where Mao was born and raised: (BACK ROW) Maurice Meisner, Edward Friedman, Tang Tsou, and Jerome Chen; and (FRONT ROW) Stuart Schram, Angus McDonald, and the author.

In January 1981, following a show trial, Jiang Qing and nine other leftist Mao associates were sentenced to various terms of imprisonment. Here Mao's widow listens to the sentence meted out to her: death, suspended for two years "to see how she behaves."

23

24

By 1982 China and the Western world were officially "friends" and it was at last possible to visit and conduct interviews at an army unit. Here the author talks with PLA officers near Nanjing in the course of filming for an Australian TV program.

25

Shen Chunyi (LEFT), a young Beijing teacher whose life was changed by study in Australia (see pages 171–176), eating with companions at the Lantern Festival in Zigong, Sichuan Province, in 1984. The western hat and tie would not have been permitted in the Mao era.

During 1984, young women in Chengdu, Sichuan Province, enjoy new consumer goods and freedoms in the atmosphere of Deng's reform era with its stress on economic progress and openness to the outside world.

26

By the mid-1980s Mao was no longer a god, but a fading memory, if still a shadow over Chinese politics. Many Mao statues were pulled down; this one was cleaned by firemen in Chengdu as nonchalantly as they might wash their fire truck.

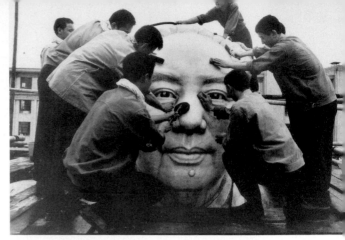

27

By 1985 Deng had two lieutenants, both in favor of political reform. A year and a half later, Hu Yaobang (LEFT) would be replaced as party chief by Zhao Ziyang (RIGHT), who in turn would fall victim to Deng's fear of democracy during the student demonstrations of 1989.

28

When Hu Yaobang died on April 15, 1989, the loss of a reformer and frustration at the contradictions of Deng's rule brought waves of students to Tiananmen Square in a call for democracy. The placard appeals to articles of the Chinese constitution that guarantee freedom to assemble, demonstrate, and publish.

29

30

Just as a hunger strike began in Tiananmen Square, Mikhail Gorbachev arrived in Beijing with his wife, Raisa, on May 15 to patch up ties between the two Communist giants. Media coverage of the historic summit also captured the rising unrest in the streets of the city.

Shen Tong, a student leader from Beijing University (LEFT) and Xiang Xiaoji, his co-chairman of the Dialogue Delegation, handled discussions with the government that at first seemed to promise a constructive response to student demands.

31

Art students erected two portraits at Tiananmen Square in front of the history museum. The Chinese characters in the center declare, "Save mankind."

32

As the demonstrations widened, tradesmen paraded their carts through Tiananmen Square with placards declaring their support for the students. "Enough is Enough!" cries one of the placards.

Passengers in buses in the streets of central Beijing, now largely policed by organizers of the democracy movement, donated funds to the students.

Because Deng was ruling enigmatically and despotically, he was likened in a parody to Ci Xi, the manipulative empress dowager of the last decades of the Qing dynasty.

35

Along Chang An Avenue, a group from the railway ministry marched to protest Deng's leadership, an act unthinkable prior to the democracy movement. The forward banner reads, "DENG XIAOPING STEP DOWN. GO AND PLAY BRIDGE."

36

Demonstrators represented the government as a corpse and urged Deng to return to the southwest, the location of his early career. Deng as yet had made no decisive move against the demonstrators.

Art students built and erected a Styrofoam "Goddess of Democracy," which resembled both Guan Yin, the Chinese goddess of mercy, and the Statue of Liberty in New York. Mercy and freedom were denied on the night of June 3–4, when the demonstrators were met with gunfire from tanks and troops of the PLA.

39 The demonstrators, fleeing in panic, retaliated as the PLA cleared Tiananmen
Square, killing hundreds and maybe thousands of activists and onlookers.

Next morning, China was in tears, the world was shocked, and Tiananmen
Square was in the hands of the military. With tanks on all sides and helicopters
above, the square's crowds were gone, its spirit crushed, its broad expanse now
forbidden territory to the public.

The Styrofoam remains of the
Goddess of Democracy, toppled by
a tank during the night, lay in ruins
in the PLA-occupied square.

42

Denounced as "counterrevolutionaries," student leaders either fled the country or were arrested. Hundreds of pro-democracy activists, most of them workers, were executed. Here two in south China are being prepared for death by a bullet in the back. Photographs of their corpses were posted as a warning.

Following the massacre, Beijing donned a mask of normalcy, but China remained repressive. As communism in Europe was abandoned as a failure, the world wondered how long the Chinese Communist Party could hold out against the tide. The octogenarian Deng awaits his "appointment with Marx" and his judgment by history.

43

1960s, and devastated further millions, had disappeared from the memory of most Chinese. Both the triumphalism and the scars, reflected in novels and poems and memoirs of the 1970s, appeared as unreal as a dream by the late 1980s, with its vacuum of philosophical values and its push to make money. The mood now was less to rehash history and theory than to live as if history and theory did not matter.

On my visit to Sichuan in the fall of 1988, a young man in Chengdu who was hard-nosed yet idealistic in an individualistic way told me of his amused contempt for a residual practice of trotting out political heroes to raise people's political consciousness. "There was this crippled veteran of [China's] war against Vietnam," he said. "They put him on TV to talk politics." The young man laughed at the memory, as if recalling the sight of a dinosaur. "Then there was a veteran cadre, back from labor in a *niu peng* [cow shed], saying that while being re-educated in the countryside he read Marx and that, despite the Cultural Revolution, he believes in the Communist party." The young man laughed again, and I began to feel quite unsurprised that political campaigns (such as those against "spiritual pollution" and "bourgeois freedom") were growing scarcer and shorter in duration.

Some of my older Chinese friends felt cultural standards were declining in the late 1980s. "Valuable theoretical works do not get published," complained Wang Ruoshui, the essayist precariously attached to *People's Daily,* when we met in Beijing in November 1988, "and musicians leave classical music for pop music to earn more money." Wang noted that the bold and probing "fifth-generation" filmmakers had lost momentum in the public eye. "They're not commercial enough, people want sex and violence," he said with a touch of bitterness. "If you want a big audience for a movie, it's best to label it 'Children Not Allowed.' "

The amazing seemed to have happened, as China lost its past moorings in a fever of business-mindedness, and the Chinese spoke up for free markets and individual self-reliance with more conviction than did most people in the West. At the same time, young Chinese did not cease to try to leave China for the West, as if Deng's abandonment of Mao's unique goals for the adoption of goals more in alignment with those around the world increased the dissatisfaction of the very Chinese people the new goals were supposed to please. Everyone was painfully learning the lesson that for China with its

Communist bureaucracy and huge population, "catching up" with Japan and Hong Kong and Taiwan would be a long, slow process at best.

Anguish amidst progress may have seemed strange, yet it was hardly without precedent in history, for people frequently are most restless when they are moving ahead. The new fluidity of the reform era raised fresh possibilities for many people, yet also brought fresh insecurities. A young sociologist in Beijing remarked to me plaintively on my last visit there before the crisis year of 1989: "Deng said it's fine for part of the people to get rich first. It's a pity he did not say how we were to get rich, and which part of the populace should be the first to get rich." Ordinary people became angry at the appearance of palpable injustice, and thoughtful people had to consider afresh the meaning of social justice in a changed society. Above all there was anguish because no one really knew what the goals of Chinese "socialism" were in its adjusted form.

In the early 1950s Mao had dined with the Dalai Lama at a celebration of the Tibetan New Year, and when told it was a Tibetan custom to toss pieces of the celebratory cake to the ceiling as an offering to the Buddha, the Communist chief threw his portion of cake aloft, and then with a grin took another piece and cockily threw it to the floor.[3] Mao's expectation of an easy triumph of socialism over Tibetan tradition, however, got lost in protracted bitterness between Beijing and Lhasa, and bloodshed in the snows of the mountain kingdom. The Dalai Lama, whom Mao thought socialism would sweep into the trashcan of history, outlasted him and would soon win the Nobel Peace Prize for his long battle against Beijing's repression.

The Chinese Communists had underestimated Nature and expected too much from Nurture. For all their devilishly thorough social engineering, they had not created a "new man," abolished hierarchy, warmed the ties between Han and non-Han, kept the loyalty of youth, canceled the regard for self-interest of the Chinese people, or kept urban Chinese from sniffing the winds of freedom that blew upon China from abroad. Human behavior is an independent variable, not the end product of socialist policies, and the Chinese citizens of the late 1980s were left with little awe for yesterday's Communist certainties, and little conviction about yesterday's Communist victories.

Beyond the crisis of communism, the issue of Chinese culture seemed more central than I had ever known it in twenty-five years of visiting China. Economists were asking themselves which aspects of Chinese culture hindered economic development, and which could aid it. Internationalists (a small band) were declaring that traditional culture was an obstacle to China's participation in an interdependent world. Marxists were still fretting that China could never be socialist until feudal ways were eliminated. Every task (however "modern") was being accomplished through a network of connections, and the web of corruption was provoking deep unease with the reform era. Many Chinese still went along with any strong wind, like a time-tested tribe that always stuck together, and such anti-individualistic ways were driving many urban youths to rebelliousness.

My mind entertained the surprising thought that the two great issues of contemporary Chinese history, the impact of the West and the problems of a Marxist-Leninist political system, were being joined by a third issue—China's problem with itself. For young people especially, the restraints upon freedom went beyond politics to Chinese cultural traditions. Some Chinese wanted to get out from under an entire cultural tradition that saw China smug behind a Great Wall that precluded give and take with the rest of the world. Tragically, ironically, as the Deng Xiaoping era peaked, some Chinese even were disgusted to be Chinese.

CHAPTER THIRTEEN

■

WARM SPRING*

AS 1989 began, the sweetest fruits of the Deng Xiaoping era were being enjoyed and yet the strains of unsolved issues were growing more acute. After forty years in place, the Communist system was less heavy-handed in its daily impact on people's lives than I had ever known it, and new and growing economic forces such as small businesses and foreign joint ventures were increasingly removed from the mentality of the party. Urban young people, individualistic, materialistic, and cosmopolitan, mostly found politics corrupt or irrelevant. It didn't cost them much to say so, and they lived their lives as if Marx and Lenin belonged in the museum.

From Beijing to the minority race areas of the dusty west, from neat Manchuria to bustling Canton (Guangzhou), many Communist policies had frayed at the edges to the point of being unrecognizable. Ideological belief had shrunk to a minority taste and many realms of life and policy proceeded without influence from Marxism. Unprecedented priority was being given to efforts to make economic progress by any available means, and steps had been taken toward laws and rules that reduced the arbitrariness of the late Mao period, when one man's word was law. With a new modesty China was holding

* To protect them against reprisals, a number of the persons quoted and described in this and the following chapters have been given fictitious names and their places of origin have been changed.

its door open to ideas and products (as well as loans and investment) from abroad.

Despite the ideological and economic changes, however, the Communist political and military organizational system was intact. In both small ways and large, the dead weight of Communist rule still lay upon much of Chinese life. At Beijing airport on the wintry evening I left China after my trip through Sichuan late in 1988, piles of materials and supplies looked as if they had been lying there for years, and the staff at the shabby desks and half-closed offices and shops dozed or glared sullenly. The airport terminal dated only from the late 1970s but had grown old in its youth. The walkways were not working and departing passengers had to grope their way across a tarmac faintly lit by the headlights of a Jeep parked nearby for the purpose, and then climb a flimsy metal stairway.

Behind the vermilion walls of Zhongnanhai, the government compound adjacent to the old Forbidden City, a disagreement over economic policy that had flared up at a seaside economic summit at Beidaihe in 1988 put proreform Communist party chief Zhao Ziyang into an ever more difficult position. The pressure on the government of public alarm at inflation that exceeded 20 percent was eased by the decision to postpone further deregulation of prices (which would have temporarily raised prices). But reformers in Zhao's circle regretted the delay. "In the long run the present complicated price situation is untenable," economist Lin Ling had said to me in Chengdu, a city once in the vanguard of economic reform. The outcome of the argument within the party over the economy was the retention for the time being of the irrational honeycomb of subsidies. "It would have been too much for the people to bear too quickly," a planning commission official in Chengdu said defensively of price deregulation.

With a reform program that could only go ahead or go backward now put in the untenable position of "pause," I felt, as I returned to Boston in late 1988, that Zhao's political position was perilous. Reforming a Communist economy, like riding a bicycle, requires constant forward motion or else peril abounds. The program Zhao felt necessary in order to harvest the full fruits of reform was not going ahead, and for the lack of fruits and attendant dislocations of an interrupted program, it seemed that he, the reformer, might well reap more blame than the more orthodox Communists, notably Politburo member Yao Yilin and Premier Li Peng, who had cut the heart out of reform by stopping price deregulation at the Beidaihe summit.

In April 1989 I returned to Beijing in the course of a trip as lecturer on board the *Pearl of Scandinavia* as it sailed up the China coast. A journalist friend in his sixties, Ni Weiguo, visited my hotel and explained the crisis he had seen building up as a consequence of halfway reform. Ni had just made a lengthy visit to his home county in Jiangsu Province, where many of his old friends were to the fore in small enterprises. "Tax is the key to their success," Ni said, "they just don't pay tax. For instance, a factory is started under the name of a middle school, earning money for the teachers, but as a school operation it doesn't get taxed. And there is a rule that a rural enterprise gets a tax holiday for the first two or three years. Well, after the two years, they change the name of the enterprise and start a new tax holiday. Local officials know this, and wink at it." But people outside the charmed circle of such white-collar fudging resented the lawlessness and injustice of it.

In Jiangsu (and the same was true in much of China) Ni found it was inevitable that the new enterprises would engage in corruption in acquiring materials and marketing. "The debate over price deregulation in 1988 raised the issue acutely," he said. "To free prices would have increased inflation, which Zhao Ziyang was prepared to do. He lost out. To keep manipulated prices, with so many products having two different prices, was to guarantee continued corruption."

Ni was sufficiently old-fashioned and thoughtful to see that the Deng era had brought a deep moral shock to socialist China. He did not like the rush to print escapist novels at the publishing houses, the scale of priorities that put money always at the top, the crudeness of the newly rich, and indeed the materialism of his own high-flying daughter, who was rising rapidly in a computer business. "Deng said it's fine for some to get rich first," Ni said, "but look at what kind of people got rich first—the worst kind in China."

Ni felt that the irrationalities and unfairnesses of halfway economic reform could only be remedied if the political structures of China changed and a free press brought the cut and thrust of debate to public policy. After he several times sharply criticized Deng, I asked him what was the heart of his disillusion with China's senior leader. "During the Cultural Revolution I did not have that high an opinion of Deng, despite what he suffered," Ni replied. "But in the mid-1970s he handled the period of Zhou Enlai's illness and death well, and he was the real alternative to the Gang of Four, whom I hated. Now, unfortunately, with political reform an absolutely essential condition for the success of economic reform, Deng stubbornly refuses to accept the least political reform!" Ni's comment reflected a sharp fall in Deng's popularity in the late 1980s.

Within and beyond the difference over economics and politics, a generation gap had opened up—as between Ni and his daughter, who in the computer business earned much more money than her journalist father and had no interest in politics, even democratic politics. Chinese parents often felt the young were dreamy, noisy, materialistic, without discipline, inclined to drop out of school, and blasé about past revolutionary struggles. The middle-aged were unsettled by youth's rock and roll, motorcycles, avant-garde art, fever to go abroad, casualness about sex, and occasional talk of suicide. Above all they were hurt by youth's insistent cry, "I will do things my way."

Youth for its part tended to find older people rigid, cautious, dull, fatalistic, hung up on Chineseness, too much in awe of education, and passively inclined to give the Communist party the benefit of the doubt. Youth's rebellious spirit was on display in an exhibition of abstract art at Beijing's main gallery early in February 1989, at which the public stared in wonderment at inflated condoms and large plastic breasts, and one young female artist fired pistol shots into her own canvas as part of the creative process. The generation gap, aside from its cultural and psychological specifics, was a signpost to China's future. "Whoever has youth in his hand will rule the future," said the demoted, semiretired Hu Yaobang, who had headed the Communist Youth League for many years. "We old men can only stretch our arms and legs and die."[1]

A professor at Beijing University told me that during a seminar on the history of China's relations with the West, including the Opium Wars and other foreign military assaults, a student rose and shocked his elders by saying: "I don't agree with criticizing Western aggression. I think *more* aggression would have been better for China. Our problem is not the West, but the dead weight of Chinese feudalism." A few months before, in November 1988, I had sat before a class at Sichuan University in Chengdu and asked what foreign books had been memorable. After the obligatory period of silence in the face of such a question from a foreigner to a Chinese class, a young woman caught my eye and burst out: "Lee Iacocca's autobiography. I liked the capitalist spirit of it. As an individual he got up and did things—so different from the traditional ways of China."

Her answer started a flood of comment that could only be described as antifeudal. "For China's future progress," another female student summed up, "new ideas are even more important than science and technology." Listen to what I have to say; consider me an equal; treat me on my merits. These were the demands of the young, and as China's cultural crisis was conjoined with political tensions over reform policy, they became iconoclastic demands. I thought of how the young Mao Zedong had also raised the banner of individualism against an authoritarian social order. As a student in Changsha just as World War I began, Mao scribbled in the margin of his copy of Friedrich Paulsen's *System of Ethics:* "Wherever there is repression of the individual, wherever there are acts contrary to the nature of the individual, there can be no greater crime."[2]

Within the broad cry of youth for freedom, there existed on campuses and elsewhere quiet but potent voices pushing for an agenda of social and political change. At Beijing University "democracy salons" were organized in late 1988 and early 1989 by Wang Dan, a history student, Shen Tong, a biology student, and others to discuss a variety of ideas for moving China away from dictatorship. With an eye to the coming seventieth anniversary of the May Fourth Movement, the fortieth anniversary of Liberation, and the two hundredth anniversary of the French Revolution, teachers and writers were also stirring themselves. Professor Fang Lizhi, the outspoken astrophysicist from Hefei, wrote a letter to Deng Xiaoping calling for the release of Wei Jingsheng, the martyr of Democracy Wall, and other political prisoners, and a large group of writers led by the poet Bei Dao addressed a parallel appeal to the National People's Congress, which was on paper China's parliament although in effect more like the "flower vase" one Beijing student called it.

Between undergraduates and professors, a middle generation of tenacious prodemocracy veterans from Democracy Wall of 1979 and other past struggles, headed by Chen Ziming and Wang Juntao, were assembling the building blocks of a "civic culture." Their Social and Economic Research Institute (SERI), a private outfit that planned research with implications for sociopolitical change, published books and magazines, and conducted public opinion surveys, served as a bridge between circles of dissent and government "think tanks" that had the ear of party chief Zhao Ziyang.[3]

Chen and Wang both had been labeled "counterrevolutionaries" after the Tiananmen Square protest of April 1976, later were lionized when Deng juggled words and called the protest "revolutionary," but got into trouble again in the Democracy Wall period. Their late 1980s activity in SERI was a fruitful linking of the social change produced by Deng's reforms with the intellectual vocation to provide ideas that could change China. SERI's "correspondence colleges," attracting two hundred thousand students nationwide, were at once a money-spinner and a prodemocracy tool. SERI, like the students and the senior intellectuals, was mindful of the coming anniversaries and began seminars at the end of 1988 to prepare for an expected new wave of action for democracy.

On April 15, 1989, Hu Yaobang died of a heart attack, and the loss of the idiosyncratic Communist who had fallen out with Deng two years before during student demonstrations produced anguish and defiance on the campuses. At Beijing University a couplet was posted on a bulletin board that very night: A SINCERE MAN HAS DIED, A HYPOCRITICAL MAN LIVES ON. A stroke of fortune had brought into focus the growing dissatisfaction in urban China with Deng. There was remorse, too, that students had not protested Hu's ouster in 1987. WHEN YOU WERE DEPRIVED OF YOUR POST, ran another poster at Beijing University, WHY DIDN'T WE STAND UP?

Hu Yaobang had reflected, like a roll of silk that flashes two different colors depending on the angle from which it is viewed, both the hope and the timidity of reform. In being a follower of Deng who halfheartedly tried to go beyond Deng, he was a tragic figure, just as reform-after-revolution itself had a noble futility about it. Hu's death gave vent to the anguish that the dualism of hope and limits on hope had stored up in Chinese society. The causes of the emotion that poured out on the campuses after April 15 could be summed up this way. Deng's open policy had brought to China a sense of comparison with the non-Chinese world, and the reform policies had brought a new stress on incentive and ambition. Together, the openness and economic reforms had given rise to new social and economic forces, such as private business, which had a vested interest in moving as far away from Stalinism as possible. Meanwhile the reforms had produced the unsettling side-effects of inflation and corruption, and students and teachers felt education had suffered from the prevailing money-mindedness. Underlying the new strains and opportunities, the decline of faith in Marxism had left a vacuum of values.

A week after Hu's death there sprang into existence an organization of students from some twenty Beijing colleges, called the Provisional Students' Federation, to spearhead a reasoned, peaceful movement for "democracy," its actual ingredients yet to be defined. Day by day scores of thousands of students marched the nine miles from the university quarter in western Beijing to Tiananmen Square. Many of them were from urban families that read books and encouraged in their children a degree of independence. Such a background also had frequently produced tension between parents and sons and daughters and led students to question their parents' values. The activist students were exposed to more Western cultural influence than their fathers and mothers had been, they did not believe much in socialism, and they were possessed by an urge for individual self-realization that transcended any political conviction. Their parents typically were opposed to their offspring's participation in the democracy movement on prudential grounds, even as they expressed a general sympathy for the students' aspirations.

In Beijing during my *Pearl of Scandinavia* trip, I asked Ma Qingguo, a psychology major at Nankai University in Tianjin, the port city a short train ride from Beijing, where a student democracy movement also began, why the death of Hu Yaobang was a spark. "Because Hu had the best ties of any leader with the intellectuals," Ma replied, "he paid attention to youth, and he was the most keen for reform." In Tianjin as elsewhere, various resentments hung in the air waiting to be channeled into a protest movement. Students living eight to a room, professors earning in one month what taxi drivers earned in a few days, young government workers on fixed salaries with no opportunity for economic advancement—all felt left behind in an age when "to get rich [was] glorious," as Deng put it. And nepotism and corruption within the government infuriated many ordinary people. "We request that the central committee answer the following questions," ran one handbill that Ma saw in Tianjin. "How much money has Deng Pufang [Deng Xiaoping's son] spent betting at the horse races in Hong Kong? Where did this money come from?"

In Beijing on April 22, the day of the memorial meeting for Hu in the Great Hall of the People, the authorities announced that Tiananmen Square must be cleared for the occasion. But the students gathered there would not leave and one hundred thousand of them formed a defiant phalanx in the square as the aged leaders arrived at the hall and slipped in by back doors or tunnels for the ceremony. Speaking to the four thousand funeral guests, Zhao Ziyang praised

Hu and glossed over his "mistakes." The hardliner Chen Yun did not attend and incidents between Hu's widow, Li Zhao, and Marshal Nie Rongzhen and Deng showed that tensions in the Politburo over Hu's softness toward "bourgeois freedom" (or "bourgeois liberalism" as the Chinese phrase can be translated) still existed. When Nie in politeness asked Li Zhao if there was anything he could do, she replied crisply, "Yes, clear my husband's name."[4] Deng approached Li Zhao to offer his sympathy, but she waved him away. As China's elite left the hall after the ceremony, students in the square shouted in their direction, "We want dialogue! Down with dictatorship!"

By now "seven demands" had emerged from a student movement that was quickly taking on a national dimension. These "demands" (the Chinese term *yao qiu* could as readily be translated as "requests") incorporated the diverse grievances of the time: restore Hu's reputation; end the drives to eradicate "bourgeois freedom"; allow a free press, free speech, and peaceful demonstrations; spend more money on education; and punish corruption among officials. By no means were the demands of April an attempt to overthrow the political system, although the coming weeks would bring a more confrontational tone and new demands of a more anti-Communist import. In an attempt to deliver the seven demands at the Great Hall of the People on the day of Hu's funeral, three student representatives knelt on the steps of the hall waiting nearly an hour for Premier Li Peng to appear, but neither Li Peng nor any other responsible official came out. Few events during the spring of 1989 made students angrier than that rebuff.

On April 23, the day after Hu's funeral, I went to Tiananmen Square to see the wreaths and memorial messages in Hu's honor left there by students. The square was the usual blend of visitors snapping photos, travelers from out of town sitting at rest with their luggage, small vendors offering cakes and ice cream, and untidy piles of bricks and planks and coils of wire. On the Monument to the People's Heroes, at the center of the square, the wreaths to Hu were sagging and the large black-and-white photos of him were dog-eared, but hundreds of people pressed close to the white marble surface to read stenciled, handwritten, and photocopied manifestos and slogans respectful of Hu, critical of Deng, and extolling democracy. Many young people with pen and notebook in hand were copying down the Chinese characters. One poster read: "Comrade Xiaoping, I would like to know something. You realized long ago that it doesn't matter if a cat is black or white; as long as it catches mice, it's a good cat. Doesn't it show a lack of logic, then, to try to distinguish between 'red' [orthodox] and 'yellow' [bourgeois liberal] thinking?"

Official Beijing in this last week of April walked a tightrope by offering praise for the dead Hu, whom Deng and many of his colleagues had denounced in January 1987, while avoiding praise for the student movement that his death had triggered. "Democracy is something everyone builds gradually on a proper foundation," I heard on the government radio one morning, "not something grabbed by a handful." By a "handful" the commentator meant the students, although a detached observer might well have found the phrase "something grabbed by a handful" an apt description of the power seized by Mao and Deng and other Communists from Chiang Kai-shek in the 1940s. I phoned Yuan Ming, a Beijing University scholar of international relations, and she said to me excitedly: "This is one of the most important moments in Chinese history." That afternoon I could not imagine events to justify Yuan Ming's remark, and indeed I was thinking less about Deng than about Mao.

For in my room at the Kunlun Hotel I sat staring with pleasure and almost disbelief at two books on the table before me. They were Chinese translations just published in China of my two biographies, *Mao* and *The White-Boned Demon,* and across the table sat Liu Luxin, a young sociology teacher who was the translator of the Mao biography. The publisher had wanted a "serious" jacket and the cover in red and black showed a Leninesque head of Mao in international statue style. Liu brought the news that the book, released only a month before by the People's Publishing House of Hebei Province, had sold more than fifty thousand copies, and he showed me a clipping from the *Tianjin Daily* saying that of all the books at the Tianjin book exhibition in the spring of 1989, my Mao biography was the "best received." One staff member at the exhibition told Liu she had sold one thousand copies of the book in a single day.

Mao, in the eight years since its original American publication and editions in six foreign languages, had never been mentioned by the Chinese press, yet now the book was springing into life in Mao's homeland ten years into the reform era. The publishers in Hebei found the tide of interest in Mao bore them along faster than expected. When the chief editor commissioned the translation in mid-1988, he said to Liu Luxin: "We won't be able to publish it for a while, we'll have to wait. But I want to have the book ready to go."

Yet it turned out that the editor did not feel any need to delay, and setting aside all worries about my "bourgeois viewpoint" and the criticisms I made not only of Mao but of the Chinese Communist party, he sped the book into production soon after receiving the translation from Liu toward the end of 1988.

How was it possible that a populace now apathetic about Marxism would want to read about Mao? Previously Mao had been a kind of religion, but the new interest in him was in Mao the man and in an objective appraisal of why he did what he did. There was also nostalgia and admiration for Mao on the part of a fresh generation that reflected disappointment with Deng and disgust at corruption among the top Communist leaders. A computer specialist who worked for a joint venture made a remark to me just after the funeral of Hu Yaobang that touched indirectly on the Mao issue. "We need a strong leader to take things in hand!" he said with passion as he criticized Deng's enigmatic role, retired from most posts but supreme, "and also to come out from behind the throne and face the people!"

Liu Luxin had often visited the Mao Memorial Hall as he translated my book and he found something of history as he stood and ruminated there, he told me, and also a great life he could respect in a world full of timid bureaucrats and mediocrity. Although my young acquaintances stressed the differences between Mao and Deng, I felt that Deng resembled the late Mao as much as he differed from the earlier Mao. Set in his ways, unaware that the new had for many turned into the old, Deng, like Mao before him, was hanging on to power long after he could properly exercise it, while distrusting any number two man whose fingers seemed to itch for the crown, all the while obsessed with how history would judge him.

My biography of Mao's widow Jiang Qing, *The White-Boned Demon,* had been published in Beijing by a house linked with the Chinese foreign ministry. Most Chinese officials I knew had criticized me for tackling this biography, even though its initial target was readers in the West, yet now the book in its yellow and black cover was on sale in the bookstores of China. It contained a prefatory note saying the work was controversial but important. In the prologue to the first edition of *The White-Boned Demon* in 1984 I had written: "Apart from a date here, a selected fact there, the story of Jiang Qing will never be published in Communist China." I was wrong in part. The book as it appeared in Beijing in 1989 omitted some 20 percent of the original—I was not consulted about the omissions—but still the bulk of the story of Jiang Qing was now before the Chinese public.*

Not all of the interested Chinese public could obtain the book, however, for one day as the student democracy movement began to rise, I discovered in a bookshop on Wang Fu Jing Street in Beijing that freedom of the mind in Deng's China was partial when the subject in question was Jiang Qing. While the Mao biography was published as a general book for regular sale in bookstores, *The White-Boned Demon* was published on a restricted basis for an "inside" readership. I knew about this distinction, which lay at the heart of a bewildering maze of Chinese publishing rules, but as the author of the book I wished to check out the regulation for myself.

On the second floor of the Wang Fu Jing bookstore, I found a separate room given over to "inside" readership books, including biographies of controversial figures such as former defense minister Lin Biao, Chiang Kai-shek, and Nikita Khrushchev, and a large pile of copies of *The White-Boned Demon,* called in Chinese "The Real Story of Jiang Qing." When I went to purchase two copies the assistant inquired, "Where's the permission from your organization to buy the book?" I confessed I did not have such a document. Then the assistant asked for my unit identification, and I explained that I was a foreigner, but that I was also the author of the book. She went away to check with her supervisor and came back to say it wasn't possible to sell the book even to its author. Stark indeed was the arrogance of censorship.

The incident reminded me of the twilight character of Deng's reform era, and of how maddening life still could be in a society that had laws and yet no law. It was a society, I felt, in which so much was wrong that the government could not but be jumpy; even a small event might trigger a large outflow of discontent. As Mao had written in a different situation in 1930: "All China is littered with dry wood which will soon be aflame . . . it cannot be long before a 'spark' kindles a 'prairie fire.' "[5] In those days the Communists were the spark, but now they were the dry wood.

The student democracy movement did indeed grow like a prairie fire, feeding upon dry wood on all sides. At the end of April Ma

* The sentence quoted above from *The White-Boned Demon* (page 19) is understandably omitted from the Chinese edition (page 7).

Qingguo, the psychology major from Nankai University in Tianjin, from which Zhou Enlai had graduated seven decades before, told me of the reaction to Hu's death on his campus. "Three hours after the announcement of his death," said Ma, "the first poster went up at Nankai." Students in Tianjin as elsewhere were uneasy at the injustices and irrationalities of half-baked reform, wished an advance to political reform, and resented the dim prospects in society for the educated person. Posters in the number three dining room attacked Communist leaders in various provinces for corruption and nepotism. One was a "revolutionary family tree" of twenty-seven senior officials and their nepotistic sprawlings. Ma helped put up another poster that inquired: HOW MUCH MONEY HAS BEEN EATEN UP BY BUREAUCRATS TO BUY FOREIGN CARS DURING THE PERIOD OF REFORM? Not one word of the activities and posters, which were coordinated by an "autonomous union" linking Tianjin's leading colleges, appeared in the Tianjin press.

"We asked permission for a demonstration to mourn Hu Yaobang," Ma went on of the Nankai movement, "and the administration said no. Still we went ahead." Although there were no rules about the contents of wall posters, Ma and other leaders of the movement at Nankai strictly controlled the slogans for demonstrations, not allowing personal criticism of leaders. On April 22, forty thousand students from five schools including Nankai marched in the streets of Tianjin, as the police stood by and watched. The students bore flags with DEMOCRACY AND SCIENCE written on one side and FREEDOM AND HUMAN RIGHTS on the other.

This new democracy movement was more trenchant and more electric, in Ma's view, than that of 1986, which had led to Hu's dismissal by Deng. "In 1986 the movement started in Hefei," he recalled, "and other campuses responded to the leadership of [astrophysicist Professor] Fang Lizhi and others in Hefei. In 1989 the student democracy movement burst out simultaneously in Beijing, Tianjin, Wuhan, Shanghai, and many other places." Another difference between 1986 and 1989, according to Ma, was that the present movement had much broader support because its goals were loftier. "In 1986 it was just students, except in Shanghai," he said. "Whereas we have many professors backing us, and small businessmen too." At the time Ma and I spoke, a strike was being planned in Beijing, Tianjin, and many other cities to press the "seven demands" that had been rebuffed the day of Hu's funeral.

As I listened to Ma talk about the movement in Tianjin, I reflected on the pleasantness of the loosened-up atmosphere of China that warm spring. Social vigor was growing at the expense of state regulation, and as the human face of China reappeared, there came to the fore not only democratic ideas but also the creative, amusing, and stoic qualities of the Chinese. At the same time I did not think Chinese young people like Ma were confident of quick deep political change. So far, they were respectfully asking the Communist party to improve itself, not signaling their intention of trying to push the Communist party aside. The awareness that change was imperative was mixed with a sense of limits on the possible scope of change that is rare among youth.

One influential graduate student leader whose thinking summed up the views of the older students was Tan Zhenzhou, a sharp-featured man of thirty from the city of Shenyang in Manchuria. "I joined the army at age fourteen," he related of the mid-1970s, "because I thought Russia and China were going to fight and I wished to help." Later he became a sailor on a Chinese merchant vessel. "First I went to North Korea and Somalia, which were both poor like China," Tan said, "then to Antwerp, which was just beautiful." He also went to Gdansk and observed the Polish Solidarity movement, but the deepest impression from his travels came in Singapore. "I had thought that all Chinese people were poor," he said as a smile crept over his face. "Under Chairman Mao, that's how we saw things. Then in Singapore I found a Chinese community that was not poor!

"There was more Chinese tradition in Singapore than on the mainland," Tan continued, revealing a second fact gleaned in Singapore that made him a dissenter. "So I could not believe the line that Chinese tradition was holding us back, and I came to the conclusion that the Communist political system was the culprit." On board ship Tan educated himself by reading books, and at the end of the 1970s when entrance exams for college resumed after the Cultural Revolution, he gained admission (although still not a high school graduate) to Fudan University in Shanghai. By the time of Hu Yaobang's death, he was a graduate student in history in Beijing and he was taking a leading role in the democracy movement at his college.

Tan felt that a democratic system was the ultimate aim of the student movement, but he distinguished between strategy and tactics, and between goals that could be reached at various stages of what he expected to be a long battle. His principal stress was on the need for a free press, not merely because of an attachment to freedom in the abstract, but because he had thought through its indispensable role in exposing corruption. "Getting rich by using power is an awful feature of China," he said, "and only when information gets out to the people can that be stopped."

The terms "political struggle" and "planned conspiracy" had become rare enough that I pricked up my ears on hearing them as I made my way through Beijing railroad station on the morning of April 26. Heading for my train to Tianjin to rejoin the *Pearl of Scandinavia,* I heard a repeatedly broadcast editorial from *People's Daily* condemning the multiplying student demonstrations, posters, and petitions. The tone was hectoring, a government was warning its people about the danger of chaos, bullying them with the bugaboo of ideological authority, telling them in haughty fashion what was right and what was wrong. "The only thing remotely like it I have ever heard in America," I noted in my diary, "were Nixon's harangues during the bitter days of the war in Vietnam and Cambodia, which contained a bit of the same them-and-us rhetoric toward his opponents on the campuses. And back then, none of us students at Harvard thought the harangues could go on for long—the gap in values was too much, the government was merely being atavistic."

The day before the editorial appeared, a meeting took place at Deng's home of an unofficial top group that heard a hardline report on the student demonstrations from the Communist party authorities of Beijing, and then a crucial speech by the senior leader himself. "This is not an ordinary student movement," pronounced Deng, "but turmoil—a planned conspiracy to transform a China with a bright future into a China without hope. We cannot let them have their way."[6] It seemed that Deng had already decided what to do about the spring demonstrations, although for the moment few knew of his resolve. He assailed the dead Hu (on whom Zhao Ziyang had heaped praise at the funeral just three days before) as "weak." He called for a forceful editorial—which duly appeared the next day—and for strict enforcement of law against the demonstrations. "It is a shame that we have wasted time," he remarked on this spring morning a bare ten days after the student stirring began. "We need to quickly use a sharp knife to cut the tangled weeds in order to avoid even greater turmoil." Yet was the knife ready, and who would wield it?

Tour guides in Mao's China used to sing variations on the theme,

"Everything is glorious—now," but in April 1989 as the *Pearl of Scandinavia* passengers walked on the Great Wall of China where it reaches the Bohai Gulf at Qinhuangdao, a tour guide, who was a student of hotel management from Qingdao, said in an addendum to his little speech on the Wall: "Unless something happens, this country is doomed." That same afternoon another guide who was a business student in Tianjin expressed the other side of the dual mood. "No, I haven't taken part in the movement for democracy," he said when I inquired. "By the way it's not turmoil [as *People's Daily* had said that morning in echo of Deng] but a movement for democracy. I'm afraid I think it's useless to join in. Yet I also think it's a good thing for people to do." That night as the *Pearl of Scandinavia* sailed into the Bohai Gulf, I wrote in my diary: "The fading of communism is not the same thing as the coming of democracy."

CHAPTER FOURTEEN

∎

POWER AND EMOTION

THE night of the day April 26, on which Deng's threat to repress the student movement was relayed to the nation—without mention of Deng's name—in the form of the editorial in *People's Daily,* police took down from the Monument to the People's Heroes all the wreaths, posters, and banners placed there in tribute to Hu Yaobang. It was a signal that mourning for the dead reformer would no longer be permitted to cloak prodemocracy agitation.

Yet the endless rebroadcasting of the harsh *People's Daily* editorial actually helped the student movement by drawing attention to a rally planned to descend on Tiananmen Square on April 27. Telling people not to join the demonstration, the government nonetheless informed them of the demonstration. That day, like a huge bonus beyond their dreams, the student organizers found on their hands a tumultuous rally of one million people that made of Tiananmen Square a district of dissent. Citizens climbed trees to shout across the street their support for the students in a display of popular will that lasted eighteen hours. The protestors' demands were trimmed to three: the government must talk with student representatives on a basis of equality, the police must apologize for violence committed against citizens outside Zhongnanhai the previous week, and the media must fairly cover the student democracy movement.

Charles Kim, a Chinese-Canadian student at the Beijing Language Institute, described the demonstration of April 27 to me. At Liubu-kou west of Tiananmen Square, police were blocking part of the marchers' route, and a crowd of citizen onlookers formed a third component. It was a tense moment as police and students pushed each other, and tellingly it was the onlookers who tipped the scales toward the students by clearing a path for the marchers to proceed. The police retreated. "We cried out, 'Thank you, police!' " said Kim, "and some students called out that they favored raising policemen's wages. We reached a group of PLA," the Chinese-Canadian student went on, "but they carried no guns, or even sticks, and did not wear belts or army boots. It was an order from above to prevent a repeat of the incident [that caused several injuries] in front of Zhongnanhai the previous week. It made us feel we were a snowball gathering momentum.

"People from all walks of life joined us," Kim went on, "and the mood was buoyant. I was amazed that in China citizens gave students popsicles and *man tou* (rolls) as they passed by." At the end of the day Kim faced a long ride home to his campus on the Number 375 bus, and he knew the last one left at 8:00 P.M. But the bus drivers told the students they would work late and drive them back on the 375 route at any time convenient. "Jammed into the bus," Kim said, "we were so happy. We felt we had won something. I thought to myself, Deng is not bad after all, Li Peng is not stupid after all."

That night the radio cried an interesting announcement from the government. "We are ready to conduct a dialogue with the students at any time," it said. "But the dialogue must be through the normal channels, not as a result of resorting to extremist actions." The next day, April 28, *People's Daily* at last published its first news report on the spring's demonstrations. And the day after that, the Communist party newspaper ran an editorial quite a bit milder than that of April 26, fairly politely asking the students to resume their classes.

Charles Kim, as an ethnic Chinese but also a Canadian citizen, had an unusual angle of vision on the motivation of the democracy movement. "Chinese students won't admit it is one of the reasons for the protests," he said, "but the comparison of themselves with the foreign students *is* one factor behind it all. The Chinese students live eight to a room, the foreigners are one or two to a room." Kim asked one of his Chinese classmates who was busy writing posters what he really wanted. "A room of my own," the young man replied, not looking up from his work on the poster. Kim pointed out that China had more than a billion people and space was limited. "Japan is crowded too," the student rejoined, "yet they live far better than us. Why hasn't the Chinese government provided a better life for us?" On this point the 1989 protests repeated those of December 1986 (and resembled student protests in other Third World countries).

Another rally in Tiananmen Square on May 4 added to the momentum of the movement. The occasion was a historic one, the seventieth anniversary of the watershed May Fourth student movement of 1919, and many people who were by no means firebrands against the government felt able to join in. After the rally, Shen Tong, the biology major who had organized seminars to discuss democracy and now was one of the student leaders at Beijing University, dropped by the house of his proud but anxious parents and overheard an exchange between his mother and his father, who was a Beijing city employee. "My friends at work were all asking me why my son is so fearless," Mr. Shen said to his wife. "And what did you say?" inquired Mrs. Shen. "I told them," said Mr. Shen, "it must be because we—the people of our generation—have been cowards for too long."[1]

After May 4, the main demand of the student movement was for a "dialogue" with the government, and thoughtful students were uncertain of the wisdom of further large demonstrations. Most of them wanted a more responsive government, more mental freedom, and an assurance that the reform process would resume and expand. It was all ad hoc, Confucian, respectful of procedures, and dictated by the outcome of intense factionalism and networking. Back in Boston, I worried about the movement's future direction. "If there is no faction within the Communist party that the students can appeal to and be encouraged by," I noted in my diary on May 6, "where does their movement go now? Judging by the two variant *People's Daily* editorials [of April 26 and 29], there could be a split in the party. Yet it may be just that old Deng is wavering, as old Mao wavered."

Deng may well have been wavering, but indeed there was a disagreement within the Communist party and the moment of decision had arrived for party chief Zhao Ziyang. If the student movement were to have a fruitful outcome, it would have to be in conjunction with the bolder elements of a divided Communist party, led by Zhao. Of the two other possible positive outcomes to the spring turbulence, a prompt dismantling of Communist rule was virtually out of the question, and the mere resignation of Premier Li Peng would not necessarily amount to much. Yan Jiaqi, the distinguished political scientist who later fled China, would issue a declaration on

May 17 calling for Deng to relinquish control of the government, but in my view Deng—like Mao before him—was too much of an emperor for "retirement" to have any meaning. Death (or utter disgrace) was the only way for his power to come to an end.

But would Zhao Ziyang put himself at the spearhead of a challenge to those who had stalled reform, and could the student movement deploy its strength in order to take advantage of any move Zhao might make? Zhao had been on a visit to North Korea in the last days of April. From Pyongyang he had apparently given a general approval to the harsh April 26 editorial, although privately and through his staff he had been expressing sympathy and understanding for the students. What was his political strategy? It seemed that after the spectacular April 27 rally Zhao decided to distance himself from Deng. On May 3, in a speech commemorating the seventieth anniversary of the May Fourth Movement, and again on May 4, before an audience of the Asian Development Bank, he contradicted Deng by making no criticism of "bourgeois freedom," saying "there will be no great turmoil in China," and declaring that the students were "in no way opposed to our fundamental system." The Communist party was speaking with two voices.

Yet Zhao and the student movement were not in harness; indeed to a degree they were a threat, as well as a source of hope, to each other. Zhao could point to student opinion as an argument to push Deng toward bold steps of political reform, but Deng could rejoin that "turmoil in the streets" would undermine the Communist party's authority and harm the economy. The moderate students could point to Zhao as a sign that change within Communist party rule was possible, but radical students (for the student movement, too, increasingly spoke with more than one voice) could recall the fate of bold reformer Hu Yaobang in 1987, and add that Zhao had helped push Hu out and that Zhao's family was as deeply into using office for profit as Deng's family.

In the fumbling yet obstinate manner of its overall response to the student movement, the government agreed to a dialogue with selected students on April 29, but treated the students with fatherly condescension. The government representatives spoke for 80 percent of the three hours and almost none of the student representatives reflected the prodemocracy views of the student union federation. Li Lu, a student from Nanjing University who was emerging as a leader of the movement, watched the dialogue on TV and felt it was like parents berating children. "You're still young," the officials were saying. "You don't really know anything about party and state affairs. We have good reasons for everything we do."[2] The generation gap was reinforcing the political gap between government and students.

After further efforts to mount a student-government dialogue in the second week of May came to nothing, a hunger strike began in Tiananmen Square on May 13, a dramatic move designed to evoke a response from a government that was hiding behind vague, delaying gestures. Chai Ling, a twenty-three-year-old graduate student of psychology at Beijing Normal University, made an emotional speech that galvanized students to fast for democracy. She had joined the movement out of anger at the rebuff to the three students who had kneeled with the "seven demands" on the steps of the Great Hall of the People the day of Hu's funeral. "My hunger strike," Chai Ling cried in a recorded speech to student groups, "is for the purpose of seeing just what the true face of the government is, to see whether it intends to suppress the movement or to ignore it, to see whether the people have a conscience or not, to see if China still has a conscience or not."[3]

Hundreds of students immediately signed up for the hunger strike. They took a fasting pledge and put on white headbands reading, GIVE ME FREEDOM OR GIVE ME DEATH. They operated their administration from a bus parked in the middle of Tiananmen Square, and used other buses for accommodations, piercing the tires and removing the steering wheels so the government could not come and drive the vehicles away. With the start of the hunger strike the movement entered an emotional stage, and won enormous public support, but did not move closer to a political goal. If there is one activity the Chinese take more seriously than any other it is eating, and the issue of food and famine runs through Chinese history like a fault line. "Save the students" became a new demand from all quarters of Beijing, as each day hundreds of fainting students were carried off to hospitals, and although the cry was extraneous to any political goal, it was more passionately supported than any other demand of the spring.

"Literary critics could be seen shouting in streets and alleys," Liu Binyan related, "famous writers ran around in a sweat, buying urinals for students."[4] With a boldness unprecedented in the PRC, journalists marched in the streets to protest the lack of press freedom and to support the student movement. THE APRIL 26 EDITORIAL WASN'T WRITTEN BY US, cried the banner of one group of demonstrating journalists.[5] Some newspaper editors marched to the door of the Communist party's Propaganda Department, which instructed and censored all Chinese publications, and shouted through the windows, "Don't call us anymore!" Meanwhile the official press grew bolder, although often still by indirection, such as the use of extraneous foreign news for allusion. Out of the blue *People's Daily* offered a story on anticorruption measures in Egypt, then a report on how President Bush made public his personal assets and a list of all gifts he had received while in office. An unusually large headline was placed over a dispatch from Iran: KHOMEINI AGED AND IN POOR HEALTH; WHO WILL SUCCEED HIM?[6]

By the middle of May Tiananmen Square had become a city of protest, a spectacular locus of a student movement that had grown into a broad antigovernment demonstration. Wang Dan, the Beijing University student leader who had conducted "democracy salons" on the campus in 1988, summed up an achievement of the movement: "[It] has made the Party realize the actual opinion of the people, and it has made the people, for the first time in forty years, aware of their own power."[7] Perhaps Deng would not be able to wield the knife after all! The writer Orville Schell, who was in the square, caught the mood of the time. "[I]t seemed almost unimaginable," he wrote, "that the old stifling order that had made Chinese feel eternally afraid of speaking out could ever again reassert itself. Even the facade of elephantine socialist buildings that ringed the square and had once looked so imposing now seemed clunky and out of date."[8]

The students with their books and music cassettes and water bottles were encamped college by college, as units in the Chinese style, and the negative features of this "unit mindedness" turned into a positive advantage of organizational strength and unity that encouraged the fainthearted to swallow their doubts and join in. One such was Lao Yujun, a graduate student whose temperament inclined him to shy away from the poles of orthodoxy and dissent. Born in a village in Shandong Province, Lao studied at Beijing University but retained the caution and shrewdness of his rural roots. He was finishing a masters' thesis on Wallace Stevens when the democracy movement arose. "I joined in the hunger strike to find out what a hunger strike was like," he would later tell me matter-of-factly, "and also because a lot of the younger students from our campus were going to Tiananmen Square, and I wanted to be there with them." Like thousands of other middle-of-the-road students, Lao became a demonstrator as, for a season, the unthinkable ideals of freedom and democracy seemed nothing more than reasonable. After three days he fainted and left Tiananmen Square.

From May 13, when the hunger strike began, Ma Qingguo forsook his psychology textbooks and worked as a "student police" in Tiananmen Square. For ten days he never left the square or bathed, and for two nights he slept under the Golden Water Stream Bridge beneath the portrait of Mao at the northern edge of the square. Part of his job was to keep open one of four lifelines (*sheng ming xian*) for ambulances to reach the hunger strikers near the Monument to the People's Heroes. "Our demands boiled down to something rather simple," Ma recalled. "That the government affirm our movement was patriotic, not turmoil, and that they talk to us and realize we were not seeking to overthrow them." If there was a tentativeness to Ma's aims, perhaps there was reason enough in the formidable state machine the students faced. In the West an opposition movement is expected to be programmatic, and from the start work toward a clear-cut outcome. In China, for many in the democracy movement, certainly for Ma Qingguo, the process of challenging a totalitarian state was more like an endless game of chess played in the dark.

"Should the students push hard?" I wrote in my diary in mid-May, as I watched pictures of the events unfolding in Tiananmen Square, surprised that Deng was permitting so much foreign television coverage of the democracy movement. "Yes, they must push, because without pressure the Communist party has too many reasons not to move ahead with reform. But the students must formulate goals as well as push," I went on. "The way to find out how strong the prodemocracy movement is would be to demand repeal of Deng's 'four cardinal principles'—which boil down to a guaranteed monopoly on power by the Communist party—and to found a new political party, a Democratic party." But this did not happen.

The hunger strike produced the first streak of angry radicalism in the movement, as well as shafts of disunity, and all the while it broadened worker support for the students. Shen Tong said he felt for the first time "opposed" to the government and on impulse on May 15 he decided to lead a group of students to "charge" Zhongnanhai. At the heavily guarded gate of the government compound, the Bohemian-looking activist cried: "I want to see [Premier] Li Peng. You have fifteen minutes." The knot of students around Shen gained access to the compound, but after insulting lower-level officials they were required to leave. At the gate Shen Tong shouted back at the PLA guards: "This place is not worth your protection. You should just go home."[9] Others were even more radical than Shen Tong. Li Lu, the Nanjing student who was deputy commander of the hunger strikers, said Zhao was "playing games" and refused to take any note of political maneuvers within the Communist party, and Chai Ling, his boss, a spellbinding orator, seemed guided as much by apocalyptic emotion as by political strategy.

In an exquisite piece of historical awkwardness, the hunger strike began just two days before the arrival in China of Mikhail Gorbachev, on a long-planned visit to bury the deep antagonism between the Soviet Union and China that went back to the days of Khrushchev and Mao. The flagging student movement benefited from Gorbachev's arrival and from the presence of twelve hundred foreign journalists in China to cover it. Here was a major reason for the extent of the world's knowledge of the student demonstrations, for Beijing had given permission months earlier for CBS, CNN, and other news organizations to bring satellite dishes and extra journalists into China to report on the Deng-Gorbachev summit.

In Tiananmen Square, instead of the expected display of Soviet and Chinese flags, there were clustered the banners of a score of colleges inscribed with calls for democracy. One proclaimed in Russian, DEMOCRACY, OUR COMMON DREAM. Another, WELCOME TRUE REFORMER, implied an aspersion upon the Beijing leadership, suggesting that in the late 1980s Gorbachev had dared to go ahead with political reform, while Deng stuck with economic reform. A third read, GORBACHEV IS 58, DENG IS 85, with reverse arrows linking the two pairs of numerals. For young people, the age difference between the two leaders was devastating. "Our rulers are all old men," a female clerk said to a foreign friend plaintively, as if she had made a fresh discovery. School pupils rammed home the point about age with a startling cry. "If you fall," they shouted to the college students, "there will still be us to take over."

Never in the history of the PRC had a visiting leader's Beijing schedule been mangled by domestic turmoil as Gorbachev's was. The welcoming ceremony, planned for Tiananmen Square, had to be held instead at the airport, the Soviet chief's visit to the Forbidden City and the opera both were canceled, and his press conference was at the last moment moved from the Great Hall of the People (outside of which one hundred thousand people were gathered to cheer the hunger strikers) to the guest house where he was staying. Copies of

Gorbachev's address to the Chinese people did not reach the press as scheduled because the photocopy machine repairman was out in the streets demonstrating. A leaflet prepared by the students said, "The Communist party's own backyard has caught fire," and it seemed to be true. By now the student movement virtually controlled parts of the city and the government, evidently hoping to undermine the students by creating inconvenience, stopped the operation of some sixty public bus routes.[10]

Gorbachev had come to accomplish with Deng a historic reconciliation between the two Communist giants, but the world was changing under the feet of both men. Zhao was not quite finished politically and he chose to use his meeting with Gorbachev to boldly turn up the heat on Deng, who was calling the shots behind the throne but saying nothing in public. "On the most important questions, we still need Deng as the helmsman," Zhao said to Gorbachev (and the press), thus putting responsibility for the crisis on the shoulders of the eighty-five-year-old patriarch. Zhao's belated decision to stand against Deng was a perilous one, and to China's great loss the student movement was not in a position to support him in that fateful step. "Our movement had absolutely nothing to do with the party struggle," a Beijing Normal University student leader, Wuer Kaixi, an education major, said later. "We didn't care anything for their internal struggles."[11] Wuer stated that overtures from Hu Qili, a Politburo member sympathetic to the democracy movement, for a coordination of efforts with the democracy movement were rejected by the student leadership, as were proposals from some military generals for a "deal" with the students.[12] Still less was the hunger strike leadership, representing the militant wing of the movement, interested in any deal with Zhao or the military.

Gorbachev's presence in Beijing and the enthusiasm of the students for him highlighted the confusion over the movement's goals. Were the students pursuing democracy or merely communism modified by political reform in the Gorbachev manner? The movement chose simply to focus on Gorbachev's open, youthful style, and use him as one more stick to beat the Chinese government. For his part, Gorbachev while in Beijing spoke in favor of "a sensible balance between the generations, combining the energy of the young in speaking out against conservatism with the wisdom of the older generation." But Gorbachev's accommodationist instincts were not necessarily those of Deng, who still kept the knife beside his trembling hand.

Although the student leaders were nearly all independent spirits, in a curious way they were institutionally very dependent, perhaps unavoidably so because of the environment of dictatorship in which they grew up and operated. There had been no such thing in the PRC as a separate business realm, intellectual activity as a free and independent vocation, an opposition political party, or a national election. Probably it was inevitable that many of the students would think in terms of "good men" rather than new structures, and act in the experimental mode of incrementalism rather than in accord with a long-term program.

A paradox about these students was that they were without awe for the Communist party, yet often they lacked political shrewdness. One veteran of Democracy Wall of 1979, looking down the years at a generation a decade younger than his own, was amazed at the 1989 youths' detachment from communism. "We were believers in communism," he said of his generation. "I was a Red Guard. We tried to work within the system. These new students seem not to care at all about the party." Then the former Red Guard, now thirty-five years of age, struck a poignant note: "Perhaps they are right. Caring about the Communist party did not save us at Democracy Wall."[13]

Yet if the students of 1989 had paid closer attention to the split within the party that opened in 1988 and widened further in early May 1989, the outcome of their passionate endeavors might have been less barren than it was. They stunned China and the world because of a purity of aim, yet the very abstraction of that purity made it difficult for their movement to be a politically successful operation. When Zhao sought to persuade the students to leave Tiananmen Square on the eve of Gorbachev's arrival, the main student leaders Wang Dan, Shen Tong, and Wuer Kaixi favored this step, which could have led to a new coalition between the students and the reform wing of the government, but these three were not able to work their will. Radical impulses at the grass roots, and the hunger strike leadership of Chai Ling and Li Lu, were increasingly in conflict with the original limited aims of the democracy movement.

The SERI group of Chen Ziming and Wang Juntao was patiently trying to build the "civic culture" whose still-limited existence also made it difficult for the student democracy movement to achieve political results. Torn between protecting their long-term goals of research, education, and networking, and on the other hand seizing this historical moment to put all they knew to a test, the SERI leaders resolved to risk participation in the democracy movement, but in a background role as advisers to the young student leaders. They formed a body called Joint Liaison Group of All Capital Circles that met daily to analyze, plan, and take action on behalf of the students. Wang Dan, Wuer Kaixi, or one of the other student leaders generally attended the daily meeting. However, the divisions of opinion in the movement as a whole were growing, and a gap yawned between the idea of changing China by building a civic culture and doing so by a hunger strike.

After five days of the hunger strike, with emotions soaring all across Beijing, the city witnessed some of the largest rallies China has known as more than a million people choked the streets on May 17 and May 18, perhaps a majority of them workers. In dozens of other cities around the nation, huge demonstrations occurred, spurred on by Chinese TV pictures of fainting hunger strikers in Tiananmen Square. Posters and banners sharply attacked Deng, taking a cue from Zhao's remark to Gorbachev. XIAOPING, THANK YOU AND GOOD-BYE, said one in Beijing, and another made a play on the Communist leader's famous maxim of pragmatism: IT DOESN'T MATTER IF THE CAT IS BLACK OR WHITE, SO LONG AS IT RESIGNS. Not all of these slogans had been approved by the original leadership of the student movement, and their sharply confrontational tone reflected the rising influence, within the sprawling umbrella democracy movement, of the hunger strikers. The sharp tone was also due in part to the intervention of senior advisers grouped in the Beijing Intellectuals Association, who wished the students to take up Zhao's sagging cause against Deng and Li Peng.

In the streets the police were nowhere to be seen, except for some traffic police working under the supervision of student marshals, and student leaders became heroes, signing autographs with one hand, scribbling a will with the other. Old women walked miles to bring salted eggs to the youths, food vendors donated their cakes and soda pop, and nurses volunteered their services after hours to tend the faint and the ill. On May 6 Zhao Ziyang as party general secretary had personally instructed Hu Qili, the Politburo member in charge of media, to ensure full and accurate reportage of the democracy movement, and on May 18, with Gorbachev still in China, the Sino-Soviet summit was only a tiny item on one corner of the front page of a *People's Daily* that was filled with vivid reports of the activities of the students. "Our Gorbachev is probably still in high school," grumbled a health ministry official to *The Wall Street Journal*. "All we've got is a bunch of Brezhnevs."[14]

"May 18 was the most difficult day," Ma Qingguo recalled of his ten days as a "student police" in the square. "With a crowd of one and a half million in Tiananmen Square, it was so difficult to protect the hunger strikers, and I had no food at all for long stretches of time." Ma was proud that no traffic accident occurred on his watch despite the crowds. "That night from my place by the Golden Water Stream I looked up at Mao and wondered what he would have thought of us," he said. " 'Too many people,' Mao would have observed, 'but all in good order.' "

The All-China Women's Federation, the Communist Youth League, the All-China Federation of Trade Unions, and other such officially approved organizations, for long mere paper cut-outs whose words sounded like tape-recorded propaganda, became breathing, walking bodies that issued statements in prose with life and meaning to support the student movement. Among the thousands of businessmen who rallied to the side of the students was the son of a professor friend of mine at Beijing University. Zhu Bingchun was an arts college graduate who in the spirit of the reform era had turned to business and now ran a furniture company. During all of the major demonstrations in April and May, Zhu's staff used the company truck, which carried on the front a placard reading DOWN WITH DICTATORSHIP, to join with the students and lend transportation help. Later I asked Zhu if he encouraged his staff to back the democracy forces. "I encouraged them, and they encouraged me," he replied.

There was something unrestrained and very proud about the days of freedom. It was as if all the things that are "true" of life in the PRC ceased to be true. People were open, polite, enthusiastic, and candid. They avidly read Chinese newspapers and watched Chinese TV. They showed no trace of obsequiousness toward foreigners. The new sense of equality with non-Chinese made it plain that the ritual of politeness to the foreigner had always been bound up with the Communist party's dictatorial hold over the Chinese people. A taxi driver said to a foreign woman who had expected the usual deference: "The students have risen against the government. We don't have to be afraid of you foreigners any more."[15]

Where a state dwarfs the people, citizenship does not exist, but in these weeks of freedom citizenship flowered. People shared and cooperated, and a misunderstanding in the street did not lead, as it usually had, to an argument or altercation, but to a compromise or an apology or a smile. Hundreds of young men on motorcycles calling themselves the Flying Tiger Brigade became a liaison team for the democracy movement, carrying messages, telling the student leaders of anything unusual they saw. Traffic gave way for them and pedestrians cheered them on their noisy way.

With Gorbachev gone, the Chinese government began its move against the demonstrators as Premier Li Peng announced martial law for most of Beijing. Li Peng was a product of the Chinese bureaucracy and the period of Soviet-China amity. Born in Sichuan Province in 1928, orphaned and brought up in the household of Zhou Enlai, he studied engineering in Moscow in the 1950s. Bespectacled and stiff, he often wore a smug look and assumed a pugnacious stance. His approach to politics stemmed from the nuts and bolts logic of his chosen field of engineering. He first entered the leadership as minister for water and power in 1981 and became premier in 1987. After the contentious meeting on the economy at Beidaihe in 1988, Li essentially took over management of economic affairs from Zhao Ziyang, but only with his speech declaring martial law did he become a household face for the people of China.

The broadening of the movement during the days of the Gorbachev visit from a student affair to an antigovernment surge with wide worker support was one reason for the government's decision to act.* Troops of eight armies began to approach Beijing. "The troops' arrival," said President Yang Shangkun in a whopping lie, "is definitely not aimed at dealing with the students." For many nights Ma Qingguo and his friends, still camped in Tiananmen Square, did not sleep but talked, and the main topic was whether to stay on in the square until the government responded properly to the demands of the democracy movement, or whether to retreat, proclaim an initial victory, and prepare for a future stage of the movement. Ma was from a farming family of five brothers, the only son who went to college, and as a cautious son of the soil he favored leaving Tiananmen Square after martial law was declared.

But the square was increasingly occupied by tens of thousands of

* A reliable source told Wang Shaoguang, a legal scholar formerly with Beijing University, that the official trade union organization had decided to call a general strike for May 20 (*China: The Crisis of 1989*, State University of New York at Buffalo conference, 1990, p. 247).

newly arrived students from outside Beijing who felt the movement was only at its beginning and were in no mood for tactical retreat. Although the hunger strike was called off with the arrival of martial law, the occupation of Tiananmen Square and the propaganda activities of the movement continued unabated. "After May 19," said Gao Xin, an activist from Beijing Normal University, "no one could have persuaded more than 10 percent of the students in Tiananmen Square of anything—not Wuer Kaixi, not Zhao Ziyang, not Wang Juntao. They just would not listen to a voice of moderation."[16] Perhaps this was a factor in Zhao Ziyang's hesitant political strategy.

"Zhao thought for four hours straight," Su Shaozhi, a researcher connected with the Zhao camp, said later, "about whether to summon a central committee meeting and seek to win support for his line by obtaining dismissals and new appointments—the way Khrushchev did in battling Malenkov and Molotov and Kaganovich in 1957. But Zhao felt the system just would not work that way." Another report hinted at Zhao's hesitation. On May 16 Defense Minister Qin Jiwei offered his support to Zhao, but Zhao rejected a military confrontation with his opponents on the grounds that it would split the party and be against the constitution.[17]

No real cooperation existed between Zhao's circle and the politics of the streets. Nor indeed did the harmonizing of tactics between young researchers and bureaucrats who supported Zhao, and Zhao himself, seem effective: at the very time on May 19 when Chen Yizi and other pro-Zhao advisers in the Beijing Intellectuals Association were appealing to the students at Tiananmen Square to end their hunger strike and heed the internal political struggle, Zhao himself was finally bested behind closed doors at leadership meetings orchestrated by Deng.[18] Zhao had declined to go along with the declaration of martial law and that put an end to his role at the head of the party.

The radicalized turn in the democracy movement was clear in Wuer Kaixi's fall from the chair of the Beijing Students' Federation on May 22 after he unsuccessfully urged a retreat from Tiananmen Square. On May 27, Wang Dan, Wuer Kaixi, and Chai Ling announced that the students, no longer on a hunger strike but still occupying Tiananmen Square, would leave the square. Within forty-eight hours that decision was reversed and Chai Ling went along with the more radical sentiment of the former hunger strikers to stay at least until the National People's Congress could meet in emergency session to review the situation. If the hunger strike had broadened the democracy movement into a vast antigovernment protest, it had also radicalized the group that now spoke for the students and thus made a political outcome—as distinct from a military one—less possible. By late May the militant core that had emerged from the hunger strike was nakedly face to face with the army.

Deng's one formal post was the chairmanship of the Communist party's military commission, and it was to a session of this body, "enlarged" with selected guests, that Yang Shangkun, president of the country and vice-chairman of the commission, gave a speech on May 24 that divulged Zhao's fall. The shadow of khaki had fallen over Beijing and Yang, a Sichuan-born Communist with a streak of the warlord in him, now eighty-two years old, spoke with authority. He picked up from the law-and-order line of Deng's remarks to the gathering at his home on April 25 that led to the tough *People's Daily* editorial the next day. "Before I came to this meeting," Yang said, "Chairman Deng gave me an idea. He said military cadres should be organized to conduct propaganda among students and citizens." This showed how much Deng was out of touch with the actual situation in Beijing, where soldiers would soon be mostly left speechless by the arguments put to them by students and citizens.

Zhao Ziyang had become weak in the face of bourgeois influences, President Yang told his audience, and even worse, he was disloyal to Deng. That really was the gist of the matter, and Yang's praise for the retired Communist party elders who had been drawn from sitting in courtyards with their grandchildren to tip the balance of power at "enlarged" meetings suggested the atavistic nature of the solution Deng had chosen to the problems posed by the student movement. "We can no longer retreat and must launch an offensive," Yang told his military audience. "Today I just want to tell you about this so you can prepare yourself mentally." [19]

On one point Yang spoke the sober truth. "There is now trouble in almost every province and city," he said. In dozens of cities all over China daily marches and demonstrations unfolded. To a degree the provinces took a lead from Beijing, starting hunger strikes after Beijing did so, yet the scope of prodemocracy activity proved that "dry wood" abounded in all urban China. In many provinces virtually every center that had a postsecondary school saw demonstrations, and most of them intensified after the declaration of martial law in Beijing. In all provinces the authorities seemed more reluctant to denounce and confront the students than were the leaders in Beijing; typically, city or province leaders supported the students' goals but opposed their methods. In few cities and towns was there much violence, in even fewer was anyone killed, and no city other than Beijing declared martial law. In the smaller cities the theme of the demonstrations often was to "support the students in Beijing," but in many large cities there were original, varied demands based on local realities. Zhao Ziyang frequently was included with Deng and Li Peng among the targets, on the grounds of his family's involvement in corruption. One poster in the Manchurian city of Shenyang showed how eclectic were the grievances aired: "Why does no one ever mention Mao's 'Serve the people'? Prices are rising . . . the population is out of control . . . Rare animals are being killed . . . marriage is a commodity . . . our rivers are polluted . . . AIDS spreads unchecked. . . . Where is China going?" [20]

In Tianjin the reaction among students to martial law was an angry one. "After Li Peng's speech of the evening of May 19," Ma Qingguo told me later, "my classmates came out in a demonstration at Station Square in the middle of the night. On coming back from the square, several students who were party members went to their department party secretary and asked to resign from the party."

"Asked to resign?" I queried.

"You can't just tear up your card and resign from the Chinese Communist party," Ma said. "You have to get permission." The next day the government of Tianjin announced that no more demonstrations would be permitted, yet it did not punish the protesters of the previous night, no troops came to Nankai or other Tianjin campuses, and police at no point beat up students.

Just as the northern China sky in May can sharply change color, the student democracy movement did so by the end of May. "Dare to Die" corps reflected the uncompromising stance of the militant leadership, and the growing presence of students from outside Beijing brought a desire for new action, even as the Beijing student organizations (apart from the former hunger strikers) were in the mood to draw back. Chen and Wang in their SERI research group put forward a proposal on May 28 that the students should leave Tiananmen Square, but their advice was not heeded.

The Communist leaders inside Zhongnanhai were enraged when students from the Central Arts Academy built and erected in Tiananmen Square a huge white Styrofoam "Goddess of Democracy," which bore a resemblance to Guan Yin, the Chinese goddess of mercy, but also uncannily recalled the Statue of Liberty in New York. A factory donated eight thousand yuan to pay for the Styrofoam, plaster, and wire. When the goddess was ready to be taken to the square, a phone call came to the Arts Academy from Section Thirteen of the police ministry saying that any truck driver who transported the statue would have his driver's license canceled for life. The art students took the goddess to Tiananmen Square in four parts on small carts. The ten-meter-high form was hoisted into the air to the accompaniment of music from Handel's *Messiah*.[21] Meanwhile tens of thousands of troops with AK-47 rifles were inching toward Beijing, and military helicopters grated across the sky, creating an ominous air.

An astonishing number of Beijing citizens from all walks of life argued with the troops or ingeniously impeded their advance. Just as the grass-roots citizen response to the hunger strike had broadened the democracy movement beyond a student affair, so the citizen resistance to the army's advance made the movement very nearly an uprising against the government. Clerks, shopkeepers, grandmothers, factory workers, drifters from outside Beijing surrounded military trucks, lay down in front of them, let air out of the tires, blocked roads with trash cans, logs, bicycles, market stalls, and concrete slabs. At Xidan market, thieves announced a strike of ten days so that they could concentrate on impeding military vehicles.

In the last week of May troops of the Fortieth Army, which was based in the Manchurian city of Shenyang, were stationed outside the gates of the college attended by Tan Zhenzhou, the former soldier and sailor—also from Shenyang—who was now in the thick of the movement. The students argued with them and sought to bar their further progress toward Tiananmen Square. Although the Beijing Students' Federation no longer ruled in the square, the federation mobilized its forces to enlist the citizens of Beijing to stop the troops in one way or another from reaching the square. Soldiers told Tan they had not seen TV or newspapers for a week and that their superiors said the reason for coming to Beijing was to make a documentary film. Some said, in a reference to another army that was based in Shijiazhuang (with what degree of accuracy and sincerity it would be hard to say): "We are here to deter the Twenty-seventh Army from firing on the people of Beijing." Tan and his classmates drew up a list of slogans and talking points for the dialogue with the troops. "The students are brothers and sisters of yours," ran one item stenciled on tissue paper. Another said: "Think carefully before you shoot at people who made the guns and artillery and tanks you are using."

Citizens who lived near Tan's college joined in the blockade and persuasion of the PLA unit. One woman went up to a troop truck and said: "My grandson is among the students camped at Tiananmen Square, and if you are on your way to kill him, here am I, kill me first." Tan and his friends showed the troops the newspapers from the "free press" interlude in the third week of May and the young peasants from far-flung parts of China were amazed. "We gave them a detailed picture," Tan said, "of how crime and traffic accidents were less during the period of the student democracy movement than they had been before. We told them that the student struggle is one for all Chinese. When they heard all these things, some soldiers said their eyes were opened and they left—they just ran away from the unit. I said to the soldiers," Tan went on, " 'If I'd stayed on in the PLA, I would be there with you.' Most of them told me their mothers did not want them to be in Beijing doing this."

In all the scores of cities where the democracy movement arose, and especially in Beijing, the students themselves realized that a violent crackdown could come at any time. It was widely expected after the threatening April 26 *People's Daily* editorial, after the May 4 rally, before Gorbachev arrived in China, and again when he left. So it was that students made wills, settled accounts with their families, and made plans for escape from China, or for an invisible existence in the countryside, in the wake of a collapse of the movement. Yet almost no one knew, in those first two days of June, what was going to happen in Beijing. Many people took the view that with Zhao deposed, reform had been set back, somewhat as it had been after Hu's fall in 1987, but not terminally so. A sense of triumph that the democracy movement seemed to be holding the army at bay was mixed with foreboding that the physical standoff in Beijing could not last for long. Most believed the student movement had run its course for the present stage, but also that behind the vermilion walls of Zhongnanhai, Chinese politics had been deeply affected by its cry from the heart.

CHAPTER FIFTEEN

■

MASSACRE

IN New York at the end of May 1989 to pick up a visa for a return to China, I asked a Chinese diplomat his opinion of the student democracy movement that had been rising and twisting in Beijing and dozens of other cities for the last six weeks. "It's all over and everything is returning to normal," he replied. It was true that many of the Chinese students felt one phase of their struggle had ended, but three evenings later on June 3 at Beijing airport, I did not find normality. Customs officials ignored my luggage and my customs declaration form; authority was absent where it had always been present. Outside the terminal there were many taxis and few passengers, yet drivers were strangely reluctant to accept my business, looking like sad spaniels, hungry but not able to eat. The first one I approached said he had never heard of the Palace Hotel, where I had a reservation, and he showed no inclination to find out its location, and a second with eyes averted asked the outrageous sum of 180 yuan to take me into the city. "It's complicated and dangerous to drive into that part of Beijing," said a third driver after we began the trip to the Palace.

With a curse my driver accepted the necessity of detouring far to the north of the main road from the airport to the city. Bumping down dusty ill-lit lanes, we were on a checkerboard of trial and error as passersby leaned toward the taxi window with advice on which streets were tractable and which intractable. As we drew near Beijing city, I saw clusters of people on the sidewalk at intersections, faces looking upward toward some kind of illuminated platforms, brushed by leafy branches, on which figures in colorful headdresses moved about speaking loudly. From a distance these "platforms" looked like open-air stages, but closer up they turned out to be the roofs of cream and red-painted public buses, placed in key positions by prodemocracy forces to try to block advancing military vehicles. The "actors" were students in their signature red or blue headbands, speaking to the crowds about government corruption and the need for democracy, and arguing to nearby troops that the army should not advance to Tiananmen Square.

"Don't go into the streets, in particular don't go near Tiananmen Square," said the Chinese-language taxi radio as we neared the Palace Hotel, a mile northeast of the square. "Citizens of Beijing, stay in your homes." Not deterred, I climbed out of the taxi, registered at the hotel's reception desk, put my suitcases in my room, and headed for the square. It was ten o'clock on the evening of June 3, 1989. "There is war!" said a pedicab driver, banging his fists together, as he quoted a fare five times the norm to pedal me from the Palace Hotel to Tiananmen Square. "I could be arrested," he added with a smile when, lacking an alternative for a quick descent on the epicenter of the student movement, I agreed to be gouged and climbed into his vehicle.

As we moved out of Goldfish Lane, which the Palace Hotel dominates, and rolled down Wang Fu Jing, Beijing's leading shopping street, the air was turbulent with shouts and sirens. When the pedicab reached the corner of Wang Fu Jing and Chang An Avenue, where the beige hulk of the Beijing Hotel watches over central Beijing, its various wings capturing in stone the mood of successive epochs since the fall of the last dynasty in 1911, my driver had to stop in the face of a huge, agitated crowd facing west toward Tiananmen. Beside me a sweating young man in a blue tank top tugged at a flagstone by the entrance to the subway tunnel that went under the wide boulevard, until he pried it loose and hurled it with a curse in the direction of an ambulance that had just arrived at the rear of the crowd. "It's not really an ambulance," a woman explained to me. "In it are plainclothes soldiers trying to get beyond the crowd into Tiananmen Square."

"Why is this crowd still so numerous and bold and well-organized?" I asked my pedicab driver. "Because Zhao Ziyang is behind them!" he answered in a conspiratorial tone. I was virtually certain that the Communist party chief had lost all power since the declara-

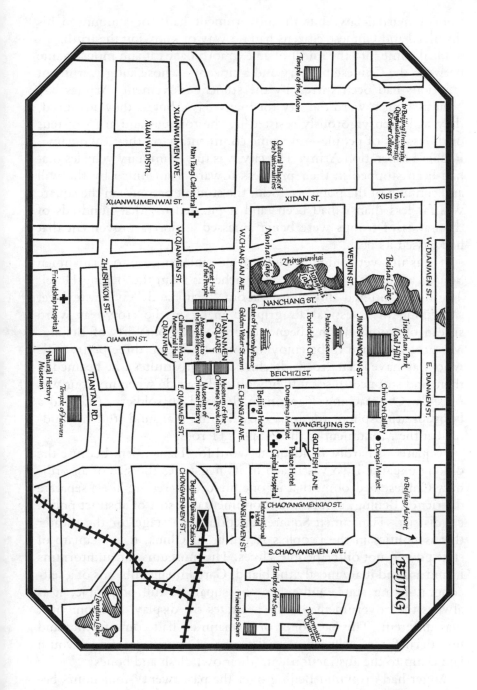

tion of martial law, but the government had not announced his dismissal and Chinese citizens had no way of knowing the truth.

I had come into the midst of an extraordinary cat and mouse game between the Chinese military and a citizenry whose antigovernment emotions had been stirred by the student movement. Armies had been inching toward the city for many days, but as they advanced, they had been vigorously resisted by the tongues and arms of tens of thousands of people—an ironic commentary on their own name, People's Liberation Army. The city was full of military vehicles that had been stopped in their progress toward Tiananmen by the will and cunning of the populace. Still, the student presence in the square was far less than it had been, and it puzzled me that hundreds of thousands of troops were being amassed against a movement that had passed its peak.

It was not yet midnight and still possible to go into Tiananmen Square, and in my pedicab I approached it from the Beijing Hotel. The driver uttered dire words about "war" and "civil war," yet something of a festival air gripped many in the crowd as word spread of troops having been stopped on the outskirts of Beijing. My driver seemed to be enjoying himself. Seeing three pretty girls who may have been "roadside chickens" (prostitutes), he beamed at them and stopped to see if they would like a ride when my tour was finished. On reaching Tiananmen, I found no soldiers at all and a buoyant atmosphere among a crowd milling around students huddled at the Monument to the People's Heroes.

"Square" is hardly an adequate word for Tiananmen, because the oblong expanse is so vast, each of its flagstones the size of an ordinary Chinese bedroom, that its one hundred acres are like a separate district of Beijing, empty and monumental, a sort of abstract political district. Tiananmen Square functions as a stage for the theater that is politics in the People's Republic of China; it is a square of state power, not of the people's lives. The museums and auditoriums in and around it are mostly the bland, Gargantuan emblems of a self-congratulating state, and when the square is full of people, it is always the government that orchestrates the display. Yet tonight it was different. The flagstones of Tiananmen had come to life, and unofficial forces eclipsed official forces as angry, emotional youth laid claim to the abstraction with their own flesh and bones.

Anger had grown in Beijing over the past twenty-four hours because, after days of peaceful argument between soldiers and citizens, on June 2 three people had been killed in a Mitsubishi Jeep "accident" near Muxidi, a few miles west of Tiananmen. The people nearby considered it a deliberate act by the military, and later that day tear gas was used in the streets for the first time in the history of Communist China. Troops surreptitiously advanced toward Tiananmen Square from west and south and east, and by the time I reached Beijing airport word had come from the west that soldiers had broken through a barricade of buses and shot at and killed people at Muxidi bridge.

Through rising coils of smoke I made out the giant portrait of Mao that hung at Tiananmen itself (the Gate of Heavenly Peace), at the northern edge of Tiananmen Square (the Square of the Gate of Heavenly Peace), and as I drew near it, the tall white student-erected statue of the Goddess of Democracy, its surface looking as smooth as marshmallow, loomed from the south. My pedicab whirred between Mao and the goddess, and Mao's pink-yellow face seemed to be suffering in silence as an angry post-Mao citizenry took the revenge of disorder upon him. On display were the symbols of two divergent philosophies of how to order society, a collectivist one and an individualist one.

Tents and placards were the most visible signs of a remnant of some thousands of students still holding the square under hourly increasing pressure. As I moved around on foot or in my pedicab, the student radio, "Voice of Democracy," spoke of democracy and of an unshakeable determination to attain it. "Democracy is something everyone builds gradually on a proper foundation," rebutted the government radio from near the Great Hall of the People. "Tiananmen Square is a sacred place."

Over the decades I had become used to the fact that in China there is always a clear political line, and that any broadcast from a public loudspeaker represents the line. Interviews in a factory, school, or commune would simply cross the t's and dot the i's of the line, and seldom until the 1980s did even a private conversation about politics vary from it. But here in Tiananmen Square, even as late as 11:00 P.M. on June 3, the amazing thing was that citizens were hearing more than one line, were being offered more than one vision of where China should be headed.

My driver said I ought to go back to the Palace Hotel, and I replied with a casual air that I would like first to have a look at the southern tip of the square. As I glided in my pedicab by the cypresses along the southeastern rim of the square, students and workers drew close on their bicycles to chat. "Where are you from?" "What do you think of our movement?" "Please take care of yourself." It was part of the camaraderie of those hours that people shared information with cheerfulness and good humor, and that the foreigner was welcomed with absolute openness.

"Have you heard the one about Li Peng?" said a rakish young man in a straw hat, and I motioned my driver to speed up to the pace of the young man's bike so that I could listen. " 'Premier Li,' says this citizen, 'how come we ordinary folk haven't benefited from all the foreign money that floats around China?' And Li Peng says, 'The people have received things—we've imported tear gas specially for them.' "

Soldiers were jogging into the eastern fringe of the square past the Museum of the Chinese Revolution. "Go home, we don't need you," a young man cried to a row of troops. "We are all Chinese," a girl shouted in an appeal against the use of force. A student whose shock of gleaming black hair fell across his sweating brow drew his bike close beside me. "Hello," he said shyly in English to start a conversation. He was a student at Beijing Normal University and his uncle was in the PLA. He heard my driver urge again that I return to the hotel, but he put before me an alternative. "If you stay awhile," he said earnestly, "you will see large numbers of soldiers arrive, and you will see an attack."

When I reached the center of the square, I got out of my pedicab and walked to the northern steps of the Monument to the People's Heroes. A female student whom I recognized as Chai Ling, the psychology graduate student at Beijing Normal University who was commander-in-chief of the Tiananmen Square operation, rose from the steps to address me. "Please go home now," she said softly but firmly. Chai meant to convey, I think, not that the confrontation in the square was none of my business, but that the danger had become overwhelming, she and her fellows were prepared to die, and others should go while they could. Later, in a videotaped speech shown on Hong Kong TV, Chai Ling would say of the final moments at the Monument to the People's Heroes: "We gave one another a hug, holding each other's hands tightly because we knew the last moment of our lives had finally come."[1] That night the hopeful scenarios had slipped from the realm of the possible and one thin, pale student (he had been a hunger striker) said to me calmly, "We have no alternative." Whether he stayed in Tiananmen Square or left, he knew he faced punishment, I suppose, and the issue of the hour was the acutely personal one of possessing or lacking the courage to face death.

The last voice I heard on "Voice of Democracy" before we pedaled east out of Tiananmen was an anguished young woman's, perhaps Chai Ling's. "This evening people have been killed and wounded," she said, her voice at one moment shrill and the next cracking. "We say to the government, this cruel slaughter will only make us struggle harder for our goals." Strains of student voices singing the "Internationale" wafted across the square's expanse.

Having come directly to Tiananmen, after flights from the United States and Tokyo, and not at first realizing the epoch-making character of the events I was witnessing, I wanted to go back to my hotel room to make some notes and check on the overall situation. My driver sighed with relief as he swung into Wang Fu Jing. "Were the Martin Luther King demonstrations like that?" he asked as we found ourselves in a more normal street setting. "I suppose they were in a way," I said, groping a little for the comparison.

"Did you have as many people in the streets as we saw here tonight?" he inquired.

"About the same," I replied.

He jerked his head sharply sideways to look at me. "You know, mister, we shall overcome too."

I suggested the revolt in Hungary in 1956 might be a better comparison than the American civil rights movement. "But you Chinese are freer than the Hungarians were to deal with the situation," I remarked, "freer to grasp its opportunities, without being interfered with from outside the country."

We passed the Wang Fu Jing department store, once a giant among pygmies in a street of two-storied shops, but now overshadowed by skyscrapers in the neighboring area. "What most strikes me tonight," I said, leaning forward to make my flawed Chinese clear above the street noises, "is that for so many years Chinese have been extremely patient and forgiving of the Communist party, but now suddenly people finally have had enough and found their voices."

"Shh, shh," the driver hissed and pointed a shoulder toward the sidewalk to our right, where twenty or thirty PLA men were standing under a tree. We had almost stopped as we were at the Eastern Market preparing to turn east, and the soldiers, my driver feared, might overhear our subversive talk. I thought these soldiers looked comparatively unferocious as they smoked cigarettes and ignored the foreigner and his pedicab driver.

We turned into Goldfish Lane. "You know, I carried the students for free," the driver said as he pocketed his large fee for our dangerous foray. "Didn't charge them a penny."

"Why?" something made me ask.

"Because they're *doing something,*" he replied. In a society where staying in line indeed had long been the norm, the student movement was like a streak of lightning that illuminated a vast terrain and brought the relief of a thunderstorm (and perhaps also its devastation) to a parched land.

As I went through the revolving doors into the Palace's lobby, troops marched along Goldfish Lane past the hotel. Some, heading east, wore bandages on wounds to the head or arm; others, heading west, looked fresher. The white-and-beige marble interior of the hotel with its pink-and-green carpets seemed unreal, a glossy illusion after the emotion and danger in the humid, dusty streets. As I sat down in my room to scribble notes, I did not seem any longer to be in Beijing, where history was being made a mile away at Tiananmen Square.

Beside my writing table lay a copy of the recently published Chinese edition of *Mao,* and as my eye lit on the book, my mind raced back through the late Mao years as if seeking to anchor itself in a more familiar Chinese reality. I thought with a stab of alarm about Liu Luxin, the book's translator. I wondered if he was involved in the democracy movement, and where he was at that moment. I asked myself what Mao would have made of Deng's dictum, "To get rich is glorious," and whether Mao would have ordered the army into the streets of Beijing in June 1989. I felt he would not have agreed with Deng's elevation of economics over politics, but also that he would not have approved of Deng's solving a political problem by military means.

In the hotel lobby as I headed back toward the streets, a green-uniformed concierge said to me: "If they kill the students, I will attack them myself." A fresh pedicab driver, making good business out of danger, used the same argument as the first to bargain with me, but with extra resonance. "It's war," he said, "war or civil war —I could be *killed.*" I agreed to pay him two hundred yuan for an hour (two months' wages for many people) and the same for each additional hour.

Angrier, now, were the confrontations between the regular troops gathering in the square and the agitated crowds backing up the students' last-ditch struggle from Chang An Avenue and other streets east of the square. On all sides there were shouts, smoke, and cursing of soldiers. Rocks, bottles, and chunks of flagstone were being thrown toward the massed troops. I could not hope to enter the square again.

Soldiers in a variety of vehicles had been streaming into central Beijing from Nanyuan airport to the south, Shahe airbase in the north, and the town of Tongxian in the east. When two public buses full of passengers dressed in identical white shirts reached a point just east of the square on Chang An, students and other citizens began to attack them with sticks and bricks and bottles. "They are not ordinary buses," a man said to me angrily, "those 'passengers' are plainclothes soldiers." One of the buses, ten yards in front of me, was ablaze and inside it pitched battles were being fought between the white-shirted occupants and furious students and citizens. "If they were just bus passengers," a woman cried, "they wouldn't all be dressed the same!"

"Look at the license plate," a voice said. "It says *Shi* [Training] before the numerals. Such a bus isn't allowed to carry passengers." Convinced the bus was a capsule of infiltration, loaded with machine guns and hand grenades to aid a coming assault on the student-held square, the crowd finished the job of subduing its occupants. The bus was now half-burned, most of its windows were shattered, and I could see figures in blood-stained white shirts inside the vehicle. Nearby, an armored personnel carrier that had been intercepted in its progress from the west was ablaze like a bonfire. Yellow light from the flames fell on the jet-black hair and sweating shoulders of a crowd of activists and onlookers.

"Stand on the bicycle seat and you'll get a better shapshot," cried a bystander as I readied my camera. I followed the suggestion— scores of people were already standing on their bike seats to get a better view—and as I photographed the wrecked buses and the armored personnel carrier, I saw smoke puffing irreverently around the Mao portrait, the Goddess of Democracy, and the magnolia bulbs of Tiananmen Square's elegant street lamps.

From the west, a move—or was it just a threat of one?—by the soldiers who now seemed to be installed in Tiananmen Square sent people scurrying. "They're going to shoot," someone called out and all of us flew eastward, bumping into one another as we turned and ran, my pedicab driver maneuvering his vehicle in the new direction as best he could. The flagstones beneath our feet were littered with the debris of street fighting.

T-T-T-T-T-T-T . . . T-T-T-T-T-T . . . T-T-T-T-T-T. For years that sound for me in China meant firecrackers, but tonight it meant gunshots, bleeding bodies, and death. The sounds were close, offensive, terrifying. Deng Xiaoping's soldiers were firing on unarmed crowds in the streets of Beijing for the first time since the revolution in 1949. "Tell the world our government has gone mad," a woman cried to me, tears running down her face.

I looked up at the middle wing of the Beijing Hotel and saw two banners in white Chinese characters on red cloth that seemed to have strayed upon the night from another time and place: UPHOLD THE SOCIALIST WAY and STRUGGLE RESOLUTELY AGAINST BOURGEOIS FREEDOM. On the streets of dozens of China's cities, students loudly backed by millions of Chinese citizens had for six weeks been trying to tell their government, and the world, that the socialist way had run into deep trouble in their country, and that bourgeois freedom was, well, freedom. Now the government was responding, shooting bodies to muffle voices. The disjunction of world views was total. It was one of those moments in history when huge opposite forces shared a stage, looking each other up and down—fleetingly, however, for one force was doomed and the other would soon shrug its shoulders and rewrite history.

For this evening at least, for those of us in the crowd, the Chinese Communists seemed as much out of touch with the Chinese people as Imelda Marcos, with her seventeen hundred pairs of shoes, was out of touch with the Filipino people the week the people of Manila began to push the Marcoses out. The old men of Beijing seemed as eerily out of touch with their epoch as were the Romanovs listening to string quartets in St. Petersburg hours before they were taken prisoner.

That night, despite the horrors, my view of the capacities of Chinese people was enhanced. The courage, humor, practicality, and sense of history of youths whom I talked with intensified my faith in the Chinese ability to fashion a rich destiny for themselves. Yet I also felt that the courage of the crowd was almost suicidal, for Communists when their grip on power is threatened have a strong tendency to behave like Communists, and tanks against a crowd without arms or a leader can hardly lose. I was not surprised at the fact of the repression of the student movement. For years I had felt, as I had written in *The Atlantic Monthly* in July 1983, "China is first

and foremost a repressive regime. The unchanging key to all Beijing's policies is that the nation is ruled by a Leninist dictatorship
that intends to remain such." At seminars at Harvard just the month
before, I had expressed the view that it was virtually certain Deng
would put a stop to the democracy movement in some way or other
and that his fury over the democracy movement's upstaging of the
Russia-China summit and the disruption to Gorbachev's schedule in
Beijing had added to his hostility toward the "liberal" students.
Deng did in Beijing on June 4, after all, only what he had already
done in Tibet three months before. But because Beijing was not
Lhasa, he could not do it as swiftly, directly, and secretly as he had
done in Tibet. Yet with all that said, I did not expect the Chinese
regime to be so desperate as to fire volleys of shots into crowds, and
that night in the streets of Beijing I could hardly believe what I saw
and heard.

A near-festival atmosphere turned into one of terror as fifty meters
ahead of me on Chang An Avenue near Tiananmen gunfire rang out
and people at the front of the crowd fell. We surged back, turned
around, and fled helter-skelter to the east. Where the crowd had
made contact with the troops, to the west, the area of the Gate of
Heavenly Peace had become an area of earthly tumult. At the rear,
rival ambulances tore around, trying to get through the crowd
to pick up the wounded. "Let them through, it's a people's
ambulance," two factory workers shouted to the crowd after
a hurried verbal communication through one ambulance's front
window.

An opposite verdict brought terror upon a second ambulance.
Back doors flapping, most of its windows smashed, this vehicle was
veering crazily along Chang An Avenue as people hit it with sticks,
threw bottles at its remaining windows, and tried to impede it with
their shoulders. Inside the ambulance a white-clad figure crouched
in fear. "It's not a real nurse," a woman said to me. "It's a military
dressed up as a nurse to get into Tiananmen." By now the driver of
the ambulance was desperately trying to retreat from the square
toward the east. More missiles hit the vehicle as cries of fury rent
the air and the "nurse" knelt on the floor, cowering like an animal,
hands covering the head, lips crying out words that could not be
heard.

I went to East Qian Men Street, which runs to the southern edge
of Tiananmen Square, and found it even more crowded than Chang
An Avenue, and the people there even more agitated. Rows of tall

apartment blocks line the broad street, and from each window a bunch of citizens leaned down to watch, many of them wailing or shouting. East Qian Men Street has fewer lights than Chang An Avenue and I felt less conspicuous, more part of the frothing crowd. On the street and sidewalks there were confrontations, gutter-level cursing, the whistle and snap of gunfire, and fury as the crowd realized that students and citizens at the western edge of the throng were dead and wounded. Again I was hardly able to believe that I was in well-ordered China, where submission to authority, however misguided, was supposed to be the norm.

My pedicab driver and I argued back and forth in a cooperative spirit. "If you stop, it's dangerous," he would point out. "You look suspicious. Let's keep moving." Hot, shocked, nervous, I would rejoin, "But I want to *talk* to people!" I would instruct my pedicab driver to take me deeper into the crowd, keeping to the darker edges of East Qian Men, then shots would crackle, cries of horror and alarm would rise from the front of the crowd, and impatiently I would urge him to turn around and flee from the danger, at times grabbing at his waist or tugging at his T-shirt in my eagerness to have him whip us to safety.

Incredulity was a major ingredient in the tumble of emotions that moved around central Beijing like a whirlwind. A worker from a joint-venture company banged his hand against his forehead as he stammered his amazement that soldiers were firing into the early morning crowds. A woman rushed around uttering variations on one sentence: "Our students, our students! What are they doing to our students!" Yet there was also fatalism, which for many people may have eclipsed fear.

Sustained, repeated crackles of gunfire close by made me retreat north along Zheng Yi (Righteousness) Street, past the Public Security building where the Gang of Four had been tried and convicted at the start of the Deng era, and about 4:00 A.M. I reached the entrance to the Beijing Hotel. Some in the huge crowd in front of the hotel were now overwrought, including a woman who sobbed uncontrollably, kneeling on the ground, as she told those around her of having seen people mown down by gunfire minutes before. "Two young people fell dead at my feet," she screamed. Holding her spectacles in her hand and looking upward from the pavement, she begged me: "Please tell the truth about our land!" Foreigners had never in the history of the PRC witnessed Chinese people's emotions so nakedly as they did at the climax and smashing of the democracy movement.

A group of thirty or forty men was trying to overturn the red-and-white metal barrier that stood between the southeastern tip of the hotel yard and the Chang An Avenue sidewalk. "One, two, three—booooommmm." Before their shouts had echoed away the barrier was down, and a crowd surged onto the hotel grounds. I could not discern any motive for this act, but it seemed, like a number of acts that night, to have the flavor of Luddism: anything in sight (and in China most property is owned by the government) was a potential target for an anguished lashing out at a resurgent authority.

At the service desk in the hotel lobby, where staff members were huddled together with faces like frightened rabbits, I asked a young woman for some notepaper. She looked startled, then relief crossed her face as the quotidian nature of the request canceled her anxiety at having to deal with a foreigner while gunshots peppered the night. She gave me a Beijing Hotel Jotting Pad, on which the rest of my notes from that night were written.

I took an elevator to the seventeenth floor, hoping to view Chang An Avenue and Tiananmen Square from on high, but a white-jacketed young man at the service desk would not permit me to look down from one of his balconies. "There's nothing to see," he said in the familiar stonewalling style of a Chinese government employee. It was the first time all night that I had been held back by a hand of authority. I had walked unchecked through customs, broken martial law regulations, watched citizens throw rocks at soldiers, come face to face with Chai Ling at the Monument to the People's Heroes as tanks rumbled to the west—but only now did the habitual restrictiveness of the PRC check my movement.

Picking at random a lower floor, the twelfth, I found a guest room open and peered inside. Four Hong Kong businessmen were on the balcony. They were speaking emotionally in Cantonese; two were almost crying. I crept into the room. So preoccupied was the quartet with the scene below on Chang An Avenue that for two or three minutes I remained unnoticed beside one of the beds near the window.

Beneath us the front entrance of the hotel was barricaded with buses, minibuses, and trucks. Smoke rose from wrecked vehicles and mysterious conflagrations along the avenue, and gunfire rang out from the south. The northern part of Tiananmen—I could not see the central or southern parts of the square—seemed almost emptied of people, but it contained massed soldiers and tanks facing eastward.

"Excuse me," I said finally, "could I watch with you from the balcony for a moment?" One of the Hong Kong businessmen replied, "As long as you're not from the press." In fact none of the four seemed to pay the slightest attention to me, so distraught were they at the latest events in their homeland. One of them burst into English, not, I think, to address me but out of mental turmoil: "It's the last straw! China is finished!"

A military presence, vehicular and on foot, had produced shouting and clashes at the intersection of Chang An Avenue and Zheng Yi Street, and I raised my camera and snapped the turbulent scene. A cry of horror went up on the balcony. "Get out," shouted the Hong Kong businessman who had waved me through the door five minutes before. "I'm sorry, I'm sorry," I mumbled in shame. "But we are so far above the street, who could possibly see or care? Anyway, I'm terribly . . ."

"Just go. *Get out!*" Evidently the Hong Kong businessmen were more wary of PRC authority than I was.

I returned to the streets and since my third and final pedicab driver and I had abandoned each other, I found myself walking ever so slowly north on Wang Fu Jing Street toward the Palace Hotel. Despite the presence of troops, at each street corner citizens clustered to report news on the night's events, quiz each other, and offer the Beijing citizen's ever-ready philosophical analysis. Not for many years had the Chinese people known such a sense of participation in news as it was being made, and the resulting feeling of citizenship did a little to mitigate the tragedy that had engulfed Beijing. People were galvanized because the students had been "doing something," as my first pedicab driver said. The flowering of unofficial China, the emergence of civil society, which had been an achievement of the new forces of the Deng Xiaoping era, had reached its peak, and apparently its end.

A hubbub arose from the entrance to the lane where the green-roofed Capital Hospital stood. Ambulances came and went, exhausted nurses and doctors mopped their brows as they moved along the verandas, and tense crowds pressed toward the hospital gates seeking news of family or friends.

Near the Wang Fu Jing department store, fifty soldiers standing by two trucks stared at me. These dark-skinned, round-faced young men obviously were not from Beijing, and also not northerners. According to martial law, declared two weeks before, it was illegal for me to be in the street so late, and with the memories of the shooting I had seen, I felt an extra furtiveness before the snarling face of Chinese communism. This particular platoon of troops was not snarling, however, but squatting, leaning against trees, and smoking. As soon as I stared at them, they looked away.

Buses, trucks, and other vehicles barricaded the Palace Hotel's doors. At ten o'clock the previous evening, the spacious front court-yard between Goldfish Lane and the hotel's revolving doors had been a path of welcome to Beijing's newest and best hotel. Now its chain of vehicles said "No" to anyone outside with the crispness of the Berlin Wall. "The buses and trucks are blocking the doors for your protection," a flustered assistant hotel manager said when I asked the reason. "The trouble in the streets could overflow in here."

Just before 5:00 A.M. I fell into bed, thirty-odd hours after leaving Boston, and there on the pillow was a chocolate mint and a card from the Palace Hotel management with a quotation from Shake-speare's *Macbeth:* "Sleep that knits up the ravel'd sleave of care, the death of each day's life, balm of hurt minds, great nature's second course . . ."

CHAPTER SIXTEEN

■

SHOCK AND FEAR

A few hours after I went to bed at dawn on June 4, 1989, I awoke to the sound of gunfire coming from several directions and the sight of black smoke rising from parts of the city. Memories of the previous night's amazing events flashed before me and I was torn between staying in the hotel, where some of my Chinese friends could find me, and returning to the scene of the massacre, to which I was powerfully drawn by a half-disbelief in the reality of what I had seen.

I had no way of knowing if the climax had been reached, or if there was more violence, political theater, and secret power struggle still to come. I did feel that the settled order of Beijing that I had taken for granted for many years had over recent weeks hung by a thread, and perhaps still did. Whether or not that was true, it seemed on this stunned Sunday morning that the mask had fallen off the face of Communist China, and that the raw edge of Communist power had revealed itself as it had not done since the civil war against Chiang Kai-shek in the 1940s. "The Chinese Communist party will pay a price for this," I noted in my diary, "and for some time China's status in the world will be lowered."

I made my way through the debris of the streets around the Palace Hotel, my nostrils assaulted by a pervasive smell of burning. Reaching a lane by Capital Hospital, on my way to Tiananmen Square, I came upon knots of people dissecting the night's bloody events in a tumble of emotion and with an openness that still made the foreigner welcome. I stopped by a wrecked minibus that smelled of burned paint to listen to one group. "What about Wang, was he killed?" asked a man in a white shirt with beads of sweat standing out on his forehead.

"Yes," said a tearful woman.

"Have you heard anything about Chen?" a voice inquired from the back of the knot of citizens. No one had. A shocked populace amidst the wreckage of street warfare was asking itself how and when China would recover from this raw confrontation. An older man said that an era was ending, the era of Deng, and that a dynasty had run its course, the dynasty of the Communist party dating from 1949. Another middle-aged man with a sallow complexion and a tiny beard said that China could not but change, yet also that China once again had proved itself incapable of change.

My mind turned to Mao and I felt astonishment—not for the first time—at the durability of the dead leader's ideas. Decades earlier he had said, "Political power grows out of the barrel of a gun,"[1] and in Beijing in 1989, despite the sleek glass towers and the pollution and the trappings of cosmopolitanism, this horrible maxim still obtained. Yet I could hardly believe that China really had changed so little and that acquiescence in such atavism could in 1989 become the order of the day. Was not society more assertive in the face of the state than in Mao's day? Had the military not suffered a loss of status after the setback on the Vietnam border in 1979 and during the money-mindedness of the reform years?

Farther south as the lane approached the hospital, a voice called out "Hullo" in English to invite conversation, and I asked the man, a worker in a steel plant in his thirties, if anyone he knew had died the previous night. "Yes, my fellow worker," he replied as I looked into his drawn face. "He worked right beside me at the bench." An older woman shopkeeper said this was the lowest point in China since the Liberation in 1949, and when I questioned if it really was worse than some of the dark moments of the Cultural Revolution, she fixed me with large sad eyes and said, "In the Cultural Revolution there were no guns and no shooting at Tiananmen Square—just sticks and stones." I flicked my eyes across the strained, sweating faces of the cluster of people and asked what could now be done for the cause of a freer China. An old man in a dark gray shirt and black pants spoke. "We have to wait," he said. "And we have to search."

At the gate of the Capital Hospital, crowds were gathered to await news of injured relatives or friends. I watched the anxious faces for a few moments and then walked past the closed shops of Wang Fu Jing Street to Chang An Avenue near the Beijing Hotel. Burned-out buses sat at diverse angles on a surface dotted with glass and bits of traffic dividers and paving stones. "Yes, he was only seven years old," a man was telling a semicircle of people around him on the sidewalk, "shot to death in front of me." The man demonstrated to his listeners with his spindly hands how a bullet had entered the boy's chest, leaving it hanging open, and how another bullet had blown away his left eye.

The lobby of the Beijing Hotel resembled scenes of a civilization interrupted in the midst of the daily round by the flow of lava from a volcano and caught for posterity in a coating of ash. On the café tables, half-eaten sandwiches, full ashtrays, and dishes of ice cream turned to liquid bespoke the rude intrusions of the night before. Chairs were strewn around or piled high, and the bar and restaurants and shops were dark and silent like morgues. I went up to the seventh-floor restaurant in the old wing of the hotel to view Tiananmen Square. "There will be no lunch," a waitress said with impeccable logic, "because there are no people."

From the restaurant balcony I saw a phalanx of tanks in the square, looking like even-toothed, murky-green dragons, with a row of soldiers sitting in front of them facing eastward along Chang An Avenue. Between Tiananmen Square and the Beijing Hotel, a further fifteen tanks were arrayed on Chang An, a very broad street that now looked even broader without bicycles or cars or pedestrians. A helicopter zoomed down to land near the spot where a dozen hours before the Goddess of Democracy had stood, and two more helicopters descended noisily toward the square from the north. Apart from the row of soldiers in front of the tanks, no human beings were visible farther west than the Museum of the Chinese Revolution, and in Tiananmen Square itself the ardent voices of students had been replaced by the metallic clink of military equipment.

I went downstairs to mingle again with the crowds, and in the hotel lobby I spoke with a thin man in his twenties wearing a black Western suit and an open-necked white shirt. Slumped on a couch in the gloom smoking one cigarette after another, he was a driver for a joint venture between a Chinese unit and a West German company who had taken refuge in the hotel during the night. "The center has gone crazy," he said of the Deng government through the smoke from his Marlboro, readily expressing his views to a stranger. "This is absolutely 'it' for me. I'm going to Australia." Beijing was in shock and normal facades and ingrained restraints for the time being did not apply.

It was about noon on that hot, humid Sunday when I went out the front door of the Beijing Hotel and positioned myself under a scraggy cypress tree on the eastern edge of the hotel's parking lot. The collection of people on Chang An Avenue at a point level with the revolution museum, although far fewer than the night before, still was numerous, and it was less of a student crowd, with fewer women, than the previous night's crowd. I wondered whether they were merely curious, like me, or intent on confronting the PLA.

Suddenly there was a rushing of people in the front part of the crowd and shots rang out, first a loud boom, then after a pause the crackles of smaller arms' fire. I saw people fall in the front rows of the crowd as shouts flew into the air and everyone turned to face east and ran with arms held high around their heads.

Under the next cypress tree two young men also watched the shooting, and as the gunfire died down and the rush of people ceased, the three of us looked at one another. "What can the Chinese people do next?" I asked the pair. One just slowly shook his head. The second looked into my eyes and said: "There's no way you can deal with tanks, but I tell you, these events will never be forgotten."

Near the entrance to the Beijing Hotel, people were talking angrily and sadly in random groups, and the Chinese words for "warlord" and "crazy" recurred. I asked a woman who said she had been in the vanguard of the crowd exactly what had happened a few minutes before. "People shouted insults at the soldiers," she replied, "and some threw rocks at them. The soldiers opened fire and shot at us, first at our feet, and then higher up. Some people were killed."

One teenager cut through the analyses of his elders with an anguished cry: "We have no guns, that's the curse of it. If only the people had guns!" An old man in tears said his grandson had just been killed. "I reckon ten thousand have died," he added, joining in the wild guessing on loss of life that was common among a populace given no hard news by its government or media. A man in a Gallic cap wearing a black armband attached to his white shirt with a safety pin addressed those of us who stood near him. "What sort of army is that?" he said. "We feed them, we pay them, we train them, and they turn and shoot us."

In Chinese characters scrawled in black over the red and white Beijing Hotel fence I found the message, KILL LI PENG, and a little farther on, THE BLOOD DEBT MUST BE PAID. In the street I twice heard the crude epithet (a traditional Chinese curse), "Fuck Deng Xiaoping's mother!" Over many years I had grown used to orchestrated denunciation of fallen Chinese leaders, but only in this brief span of the 1989 crisis did I witness open denunciation of leaders still in office and in power.

A man in his thirties who said he worked in the foreign trade ministry went up to every foreigner he saw and said: "Tell the world the truth about what is happening in China." He said that from his own observation some three hundred people had been killed around 3:00 A.M. the previous night in the vicinity of Tiananmen Square. I could not tell how many people died and even later I doubted the true toll would ever be known. It was partly because of the savage, dispersed, and unexpected nature of the assault, partly because in the streets and alleys emotions ran riot and imagination at times took the place of investigation, and partly because from the very beginning the government (and a few citizens) told lies.

"If you were close enough to count the dead," said a young Beijing University teacher who participated in the democracy movement when we ran into each other some weeks later, "you would have been dead yourself." I did know that hundreds of people at least were killed and maimed, and this was because in the weeks after the violence I heard or overheard bits of information that could only be part of such a large mosaic of bloodshed. On a train between Beijing and Shijiazhuang, a man who worked for the railroad ministry told a companion within my hearing that his girlfriend, a nurse, arrived for work at People's Hospital on June 4 to find "scores of bodies" shot to death. A physical education student who lived with his family in a high rise in Muxidi told me "twenty-odd" died at Muxidi bridge.

In the eastern Beijing neighborhood of a close friend of mine, an old man sitting at the door of his house reading a book was hit by a bullet and killed instantly. "Last night near my house in the Dong Dan area," a barman at the Palace Hotel told me on June 5, "a young man who had just returned from studying in Europe was at a street corner talking about foreign bank accounts of Chinese government leaders. Bullets whizzed through the air and killed him." It was a sign of much loss of life that a number of doctors were killed while rescuing and tending the wounded in the streets.* In addition to the deaths among Beijing people, students and others from outside the capital were killed in the massacre, such as the known fourteen from Jilin University in Changchun in the northeast.[2]

I also realized the death toll would be understated by anyone pronouncing on the matter on the basis of documentary evidence. The young Beijing University teacher told me of a man he knew going to a hospital to claim the body of his son killed west of Tiananmen Square in the early hours of June 4. Hospital authorities said they were required by a new state council rule to have the father sign a paper acknowledging that his son died of natural causes. The father declined to lie and the hospital declined to hand the body over to the family. A friend who worked at Friendship Hospital said the hospital itself decided to destroy many of its records of treatment of the wounded in order to impede the tracking down of participants in the democracy movement. When police came to inspect the files, there was very little under the heading of June 4 and following days, and the verdict offered to outsiders and posterity was that almost no one was treated for gunshot wounds at Friendship Hospital in the aftermath of June 4! A teacher friend told me that one of his students was shot in the stomach near the Great Hall of the People as he crouched in the darkness watching the arrival of soldiers. He was taken to the nearby Red Cross building. His medical care cost several thousand yuan, all paid for by his college, but on the medical papers there was no mention of bullet wounds. "To avoid political trouble," the teacher said to me with a shrug of the shoulders.

As smoke from a night and day of violence curled into the sky on that Sunday afternoon of June 4, I left the area of the Beijing Hotel, torn with emotions and bristling with questions, and went to the

---

* The *Time* magazine book *Massacre in Beijing* (New York: Warner, 1989) said at least nine doctors died "in and around Tiananmen Square" (p. 55). A doctor rushed up to Li Lu and said of the army men, "They are thousands of times worse than the Fascists. They are even killing doctors" (Li Lu, *Moving the Mountain*, London: Macmillan, 1990, p. 196). A later Chinese government statement said, "Doctors and other people who were carrying out various duties on the spot" were killed (Chen Xitong's speech to the Standing Committee of the National People's Congress, June 30, 1989, in Yi Mu and Mark V. Thompson, *Crisis at Tiananmen*, San Francisco: China Books, 1989, pp. 194ff.).

Catholic cathedral, Nan Tang, southwest of Tiananmen Square. Mass was over, there were few people in and around the sanctuary, and the cathedral compound was a welcome place of retreat from the soldier-studded streets. I found a youth sitting in meditation within the gray stone walls of the compound and drifted into conversation with him. Zhu Yasheng was a sixteen-year-old middle school student who had been involved in the protests. At one rally he had marched with other Christians behind a banner that read, THE LORD LOVES YOU, LONG LIVE DEMOCRACY. Zhu's father was a master chef for senior government leaders, his mother worked in the Communist party secretariat of Beijing City, and no one else in the family —only Yasheng—was a Catholic. "Buddhism enjoys a certain security," he said to me. "Why are the Communists so hostile to Christianity?" I asked Zhu why he had become a Catholic. He smiled a little at the question, a smile that suggested both innocence and passion, and replied, "Because in China there is nothing you can believe in." I gave Zhu my number at the Palace Hotel and invited him to call me.

From Wang Fu Jing Street, as I walked back to the hotel in midafternoon, I heard the sounds of renewed shooting from the direction of Tiananmen Square. "In 1949 Beijing was taken without a shot," I wrote in my diary, "and only now after forty years do shots have to be fired at people in the streets. Who is the people and who is the enemy?" I went on. "Deng Xiaoping in his critique of Mao a decade ago said Mao confused the two—a pretty basic error, I felt at the time. Now Deng himself is doing the same thing."

That afternoon, June 4, the last uncensored piece of reporting came from Radio Beijing as the English-language service said, "Thousands of people . . . were killed by fully armed soldiers when they forced their way into Beijing. Among the dead are our colleagues at Radio Beijing." At the end of the account of the night's violence, the newsreader said, "Because of the abnormal situation here in Beijing, there is no other news we can bring you." Then Beethoven's Fifth Symphony was played, and that was just about the end of Beijing's brief season of relative press freedom. The June 4 issue of *People's Daily* contained some final bitter gestures of rebellion by the staff. A trivial story about a problem of pesticides in a village carried the sensational headline, HOW LONG CAN THE MASSES BE CHEATED?; another on a handicapped person winning a sports medal was presented under the florid headline, THE PEOPLE'S HEARTS WILL NEVER BE CONQUERED.[3]

On the evening of June 4 I decided to venture out of the Palace Hotel, despite advice on all sides not to do so, and hired a man and wife team who, in the absence of regular taxis, were moonlighting with a vehicle from their factory unit. Under an overcast sky the van crawled along streets littered with stones, broken bottles, shell casings, bits of building materials that had been hauled into use for combat, and twisted traffic barriers and railings that had served as barricades. We passed burned-out buses and several military trucks with hoods open and parts of the engine missing, so I learned of one more method people had used to prevent many PLA from advancing to Tiananmen Square.

I stopped at the Kunlun Hotel to go swimming with Yuan Wei-gong, the young computer specialist who worked for a European company, and who lived nearby in this eastern part of the city. "Beijing does not need these peasant soldiers," Yuan said with a gesture of disgust toward the military in the street outside the hotel. "Beijing people know what real life should be. Don't the soldiers understand we do very well without them?"

Few staff members were at work at the Kunlun Hotel sports club as they had not been able to get transport through the devastated streets of central Beijing, and those who were on duty spent most of their time on the telephone trading news of the massacre. One life-guard at the swimming pool received a phone call from a friend in the military and relayed the gist of the alleged report to Yuan: some dead bodies, and several not quite dead, had been burned right in Tiananmen Square by the PLA in the early hours of Sunday morning. "I wonder," I said to Yuan, "if Deng Xiaoping went through Beijing hospitals this evening and saw the results of last night, would he regret the decision to shoot?"

"If he went to the hospitals," Yuan replied, "he would not get past the door, he'd be killed—stabbed, stoned." My friend had never struck me as being very interested in politics, and his vehemence against Deng took me aback. "He's a serpent," Yuan went on. "We warmed him at our chest in 1979 [a reference to public support for Deng's climb to power over the top of the sinking Hua Guofeng], and now he bites us."

In Yuan's neighborhood there was despair. "The men are all half-drunk on local liquor," he said. "And tempers are short." One of the few incidents to have amused Yuan over previous days had been the spectacle of "hicks" of the PLA, not knowing one side of Beijing from the other and, asking directions on June 2 and 3, being directed by gleeful citizens, not to Tiananmen Square but to a variety of other unwanted destinations. The spectacle reflected faults in the PLA assault on Tiananmen that were due to poor coordination, shaky military morale, and perhaps political hesitation.

Yuan said his European boss had decided to close the office until further notice and no one knew when normal commerce would resume in Beijing. The thirty-year-old regarded the previous night's assault as the worst event of his life. He and many of his friends wished to leave Beijing for the homes of friends or relatives in other parts of China. "My mother doesn't want me to go," he said, "though my wife agrees. My mother says 10 million are staying, so why should I not also stay."

Yuan and I kept in touch over ensuing weeks. "We can still talk," he said a week later, "but only in a swimming pool." In the water and the locker rooms of various sports facilities we found an oasis of anonymity. Yuan, an unabashed cosmopolitan with an interest in technical knowledge that knew no cultural boundaries, told me an acquaintance of his attended a briefing at which hardline Politburo member Yao Yilin said: "If the crisis drives the Americans away and we lose their trade and technology, it doesn't matter. We'll turn to the Soviet Union." Sneered computer specialist Yuan: "And what would we get from them—potatoes, I suppose!"

"Everyone says now the smart thing is to tape your mouth," Yuan said one day. "When people meet they avoid 'this topic.' No one likes the matter, so it's better to keep quiet about it." Nearly everyone felt they should "get into line" (yao pai dui). Yuan decided not to leave Beijing, but only because his chosen place of retreat, in Jiangsu Province, would have routed his train trip through Shanghai and other cities where railroad disruptions were at that time frequent.

Just past midnight on June 5, a group of battered, dirty foreigners came through the revolving doors of the Palace Hotel. There were three Swiss travelers, an American music student, a journalist from the Italian newspaper Espresso, the thirteen-year-old son of the Pakistan air attaché in Beijing, and a few others. Together with a CBS reporter and cameraman, they had all been nabbed by the army in the western part of Tiananmen Square toward dawn on June 4 and held for eighteen hours in the middle school within the Workers Cultural Park just north of the square.

"We had broken the rules of martial law," said the music student, Valerie Samson, as I ordered coffee for her and the three Swiss, "by taking photos in the central part of Beijing. In captivity we were not allowed to make any phone calls, because only if you are arrested can you do that, and we had been not arrested but 'detained.' " Explaining martial law to Samson, a PLA man said to her, "Do you realize China is an independent nation with its own laws, and that you are in China?"

Some of the tired, stunned foreigners who sank into the green-upholstered chairs of the Palace Hotel lobby had been beaten, including the Italian journalist, Frederico Bogno, who was cut about the face. While in detention the group saw heavy brutality toward young Chinese detainees. "Two Chinese boys were lying in a truck," Bogno told me. "They had already been beaten, and soldiers began to beat them again with rods and sticks, though they were lying down." In the middle school, PLA men cried, "Kill them! Kill them!" as they beat Chinese youths, whose hands were tied behind their backs. "They relished beating the Chinese," Valerie Samson said, "spurring each other on." As for the foreigners, she went on, the soldiers would peer into their room and swear at them, calling them *huai dan* ("bad eggs"), but mostly not touching them.

"The soldiers said we were safer in custody than we would be out on the streets," Bogno recounted with a wan smile. "They did not think we would make it to the Palace Hotel." The Pakistani air attaché arrived to collect his son. "Your mother is worried," he said to the boy brusquely, and the boy looked as if he was going to cry.

For a few days after June 4 there was no public transport, postal service, garbage collection, or domestic flights. Beijing essentially turned aside from usual pursuits and became a vast seminar of post-mortem on the military crackdown. All the while not a single word on any subject was spoken to the people by any Politburo member. It was common at the time to take the nonappearance of the Chinese leaders as a sign of weak or even nonexistent government, but this was not my view. "Guns are a government," I noted in my diary.

The Chinese staff of the Palace Hotel, like people in the street, remained open to frank conversation with a foreigner. On the afternoon of June 6, I was sitting in the lobby with a cup of tea as a tour group called China Experience readied itself for a departure to the airport. The travelers were ashen-faced, yet some permitted themselves a small smile at the imminent prospect of putting their "China experience" behind them. Suddenly a commotion began outside the hotel entrance and people from the street ran toward the glass re-volving doors. Chasing them from behind were army men in plain white shirts—a familiar sight in the streets—and stopping them at the hotel doors were cursing Palace Hotel staff members in their handsome green uniforms and caps. The citizens did not gain admit-tance to the hotel and I did not see what became of them.

When calm returned, the China Experience tour group, even more ashen-faced than before, boarded their bus and left for the airport. A hotel staff member whom I had talked with several times previously said as he cleaned dirt off his white glove: "I wish Amer-ica would come in with guns and knock down this government." A bellboy swore at the army men, sighed, and said: "The people have no guns, but I think people will resist in the alleys even without guns. They will sabotage the army when no one is watching."

On June 6 in the lobby of the Palace Hotel, a Canadian TV jour-nalist asked a German hotel manager if any more tourists were arriv-ing in Beijing. The reply was itself like the bark of a rifle. "Tourists are leaving!" the German snapped. With shots being fired into the windows of apartments in the diplomatic compound at Jianguomen-wai; foreign reporters being roughed up, detained, and expelled; and persistent rumors of imminent civil war, even resident foreigners were leaving Beijing by the minute. Several Western nations and Japan arranged evacuation flights and urged all their nationals to depart. American ambassador James Lilley, a steady man in no way inclined to anti-China sentiment, was on the phone to Washington demanding a decision on the spot to evacuate the American women and children whose lives seemed to be at risk. Had Americans been killed—and it was a miracle no one died in the Jianguomenwai shooting—he might well have been criticized for not arranging an evacuation plane sooner.

On the evening of June 6 I went up to the roof of the hotel to stroll in the open air—not being permitted to go into the streets—and there I ran into three middle-aged cleaning ladies in their beige uniforms and white caps. When I smiled and said hello, they began to talk with agitation. "The government is trying to trick the peo-ple," exclaimed one round-faced lady. "The TV tonight said only twenty-three students were killed, but that's wrong." Another chimed in as she leaned on her broom: "We saw scores of bodies at Xiehe Hospital!" It was astonishing by the standards of China over the years to hear cleaning ladies denounce their government to a foreigner they had met two minutes before. A third lady inquired sadly: "Will all you foreigners now go home? Do you think our Palace Hotel is finished?"

In the streets there still were subtle signs of resistance, such as the black and yellow paper strips on bus windscreens with the characters *Wei min tong che* ("Run buses for the people"). It was an unexceptionable sentiment except for the explosive fact that the character for people was not *ren min*, the Communist term, but simply *min*, the traditional Chinese word for people that carries nothing of the Communist sense of "the people" serving as passive ideological scenery for a dictatorial regime. Bus drivers were telling the government they still possessed a mind and will of their own. In the alleys, posters could be found on the theme of a people disgusted with the ill deeds of tyrants. One young bank clerk who lived in Xuan Wu District copied out for me a long poem put up on a wall near his home. It spoke of Deng and President Yang Shangkun "eating the people's production, and filling their own kitchens." It said of Premier Li Peng that he "only bowed to old Deng, making himself Deng's gun." The young man thrust it into my hand with the remark, "I could be killed for giving you this."

Leading figures of the student movement and their advisers from university faculties, research institutes, and government organs were paralyzed by sadness and fear, in hiding, or on their way out of the country. The chief aide to Zhao Ziyang, Bao Tong, was imprisoned and the various think tanks that Zhao had encouraged were decimated by arrests, closings, seizing of materials, and intimidation. Truckloads of armed police and soldiers raided the offices of SERI, the civic culture group of Chen Ziming and Wang Juntao, seizing the fruits of years of work, and soon most of the SERI leaders, who ironically had urged moderation and gradualism upon the student movement, were arrested as "counterrevolutionaries."★

Broadcasts said that all leaders of student and worker organizations now declared illegal must report to the police about their "crimes," and that those who came forward quickly would receive

---

★ The ironic contradictions of the collapsed reform era were caught in an exchange between Gao Xin, a student leader who was arrested after the crackdown, and one of his prison mates. "Are you in the [Communist] party?" Gao asked.
   "Yes."
   "What are you in prison for?"
   "For committing corruption [*guan dao*]. And what are you here for?"
   Gao Xin replied, "I'm in for opposing corruption" (Gao Xin's talk at Harvard University, April 16, 1991).

"lesser punishment." A special phone number to call in with reports of people having committed "counterrevolutionary acts" ran hot as many sought to save their own skins by pointing a finger at others. Words and phrases that had been rare over recent years, such as comrade, dictatorship of the proletariat, and serve the people, returned like cockroaches from a dark corner, as people out of fear fell into line with a new "truth."

Outside Beijing it took longer for the new truth to smother contrary voices, and in Shanghai, Hangzhou, and many other cities news of the Beijing massacre produced intensified demonstrations. At a Democracy Forum wall that was a feature of the movement in the northeastern city of Shenyang, a notice went up after June 4 that said, "Five million Shenyang citizens say 'Down with those bastards on the central committee!'" and on June 6 a huge rally gathered in Shenyang's main square. In Shanghai, Mayor Zhu Rongji discussed the crackdown for a full two weeks without ever using the term "counterrevolution" (he first used it on June 18), and in Chongqing my old friend Xiao Yang, the party chief, tellingly chose to depoliticize the trouble by calling it "purposeless commotion" (luan dong) rather than "turmoil" (dong luan). The Shanghai mayor closed the books on June 4 with a Delphic statement: "Things that occurred in Beijing are history. No one can conceal history. The truth will eventually come to light."[4] Wang Dan, Shen Tong, Wuer Kaixi, and other student leaders could have summed up the massacre in the same words.

Still, by late June the entire nation fell in behind Beijing's chosen course, and provincial leaders, however reluctantly, stood on their heads and meted out harsh punishments to students and others they had so recently praised as patriotic. In Hangzhou, a student who had telephoned the Voice of America to say the authorities had lowered the Chinese flag to half-mast after June 4 in response to student demands (in fact another student had climbed onto the roof of the building and moved the flag) was sentenced to nine years in prison for counterrevolutionary propaganda and sedition. Like Beijing, the provinces punished worker activists more harshly than student activists.

Some Western media spoke of former participants in the democracy movement "disappearing," as if that meant arrest, but the reality was more complex. In Chinese society there are many ways of being intimidated short of arrest, and many ways of disguising noncooperation in a packaging that is politically acceptable. One friend of mine "disappeared" from his neighborhood out of prudence and stayed with a classmate in a different part of Beijing. Another told her office she was ill and retreated to an aunt's house south of the city. A third vanished from his room at People's University and went back to his home village in Shandong. All three turned up later safe and sound.

The crisis and its aftermath were full of Chineseness, as family networks proved important in protecting, or incriminating, the individual, and as the government, like the emperors of old, treated politics as theater and the citizens as props for the dramas of the court. The army in late May and early June used entrapment techniques and delaying tactics that were straight from the pages of *The Art of War* by Sun Zi, who wrote, "When capable, feign incapacity."[5] Zhao Ziyang "waved the red flag to oppose the red flag" in "praising" Deng to Gorbachev as a way of blaming him for an untenable situation. "My cousin, who is a policeman, isn't going to work," a student friend told me a few days after the massacre. "His pretext is that he has to take care of his hospitalized aunt." In China it was an ironclad excuse because it appealed to family values. When a young researcher tried to explain to me the fatalism that resettled upon Beijing by the end of June, he remarked: "We really do never forget that we are Chinese!"

Before Beijing folk began to say the opposite of what they believed, there was a brief transition period when many of them declined to talk but candidly stated why. At a construction site in the north of the city—the sounds of the hammers startled me as I momentarily thought they were gunfire—I chatted with three workers about daily matters, but when I asked their opinion of the student democracy movement, a short, cheerful character in blue overalls said: "On that, it's not good to talk—there are guns around."

A curfew was announced for our East District of the capital and we were supposed not to go out of the hotel after 9:00 P.M. Many streets were deserted after dark, and I felt the soul had gone out of the city of Beijing. Loudspeakers late at night declared, "You should not be on the streets," and told people to "leave or accept the consequences." One night Peter Meade of WBZ radio station in Boston phoned to interview me, and his first question was about the situation in Tibet, but I could not even go as far as Tiananmen Square, let alone to Lhasa.

I began to see the Palace Hotel as a symbol of the strains and contradictions of the reform era of Deng. The twelve-story structure in beige and cranberry tile, its green eaves curved upward in semi-Chinese style, was a joint venture between the Chinese army and a Japanese-Filipino company, and each day the foreign managers would sit down with PLA officers for a meeting; military officers of a Leninist state face to face with business executives from free-market economies. With great fanfare the hotel had opened just two months before the crisis. Now the flow of tourists and businessmen to China stopped; not for the first time, Beijing had cut off with the left hand of politics what it had cultivated with the right hand of economics. The Palace with its 578 rooms became a tomb within a week of June 4, and at the daily management meeting arguments took place between the PLA and the foreigners on the problem of hotel staff members (vastly outnumbering the guests) being "contaminated" by watching Cable News Network programs on TV as they went about their duties in the rooms. Fresh from insisting at the meetings that the corrupting Western influence of CNN be cut off—which it was for a time—the fat PLA officers in plain clothes would come to the lobby restaurant and gorge themselves free of charge on roast beef and apple pie à la mode.

In the first week of June I saw that anger was a powerful force, and in the second week of June I learned that fear was even more powerful. Deng finally appeared on TV on June 9, to bestow his congratulations on the military commanders who had crushed the "counterrevolution," and the occasion was a watershed, signaling intensified repression. The televised scene in the Huairentang Hall at Zhongnanhai recalled the parlor of a nursing home as Deng's old comrades gathered around him. His hands trembled, his voice faltered, and Li Peng prompted him with words and phrases when his mouth opened but speech failed him. "The storm was bound to happen," Deng croaked to the army men in remarks that blended militarism with nationalism. "For it to occur now is an advantage for us—while we still have a large group of old comrades who are living and healthy."

Deng spoke of the student demonstrators as if they were the Japanese or Nationalist enemy that he and Mao had fought against in military campaigns of the 1930s and 1940s. "Never forget how cruel our enemies are," he told the commanders. "We should have not an iota of forgiveness toward them." Deng showed himself extraordinarily nervous about the strength of his cherished socialist system in the face of a "handful" of bad people instigating the masses. He almost gave the impression that the Communist party doubted its own legitimacy—like a man who has taken his wife from another man and must watch out that the same thing does not also happen to him. Deng's lame instruction for the future was to intensify propaganda work.[6]

"I find China in a most Sinocentric mood," I wrote in my diary the evening of Deng's speech. "Mao was Sinocentric, but he never sounded like the head of a fearful military junta, as Deng now does. Mao spoke of history's direction, of the world's future; Deng talks like a police chief."

The government radio announced that gatherings at street corners were forbidden, and that anyone hearing of others spreading rumors must report such persons to the police. The Palace Hotel dutifully put on the garments of political rectitude. PROTECT THE LARGE PICTURE, said a banner draped down one side of the front entrance; PROTECT STABILITY, said its twin on the other side. Day by day, tongues that had been loose ceased to move, the phone rang less, people found it safer to talk little with each other, and Beijing became a city of silence.

The mood in the streets, which before the June 4 violence had been buoyant, candid, and warm toward the foreigner, now was sullen and there was not only a fear of contact with the foreigner but a Chinese fear of Chinese. The morning after Deng's speech, I was riding in a pedicab near Chongwenmen and found myself moving parallel to a young man in a green jacket on a bicycle. He was a twenty-seven-year-old worker in a clothing factory on his way home after night shift. I asked what he thought of the condition of China. "Not clear about that," he mumbled, and when he asked my opinion I gave the same handy, evasive response. Then the clothing factory worker, a plastic bag clutched in one hand as he wove through the traffic, indicated with sign language that he was concerned about my pedicab driver overhearing our conversation. I rashly remarked that the driver was a good friend of mine, and then the worker said earnestly, "China is without hope. Like many workers, I supported the student democracy movement, but now there is just nothing." I observed that many foreigners had left Beijing and the young man said with a bitter laugh, "Of course they would leave!" Then he hissed me to silence; our two vehicles were drawing near a large Public Security building, which was heavily guarded by soldiers. The worker said no more and his bicycle quickly slipped back to the rear of my pedicab. I turned around to look at him and saw that his face had gone pale.

Rumors flew, for the good reason that people were kept in the dark about many important matters by the government, and when the government did speak, few believed it. To exchange rumors was also a way of keeping alive some ray of hope; a "reality" could be invented that was an improvement on observed reality. "Li Peng has been shot . . ." "Deng has died of prostate cancer . . ." "The PLA is mounting a coup against Li Peng . . ." There even was talk that the Guomintang was on the way from Taiwan to retake the Mainland, which prompted me to reflect in a June 7 note to Ted Koppel of the ABC *Nightline* TV program, which I was assisting on a special devoted to the China crisis, "If the Chiang Kai-shek Nationalists were to come to Beijing this week, they would be thought of as liberators."

One night on the TV news a law professor from People's University jumped around the screen in his eagerness to spin the line that a "handful of hooligans" had caused the crisis. But the next moment the news program blamed the outside world for the crisis, offering film from secret cameras that purported to show "Taiwan Guomintang" agents among the demonstrators at a May rally. All credibility departed from the news programs as words were cut out of midsentence from interviews with people in the streets who were presented as supporting the "hooligans" theory of the crisis.

The most gruesome pictures I had seen on television anywhere were shown of two soldiers who had been attacked and killed by furious crowds. One of them, Liu Guogeng, had been surrounded in his Jeep by a mob that managed to overturn the vehicle. Liu thereupon shot and killed four of the crowd (Chinese TV omitted this part). Others in the crowd then grabbed Liu, stripped him, disemboweled him, and hung his dripping corpse from the top of a bus. The spectacle of the maimed corpse, including the remains of Liu's genitals, was shown repeatedly on Chinese evening TV.

"Everything is back to normal," purred an official spokesman, yet my acquaintances in the government did not answer their phones, I had to pass by troops with fixed bayonets in order to keep appointments at offices and institutes, my car was often stopped at night and searched by soldiers, and my close Chinese friends were leaving Beijing one by one. "How can the world believe the Li Peng government line?" I noted in my diary. "China itself does not believe it." Meanwhile, the government took pains to invite tourists and foreign businessmen to resume their activities in a newly stabilized China.

There were times when I felt I was back in the Australian army, a world where (as in all armies) guns and morality and team spirit were supposed to go neatly together. The soldiers became not only the emblems of order but the moral center of gravity of Chinese society. They were back at tasks both heroic and mundane, from praising Deng and defending socialism to darning their own socks and giving therapeutic massage to elderly citizens. Ministers laid wreaths to honor dead PLA, scurried to hospitals to visit wounded soldiers, and each day thanked the PLA for saving Beijing from "counterrevolution." Meanwhile PLA spokesmen tersely appealed to the people of Beijing to return all weapons seized from soldiers and military trucks "within forty-eight hours."

During breakfast at the Palace Hotel the music of Wagner was introduced, providing an apt feeling of swirling clouds, turbulent emotions, and hidden dark forces. "The regime looks and acts like a frightened Central American junta," I wrote in my diary. "How will they get out from under all this? It won't only be a case of explaining Tiananmen Square. There are now tremendous complications from the fact that the military has become the political heart of the nation. The worst scenario I can see," I went on, "would be a militarized China with conflicts developing between regions and factions, adjudicated by the gun. The best scenario I can see is a period of leftist stagnation."

Beijing had seen three epochs within the span of three weeks: a festival of Jeffersonian freedom in late May; guns and Molotov cocktails and bleeding bodies and the wail of ambulance sirens on June 3 and the following days; an Orwellian repression in mid-June as silence marked the victory of power over truth. From the authoritarianism of the Deng era, China seemed to be back at the totalitarianism of the Mao era. The awesome power of the state was matched by an official ideology that reached into every corner of life.

In those June days, as I listened on Chinese radio and TV to talk of "class struggle" and "monopoly capitalism" and watched new slogans go up on red and white cloth strips on the streets, I had an eerie feeling I was living in the Mao era, or even earlier when the last dynasty still stood and the rulers of China thought they were the center of the world, caring little for the thoughts and deeds of non-Chinese unless they should inconvenience the Middle Kingdom. One evening Mauritania was at the top of the news because its leader had announced "unswerving" support for China's foreign and do-

mestic policies. Like the Middle Kingdom of old, Beijing, in ritu-
alistic dealings with tiny states or selected "distinguished guests" of
no weight in their own country, paraded them and caressed their
feathers as if they represented the full panoply of world opinion.

The torrent of lies from the government in the name of opposition
to "counterrevolution" made Marxist rhetoric even more bankrupt
than I had found it to be at the height of the Deng era. "To say the
shooting was the Beijing citizens' fault as the government does," I
noted in my diary, "is like saying a conflagration is the fault of the
house being burned." So it was that the problem of a vacuum of
values in Chinese society became even more intense than it had been
before June 4.

Literary magazine editor Liu Xiaoyan, daughter of the prominent
dissident journalist Liu Binyan, came to the Palace Hotel to see me
and said, "No one is talking, phoning, or exchanging information."
Her father's name had twice been mentioned on the radio in recent
days and she was expecting trouble. "Not just yet," she said calmly,
"but after some weeks." As in the Maoist days, authorities at the
front door of the hotel required each visitor to fill out a form about
the purpose of the visit. Xiaoyan's eyes flashed with irony and a
bemused expression crept across her mouth as she smoothed the
flimsy piece of paper on the table in front of us for me to sign,
reporting to the police not only her own name, but also the name of
the person she had come to visit.

The classic modes of a totalitarian state trying to shore up its
legitimacy were evident each day: "enemies" were everywhere, the
government bristled with righteous indignation at them, and an
appropriate "truth" to explain the government's crusade to rout
them was created by the hour. What amazed many in Beijing during
those weeks was the absurd contradiction at the heart of the newly
manufactured truth. "A handful of hooligans" was said to have
caused the entire crisis, yet a huge military force enveloped Beijing;
never had so much been needed to quell so little.

In an atavistic lunge, the Communist leaders had picked up the
old formula of the Chinese realm as a *jia,* a household, which was
hierarchic and paternalistic, and which lived according to one strict
set of values. The terrifying thing was the power the formula had to
enlist the passive support of so many members of the *jia.* Not only
did the government rewrite history after the shots had died down,
but many of the Chinese people, like children echoing their parents,

cooperated in the rewriting, whether out of the habit of conformism, or to protect themselves, others, or the future.

In dynastic China the Mandarins were sometimes known as "father and mother officials" *(fu mu guan),* and this same concept was carried incongruously into the modern era by the Communist party. Meanwhile a whole generation of Chinese youth had mounted through the 1980s a cry for individualism, asking to be treated not paternalistically but as human beings with rights of their own. Now in mid-1989 the Communist leaders offered youth the mere incantation, "We cherish you," and the gesture was not so much a lie as irrelevant—like the head of the *jia* saying, "I love you, son," while also conveying to the son the message that the parent knows what is good for him better than the son knows himself, and will beat him up if the son does not obey. It was all as if the social awakening of the reform era had never taken place.

The Communist Youth League, which in mid-May had urged Li Peng to mount a dialogue with the student movement, now cried out its support for martial law and congratulated the soldiers upon their entry into Beijing. The All-China Federation of Women, which had also smiled upon the movement, called on women all over China to "support and cherish and love" the PLA that had crushed it. China's two living marshals, who had asked Deng not to bring troops into Beijing, now wrote letters of congratulation and support to those troops. "If the ordinary people of Beijing could show such courage in confronting the PLA," I wrote sadly in my diary, "might one not expect that the vast army of white-collar government servants would express their true feelings to their bosses —and that the journalists would refuse to write lies?"

The threat of the vague came back in all its maddening power. Just what was a "counterrevolutionary" in the China of 1989, forty years after the revolution? I recalled with a wry smile to myself how in the spring of 1976 when Deng was labeled by the Chinese government a "counterrevolutionary," Chinese diplomats in Washington angrily said that if I did not understand this, I knew nothing of China. "Small businessmen who are exploitative will be restrained," the government said in mid-June, "those who are not will be free to continue." But how was the distinction to be drawn and who was to draw it? So much in China was illegal that if a person read the fine print of the rules—and remembered past experience—he might hardly dare to venture outside his own door. It all boiled down to the Communist party's persecution mania approach to the sacred task of maintaining its own monopoly on political power. As the old quip ran in definition of what was permissible: "You may say what you please, as long as you please the Communist party."

CHAPTER SEVENTEEN

■

FRIENDS LOSE
HOPE

FOR all the disappointment and fearfulness in the wake of June 4, I experienced in the following weeks an unprecedented sharing with Chinese I knew well. Helping a student search for a missing friend, I could feel her loss and anxiety. Walking in the street with a teacher who stiffened when he noticed we were being followed, I gained an extra sense of the intrusion of the state into private life. Together we sadly watched intimidation, dismissal, arrest, execution, the pruning back of foreign influences, and a clampdown on the life of the mind. Between June 4 and the beginning of August, tens of thousands of people who were involved in the democracy movement across China were put in prison.[1] My Chinese friends' dismay, fear, and dashed hopes pulled me from the grooves of my role as a "China watcher" and put me beside them as I had never felt myself to be before.

"None of my friends has cried in my presence," I noted in my diary, "and that is part of what terrifies me." In the streets on June 3 and June 4 I had seen tears, and on TV in the aftermath of the massacre people cried for dead or wounded soldiers like professional mourners who had rehearsed for weeks. But the Chinese I knew well had internalized their grief and sadness and anger; bent upon analyzing their situation, taking steps to cope, and planning for the future, they never embarrassed me by wringing their hands in fury or despair.

On June 5 there was a knock on my door at the Palace Hotel and there stood Ma Qingguo, the graduate student in psychology at Nankai University in Tianjin who had been a leader in the student movement. He looked exhausted and his clothes were dirty and rumpled, but I was relieved to see him in one piece. On May 22 he had left Tiananmen Square and returned to Tianjin, and only that morning had he come to Beijing. "I could not buy a train ticket," he related. "I still had my black armband on and they refused to sell me a ticket. I walked down the track and got on the train anyway." He paused, and then said quietly, "None of us thought the troops would shoot and kill as they did."

I could see a deep tiredness in Ma's eyes behind his spectacles and for a moment he slumped silent in his chair. "I don't know if my cousin is safe," he said softly. "He is more excitable than me. I'm going off to see if I can find him." Over the next weeks Ma came often to talk with me and by mid-June plainclothes police hovering in the hotel lobby stopped him each time. "Why are you here again?" they would ask in an effort to intimidate him that did not succeed.

Ma Qingguo's experiences in Tianjin revealed the shape of the repression that descended upon China. As soon as he had boarded the train from Beijing a few weeks before, he was drawn aside by six police and three plainclothesmen. Why had he come to Beijing, they wished to know, and what had he done there? Ma said he had come to Beijing to see his sick cousin. Had he not taken part in the student demonstrations? "Several times, yes, in Tianjin, not in Beijing," Ma lied to the police, who thereupon searched his bag and found notes and photos of the student movement both in Beijing and Tianjin.

Ma explained to the police that it was his habit to take notes on current events, as he was a student of social science. "This is not a good thing to do," the police advised. In Ma's notebook the police found slogans copied down from the spring demonstrations in Tiananmen Square that aroused their ire; from the book (which they later confiscated anyway) they angrily tore out pages that bore the slogans, WHAT SHOULD THE NEWSPAPERS TELL THE PEOPLE? and WHERE IS THE CHINESE LECH WALESA?

"Where did you find these statements?" the police asked Ma. "On the wall of the number three dining hall in Nankai University," he replied impassively. Ten minutes before the train arrived at Tianjin, the police allowed the graduate student to return to his seat—minus his records of the democracy movement.

At Nankai University Ma visited seven professors and all but one of them talked candidly about the student movement, but on the train back to Beijing notes from these conversations were also confiscated. No reason was given other than to say again, "It is not good to keep notes like this." I asked Ma if he had protested the searches and the taking away of his notes. "I didn't protest because it is useless to do so," he replied. Ma could have fared much worse; and the notes and photos, had he retained them, might well have gotten him into serious trouble later.

By the end of June, Ma Qingguo was a person matured and emboldened by the three-month experience of the rise and fall of the democracy movement. When a close friend of his in Tianjin was arrested, Ma came to feel that his own fate might be the same as his friend's. "This made me less scared in a way," he told me. "I just feel a destiny to go on with this." Earlier in 1989 Ma had been considering applying to join the Communist party, but now he had changed his mind. "I don't think I want to join the party," he remarked. "I can believe only what I see—not what I am told to believe."

Ma now had a vision of undermining Chinese dictatorship by a committed pursuit of social science. "The Chinese people's minds have got to be opened," he said. "If you give a person a computer, after three months they can use it, but their world view does not necessarily change. But when a person investigates society, his eyes are opened onto the nature of authority." Ma's hope in the capacity of knowledge to budge power reminded me of the rationalistic optimism of the early decades of social science in Europe in the late nineteenth century.

Another friend who had been active in the democracy movement, Lin Mu, was a recent mathematics and sociology graduate from Wuhan University who now worked for the government. A small, energetic twenty-six-year-old with a sharp sense of humor, Lin came from a "bad background" (which meant an upper-class one), and in part because his father was ridiculed for his landlord heritage, his mother divorced him, and Lin at age two was sent to live with a grandmother. At college he took up sociology as a means to try to understand his unhappy childhood. He lived with his wife, Chen, a twenty-six-year-old of birdlike grace who had been his classmate at Wuhan University, in a single room of eleven square meters. I was relieved to see him arrive at the Palace Hotel, although he had to sign in at the front entrance in the old 1970s way.

"I saw a man die for the first time in my life," Lin said, as black smoke curled into the sky outside the window. "It happened in Qian Men Street near a well-known bicycle shop. The left side of his face was blown away by a bullet. He was probably just a bystander." I asked him if he threw any rocks or Molotov cocktails. "Not exactly," he replied softly. "But I used a metal bar—the sort a cook uses to mix a large pot." I looked across at Lin's profile and his face had tensed. "I hit a soldier on the head with it." A silence stretched between us and then Lin went on: "I was angry—the soldier had just shot that man."

Did the soldier die? "I only wounded him," Lin replied, his voice even quieter than before.

After hitting the soldier, Lin ran into a lane. "I felt Beijing was finished, and China too," he said to me. "There seemed no point in staying on and I felt I should go home to my wife." But after ten minutes he felt he could not go home, and by chance he ran into a classmate from Wuhan. Like many others, the two of them tried to build makeshift barricades to stop the progress of the tanks. "Troops started pouring out of the subway station [at the southern edge of the square]," Lin said. "We threw stones and sticks at them as they emerged. The soldiers had guns, but apparently no bullets. They just picked up the things we had thrown at them and hurled them back at us. It was strange—some PLA were firing, some were not."

About 2:00 A.M. Lin and his Wuhan friend went to the northern rim of Tiananmen Square near Nanchang Street. "There were lines of PLA facing a wave of people," he said, "not far from Golden Water Stream. Some in the crowd shouted 'Zou gou! Zou gou!' ['Running dogs! Running dogs!'] at the soldiers. In the front row, four or five soldiers fired point-blank into the crowd at chest height. People fell down.

"It was like fire and water," Lin went on, "the crowd was a body of water going in waves and the soldiers were a wall of fire. The fire crashed at us and the water flowed away. I think the PLA were scared because there were so many people. I noticed that not all of the soldiers dared to fire—just some of them." Step by step the army took over more of Chang An Avenue as the young pair watched. "But I had felt the power of the people," Lin said. "One man with blood running out of his back kept running around, excited, hardly noticing that he had been shot."

Lin had not done any work for weeks although he went in periodically to his office in a government ministry. In the stillness of the hotel room he lit a cigarette and inspected it. "These are our drugs," he said as he held it before his face and the smoke clouded his pale eyes, "like cocaine and marijuana for you in the West. Comfort for the spirit [*xinli anwei*].

"I have also taken up Mah-Jongg," Lin said. "I always thought of it as an old man's game, but now it's my game too. You see, Mah-Jongg is a good escape from reality. It has strict rules and everyone starts equal."

Lin felt deeply discouraged about the role of educated young people after a decade of reform and its rude denouement. "I didn't spend eighteen years going to school in order to have guns pointed at me," he said. "There are only two ways out for people like us: go abroad or go into business." To Lin it seemed useless to study in the face of mindless political power and economic priorities that discounted the realm of knowledge. "What significance does social research have," he asked me, "when the results are never implemented?" Lin recalled his past enthusiasm for acquiring knowledge. "When we were young, every penny we could get we spent on books. Now, I seldom have money for books—and anyway, I have come to wonder whether there's any point in studying." I thought of a remark the bold journalist Wang Ruoshui had made to me on a previous occasion. "It doesn't pay to speak," he had said, "and also, to have spoken proves of no use."

Lin showed me a letter he had received from his father, who had become an architect in order to transcend his "bad background" and had never trusted the Communists. "Please leave Beijing and don't have anything more to do with the democracy movement," the elder Lin wrote. "In China intellectuals are always getting out ahead of the ordinary people. It makes trouble—and it makes you young intellectuals vulnerable." The father, who as a landlord's son had been a Cultural Revolution target, felt talk about democracy for China was unrealistic.

"The crisis of 1989 was a small crisis, son, compared with the big crisis of the Cultural Revolution," the father wrote. "Just study, and try your best to scrape out a living [*huo ming*], for there are so many dangers." Concluded the father in his letter to his son: "China is China. Democracy can't come here as readily as in many other countries. No recipe for China's problems can neglect our long traditions, our backwardness, or that most Chinese are farmers."

Lin Mu, an only son, listened respectfully to the advice and views of his father, but did not agree with them. "Study, yes, but June 4 was not a 'small crisis,' " he said to me. "I am not content to live a life little different from the animals." He did not intend to leave the capital. "I want to see how history changes in Beijing," he explained, and then he gave me three reflections on the crisis. "Never forget that China is a Third World country, and it has a military to match," he said. "In China the military situation *is* the political situation." Lin's second point was equally sobering: "Economic reform without political reform mainly benefits the bureaucrats." His third was that there are two kinds of reform, reform from above and reform from below. "In China, reform from below is difficult because of the horror of disorder that Chinese have," he said. "But now reform from above is also stalled."

With Lin Mu, as with other friends, I found that the strain of the tight political atmosphere grew as June progressed. "Last night I thought hard about whether I should come and see you today," he said one morning in the third week of the month. "Back and forth, I pondered the matter." Lin's wife said to him, "Be careful! Trouble comes from the mouth. In China, telling the truth is hazardous." But Lin resisted her words. "Because people died at Tiananmen," he told me, "I felt I would come." I did not feel able to reassure Lin, nor did I wish to try to influence his decisions.

"A Westerner could not believe the current situation in Beijing," Lin said. "The power of the state in China is just overwhelming." He did not see anything weak or unstable about the government of China in late June 1989—nor did I—but he felt the regime had no moral legitimacy. "When you have stolen something," he remarked in an application of an old saying, "your heart is empty; Li Peng has stolen the hope of the Chinese people."

One day Lin brought with him to the Palace Hotel a toy tank that he had bought at a department store. "I am saving it to give to my first child when I have one," he said. "It will serve to remind him of something he must understand and should never forget." I asked Lin to buy me one and bring it on his next visit. A week later Lin and his wife came in with the news that toy tanks were sold out all over Beijing. Many Beijing folk, mindful of history and used to making small things play a large symbolic role, had done as Lin did and bought a toy tank.

Lin was wearing a baseball cap, which I had never seen on him before, and Chen wore a colorful dress. "I read that Goebbels said if you tell a lie a thousand times, it becomes the truth," the young sociologist said. "That is what we are seeing in China now. Guns, lies, I hardly know which is worse." Nevertheless Lin soon was talking about the road ahead and the need to unite with rural folk for the next challenge to Communist rule. Chen felt such talk was a waste of energy. "What's the point?" she kept saying between sips of Coca Cola. "One or two people are nothing," Lin rejoined to his wife, "but banding together we can build something for tomorrow."

Lin asked me two arresting questions on that sunny June morning. "How is it that although China is so poor, we Chinese love our country so much?" he said softly. "And how is it that, although China is so miserable, Westerners still are so interested in China?" I said I would think about these questions and give my answers the next time I came to Beijing. Lin lit a cigarette and he and Chen went out into Goldfish Lane and took a bus home. Later he sent me his own toy tank and I brought it back to Boston so that I, too, should not forget.

Tan Zhenzhou, the graduate student from Shenyang who had been a youthful soldier and a merchant marine, also met me some days after the massacre. He said the PLA unit with which he and his classmates had reasoned for three days never got to Tiananmen Square. The students themselves brought back to these troops at the college gates the news of the massacre in the central parts of Beijing. Hearing it, the officer in charge of the unit that had been outside the college gates said to Tan: "Thank you for stopping us. Had we gone in toward Tiananmen Square, we would have participated in what happened."

Tan's background, like Ma Qingguo's, was rural and he had been among the more cautious of the student activists. In common with many other graduate students, he felt the occupation of Tiananmen Square should have ended late in May. "Everyone knows the government was wrong to shoot," he said, "but we could have avoided it by leaving earlier. We should have gone back to the campuses, happy with two victories; people in the streets had supported us, and we'd learned that a citizens' movement has power to influence events. Then at intervals we would have mounted further city demonstrations, building ourselves up. In South Korea it took twenty years of this activity to break down authoritarianism."

Of the student movement activists I knew, Tan was one of the more thoughtful about long-term goals. "You can't cry out, 'Down with the Communist party,' " he reasoned, "because another party doesn't exist in China—we just have to move step by step." He took the view that "there are different views in the Communist party, and we democrats should take advantage of this fact." Tan felt keenly the tragedy of the totally inadequate links between Zhao Ziyang's camp and the street politics of the student movement.

"Now is the worst time in my life," Tan said before he left Beijing for Shenyang. Not one to brood for long, he brightened after a bit and added, "The sweetest time of it all was from May 15 until May 20, when the newspapers published the truth and we really believed democracy was quickly coming." Tan told me he was afraid of the guns but he was not afraid of going to prison. "There is always something you can do in your cell," he said. "I won't be arrested now, but probably in two or three weeks."*

Ni Weiguo, the journalist who had described the ugly features of corruption in explaining to me the roots of the democracy movement, arrived at the Palace Hotel, and I had never seen him so stirred up. "I've started smoking again," he said with a wan smile. "This event has been more painful than the Cultural Revolution. In 1966 I had already lost illusions about Mao, but in 1989 I guess I still had a few illusions about Deng."

Ni looked around at the walls and ceiling of my hotel room and then took a piece of paper and a green pen that were lying on the coffee table. He wrote the English words: "Nearly all the journalists of Beijing are unable to accept the line of the government." I realized Ni would feel more comfortable elsewhere, so we went downstairs to a restaurant, and after I had ordered beer and noodles he leaned across the table to my notebook, took from inside it the sheet of paper with his words in green ink, screwed it up, and put it in his pocket.

The net result of the government response to the student democracy movement, in Ni's view, was that the Li Peng regime had become a junta. "The line of today is more hollow than that of 1976," he said in a reference to Mao's last year, "because the Gang of Four did have convinced followers, but these people have almost none." As we looked to the future, Ni expressed the view that in some ways the egalitarianism of the socialist ideal was more deeply rooted in China than in the other countries of the Marxist bloc, and that it was not easy to see beyond it to a loosened-up system with which the majority of Chinese people would really be content.

* Tan was not arrested and I saw him again when I returned to Beijing in December 1989.

As Ni Weiguo prepared to take his leave, I asked if there was much evident resistance to the Li Peng regime. "Resistance is everywhere!" he replied, "but there is no leadership. Everyone is waiting for the death of a few old men—that is China's tragedy." Ni summed up the rise and fall of the democracy movement: "Old Deng underestimated the people, and the people underestimated old Deng." From the front door of the Palace Hotel I watched him walk out into the evening, with his measured step and his black satchel under his arm. I felt he would be resuming a life of caution and subterfuge that had seemed to both of us a thing of the past.

Zhu Yasheng, the middle school student I had met at the Catholic cathedral the day after the massacre, was not permitted by his family to have any contact with me for a while, but late in June he phoned me and we met at the Palace Hotel. Still bright-eyed but looking tired, he brought the sad news that a close friend, a classmate who participated with him in the demonstrations, had just been arrested in Shijiazhuang after fleeing there from Beijing. "He attacked a soldier," Yasheng said of the sixteen-year-old, "and it turned out this action was recorded by a secret camera attached to a lamppost." Thousands of other young Chinese were arrested, harassed, or discriminated against on the basis of film from these ubiquitous secret cameras (which the Chinese government had bought from Britain for the purpose of monitoring traffic).

Not long afterward news reached me that Zhu had suddenly gone into the military, and I would later go to the Zhu family house to seek light on this unexpected twist. Zhu's father, the master chef, could not have been nicer—although perhaps he could have been more candid. "Yasheng is fine," he said. "He is at an air force base south of Beijing. The discipline is good for him. You see his grades were poor and his middle school thought the military would have a good effect on him."

I was surprised because Yasheng had told me his grades were excellent, at least before the Beijing massacre, and because I knew how much the arrest of his classmate for the crime of "attacking a soldier" on June 4 had upset him. In Yasheng's room Mr. Zhu proudly showed me books and photos of school events and family outings. There was no sign of Yasheng's Catholicism. Where was the Bible he had asked me to send him from Boston? Perhaps he had it with him at the air force base, but that seemed unlikely.

I asked Mr. Zhu if his son kept up with his religious observances. "When he visits Beijing he does," Zhu replied, "but he can't at the air force base." I got to the point. "Did the school send Yasheng into the military as a punishment for his participation in the democracy movement," I asked, "and to try to knock Christianity out of him?"

"No, no, no," said Mr. Zhu with a broad smile. "It was his low grades."

Later I showed a Chinese friend the address which Mr. Zhu gave me for his son. "Strange," he said as he looked at the Chinese characters. "It's an invalid address. The code he has written down is for Xuan Wu District, here in central Beijing, where I myself live. Nanyuan, the air force base, is well to the south and must have a different code."

Beijing University was a quiet, smoldering place in the midsummer of 1989, its voices stilled, its gates monitored, its spirit in mourning for students dead and a movement crushed. Rows of smart and well-stocked computer and electronics stores near the campus seemed to symbolize the division between an emerging modern China and a last-gasp backward China—led by "bullshitters with low IQs," as one student said—that had met ideas with bullets.

On June 16, Ted Koppel of ABC News boldly took me to the campus to film a *Nightline* program and at the gate our van with half a dozen people in it was refused entry. A little later Koppel and I returned alone on foot and to the police at the gate I said in Chinese that we were professors visiting from Harvard. We were waved through ("That's the first time," said Koppel, "that I have heard anyone speak Chinese with an Australian accent"), but within half an hour Koppel, using his Video Eight camera, was detained by soldiers. He was released, but few students or teachers would talk to us. (Koppel made a *Nightline* program largely out of conversation between the two of us.) A week later I understood why, after a meeting at the campus with a philosophy teacher and a history teacher. The pair expected that at any moment the PLA might occupy the university. Political indoctrination was taking the place of most normal intellectual activity on the campus, and these teachers expected the autumn enrollment of new students would shrink or even be canceled. It seemed likely to them that any new students entering the university would first have to undergo military training. "If they teach them how to use guns," the historian joked, "maybe the outcome of the next student democracy movement will be different."

"I would be glad to hear the news that Deng Xiaoping is in good health," remarked the philosophy teacher, "because if his mind is clear, he must see that the crackdown is wrong." The history teacher had a different view. "Deng Xiaoping is in charge and he is behaving like a man whose house is on fire," he said. "He rushes from room to room beating out the flames, and nothing outside the house, let alone farther down the street, matters to him at all." At that stage the historian felt the government still had a choice. "They can treat the root causes of the dissenting movement," he said, "or they can simply punish those who were part of it."

Soon after the massacre I tried to phone my Beijing University friend Professor Zhou Yiliang, who had talked with me about the problems of Deng's reforms the year before, and about Mao and the Cultural Revolution many times before that. But on each occasion an operator said the line was "out of order," and by mid-June the response was that the line was "cut off." Eventually I got into a taxi and drove out to Zhou's spacious house on the campus.

"How did you get through the gate?" asked the son of Professor Zhou as he greeted me with a surprised look on his face. He explained that his father was in New York attending a conference. "Hu Yaobang and Zhao Ziyang were the two arms of Deng Xiaoping in pursuing reform," the younger Zhou said in summing up the crisis. "Deng wants reform, but he has allowed the old revolutionary guard—who want reform to fall short of political reform—to cut off his two arms, Hu in 1987 and Zhao in 1989." Zhou explained that on the night of June 3, three hundred phones at Beijing University were put out of order. "Since then no one has been able to phone in here," he said with a shrug of the shoulders.

By late June it had become a widespread theme inside the government and outside that "China is not ready for democracy." It suited the government to embrace a variation of this theme and many older Chinese people—like Lin Mu's father—basically agreed with it. The notion that democracy was beyond China's reach even appealed to many participants in the student movement who were groping for an explanation of their failure. The cry "China is not ready for democracy" seemed to me to express an endemic fatalism in Chinese society that transcended any political analysis. Charles Kim, the Chinese-Canadian student who had described the April 27 demonstration to me, summed up the mood on his Beijing Language Institute campus this way: "People say we had our big bang, but now it's back to our senses. We are after all not living in the U.S.A.—we are Chinese. We don't have emperors any more, but we do have dictators." From its perspective, the government tried to appropriate this streak of fatalism and put it alongside an unsavory nationalism. "Fang runs to the house of foreigners," Chinese officials said of Professor Fang Lizhi's decision to seek refuge within the American embassy. "He has forgotten that he is Chinese."

It must be said that a vast number of Chinese by late June accepted with equanimity the crushing of the democracy movement and the resurgence of leftist totalitarianism. One night I took a taxi from the Great Wall Hotel back to the Palace Hotel and the driver said just before I got out of his cab: "I supported the democracy movement, and now I support the government. The students were correct about corruption, but, you see, in China democracy is impossible." An energetic spring had turned into a listless summer, and some people had shed their spring opinions as readily as their spring garments.

Yet some students found stratagems to express the view that justice had not been done and the government was not serving the people. In Xian at the graduation ceremony of Northwest University, the students as they walked from the campus to the theater requisitioned for the occasion began to sing the "Internationale." Inside the theater they continued for an hour to sing this technically harmless anthem, which nevertheless had been a theme song of the democracy movement. At length the university president was able to achieve silence and began his speech, and like virtually every oration in the nation after June 4, it contained a pious denunciation of the "counterrevolutionary riot." When he reached this phrase, the audience burst into orderly, sustained applause, bringing a long interruption to the speech. The head of the Communist Youth League rose to make his speech and when he began a sentence about the "counterrevolutionary riot," applause again broke out and continued for so long that the poor official had to abandon his speech and resume his seat.[2]

In Beijing, Tiananmen Square was empty of people and tanks alike. At its northern edge along Chang An Avenue, soldiers were busy tending the trees and shrubs and grass that form a belt of transition between the public street and the forbidden zone of

Zhongnanhai. That both sides from the early June confrontation had gone from the square seemed a symbol of the sad reality that everyone had lost on June 4. "Most of the young are for the moment demoralized," I noted in my diary, "and at the top, there is a government and a 'line' that is simply waiting to fall." Given the age of the Communist leaders, and the fact that the number of young people in China between the ages of fourteen and twenty-seven equals the entire population of the United States, an eerie disjunction seemed to exist between the present and the probable future.

Calls came to my hotel room and the caller would say nothing or mumble about a wrong number and hang up, a probable sign of police surveillance, yet I was not required to leave China (as I had been required to leave Poland years before in a less tense atmosphere) and I wondered why. From the government point of view, I was a negative force, gaining information each day from Chinese whom I trusted and who trusted me, providing for them a window to a saner world beyond China, and giving occasional interviews to Western TV and radio (sometimes on my hotel phone) that provided a bleak view of China's condition and policies.

I think there were two reasons why the axe did not fall. The government of Li Peng had so much to do of a life and death nature that anything concerning foreigners was probably not focused upon with the usual attention. A policy of stifling the foreign press existed —no more entrance visas were issued after June 8—but it was limited in scope by a desire not to scare foreign business, and at the middle levels of the bureaucracy, especially in the foreign ministry, there was foot dragging in the implementation of the anti–foreign press line.

So it was that I could hang on throughout June, until most of my Chinese friends had left Beijing for safer spots and the refurbished machine of leftist totalitarianism was back in operation. By late June the government may positively have wanted foreign TV to report from Beijing in the hope that a message of a return to normalcy would come over to the world. It was indeed hard in those days for cameras to record anything other than soldiers sweeping the streets and helping elderly pedestrians cross the road. But I found the fruitfulness of my own encounters diminishing by the day and prepared to depart.

After all the violence and sadness and tension, I wanted to spend an hour at the surpassingly beautiful Temple of Heaven before leaving Beijing, not knowing how long it might be before I would come to China again. It took the taxi half an hour to go a few blocks from north of Chang An Avenue to the area south of it and the driver cursed the PLA that was largely responsible for the obstruction. "Tanks around you, helicopters above, the only thing lacking is atomic bombs," he snarled. "If Mao were alive, this wouldn't happen."

At the Temple of Heaven, I felt again the sense of a tie between man and nature that is one of Chinese culture's attractive traits, and that had been eclipsed in the Beijing of bullets and class struggle. Under a cypress tree not far from the Hall of Prayer for Good Harvests, a young man was curled up on a park bench reading a book, and I thought the black cover with red endpapers looked familiar. It was my *Mao*. I introduced myself and asked the reader to compare Mao and Deng. "Mao was far greater," he replied. "There were so many sides to Mao's talent and his interests. Only in one respect is Deng superior to Mao—economics." Yet that one brilliant feather in Deng's cap seemed likely to fray in the aftermath of the military crackdown, as Western nations recoiled from China and blueprints for reform were put back in locked drawers.*

I drove in silence from the Temple of Heaven east to the airport. Check-in for my flight on CAAC to Guangzhou was in one building and the departure gate in another building far away. Although I had a reserved seat, I was told the flight was full and only when I breached the rules of the check-in counter, marched across the luggage scales to the supervisor's office, and shouted in very poor Chinese, "Are you an airline or a circus?" was I given a seat. I flew south and in the commercial bastion of Guangzhou, which was shabby but not dead like Beijing, while dining in a restaurant of the White Swan Hotel at a table beneath a cage of live birds, I opened a copy of the Guangzhou paper *Nan Fang Ribao* ("Southern Daily") and found that the Communist party had reached a verdict on Zhao Ziyang. Under a headline in large red characters, the communiqué of the fourth plenum of the thirteenth central committee said Zhao had "split the party" and he was dismissed from all his posts. The judgment was far more serious than that on Hu when he was forced

* Interestingly, in the light of inevitable Mao-Deng comparisons, my biography of Mao continued to sell strongly after June 4, 1989, and by October 1991 had sold in its Chinese edition within China more than one million copies.

out as Zhao's predecessor in 1987, and approximated that made by Mao on Deng in 1976.

It seemed that Zhao had not fully confessed and not agreed to go gracefully, for the communiqué said further investigation of his errors would be undertaken. Zhao was made out to be Deng's enemy, in the time-honored tradition of the Communist party, which makes loyalty to the leader a fetish and interprets disagreement over policy as disloyalty. The only hint of compromise on the part of Deng was that the new party chief was not to be Li Peng, but Jiang Zemin, a Soviet-educated engineer from Shanghai, who was less hated in Beijing than Li Peng simply because he was less known and may not have been involved in the decision to shoot at the crowds.

I arrived at Guangzhou airport for a flight to Hong Kong, with photos and documents from the democracy movement secreted in various parts of my shirt, trousers, jacket, and socks. I hoped that nothing would give rise to a body search, yet, alas, as I passed through the X-ray machine a stapler inside my attaché case set off the alarm. After all I was to be searched! But the leaflets and poems and snapshots inside my garments were not detected. A second obstacle was my lack of a stamped customs form—due to the customs officers' inattention to arriving passengers at Beijing airport on the evening of the massacre—but this was surmounted by a posture of innocent helplessness. I sank onto a dusty brown couch and looked back on Zhao's fall and the collapse of the democracy movement.

No one I knew of inside China or outside expected Deng to order shooting at the demonstrating students and citizens, yet very few people believed—I certainly did not—that the democracy movement would result in the downfall of the Communist party. This was not only because the grip of the party on huge, rural China was still firm, but because unlike Poland (where Solidarity existed) and the Philippines (with Cory Aquino waiting in the wings) there was in China no incipient opposition force that could step into the halls of government.

Nor was it the aim or expectation of the student movement to get rid of Communist party rule in one season's lunge. The students did not seek to occupy government offices, take over TV stations, or accumulate weapons. One should not forget Wuer Kaixi's words (despite his uttering some contrary words): "Our purpose was to make the government listen to us and talk to us. That was our only real demand."[3] For the most part, and until the last two weeks of the movement when division in the student leadership became a

major factor, the students were petitioners at the court, conscious-
ness-raisers for the nation, not politicians-in-waiting. This does not
deny the fact that emotional radicalism often dominated the movement after the hunger strike began. But if the *posture* of the hunger
strike leaders was confrontational, they lacked a strategy for bringing about systemic political change.

It is true that revolutions sometimes start with banal issues—in
the case of the French Revolution, the simple demand for bread—
and it would be wrong to assert that the circumstances triggering
the Beijing Spring (Hu's death) and the issue that won broad support
(anticorruption) predetermined that structural political change
would not result. Nevertheless, the overall strategy, national mobilization, and physical instruments required for an overthrow of the
Communist regime did not exist.

In Beijing I had encountered four political cries: down with Communist rule; down with Li Peng and such hardline leaders; a plague
on both government and students as it's all just a dog-eat-dog
struggle; curse the student movement for setting back the cause of
reform. Of these four standpoints the first, the root and branch anti-
Communist one, was the one least often expressed to me, and the
second, calling for the ouster of Li or Deng, did not exist at the start
of the movement, but only after Zhao made his remark about Deng
to Gorbachev, and after Li announced martial law.

A revolution would have required revolutionaries, and the only
revolutionaries in Beijing were the retired old men keeping their
cards close to their chests behind the vermilion walls of Zhongnanhai. The student democracy movement was a partly planned, partly
spontaneous drive to urge upon the Communist party the accelera-
tion of the reform process. In light of this, Deng's violent response
was an evil act, and in the long run perhaps a stupid one. Why in
early June, when most of the students had ceased demonstrating,
did the army move toward Tiananmen Square and eventually spray
city streets with gunfire? In part it was an act planned well before
and delayed by Zhao's resistance. And perhaps the citizens' fury
displayed toward soldiers, and the divisions within the military,
made the violence greater than Deng, Yang Shangkun, and Li Peng
intended. Yet, beyond these two points, the shooting of June 3–5
was a calculated act of terror to make the point to all of Beijing and
all of China, for years to come, that Communist party rule was a
given that no one should dare question.

The struggle inside the Communist party was crucial to what

happened in the streets, and basically it was a struggle for the succession to Deng. Zhao tried, but failed, to stake out ground for his own post-Deng leadership of China (as Hu had tried and failed in 1986). That in many cities outside Beijing, Zhao had been a target of the April–May protests, hardly less than Li Peng and Deng, suggested that the policy differences between Zhao and Li Peng were not as important as their varying degrees of *loyalty to Deng* (a fact fairly well known in inner Beijing circles). Indeed, the analysis of the crisis in late June by Chen Xitong, the hardline mayor of Beijing, put extraordinary stress on the *insult to Deng the man* presented both by the student movement and by Zhao's low-key response to it.[4]

Looking back, I felt two developments could have forestalled a suppression of the movement. If Zhao had made an earlier and more resolute challenge to the colleagues he disagreed with, and won Deng's support, the result of the democracy movement would have been a strong renewal of the reform process, which had been stalled since Zhao lost out on price reform and other policies to Yao Yilin and Li Peng in the summer of 1988; the democracy movement would have proved itself the key constituency in favor of invigorated reform. Perhaps Zhao could not have won support for going full speed ahead with reform, but how hard and skillfully did he try to mobilize top colleagues? And why in the days of press freedom did he not take his case directly to the nation in TV speeches?

Suppression might also have been forestalled if the student leadership had decided to beat a tactical retreat after waves of demonstrations had proved the weight of antigovernment feeling. Around May 19, many of the students wished to declare an important stage of the movement concluded, with major victories to its credit, withdraw from Tiananmen Square to the campuses, and await an opportunity for the next stage of the movement. Substantial sections of the student ranks, and also most of the senior advisers to the movement, favored a retreat, but the emotion of street politics won the day for continued defiance.

If a move out of Tiananmen Square had come alongside a growing Zhao ascendancy, the tactical retreat by the students would have been a heavy defeat for the leftist party elders. Without Zhao still fighting strongly in the Politburo, on the other hand, a student withdrawal from Tiananmen Square around May 19 would have been a more dangerous and ambiguous step. In that event Deng would have taken steps to punish the student democracy movement, but not with bullets. The resulting standoff would have brought the prospect of further challenges to the government and further zig-zags in reform policy; China at least would have avoided the roll-back of reform that occurred after June 4.[5]

The political crisis, shooting, and repression of mid-1989 halted some of the most important items on Deng's agenda of reform and reasserted the continuity of a Leninist system in which power and publicly expressed ideas alike are monopolized by the Communist party. The backward segment of China ("diehard feudal spiders," in the words of one student poster), after some agonizing hesitation, sank back to the use of primitive force against a budding progressive segment of China. The ideas of Marxism may have long faded, but the straitjacket of Leninism stayed in place. A husk that had lost vitality remained clamped upon society, a dictatorial elite held the body of China tight even as it failed to sway the mind of China.

"Tell the world our government has gone mad," the woman had cried near Tiananmen just after midnight on June 4. But the government had not gone mad. It was preserving its power by the dictates of Leninism. It could be expected to put the maintenance of its own power ahead of all else at moments of crisis in the future as in the past. That did not mean it would necessarily prevail in the next crisis, or any succeeding crises.

"Is June 4 the beginning or the end of something?" I wrote in my diary at Guangzhou airport. "Maybe both. It's the end of the balancing act of reform-after-revolution performed by pragmatic Leninists, and the imperceptible start of a socially based movement to look clear beyond Leninism." Although many people accepted the change of wind after June 4, substantial numbers of Chinese urban folk had made a total inner migration away from influence by the ideas of the Communist party. In the support given to the student movement of April and May, a step away from docility was surely taken, for millions of people joined a movement they knew was against the Communist party's wishes, and in particular young people felt their power as China's next generation. "If silence is like an escaped animal that can be recaptured," two Shanghai-born scholars remarked, "ignorance is not."[6]

But for the moment, the terrible cost of the crackdown was the death of hope in Beijing. It had taken a degree of hope to march for change, even some hope from the direction of the Communist party. Now hope was gone and no one could foresee a better tomorrow. So no one tried, and no one cared.

CHAPTER EIGHTEEN

∎

THE PROBLEM OF CHINA

BY 1990, the bloodstains on Chang An Avenue were washed away and the gashes in the asphalt caused by the tanks' chains were filled in. As Beijing hosted the eleventh Asian Games in the fall of that year, Tiananmen Square looked like a stage set, adorned with birds and animals in replica, potted plants, an illuminated fountain, and balloons dancing overhead. It was a great show, sport as theater, with Tiananmen Square once more safe for empty ritual, and the Asian Games as a sprawling banyan tree, every branch serving a political purpose in a struggle to build legitimacy for a government that seemed afraid of its own people. A fashion designer friend of mine snorted as we strolled around the square during the games: "It's a circus. The Communist party is the impresario and the Chinese people are the animals."

That same fall I visited Hong Kong to see my old friend from the 1970s, Zhou Nan, who was now the Chinese Communist chief in that British colony. "China will be China," he thundered, as he sat beside me on a sofa, elegant in his dark Western suit, vowing that the erosion of communism in Eastern Europe in 1989 and 1990 foretold nothing about China's future. "Chinese culture has a great unifying power," he declared and went on to regale me with past injustices done to China, such as the Opium War. In the face of the bleak outlook for world communism, he urged me "not to get lost in current trends," and not to forget the historic achievements of the Communist party in China.

"Will the tattered clothes change Beijing," Mao had asked himself as the youths of the Red Army in their sandshoes "liberated" the city in 1949, "or will the change run in the opposite direction?"[1] The changes that began with Mao's rule cut both ways, and what was new did not always improve upon the old, nor did all of it stand for long. The "impresarios" Mao and Deng betrayed an endemic Chinese tendency to divert attention from ruthless maneuver by treating politics as a show, in which the people were cast as "animals" required to spring this way or that by the circus master.

A symbol of the decadent and chaotic pre-1949 past was venereal disease, and it was one of Communist China's proudest boasts that VD had been wiped out. This impressive medical drive was headed for some time by George Hatem, an American-born physician long resident in China. Despite the Cultural Revolution, I always found Hatem full of optimism about China, and advances in health, including the disappearance of VD, often came into the analyses of social trends that he offered me. After he died in 1988, I went to his Beijing home to extend condolences to his Chinese widow, Su Fei, and we were joined by a Mr. Sun, a medical worker and family friend, who remarked that "the eradication of VD from China" was Hatem's "greatest achievement."

"Syphilis was gone by 1950, really," said Su Fei as she brought a tray with cups of tea. "Some years later we could say that all sex diseases were totally eliminated," added Sun.

"Was it a permanent victory?" something made me ask.

Sun became agitated and a somber look came to Su Fei's face. "Until the open policy [of Deng] we could say it was permanent," Sun said. "But since the open policy we have had many VD cases. Some very serious," he added in a probable reference to the growing problem of AIDS in China. Perhaps human nature is more of a constant than the Chinese Communist social engineers realized. Probably the openness of China to the outside world was not the entire explanation for VD's return. Surely sex diseases came back in the 1980s because some sexual freedom came back.

The advent of Communist rule in 1949 did not bring a true human liberation—the self-realization of the individual achieved in an atmosphere of freedom on the basis of sovereignty residing with the people. A true human liberation would have been indivisible, offering freedom for the Tibetans and the homosexuals as well as for the rickshawmen and the silk spinners. But Mao's liberation was of another stripe. It was in the strong-man tradition of Zhang Zhidong

(1837–1909) who sought wealth and power for China by a variety of means. It was in the vengeful tradition of French and Russian revolutionaries, for whom the manifest injustice of the ancien régime was all that counted; anything aimed at benefiting the "proletariat" as the chosen class could be justified in the name of skewering it.

Over the years Marxist policies indeed changed some basic things. Old power and wealth agglomerations were broken up and a social leveling-down occurred. Yet as the Marxist tide ran out to sea, the reappearing shoreline was astonishingly familiar to a prerevolutionary eye; the rocks of an ancient culture that fell behind the West and Japan in modern times had withstood the frothy waves of a modern ideology. Still today, informal networks of influence count more than formal political structures. The individual can do little without taking into account his family's interests and wishes. China remains Asia's poor giant; of Zhang Zhidong's two hopes, "wealth and power," Mao and Deng achieved power for the Chinese nation but not wealth for the Chinese people. In 1964 Chinese officials had told me in confident tones that pedicabs were being phased out as "relics of imperialism," but twenty-five years later on the night of June 3–4, 1989, I scrambled from place to place amidst the tumult of the Beijing massacre in just such a despised relic.

Communism itself has become "the old" from which a people seek a new Liberation. It seems that by the year 2000 many Chinese may take the evils of the Marxists as a given, just as the evils of Chiang Kai-shek's Nationalists were taken as a given by many in the 1940s. People I know well in China—those who still *are* in China—possess little faith in their hectoring, fearful, intolerant government, and they betray an awareness that a China under the Communist party, despite successful pockets of penny capitalism, is becoming a backwater in a world hurtling on to fresh frontiers.

While the cream of a young generation have lost hope, and many of them are abroad, the old monks of the Chinese Communist party sit around in the temple with their ancient texts of Marx and Lenin and Mao. Deng and his fellow monks grope for the new, but they also want to preserve their own political power, and so the new does not come, but only a recycling of the old. The state holds society—if not the economy—tight and lifeless in its python's grip. But this bleak solution to the contradictions of reform-after-revolution only stores up trouble for the future and guarantees that China will fall even further behind the dynamic capitalist societies of East Asia.

Meanwhile the Chinese man in the street goes about his austere daily round with quiet ingenuity and cynicism's half-smile. China in 1992 lumbers on, but no one is very sure where the clouded, twisting road is leading, and most Chinese expect a crisis when Deng dies.

A dictator with a mixed record approaching his death recalls to my mind that Goddess of Democracy in Tiananmen Square. Towering, eloquent in connotations, and fearsome to foes—yet on the other hand only a shape in the air, vulnerable to nature's laws, and when toppled an unlovely sight. Mao was tormented by his own mortality (and that of the Chinese Revolution), and Deng likewise tries to transcend his mortality by winning "once for all" victories that will prove nothing of the sort. Mao's dictatorial excesses in the end brought heavy blows to the Communist party's prestige, and Deng's dictatorial excesses may, after his death, bring an end to Communist party rule itself.

The playwright Wu Zuguang has told a story about an ancient town in which all the men were said to be scared of their wives. One day, to test this tradition, the town magistrate summoned his staff, lined them up, and asked those who were frightened of their wives to stand to one side. All except one did so. The magistrate turned, impressed, to the lone holdout. "Are you not scared of your wife?" he asked the man. "No, it's not that," the man replied. "It's just that my wife told me to keep away from crowds." Playwright Wu, who comes from Beijing, went on to remark: "All of us men are like that, where I am from. So I thirst for freedom. Why exactly are we scared? Because they won't leave us alone. So I long for an environment where I can be left alone. That for me is freedom."[2]

The Chinese have long possessed certain admirable traits, among them industriousness, rationality, strong family ties, and a stoical posture in the face of the twists of fate. Yet the progress of China and its solidarity with the non-Chinese world, even with the former Communist bloc of the Soviet Union and Eastern Europe, have repeatedly been hindered by two blind spots. A lack of individual autonomy has made the Chinese conformist and vulnerable to collectivist passions, and an obsession with Chineseness has made the elites and people of China self-conscious in the face of the foreign world. The two blind spots are closely linked, for the tribal pride of the Chinese lies behind both, obstructing the individual's search for his own truth, and making give and take with the non-Chinese world difficult. The American citizen's view of loyalty stems from his ideals as an individual. The Chinese is no less loyal, but his nationality and family ties so define his loyalties that, to an American, he may seem to lack loyalty as an individual person.

The Chinese person is never left alone, as playwright Wu complained, and the weak sense of individualism is ultimately due to the fact that the nation views itself as a household, a *jia*. The Chinese family is not the simple arrangement of parents and children of a Western family; this is clear from the host of different terms for "older brother," "aunt on the father's side," "senior uncle," and so on. The multitude of branches on a Chinese person's family tree represent complex bonds of mutual obligation.

China long was a huge empire of numberless villages, under the rule of an emperor who was father to the people and also aspired to cosmic significance as the Son of Heaven. A sedentary agricultural life put a premium on family ties and gave people a strong sense of place. In this tradition, the questing individual of Western society was hardly to be found, for to roam, inquire, and conquer the new was not consonant with the fulfillment of the obligations of family farming. Chinese political culture became obsessed with order, narcissistic about its uniqueness, secretive in the way a household is secretive, and given to an Idea of China (as united and benevolent) that soared above the facts. The sense of the nation became an extension of the bonds of mutual obligation of the family, and the Communist party tightened the bonds of the *jia* by politicizing culture, law, economics, and even private life.

At the height of the demonstrations of 1989, a student of computer science in Beijing, seeking to explain why the April 27 demonstration did not raise slogans calling for the overthrow of the Communist party, wrote in a poster: "You may say that a mother acted wrongfully with good intentions, but you absolutely may not say that your mother is not your mother. Isn't this so?"[3] Some day the Chinese people will no longer accept dictators in the guise of parents.

One morning in 1988 at the Summer Palace on the outskirts of Beijing I watched a huge crowd snapping photos of the Empress Dowager's chambers and of each other. Lunchtime came and with my two companions, Miss Song and Mr. Zhang, I entered the musty golden magnificence of the Pavilion for Listening to Orioles

Restaurant. "This way please," chirped a voice like an oriole's, and the waitress led me to a small round table for one behind a carved wooden screen.

"I am sorry," Miss Song said as she and Mr. Zhang departed to take lunch in a collective room, "we would like to dine with you, but the rules of the organization that is dealing with you [China International Travel Service] still prevent us eating with you." In front of my array of dishes, I sat there thinking how hard it is for the individual to express himself in China. Out in the courtyard I could see Chinese tourists dressing up with great excitement in the yellow imperial garments available from the Pavilion for Listening to Orioles Restaurant for photo taking. A man struggled into brilliant robes and his wife plumped on his head an emperor's three-cornered hat. A daughter focused the camera.

"Wan sui," cried the wife as the man grinned and the camera clicked. This same phrase, "Ten thousand years!" (or "Long Life!"), was addressed to Chinese leaders for centuries, and it became famous to the non-Chinese world when weeping Red Guards greeted Mao with it in the 1960s ("Long Live Chairman Mao!"). Unchanged down the years is the fascination of the Chinese with the rituals, sayings, and excesses of their rulers, past and present. I believe that the crimping of the individual is bound up with this backward-looking awe for the hierarchies, precedents, and stratagems of tribal memory.

On the evening of the 1988 American presidential election, I found myself at the Sheraton Great Wall Hotel in Beijing for the American embassy's reception to watch a telecast of the election results. TV screens offered the ABC News telecast in simultaneous Chinese translation, and hundreds of Chinese clustered before the screens, at breakfast time by the Beijing clock, some silent, some in animated conversation with companions, some taking notes about the fortunes of *Bu Shi* (Bush) and *Duka Jisi* (Dukakis) on little pads.

"Who did you vote for?" a Chinese acquaintance asked me un-blushingly, and the same question was put by my driver and others whom I had never met before. To them the election was nothing to be coy about. It was a wondrous process and the voter would naturally boast of his choice. Never in their lives, I realized, had these eager, intelligent people voted for anything or anyone important, and I wondered when they would get their turn at elections.

A couple of weeks before, in Chengdu, I had cast my ballot, and as always at election time I had felt that sense of participation in a quadrennial participatory rite, when a compact between people and government (joined by the press as well) is renewed. At the Sheraton Great Wall Hotel reception I saw the overwhelming contrast between a rigid polity that looks backward and is not responsible to the populace, and a flexible polity that of necessity always looks ahead to the verdict of the next election.

Among the mystifications of the Beijing government, it is easy to find parallels at this or that point with some extreme cases of political deception in the West. Our politicians, too, dress up power struggle as debate over policy and principle, and in our bureaucracy as in China's, a big fish who is guilty of a mistake may try to slough off blame onto a smaller fish lower in the waters than himself. But two fundamental differences exist. In the United States if we see abuses, we complain in loud voices, and indeed if the daily airwaves were not generously sprinkled with complaints against actions of those in authority, we would probably feel uneasy. In China complaints are no index at all of problems in society because press and people are afraid to complain.

And in America the power of the leader has to be sought from the people at the ballot box. Hence the whole paraphernalia, tiresome in its excesses, of primaries and advertising and poll taking. In Communist China, under Deng as under Mao, not even in theory does sovereignty lie with the people. Sovereignty, like rectitude, stems from the Chinese Communist party. It is very nearly the polar opposite of the democratic way, for instead of the people choosing their leader, the leader—a good leader—is supposed to put his stamp upon the people.

Many paths in the complex forest of China's problems and prospects lead to the weak degree of individuation. The Communist party's fear of foreign influence is ultimately a fear that a widespread process of individuation in China would make paternalistic central control of the realm difficult if not impossible. When Zhao Fusan, the former pastor, told me the movement toward individualism in the late 1980s had "gone too far" and threatened family ties and good order, I recalled a conversation with him about his years in prison and at a labor camp, in which he confessed that at the time he thought the charges made against him of being a "capitalist roader" must have been true. It was very hard for a Chinese of that generation to conclude that the public policy of the moment simply was wrong; he was more likely to blame himself, for imprudence, error, or straying into a realm he was better out of: His private convictions, in a word, were a weak force alongside the public truth of the time. It was no wonder that Zhao Fusan could not accept the cry of young people for individual self-realization.

The Communist party's endless search for "enemies," against which the *jia,* as a householdlike collective force of the "politically correct" must do battle, is wearing threadbare for a generation that wants to live and love as human beings. "China has had three foreign policies within the space of two years," a young government official said to me furtively late in 1990, on the eve of the violent death of the Beijing government's feted friend Nicolae Ceaucescu of Romania, "all because of the search for an Enemy." The Communist party's perpetuation of the imperialist myth long after imperialism ceased to be the key fact about the world has the sad effect of maintaining the gulf between China and much of the non-Chinese world. During 1990 and 1991, party chief Jiang Zemin and Premier Li Peng railed against the West as "imperialists" and said the West was trying to spur a "peaceful evolution" in China that would replace communism with capitalism. But even as they spoke the bulk of the Communist bloc did its own "evolving" away from communism. Eastern Europe and the republics of the former Soviet Union turned toward capitalism, but "imperialists" did not cause the change and for the Chinese government to tell its people they did only put Beijing outside the mainstream of international political discourse.

It is as if the struggles of the May Fourth era have to be mounted all over again. To the youth of the Deng era, as to the May Fourth students in 1919, individual self-realization is a goal of absolute importance and the dynamism and openness of the West are immensely attractive. Decades ago the American foreign correspondent Agnes Smedley, who had spent much time in China and was deeply attached to the country, lashed out with a sharp critique of Chinese culture. She said she found a lack of friendship between men and women in China and she complained that "love" meant just sexual intercourse. Smedley desperately missed in China the individualism that, for all her hostility toward the Western establishment, she admired in Western society, and she came to call China "an emotional and human desert." Her critique of China (given in a letter to Freda Utley in 1939)[4] would win much more support from Chinese circles in the 1990s than it could have done in the 1930s. Her cry in the wilderness for individualism would seem obvious good sense to the young Chinese of the Deng era, who sometimes feel Chineseness is an oppressive box.

The Chinese do not equate their culture readily with universal ways, as Americans do, and the Chinese, like the French, cultivate their uniqueness. While Americans take it for granted that non-Americans will understand them, Chinese assume that the foreigner will not understand them; so while Americans often expect to be able to talk in English with Europeans or Asians, Chinese are generally astonished when they come upon a foreigner who speaks and reads Chinese.

A century ago the nationalist Zhang Zhidong, a pioneer in dealing with China's problem of a West that was at once bullying and seductive, set out a formula for negotiating the China-West gulf. Practical function *(yong)* would be drawn from the West, while cultural essence *(ti)* would remain Chinese. In other words, according to Zhang's "self-strengthening" formula, technique from the West would put strength back into China's matchless but temporarily ailing civilization. Alas, the formula, an attempt to keep the West at bay, was hard to apply, for machines were not separable from the humans who created and operated them. Even the British gunboats on the Yangzi River seemed to smell of a world view.

The China of the early 1990s, still trying to keep the West at bay, jumps around on the issue of Western culture as if a hundred years of experience have resolved nothing. Li Peng sometimes wears a Western-type suit and says this sartorial choice has no philosophical significance. But when Shanghai youth wear jeans he says *that* sartorial choice does have (an ominous) philosophical significance. His gray suit merely expresses Western "function," he seems to believe, clinging to Zhang Zhidong's formula, while youth's jeans express Western "essence." The distinction is nonsense. The Chinese Communists make it because in order to hang on to their own political power they feel they cannot yet be relaxed about grass-roots China-West cultural intercourse. They fear "spiritual pollution," which really means the West's freedoms.

I once asked the neo-Mandarin Zhou Nan what the Chinese government hoped for from a visiting writer. We were in the middle of our month-long tour together as China began to open up in 1971 and I was curious about the motivation of Zhou's attention to me. "An unbiased view of China," he said. Today I realize that is probably impossible to achieve. The quest for an understanding of China is never completely objective. China is not a rock or a beetle, but a slice of humanity, and so are observers of China. A relationship inevitably develops between the phenomena of China and the analyst of China and it changes over time as developments occur on both sides of the relationship.

Zhou Nan gave a second answer to my question: "And we hope the foreign writer will not only see things but also understand them." That, too, is extremely difficult, and I sometimes wonder if I can ever understand China. Back in the early 1970s, John Fairbank organized a small dinner party at the Signet Society clubhouse at Harvard for John Paton Davies, a China Hand hounded from the diplomatic service when China went Communist. After dinner Harold Isaacs, an author and professor who also had long experience in China, asked Davies what had he really thought of the Chinese during his many years in China, and what had they thought of him. Davies confessed that in retrospect, although China had been his life, he became close to few Chinese. Harriet Mills, the daughter of missionaries and a scholar of Chinese literature, who was arrested in China in the early 1950s as China-America relations reached a low point, once told me: "It was in prison that I came to understand and love the Chinese." In what other country, I wondered, would a period of imprisonment kindle affection and respect for the society? Mills, too, felt that her years of living with the Chinese as a missionary's daughter had not brought her very close to them.

Indeed for Westerners the quest to understand China and become close to the Chinese can be long and fraught with perils, yet the goal is not impossible and the quest always brings rewards. "China obscures," Pascal said a long time ago in his *Pensées*. Today Communist China obscures even more. Yet Pascal's full remark suggests the fascination as well as the exasperation that grips many an observer of China: " 'But China obscures,' you say; and I reply, 'China does obscure, but there is light to be found. Look for it.' "[5]

The Chinese language itself gives rise to fascination and exasperation. It is tyrant, mistress, and illusionist all at once. Characters that have evolved from pictures possess a power to sweep you into a special world with its own values. Most Chinese words are not just sounds that have a meaning, but a line drawing of that meaning. Not being alphabetic, written Chinese taxes the memory. Many are the "walls" between China and most of the rest of the world, as Isaacs, Mills, and others of us have found out, and the Chinese ideographs are among the sturdiest. One reason why China has kept its secrets better than the Soviet Union and Eastern Europe did is the singularity of the Chinese language (another is the loyalty of Chinese outside China to their motherland).

The language's power of exclusion is matched by its power of inclusion: the ideographs bind Chinese people together. They are as much a force for unity within the Chinese realm as are the numerals within the various linguistic zones of Europe. "Four," "quatre," and "quattro" have different sounds, but when an Englishman, Frenchman, or Italian write the numeral "4," they write it identically. So it is in China. A Cantonese and a northerner speaking Mandarin cannot readily comprehend one another in conversation, but the words they pronounce differently are written by them identically. The existence of various dialects only adds to the weight of the written language.

That China has often been like a mirror, with the observer seeing aspects of his own concerns when he approaches it, is due to China's elusiveness, an assumption within the Middle Kingdom that it is better for non-Chinese not to understand how things work in China than for them to understand. In China truth and intimacy are seldom immediately available, because of the singularity of the language, the attachment to ritual, the importance of connections, and the paranoia of the Communist party. Unfortunately a China that hides itself becomes a prey to the mental constructs of the ingenious foreigner. The sense of betrayal that foreigners have repeatedly felt in their dealings with China, in Isaacs's case because his faith in the Chinese Trotskyist left proved unwarranted, for missionaries like Mills's family because few Chinese embraced liberal Christian ideas, and most recently because of the crushing of democratic aspirations by the tanks and bullets of June 4, 1989, in part stems from illusory mental constructs.[6]

If foreigners often peer at China through a glass darkly, the same two Chinese blind spots help mightily to bring this about. We are inhibited in our understanding by the Chinese person's tendency to hide his individuality behind various collectives, and by China's self-consciousness about the China-West gulf. In 1991 it is unsettling to behold a person spouting the Li Peng line, dealing ritualistically with the foreign visitor, stonewalling on any question of substance, and then, when Chinese colleagues disappear and the person is alone with a foreigner, to hear him bemoan the state of affairs in Beijing, express his convictions bluntly, and beg the foreigner's assistance in fleeing China for the West.

The tight nationalism of the post–June 4, 1989, period depresses everyone who wants individualism and cosmopolitanism in China, as it seems a desperate means of reasserting control within the *jia,* and an escape from the difficult task of finding a balance between Chineseness and deracination.

The Deng Xiaoping era set in motion a line of solution to two fundamental problems of modern China: is the Chinese past a heap of dust or a usable tradition? Will the quest for prosperity and efficiency infect China with Western values? There is no self-conscious, prescribed-from-above answer to the question of "what to do" with Chinese tradition, or to the gulf in values between China and the West. Yet, independent of the will of China's authoritarian politicians, the new economic forces unleashed by them began to soften these hard choices. Young people came to be far more relaxed about both dichotomies than their elders.

But Deng could not allow the line of solution to go on to its natural conclusion, because his own grip on political power is threatened by the rise of civil society, the individuation of the urban population, and the growing demand for democracy. It is absurd to say that Western culture is a threat to Chinese culture—Chinese culture is not so weak or lacking in appeal!—but it is true that Western ideas are a threat to the *Communist grip* on Chinese culture.

In a China that is free, Chinese culture and influences from foreign countries will be able to interact in a natural way, as occurs among various cultures within the societies of Europe and America. The Goddess of Democracy will not threaten China's identity any more than the Chinatowns of New York and San Francisco threaten America's identity. A free system, in other words, will transcend the self-consciousness of the China-West gulf. But saddled with a Communist political system and the residual influence of an emperor system from the past, China finds it difficult to join the community of modern nations. And it seems just as difficult, at an analytical level, for older Chinese like Zhao Fusan to distinguish between "the West" and "freedom" as beacons of hope, and to assess the contributions of each to China's future development. Only as free individuals emerge and make their own choices, I believe, will the issue of rejecting or adapting Chinese tradition, and that of rejecting or accepting some Western influence, be capable of resolution.

Mao in his youth was attracted to the Qing dynasty reformer Kang Youwei's search for a "truth to save the nation," and this became his quest too, but the notion of a truth to save the nation was a casualty of the stubborn resistance of Nature (especially human nature) to Nurture. Mao later acknowledged that Kang had had a truth, called *Da tong,* or Great Unity, to offer China, but he said Kang could not find the method to realize this unity.[7] What sort of truth, however, does a nation need in order to progress socially and economically (as distinct from the tools or philosophy it needs to be saved from an aggressor or a benighted obscurantism)? It is to Deng's credit that he gave up the idea of a truth to save the nation, but it is his grave failing that in order to hold on to the Communist party's monopoly of power, he appeals to that same tattered truth's authority. In Beijing after the massacre I talked with Lin Mu, the government official who had hit a soldier with a cooking rod, about the idea of a truth to save China and he said truly: "The trouble with so many Chinese leaders is they have thought the people must be *given a truth.* What we really need is to be taught to think, and then by ourselves, in freedom, we will find our way to the truth."

After four decades and more of the Chinese Communist Revolution, I feel discouraged by the entrenchment of the Leninist system, and not sure how soon democracy can root itself in China. But still I am absorbed by the modes and meanings of the search for China. Finding out the truth about China requires putting everything seen and heard within a structural understanding of a Leninist state's clamp upon a society. Any alert person in the West knows that "something" is hamstringing the Chinese people. He looks at the skill and industry of Chinese people outside China; he then considers Communist China and sees that a great people is being held back from its potential. It is not just that "human rights abuses" exist in China, but that the entire dictatorial system is a fundamental denial of human rights. As Wei Jingsheng, the still-jailed hero of Democracy Wall, wrote of political imprisonment in his country, "[W]e are dealing here not just with the humanitarian implications of imprisonment for the individual, but with the significance that such imprisonment has for the basic rights of the people as a whole."[8] China's Leninist system is that "something" holding the Chinese back.

To Chinese youth, one of the best-known people in the nation is the rock singer Cui Jian, a slight, diffident twenty-eight-year-old of Korean race. He began as a classical trumpeter but was dismissed from his state troupe for experimenting with rock. The pop-rock scene makes the government uneasy because it came into existence not by state fiat but spontaneously, and because of its soul-stirring emotionalism and links with the non-Chinese world. After the Beijing massacre, Cui played a cat and mouse game with the authorities; able to give some concerts, but denied access to TV, he walked a fine line between conformity and dissent.

"Politics is physics," Cui told me over a drink in a dark Beijing nightspot in 1990. "Culture is chemistry—we need more of the chemical side." Cui was influenced by Western music as a boy and he became passionately attached to the idea of music as the coinage of cosmopolitanism. "The important thing is to express my real feelings," he said, as if summing up the spirit of Chinese youth and its chief quarrel with the old monks of the Communist party.

Cui, whose song "Nothing to My Name" became an unofficial anthem of the student democracy movement in 1989, assailed the fatalism that is thick on the ground in China. "One's mind is like a computer," he said. "When someone inserts software that says you are a dog, then you will live like a dog. I think Chinese youth should try to live with self-respect." A haunting song of Cui's is called "It's Not That I Don't Understand, It's That the World Is Changing Too Fast," and in talking with the singer I found out that his Delphic meaning is not that the world is changing too fast, but that China is not changing at all.

"Nationalism will give way to internationalism," Cui Jian said when I asked him about his vision of the future. "I don't want China to be thought of as a country that can offer Chinese food and nothing else. I'm interested in what Chinese culture can contribute to the world." Cui and his generation love China, but not in the old way of self-strengthener Zhang Zhidong and neo-self-strengtheners Mao and Deng. They do not remember past bullying of China by the West and Japan, and their patriotism is not an automatic defense of the citadel. They want a rich future for China that will flow from their own self-realization as Chinese individuals. They often transcend the cultural pessimism that entered the Chinese people's assessment of their future prospects in the post-Mao era by an unselfconscious leap to cosmopolitanism. In their view, even the nation is not more important than the freedom of the individual.

Years ago as a graduate student I had come to Harvard with youth's high ambition, seeking to make a unity of things, to fit the Vietnam War and China and my experience in the Australian Labor party into a framework of public values. I was unwilling to ignore China and reluctant to confine it to the realm of the merely exotic, as my German-born teacher of political philosophy Carl Friedrich seemed to do. "Mao does not understand Aristotelian logic," he complained to me one day after class when I raised the topic of Chinese Marxism. Eager to find connections between Chinese wrestlings with issues of power and principle and Western experience of the same issues, I both tackled China studies and took as my thesis topic the democratic socialist ideas of R. H. Tawney. Inspired by Tawney, I focused on the twin problems of too much concentration of power (the curse of communism) and too much concentration of wealth (the weakness of capitalism).

In our time, most capitalist societies have substantially broken down the concentration of wealth, but none of the Marxist or former Marxist societies conquered or even alleviated the evil of centralization of unaccountable power. Marxism has kept China separate from most of the rest of the world. It has held the economy back, while the rest of East Asia surged ahead, and it has restricted the flow of people and ideas in and out of the country. It has helped confine China to an "exotic" realm by keeping it distant from the West.

It is only possible to "make a unity of things" within an atmosphere of freedom. An unfree China has been unable to make much contribution to international issues that are of human importance, and likewise the people inside China have found it all but impossible to deal in the coinage of universal ideas that point the way to world citizenship. The present generation of Chinese youth are the first generation of individualists and cosmopolitans in the history of the PRC. Deng's policies of economic reform and the open door helped produce them, but his political repression has driven hundreds of thousands of them to leave China. The concerns of Chinese youth converge with those of youth around the world, but the Chinese nation remains as if in a time warp, with a government that does not seem to care that its best and brightest can find fulfillment only outside the suffocating *jia* of Communist paternalism.*

* Lin Mu, the young official who had joined in the democracy movement, left China in 1991 and became a graduate student in the United States. He had had no intention of leaving China before June 4, 1989, but the repression that ensued wore down his optimism about the PRC. "I would like to have stayed in my motherland," he wrote to me, "if I could read, talk, and think as an ordinary intellectual can do in a normal society with democracy and law. But in China, telling the truth means making trouble. It is very sad to think that a Chinese cannot be a full human being by staying in his own country."

. . .

Marxism's failure to win minds and fill stomachs, together with the extra blows Mao dealt to Marxism by personalizing the Chinese dictatorship during the Cultural Revolution, has brought a new challenge to Chineseness. China, having married Marxism, is losing face as divorce looms; after the failure of Marxism in China, the Middle Kingdom will have to view itself, not as the middle, but as peripheral to the major forces of creativity and prosperity at the end of the twentieth century. The proud Chinese, covered in the ashes of their disastrous affair with communism, will either have to scour the world for inspiration, technique, and capital, or sink back into a quagmire of cultural nationalism, calling out curses upon the West. The Communist bloc of which they were a part no longer exists, Western ideas are a lure for Chinese youth, and China is on an open sea before the winds and currents of universal values.

In a way it is a good thing that Marxism fails, but China is not Eastern Europe, nor yet the former Soviet Union, and it is not easy to see an alternative to the Communist organizational system in a nation that zipped from despotism to peasant communism in a couple of generations. Philosophically, a vacuum of values exists, and within the elites of Beijing a desperate pragmatism reigns. The secret lust of the people is for individual advancement, and perhaps the only collective enthusiasm left in the nation is that of the minority races in their smoldering hatred of Han Chinese domination.

The failure of Marxism does not mean the ushering in of democracy. Just as for a time many people thought if only China got rid of Chiang Kai-shek's Nationalists, justice would come, so some feel in the 1990s that if only China gets rid of Deng's Communists, freedom and democracy will stand there at the door. It is not so simple. The Liberation of 1949 did not lead to a sustained era obviously superior to what preceded it; nor will the liberation of China from its Communist dynasty necessarily do so. China's history has not been a story of progressive improvement, any more than that of many other parts of the world; splendid epochs, such as periods of the Tang dynasty, were followed by long stretches of tyranny or chaos. Nor does the experience of the Soviet Union, Romania, and other Eastern European societies suggest that democracy follows the collapse of communism as night follows day.

One reason for the near-invisibility of Chinese dissent over much of the four decades of Communist rule, despite numerous disappointments under both Mao and Deng, was the pro-Beijing posture of many influential Chinese living in the West. In contrast to the outspoken anticommunism of expatriate Poles and Russians, this sympathy for the Beijing government blocked a natural channel for the communication to the West of dissent from inside China. The tanks of Tiananmen did much to change that. As a result of the massacre the Chinese government faces an organized antigovernment Chinese patriots' movement in exile in the West for the first time since 1949. Yet the movement in exile is divided, many of its members are in transition to a permanent life in the West, and the expectations among democratic forces within China from the exiles are strangely low.

Democracy has been on the agenda for many urban Chinese since the Democracy Wall of 1979, but it seems unattainable within any short-term future. The student democracy movement of 1989 was successful in reaching out to the urban citizenry, but this very success brought into relief the nonchalance about democracy of the rural hundreds of millions. I feel democracy will take hold in China one day, in some form, but that it will be a difficult process because the economic and sociopsychological preconditions of democracy do not yet exist in many parts of the country. Of all the political storms that destroyed the Communist regimes in the Soviet Union and Eastern Europe, the violent one in Romania, the most backward nation in the former European Communist bloc, the least industrialized and the most bereft of a sociopolitical alternative to the Communist polity, gives the nearest clue to the convulsion that could engulf a post-Communist China.

The power of nature is great in China, and the thinking of rural people in particular encapsulates it. This power derives from the crucial role of harvests, the capacity of rivers' tantrums to adjudicate life and death, the sheer size of China, and the long corridor of time down which peasant wisdom has evolved in dialogue with the natural order. In the year of Mao's death, an earthquake centered on the city of Tangshan killed 242,000 people in a few hours, seriously injured 160,000 more, and demolished 97 percent of the city's structures.[9] China absorbed this unspeakable tragedy with amazingly little fuss and even declined outside aid. There were many reasons for this, some of them unpleasant, but one was that the Chinese have learned to live with and accept the power of nature over their lives.

In most of the villages, Beijing generally seems far away, although not entirely to be disregarded, while the rivers and mountains and storms are immediate, if not always benevolent. Peasant China has twisted many an incoming ideology into a cozier shape. Otherworldly Buddhism from India was brought down to earth by an infusion of Confucian filial piety and Taoist sense of nature. Marxism from Germany and Russia was shorn of its linear view of history and given a modest place in the Chinese cyclical view of history. In the countryside, from the 1930s to the 1950s, Marxism was a useful weapon to undermine landlord power. Thereafter the farmers of China have often turned their backs on its pretensions, while still bowing a knee on necessary occasions to the Red Emperor of the moment.

Rural China is a place where the overriding imperative is to survive, and that explains the naturalistic world view of the farmer. Nature's power makes for fatalism, and it leads to what city people see as apoliticism. Mao attached high importance to overturning nature's obstructing power. He covered the face of the countryside with red and white slogans about class struggle and world revolution. He ordered rice planted in the north, and wheat in the south, in disregard of rainfall levels and soil quality, and sent city graduates to remote barren areas and told them to create prosperity from nothing by sheer willpower. In traditional Chinese painting, the landscape was dominant and human beings were tiny. By contrast, Mao's Communists sponsored a painting style in which nature receded and burly steelworker heroes loomed from the canvas.

But Nurture did not win many victories over Nature. Rural society has its own sedate dynamic, evolved over millennia, and Beijing politics seldom cuts its flow. A portent from heaven such as a meteorite is just as likely as a *People's Daily* editorial from Beijing to convince farmers of a political point or shift. The Tangshan earthquake convinced untold millions of Chinese farmers that Mao was about to die, and his death a bare two months later proved to them the infallibility of nature's portents. During the Deng era, Beijing's grip on the countryside loosened and the natural order and the religions and philosophies flavored by it reasserted themselves. Chinese communism lost its credibility in the villages years before it lost it in Tiananmen Square.

The students in 1989 learned the painful lesson that China's center of gravity lies not in its cities but in the countryside. "Next time we will go to the villages," Tan Zhenzhou, the graduate student of history who argued with soldiers outside the gates of his college, said to me in Beijing on the morrow of the massacre. "We will seek the farmers as allies." Not an easy task, and yet China cannot really change unless the farmers are involved in the movement for change. Far more than Eastern Europe, it is India, huge, proud, old, and rather poor, that makes the most instructive comparison with China on the question of capacity for political and social change.

A way of saying "How are you?" in Chinese is the striking "Have you eaten?" *(Ni chi le ma?)* and a way of asking how many people there are in the family is, "In your home, how many mouths are there?" The term for "population" is "human mouths" *(ren kou),* also suggesting the centrality of food in Chinese life. The Cantonese, it is said, eat everything on four legs except the kitchen table. The Sichuanese, it seems to me, essentially eat their environment; look around the countryside, and everything you see is turned by the Sichuanese into food, from the branches above your head to the roots under your feet.

Historically, a China eating well has been a stable China, and a China short of food has been a China in chaos. When a foreigner visits the country, food is a stabilizing factor as mealtimes, regular as clockwork, bring smiles, soothe frayed nerves, and reassert the Chineseness of the context over against any tendency of the foreigner to take refuge in his autonomy. Visiting China I propose postponing or skipping a meal only for a foolproof reason. I find well-being in eating three square meals at fixed times. I listen with fascination to tales of Ming dynasty emperors inventing spectacular dishes and Tang dynasty poets dining memorably at beauty spots. I come to think that for the Chinese eating helps take the place of all sorts of diversions and excitements that are common in the West but lacking in China.

The centrality of food in Chinese life ultimately reflects the blunt fact that there are too many people in China, whose territory is huge but only 11 percent cultivable, and the weight of numbers fuels the fatalism and despair that periodically grip the Chinese. Whatever the post-Communist era brings, the agricultural realm will be central to public policy, survival will be the chief concern of most of the population, and for a long time food will continue to lie at the heart of the Chinese experience.

There will never be fundamental change in China unless the new order is based on the idea of sovereignty stemming from the people. This will mean a revolution in the communal psychology of the Chinese, the rise of a civic culture, a greater social individualism, and an end to politics as the paternalism of the *jia*. The dynasty of communism is probably drawing to an end, and at fifty years or so it will be a relatively short dynasty, but whether it will give way to a freer, still united China, rather than a long period of struggle, disunity, or even civil war is far from certain.

One great lesson from the disintegration of the artifact of the Soviet Union for the coming crisis in China is that empire cannot survive the breaking down of a Communist party's monopoly on power. An overarching "idea of China" is a powerful myth in the minds of many Chinese, eclipsing the reality that Chinese-speaking people are almost as diverse as English-speaking people, and that scores of millions within the borders of the PRC are not even Chinese. It seems likely that the strains of any transition away from communism will put in question the unity of the PRC, especially its essentially colonial hold over Tibet, Xinjiang, and other non-Han areas. Few savor more keenly the meaning of "liberation" than these peoples who still await it. Empire is inseparable from autocracy, and when the palaces of Beijing burn with the lights of democracy, the dismantling of the Han-led empire may come like a thunderclap.

Chinese foreign policy has been very changeable, from the anti-Americanism of the 1950s when Mao said "Russia's today is China's tomorrow," to the late 1970s when for Deng the Soviet Union was the source of all evil. China has been continuously friendly with almost no country since 1949, and the most intimate ties (with Albania and Vietnam) turned into the most bitter. The historic change in Moscow in 1991 closed a foreign policy door in China's face. An isolated Beijing has only Cuba, North Korea, Vietnam, and Laos with which to cry in its Marxist cups. Rhetorically, the Chinese Communists can play the "Third World card," in a war of angry words against the West it loves to hate, but in power terms this is no substitute for the triangular game they played in Cold War days. For the first time in our era, the China-Russia relation has ceased to be a major factor in world politics. Beijing's and Moscow's main concern in dealing with each other in the coming years will be to protect their parlous domestic situations.

But whatever the direction of China's foreign policy in the post–Cold War years, China will surely be hamstrung by its economic backwardness and overpopulation, rendering it a peculiarly passive great power. In a certain sense it is inevitable that China will become a superpower, but a bogged-down one. Its gross national product may well pass that of the former Soviet republics in the first part of the twenty-first century, but with a far greater population than Russia and its fellow states, China will still be poor. And so long as the Leninist system endures, China will be no better than the Soviet Union was at creativity and innovation for a postindustrial age. China will remain Asia's geopolitical centerpiece, but somewhat like a vast stegosaurus installed in Asia's front yard, opening an eye now and then, occupying a terrain rather than doing much with it.

Yet being rather poor and uninventive will not prevent China from becoming assertive in the world, and much of Asia will have to view China as a superpower. A China that has shed some of its former ideological view of the world will behave as any other great power, trading in arms and drugs, stocking up on nuclear weapons, and bullying neighbors. I never expected, and still do not expect, an ideologically threadbare and nationalistic China to be softer to deal with than a Maoist China.

When I began to teach Chinese politics in 1970, there were three near-certainties in academic circles specializing in contemporary China that today look much less certain. Communism was in China to stay, we nearly all believed, the Nationalists had lost the Chinese mainland to the Communists once and for all, and the Russia-China split was such a potent fact of international life that, since Moscow was the West's sworn enemy, China could serve the West as a balance against Russia. Yet, after all, communism may not be a fact of life in China into the twenty-first century. If a future role for the Nationalists on the mainland is uncertain, Nationalist rule in Taiwan has never looked better than over recent years. And the West would seem to face more fruitful opportunities of cooperation with the republics of the former Soviet Union than with Stalinist China.

Still, if China no longer has yesterday's strategic importance to the West, it could be even more important as a problem for the West, either because it gives itself over to the throes of nationalistic resentment or because it descends into a chaos that entices Japan or Russia (once more), or others, to reach into the Chinese landmass. With China the dinosaur of the former Communist bloc, and Beijing the bleakest large city in the world for the life of the mind, there is a tendency to simply remove China from the screen of our consciousness. Yet an isolated, troubled China is too big to be disregarded, as a Haiti, Albania, or Somalia might be disregarded, and it is too proud to accept its backwardness and isolation without rumblings of defiance and even aggressiveness (perhaps toward Taiwan). China is like a huge old man in a village, of whose death everyone is afraid because if he dies, he will topple over and crush the normal-sized folk around him. Deng went so far as to warn the world in 1989 that unless he is permitted to rule China his way with an iron fist, 100 million refugees from China will flood the world. Like the huge old man in the village, Deng was saying, "Look after me, because if I die, you will die too."

Into the twenty-first century, however authoritarian the Beijing polity may be, we will have to live with centrally placed China and its 1.1 billion people. I believe we should refrain from throwing China around as a weapon in abstract ideological battles, avoid the condescension that is involved in a "double standard" for assessing China on the one hand and the former Marxist countries of Europe on the other, and look at Chinese culture not only in its contemporary form but down the long corridor of the centuries. We should resist Beijing's political and cultural pressure to set the agenda of issues and the definition of terms in China-West relations, and try to transcend our Western impulse to maintain an image of Chinese exoticism. It is not reasonable both to hope China will become more like ourselves and to keep China confined within a magic box of the exotic. The student movement of 1989 did something to destroy the image of China as exotic, for the aspirations of the young in Tiananmen Square were recognizable to people all over the world.

Eventually the perception of China's exoticism will break down before the universals of the human condition, and the knowledge of China will merge with the knowledge of ourselves; the bridge between us will be freedom and democracy. I do not think social individualism and political pluralism will come to China ready-made from the West. The impulse and demand for them will burst out within China, not offered from on high but grabbed from below, and in the bright light of freedom, the Chinese will discover their solidarity with everyone else around the globe.

ACKNOWLEDGMENTS

In China I enjoyed the cooperation and advice of Wu Zhenzhou, Li Yanning, Xu Ruigang, Chen Mingming, Deng Yiming, Zhang Ling, Song Xinxin, and others whose political views make it unwise for me to mention them.

In Hong Kong, Zhou Nan and David Wilson helped me look back on earlier events in China.

That I found myself on the spot in Beijing during June 1989 was due to the enthusiasm for my project on Chinese Youth of editors at the *National Geographic,* especially Charles McCarry, William Graves, and Robert Poole.

For reading an earlier version of the manuscript with a skilled and critical eye, I am grateful to Paul Cohen, and for reading portions of it, to Liu Luxin, James C. Thomson, Jean Oi, David Zweig, Shen Tong, and Li-li Ch'en.

At the Harvard-Yenching Library of Harvard University, Eugene Wu, Raymond Lum, and others were exceedingly helpful, as was Nancy Hearst at Harvard's Fairbank Center Library. Others who helped in a variety of ways include James Seymour, Yang Bing-zhang, and Mark Baker.

Over the years, colleagues at the Fairbank Center for East Asian Research at Harvard University—too numerous to list here—have provided a community of dialogue without which my writing on China could not have been accomplished.

My literary agent, Barbara Lowenstein, spurred me on, and at Simon & Schuster, I benefited from the wonderful editorial team of Frederic Hills and Burton Beals, assisted by Daphne Bien.

NOTES

PROLOGUE

1. Mao Zedong, "Introducing a Cooperative," *Hongqi,* Beijing, June 1, 1958.
2. My interview with Kukrit Pramoj, who visited Mao while prime minister of Thailand in 1975, in Bangkok, November 10, 1979.

CHAPTER ONE

1. Mao Zedong, *Mao Zedong xuan ji* (Beijing: Ren min chu ban she, 1964), p. 1329.
2. Herbert Spencer, *Principles of Sociology* (New York: Appleton-Century, 1914), passim. Mao used the term "revolutionary machine"—*Selected Works,* Vol. 3 (Beijing: Foreign Languages Press, 1965), p. 86.
3. Theodore White and Annalee Jacoby, *Thunder Out of China* (New York: William Sloane, 1961 edition), p. 129.
4. Stuart Schram (editor), *Chairman Mao Talks to the People* (New York: Pantheon, 1974), p. 45.
5. *Khrushchev Remembers: The Last Testament* (New York: Bantam, 1976), p. 288.
6. Jules Archer, *Mao Tse-tung* (New York: Hawthorn Books, 1972), p. 147.
7. David Milton and Nancy Dall Milton, *The Wind Will Not Subside* (New York: Pantheon, 1976), p. 270.
8. Geremie Barmé and John Minford (editors), *Seeds of Fire* (New York: Hill and Wang, 1988), p. 136.

9. Zhen Donglei, "Lei Feng, a Fine Example of Chinese Youth," *Evergreen,* Beijing, Number 2, April 1963.
10. Charles Taylor, *Reporter in Red China* (New York: Random House, 1966), pp. 140–41.
11. The Chinese Communist army's involvement in opium smuggling is mentioned in Zhang Zhenglong, *Xue bai, xue hong* ("White Snow, Red Blood"), (Beijing: Jie fang jun chu ban she, 1989).

CHAPTER TWO

1. F. Geoffroy-Dechaume, *China Looks at the World* (New York: Pantheon, 1967), p. 47.
2. Kevin Rafferty, *City on the Rocks* (London: Viking, 1989), p. 14.
3. Paul Theroux, *Riding the Iron Rooster* (New York: Putnam's, 1988), p. 143.
4. *Parliamentary Papers,* House of Lords, London, 1843, VI, No. 143.
5. Xiao San, *Mao Zedong tong zhi de qing shao nian shi dai* (Beijing: Ren min chu ban she, 1951), Chapter 1, VIII.
6. Yugoslav diplomat to the author, Peking, 1971, citing a conversation between Mao and the Yugoslav ambassador some years before.
7. Malraux passed on the gist of this remark to President Nixon in 1972—Richard Nixon, *RN: The Memoirs of Richard Nixon,* Vol. 2 (New York: Warner, 1978), p. 24.
8. Immanuel C. Y. Hsu, *China's Entrance into the Family of Nations* (Cambridge: Harvard University Press, 1960), pp. 106–107.
9. *People's Daily,* September 25–30, 1962.
10. *Jiang Qing tong zhi lun wen yi* (Beijing, no publisher, 1968), p. 24.
11. Ross Terrill, *The White-Boned Demon* (New York: Morrow, 1984), p. 249.
12. Richard Crossman (editor), *The God That Failed* (New York: Bantam, 1952), p. 8.

CHAPTER THREE

1. Mao Zedong, *Poems* (Beijing: Foreign Languages Press, 1976), p. 23.
2. André Malraux, *Antimémoires* (Paris: Gallimard, 1967), pp. 522ff.
3. The poem is called "Reascending Jinggangshan," in Mao Zedong, *Poems,* p. 49.
4. Milton and Milton, *The Wind Will Not Subside,* pp. 103ff.
5. Roderick MacFarquhar, *The Origins of the Cultural Revolution,* Vol. 2 (New York: Columbia University Press, 1983), pp. 207ff. The involvement of theater with the Hai Rui story is brilliantly traced by Rudolf

Wagner in "In Guise of a Congratulation," *Australian Journal of Chinese Affairs,* Number 26.

6. *Joint Publications Research Service,* Number 61269-2, p. 347.

7. Information from Melinda Liu of *Newsweek.*

8. Gao Yuan, *Born Red* (Stanford, Calif.: Stanford University Press, 1987), pp. 318–19.

9. *China Quarterly,* London, Number 35, p. 59 and passim.

10. Speech in Canberra, Australia, February 19, 1966.

11. *Quotations from Chairman Mao Zedong* (Beijing: Foreign Languages Press, 1966), Foreword by Lin Biao (no page number).

12. Lowell Dittmer, *Liu Shaoqi and the Chinese Cultural Revolution* (Berkeley: University of California Press, 1974), pp. 208–209.

13. Uli Franz, *Deng Xiaoping* (New York: Harcourt Brace Jovanovich, 1988), pp. 192, 198.

14. *Facts and Features,* Taipei, September 4, 1968.

15. Stanley Karnow, *Mao and China* (New York: Viking, 1973), p. 487.

16. Samuel Huntington, *Political Order in Changing Societies* (New Haven, Conn.: Yale University Press, 1968), p. 342.

CHAPTER FOUR

1. Theroux, *Riding the Iron Rooster,* p. 93; Anne F. Thurston, *Enemies of the People* (Cambridge, Mass.: Harvard University Press, 1988), p. 131; John Avedon, *In Exile from the Land of Snows* (New York: Knopf, 1985).

2. Thurston, *Enemies of the People,* p. 134.

3. Gao Yuan, *Born Red,* p. 298.

4. Information from a fellow prisoner of Liu Yunruo, and from *Zheng Ming,* Hong Kong, Number 12, 1979, pp. 20ff.

5. Anna Louise Strong, personal communication from Beijing, July 1966.

6. Gao Yuan, *Born Red,* pp. 77–78.

7. This dimension of the Cultural Revolution is explored in Lynn T. White, *Policies of Chaos* (Princeton, N.J.: Princeton University Press, 1989). He observes, "The 'important people' were not the only important people, in the making of this event" (p. 311).

8. C. P. Fitzgerald, *The Empress Wu* (Melbourne: Melbourne University Press, 1955), p. 32.

9. Edgar Snow, *The Long Revolution* (New York: Random House, 1972), p. 70.

10. Cathy Yeh (former Red Guard) on BBC's *Panorama,* April 18, 1977.

11. Dittmer, *Liu Shaoqi and the Chinese Cultural Revolution,* p. 101; C. B. Kok, *Duan tou tai xia zhi Jiang Qing* (Hong Kong: Chinese Cultural Center, 1976), pp. 146–58.

12. *China Quarterly,* Number 103, p. 505.

13. *Joint Publications Research Service,* Number 42349, August 25, 1967.
14. Schram (editor), *Chairman Mao Talks to the People,* pp. 277ff.

CHAPTER FIVE

1. The story is told in the French diplomat's memoirs, Etienne M. Manac'h, *La Chine* (Paris: Fayard, 1980), pp. 382–83, 405, 408, 419–20, 421, and in former prime minister Whitlam's memoirs, E. Gough Whitlam, *The Whitlam Government* (Melbourne: Penguin, 1985), p. 55.
2. Henry Kissinger, *White House Years* (Boston: Little, Brown, 1979), p. 703.
3. John Maxwell Hamilton, *Edgar Snow* (Bloomington: Indiana University Press, 1988), p. 272.
4. Kissinger, *White House Years,* p. 744.
5. Ibid., p. 748.
6. The Richard Hughes report was carried by the *Melbourne Sun,* August 3, 1971.
7. Ludwig Feuerbach, *The Essence of Christianity,* cited in Robert C. Tucker, "Marxism—Is It Religion?" *Ethics,* January 1958, p. 130.

CHAPTER SIX

1. *New York Times,* June 23, 1971; *Wall Street Journal,* June 23, 1971.
2. The piece ran on the front page of *The Washington Post* on July 22, 1971.
3. Hamilton, *Edgar Snow,* pp. 237ff.
4. Chen Dunde, *Mao Zedong, Ni Ke Song zai 1972* (Beijing: Kun lun chu ban she, 1988), p. 290.
5. Nixon, *RN: The Memoirs of Richard Nixon,* Vol. 2, p. 52.

CHAPTER SEVEN

1. A source in the Chinese foreign ministry to the author in 1978.
2. Schram (editor), *Chairman Mao Talks to the People,* p. 297.
3. *People's Daily,* July 1, 1971.
4. It was only in 1988 that a Chinese official on the record gave some details of Lin's plane crash. See *Wen Hui Bao,* Hong Kong, January 12, 1988, and following days.
5. Zhou's resistance to some of Lin's plans, even to the point of requiring Mao's adjudication between them, is detailed in a book by Lin's former secretary, Zhang Yunsheng, *Mao jia wan ji shi* (Beijing: Chun qiu chu ban she, 1988); see pp. 98–99 and passim.
6. *Qi shi nian dai,* Hong Kong, Number 3, 1977.
7. These and other words from Whitlam's talk with Mao come from my

perusal of a transcript of the conversation at the Australian ministry of foreign affairs.

8. Angela Terzani, *Chinese Days* (Hong Kong: Odyssey, 1988), p. 138.

9. Thurston, *Enemies of the People,* p. 35.

10. Julie N. Eisenhower, *Special People* (New York: Ballantine, 1978), p. 153.

11. Mao Zedong, *Poems,* pp. 50, 52.

12. The two statements appeared in *People's Daily,* January 1, 1976, and were repeated in subsequent weeks and months.

13. Lee Kuan Yew, letter to the author, November 28, 1979.

14. *Zhong fa,* Number 24 (translated in *Issues and Studies,* Taipei, October 1977).

15. Deng Xiaoping, *Deng Xiaoping wen xuan* (Beijing: Ren min chu ban she, 1989), p. 305.

16. For the origin of the poems, see Ross Terrill, *The Future of China* (New York: Dell, 1978), pp. 296–97.

17. *Beijing Review,* May 14, 1976, p. 4.

18. *Zhong fa,* Number 24 (translated in *Issues and Studies,* Taipei, November 1977, p. 102).

CHAPTER EIGHT

1. *Ming Bao Yue Kan,* Hong Kong, November 1976.

2. Transcript read by the author at the Beijing National Library. The remark appears in *China Quarterly,* Number 103, p. 504.

3. Si Ma Zhang Feng, *Deng Xiaoping fu zhi shi mo* (Hong Kong: Bao wen shu ju, 1980), p. 198.

4. *New York Times,* February 6, 1979 (report on Helen Foster Snow's trip to China).

5. Ross Terrill, *Mao* (New York: Harper and Row, 1980), p. 379. These and other words from Whitlam's talk with Mao come from my perusal of a transcript of the conversation at the Australian ministry of foreign affairs.

6. Anthony Tang, "Agriculture in China: Problems and Prospects," in Norton Ginsburg and Bernard Lalor (editors), *China: The 1980s Era* (Boulder, Colo.: Westview Press, 1984), p. 158.

7. It is well known in Singapore political circles that Deng said this to Prime Minister Lee Kuan Yew. According to *Asiaweek,* July 1, 1988, p. 6, he made a similar remark to the president of Mozambique.

8. The trial is recounted in *Li shi de shen pan* (Beijing: Qun zhong chu ban she, 1981); *A Great Trial in Chinese History* (Beijing: New World Press, 1981); and *Beijing da shen* (Taipei: Investigation Bureau of the Justice Ministry, 1981). I viewed audiovisual records of the trial at the Investigation Bureau in Taipei.

CHAPTER NINE

1. After his defeat in the 1976 election, Ford told Millicent Gates, the widow of Tom Gates, who had been Ford's representative in Peking during 1975–76: "There was no doubt in my mind, had I been reelected in 1976, that we intended to push vigorously for normalization with the PRC on reasonable terms in 1977." Millicent Anne Gates and E. Bruce Geelhoed, *The Dragon and the Snake* (Philadelphia: University of Pennsylvania, 1986), p. 193.
2. Related to me by John Fairbank, who was present at the dinner.
3. Kissinger, *White House Years,* p. 741.
4. Richard Bernstein, *From the Center of the Earth* (Boston: Little, Brown, 1982), p. 219.
5. I wrote about Shen in *The Boston Globe Magazine,* August 15, 1982, but called him "Mr. Li," for at that time he still was in Beijing. Shen has since come to the United States.

CHAPTER TEN

1. Terrill, *The White-Boned Demon,* p. 333.
2. Terzani, *Chinese Days,* p. 163.
3. Karel Kovanda estimated in 1983 that not more than two hundred of the PRC's twenty-three hundred counties had ever welcomed a foreign visitor ("Chasing China's Shadows," *Problems of Communism,* January–February 1984).
4. *China Quarterly,* Number 116, p. 556.
5. *Statistical Yearbook of China, 1986* (Beijing, 1988).
6. "Bo Yang tan Zhong guo yu Zhong guo ren," in *Jiu shi nian dai,* Hong Kong, 4/1987.

CHAPTER ELEVEN

1. I gave the article this title—drawn from its closing line—but several newspapers that published it found the title too sharp and chose another. *The Boston Globe* used the heading, "What Fate for Britain's Golden Goose?" (November 27, 1983), and the *Los Angeles Times* chose "Midnight Draws Nearer for Free Hong Kong" (March 4, 1984).
2. Harry Harding, *China's Second Revolution* (Washington, D.C.: Brookings Institution, 1987), p. 106.
3. Terrill, *The Future of China,* p. 268.
4. Bette Bao Lord, *Legacies* (New York: Knopf, 1990), p. 4.
5. *People's Daily,* December 7, 1984, and following days; *New York Times,* December 11, 1984.
6. *Boston Globe,* January 2, 1987; *Miami Herald,* January 4, 1987.

7. The Criminal Code is translated in Foreign Broadcast Information Service, Daily Report, PRC, July 27, 1979 (Supplement); see also *Beijing Review,* July 13, 1979.
8. Edgar Snow, *Red Star Over China* (New York: Grove Press, 1961), p. 128.

CHAPTER TWELVE

1. *Beijing Review,* November 9–15, 1987.
2. Ibid.
3. Dalai Lama, *My Land and My People* (New York: McGraw-Hill, 1962), p. 121.

CHAPTER THIRTEEN

1. *South China Morning Post,* June 28, 1989.
2. Li Rui, *The Early Revolutionary Activities of Comrade Mao Tse-tung* (White Plains, N.Y.: M. E. Sharpe, 1977), p. 38.
3. "Rough Justice in Beijing," *News from Asia Watch,* January 27, 1991, pp. 7ff.
4. Michael Fathers and Andrew Higgins, *Tiananmen: The Rape of Peking* (London: The Independent, 1989), p. 31.
5. Mao Zedong, *Selected Works,* Vol. 1 (Beijing: Foreign Languages Press, 1965), p. 121.
6. Liu Binyan, *Tell the World* (New York: Pantheon, 1989), p. 15 (translation adjusted); Michel Oksenberg et al. (editors), *Beijing Spring 1989* (Armonk, N.Y.: M. E. Sharpe, 1990), pp. 203ff.

CHAPTER FOURTEEN

1. Shen Tong, *Almost a Revolution* (Boston: Houghton Mifflin, 1990), p. 222.
2. Li Lu, *Moving the Mountain* (London: Macmillan, 1990), p. 123.
3. Han Minzhu (editor), *Cries for Democracy* (Princeton, N.J.: Princeton University Press, 1990), p. 198.
4. Liu Binyan, *Tell the World,* p. 25.
5. Han Minzhu (editor), *Cries for Democracy,* p. 195.
6. An analysis of *People's Daily* coverage from an insider's perspective by Frank Tan appears in *Pacific Affairs,* Summer 1990.
7. *Washington Post,* May 14, 1989.
8. *New York Review of Books,* June 29, 1989, p. 6.
9. Shen Tong, *Almost a Revolution,* p. 262.
10. Che Muqi, *Beijing Turmoil* (Beijing: Foreign Languages Press, 1990), p. 29.

11. Fathers and Higgins, *Tiananmen: The Rape of Peking*, p. 57.
12. Lawrence Sullivan's essay in the volume *China: The Crisis of 1989*, from a conference in 1990 at the State University of New York at Buffalo.
13. *Los Angeles Times*, June 3, 1989.
14. *Wall Street Journal*, May 19, 1989.
15. Shen Tong, *Almost a Revolution*, p. 292.
16. Gao Xin, talk at Harvard University, April 16, 1991.
17. Tony Saich in *Australian Journal of Chinese Affairs*, Number 24, p. 202; Su's talk at Harvard, Spring 1990.
18. Saich, *Australian Journal of Chinese Affairs*, Number 24, p. 205.
19. *Ming Bao*, Hong Kong, May 29, 1989.
20. Anne Gunn, *Australian Journal of Chinese Affairs*, Number 24, p. 251. *Jing xin dong po de wu shi liu tian* (Beijing: Da di chu ban she, 1989), passim.
21. Information on the goddess from David Zweig of Tufts University, who interviewed art students involved in the project.

CHAPTER FIFTEEN

1. Han Minzhu (editor), *Cries for Democracy*, p. 363 (translation adjusted).

CHAPTER SIXTEEN

1. Mao, *Selected Works*, Vol. 2, p. 224.
2. Account by Roger Howard, *Australian Journal of Chinese Affairs*, Number 24, p. 240.
3. Tan in *Pacific Affairs*, Summer 1990.
4. Anne Gunn, Shelley Warner, Anita Chan, and Jonathan Unger in *Australian Journal of Chinese Affairs*, Number 24, pp. 254, 276, 313; and Keith Forster, ibid., Number 23, pp. 100, 114.
5. Sun Zi, *The Art of War* (Oxford: Oxford University Press, 1963), p. 66.
6. A version of Deng's June 9 speech appears in Han Minzhu (editor), *Cries for Democracy*, pp. 369ff.

CHAPTER SEVENTEEN

1. Liu Binyan, *Tell the World*, p. 63, says 120,000 were imprisoned.
2. Joseph Esherick, *Australian Journal of Chinese Affairs*, Number 24, p. 234.
3. Fathers and Higgins, *Tiananmen: The Rape of Peking*, p. 36.
4. Chen's speech may be found in Yi Mu and Mark V. Thompson, *Crisis at Tiananmen* (San Francisco: China Books, 1989), pp. 194ff.
5. A brilliant analysis of how the politics of the streets never was aligned with the closed-door maneuvers of senior political levels, and the historical and cultural reasons for this gap, may be found in "Acting Out Democracy:

Political Theater in Modern China," by Joseph Esherick and Jeffrey Wasserstrom, in *The Journal of Asian Studies,* November 1990.
6. The words of Zhao Xinshu and Shen Peilu.

CHAPTER EIGHTEEN

1. J. Kinoshita, "The World Viewed from China," *Sekai,* Tokyo, September 1963.
2. Wu told the story at a seminar at Harvard in 1986. It also appears in Barmé and Minford (editors), *Seeds of Fire,* p. 407.
3. Han Minzhu (editor), *Cries for Democracy,* p. 94.
4. Freda Utley, *Odyssey of a Liberal* (Washington, D.C.: Washington National Press, 1970), pp. 206–207.
5. Blaise Pascal, *Pensées de Pascal* (Paris: Dezobry et E. Magdeleine, 1852), Article XXIV, Number 46.
6. See James C. Thomson, Jr., "Jilted Again," *Gannet Center Journal,* Fall 1989, for a fine account of U.S. media's "courtship" of democracy in China.
7. Mao, *Selected Works,* Vol. 4, p. 414.
8. *Tansuo* ("Exploration"), Beijing, March 1979.
9. *Tangshan—Six Years after the Quake* (Beijing: Beijing Review Publications, 1983).

INDEX

Acheson, Dean, 117
Acton, Lord, 154
Afghanistan, 164, 165
Africa, 36–37, 48, 100
agriculture
  modernization of, 217
  and public policy, 333
  see also farmers
AIDS, growing problem of,
  316
All-China Federation of Trade
  Unions, 254
All-China Federation of Women,
  254, 295
Alley, Rewi, 178
Amnesty International, 37
Anderson, Donald, 168
anti-Americanism, 48–51, 53, 116,
  118, 334
anti-imperialism, 29, 31, 32, 223
anticolonialism, 35, 36, 69
anticommunism, 68, 312
antifeudalism, 29, 31, 32
Aquino, Cory, 311
Armacost, Michael, 165
Arrow War, 52
Association for Friendship with
  Foreign Countries, 114

Atlantic Monthly, The, 95, 99, 115,
  117, 119, 129, 183, 270
Attwood, William, 107, 113
Australia, 21, 36, 42, 43, 44, 49, 51,
  61
  Chinese culture in, 46–47
  and Chinese foreign policy,
    105, 106, 107, 114–15, 118,
    124
  communism in, 54
  cultural exchanges with China,
    134, 172, 174
  Labor party in, 67, 95, 97, 105,
    106, 328
  trade with China, 39, 95
authoritarianism, 93, 159, 197, 232,
  293, 303, 326, 336
  and Chinese culture, 153
  and democracy, 172
  and economic progress, 123
  and reform, 196
  vs. totalitarianism, 73

Bao Tong, 287
Bastid, Marianne, 42–43
Beer, Samuel, 94
Bei Dao, 232
Beijing, *see* Peking

Beijing Hotel, 262, 264, 270, 272, 278, 279, 281
Beijing Intellectuals Association, 253, 256
Beijing Students' Federation, 256, 259
Beijing University, 223, 224, 231, 232
  democracy movement at, 232, 233, 245, 248, 254
  in midsummer 1989, 306
Belden, Jack
  China Shakes the World, 28, 104
Beveridge, William, 73
birth control, 152
Bo Yang, 193
Bogno, Frederico, 284, 285
Bogunovic, Branko, 66
Boston Globe, The, 136, 200
Boxer Rebellion, 24, 44
Brezhnev, Leonid, 61, 126, 254
British Broadcasting Company (BBC), 102
Broinowski, Richard, 221
Brown, Harold, 164, 165, 168
Brzezinski, Zbigniew, 164
Buck, Pearl
  The Good Earth, 28
Buckley, William F., 121–22
Buddhism, 44, 85, 102, 187, 212, 213, 282, 332
bureaucracy, 33
Burma, 222
Burns, Tom, 108
Bush, George, 140, 196, 320
Butterfield, Fox
  Alive in the Bitter Sea, 152

Canada, 95, 97
Canton (Guangzhou), 46–56, 117, 167, 185, 228, 310, 311
  compared with Saigon, 69
  Cultural Park in, 152–53
  eating habits in, 333
  in 1960s, 15
  trade in, 47
  Treaty Port, 52
  Yang Cheng Hotel in, 48, 49, 50

capitalism, 73, 150, 172, 175, 322, 329
  and corruption, 199
  monopoly, 293
  and small business, 218–19
  vs socialism, 53, 217, 218, 219
Carter, Jimmy, 161, 162, 163, 164, 165, 166
Ceaucescu, Nicolae, 322
Chai Ling, 247, 250, 252, 256, 266, 267, 273
Changsha, 46, 53, 108, 116, 117, 134, 147, 155, 156
Chen, Jerome, 155
Chen Aiqing, 175
Chen Boda, 88, 157
Chen Duxiu, 27
Chen Xitong, 281*n*, 313
Chen Yi, 23, 71, 82
Chen Yizi, 256
Chen Yun, 199, 235
Chen Ziming, 232, 252, 258, 287
Chengdu, 185–90, 187–88, 189–90, 205, 214, 216, 220, 225, 320
  economic reform in, 229
  Jin Jiang Hotel in, 185–86, 190, 191, 210
  West China Coffeehouse in, 203, 210–11
  see also Sichuan Province
Chengdu Women's Federation, 190
Chiang Kai-shek, 27, 55, 107–8, 158, 190, 223, 238, 317, 330
  and Christianity, 44
  and Communists, 30, 31, 38, 126, 165, 236, 276, 292
  on Communists, 31
  defeat of, 13, 48, 61
  early life of, 31
  and Liberation, 35
  and Mao Zedong, 34, 60, 119
  as president of Republic of China, 31
  U.S. support of, 23, 51, 53, 117, 120, 189
Chiang Kai-shek, Madame (Song Meiling), 31
childhood, Chinese, 152

China International Travel Service, 22, 23, 320
China Quarterly, 121*n*
Chinese Academy of Social Science, 151, 153, 156
Chinese Communist party, 30, 33, 38, 58, 70
  attitude toward imperialism, 322
  authority of, 159, 218, 219, 296
  cadres of, 150, 154
  campaigns against "spiritual pollution," 181, 183, 225
  as circus impresario, 315, 316
  credibility of, 110, 202, 332
  cynicism about, 192
  and democracy movement, 246, 252, 258, 267, 276, 299, 304, 312, 319
  failure of, 131–32
  fiftieth anniversary of founding of, 115, 127
  leadership of, 31–32
  loyalty to leader in, 311
  and Mao's succession, 147–48
  and modernization, 112
  monopoly over public life of, 177, 215
  and Nationalist party, 126
  Ninth Congress of, 125–26, 147, 157
  opposition to, 154
  paranoia of, 325
  and reality, 134
  and reform, 195–96, 249
  and rural struggle, 30
  and sovereignty, 321
  Stalinism in, 18
  struggle within, 312–13
  Tenth Congress of, 148, 157
  Thirteenth Congress of, 216
Chinese Export Commodities Fair, 47
Chinese Revolution, 22, 61, 83, 102, 130, 143, 212, 318
  impact of, on Asia, 68
  purpose of, 47–48, 131, 194, 218
Ching, Frank, 189

Chongqing, 33, 79, 152, 190, 211, 214, 215, 217, 218, 288
  Cultural Revolution in, 83, 84
  People's Hotel in, 181, 208–9
Christian Peace Conference, 45, 85
Christianity, 13, 43–46, 57, 85, 109, 213
  and failure of Marxism, 212
  and imperialism, 46
  rejection of, by Chinese, 44, 325
  and Western achievements, 188
Churchill, Winston, 145
citizenship, American, 168–69
Civil War, Chinese, 23, 28, 53, 69, 126, 168
class struggle, 17, 65, 72, 107, 110, 134, 143, 144, 154, 293, 310
  in Cultural Revolution, 76
  and power struggle, 198
  see also Mao Zedong: and class struggle; Marxism
Coe, Frank, 179
Coe, Ruth, 179
Cohen, Jerome Alan, 96, 161
Cohn-Bendit, Daniel, 133
Cold War, 84, 334
collectivism, 75, 132
  failures of, 28
  and party control, 39
  and poverty, 101, 187
  vs. individualism, 29, 174, 175, 218, 265, 318, 325
  see also communes
Collingwood, Charles, 119, 120
colonialism, 37, 222, 223
Committee For Australia China Relations, 134, 136, 169
communes, 32–33, 59, 65, 101, 125
  breaking up of, 149–50
  in 1960s, 85
  wages on, 32
communism, 32, 92, 159, 242, 317
  achievement of, 48
  as altruistic faith, 69, 212
  building of, 57, 216
  and Chinese society, 14
  crack-up of, 18–19, 315
  end of, in China, 334

communism (*cont.*)
  and freedom, 101, 174–76
  and modernization, 57, 131
  paternalism of, 18, 329
  and religion, 44
  Russian, 14
  and student protesters, 252
  survival of, 19, 335
Communist Youth League, 133–
  134, 198, 199, 231, 254, 295,
  308
Communists, 13, 25, 26, 75, 96,
  330
  Chinese vs. Russian, 74
  and domestic control, 16
  hostility to Christianity, 282
  Japanese, 66–67
  long-term goals of, 35
  victory over Nationalists, 131
Confucianism, 50, 79, 103, 142,
  205, 223
  and Chinese Communists, 63,
  192, 197, 245
  and filial piety, 44, 332
Confucius, 27, 44, 135
Conspiracy and Death of Lin Biao,
  128
constitutionalism, 169, 170
corruption, 234, 237, 239, 258,
  287n, 304, 308, 312
  and capitalism, 199
  and free press, 240
  and reform, 230, 233
cosmopolitanism, 326, 328,
  329
counterrevolution, 157, 158, 171,
  232, 287–88, 290, 293, 294,
  295, 308
crime, 204–8, 211
Crisis at Tiananmen (Yi and
  Thompson), 281n
Cronkite, Walter, 119
Cui Jian
  "Nothing to My Name" (song),
  327–28
Cultural Revolution, 32, 65, 76–93,
  100, 163
  and anti-Americanism, 50

  and belief in Communist party,
    225
  book burning in, 188
  and capitalism, 150
  compared with Tiananmen
    Massacre, 277, 304
  duration of, 111n
  family life in, 80, 82
  fascism in, 79
  foreign journalists in, 66
  last phase of, 128
  launching of, 16
  and Mao Zedong, 17, 61, 62, 69,
    70, 71, 74, 75, 83, 84, 87, 93
  and Marxism, 76
  mythology of, 108
  participation in, 82–83, 93, 147,
    178
  personal meaning of, 86
  politics of, 180
  and power, 73
  recovery from, 100–102, 111–12,
    120, 123, 124, 125, 140
  slogans of, 158
  subjectivism of, 110
  and universities, 240
  victims of, 76–80, 129, 130, 158,
    167, 174, 178, 197, 201
culture
  as chemistry, 328
  Chinese, 75, 120, 153, 175, 195,
    213, 226–27, 310, 315, 317,
    322, 323, 326, 328, 336
  civic, 252, 253, 287, 333
  Russian, 38, 39
  Western, 190–91, 323, 326
Czechoslovakia, 61, 72–73, 216,
  220

Da tong (Great Unity), 327
Dalai Lama, 226
Dalian (Manchuria), 129, 132, 192,
  204–5
Darwin, Charles, 103
Davies, John Paton, 324
de Gaulle, Charles, 25, 60, 145
Declaration of Independence,
  American, 216

democracy, 27, 103, 154, 173, 176, 192, 236, 239, 265, 336
  bourgeois, 219
  in China, 172, 301, 307, 308, 326, 327, 330
  and collapse of communism, 242, 330
  and leaders, 87
  and reform, 195–96, 200, 217, 219
  and science, 27, 171, 239
  as synonym for "happiness," 175
  see also May Fourth Movement
democracy movement
  of 1986, 199–200, 239
  of 1989, 18, 232–36, 238–39, 240–42, 305, 336
  arrests for participation in, 297, 305
  attitude to foreigners, 254
  businessmen in, 254
  Chinese journalists in, 247–48, 304
  and citizenship, 254–55, 274
  and Communist party, 240, 311
  countrywide, 257–58, 260, 331
  crushing of, 308, 325
  and declaration of martial law, 255–56, 258, 264, 275, 284–285, 312
  and foreign journalists, 249, 250
  repression of, 298–99, 313
  slogans of, 247, 250, 253, 254, 280, 282, 298
  unofficial anthem of, 328
Democracy Wall, 170–71, 201, 219, 232, 233, 252, 327, 331
demonstrations
  anti-American, 23, 43
  student, 199–200, 209, 219, 241, 243, 245, 319
  see also Tiananmen Square
Deng Lijun, 218
Deng Pufang, 234
Deng Xiaoping, 33–34, 56, 60, 63, 66–67, 185, 188, 213, 227, 228, 317, 326, 336
  on Asia-Pacific region, 34
  compared with Gorbachev, 220–221
  compared with Mao Zedong, 237, 310
  as counterrevolutionary, 141, 295
  criticism of, 230, 237
  in Cultural Revolution, 71, 72, 82, 83, 91, 93, 129, 130, 149, 230
  and democracy movement, 235–236, 241, 243, 244, 245–46, 248, 249, 251, 253, 256, 257, 271, 305
  and Democracy Wall, 171, 172, 219, 232
  and diplomatic relations with United States, 163
  and economic development, 177, 179, 198–99
  foreign policy of, 141, 164, 167, 221, 222
  four modernizations of, 170, 192, 249
  at funeral of Hu Yaobang, 235
  and future of CCP, 318
  on Gang of Four, 199
  on getting rich, 150, 234, 268
  on Hu Yaobang, 241
  as impresario, 316
  and industry, 183
  on Jiang Qing's operas, 56
  and Leninism, 196
  and Liu Shaoqi, 71, 82, 200
  and Mao Zedong, 70, 71, 83, 92, 93, 94, 139, 143, 144, 146, 215, 225, 282
  and Maoism, 193, 194, 195
  on Marxism, 150
  meeting with Gorbachev, 250–251, 271
  militarism of, 290–91
  and military, 257
  and nationalism, 192, 194
  and privilege, 189
  reforms of, 17–18, 176, 177, 195, 196, 202, 203, 211, 215, 217, 219, 220, 226, 233, 307, 329
  return of, 129–30, 146, 149

Deng Xiaoping (*cont.*)
  rise to power of, 17
  and Soviet Union, 334
  struggle for succession to, 313,
    318
  as successor to Mao, 138, 139–
    140, 152, 175, 198
  and Tiananmen Square massacre,
    166, 270, 278, 283, 287, 292,
    307, 311
  and trial of Gang of Four, 157,
    158, 197, 198
  and "truth to save China," 327
  at United Nations, 140
  and Vietnam, 165, 166
  visit to United States, 163, 165
  and war, 165–66
Deng Yiming, 211
Dong Fengchong, Dr., 139, 184–
  185
Dubcek, Alexander, 72–73, 74, 216
Dukakis, Michael, 320
Dulles, John Foster, 23, 74, 119
Dunn, Hugh, 116

"East Is Red, The," 65
Eastern Europe, 14, 15, 22, 23, 61,
  72–73, 315, 322
  and China, 318, 330
  and Russia, 123
economic development, 133, 149,
  155, 177, 184, 197, 210, 221–
  222
  and political change, 155, 199,
    202, 209, 326
  Stalinist urban, 150
economy, 195, 198, 214, 218
  bureaucratic, 180
  free, 180
  and inflation, 215, 229, 230
  and price regulation, 229, 230
800,000,000: The Real China
  (Terrill), 121*n*, 129
Eisenhower, David, 137
Eisenhower, Dwight D., 49
Eisenhower, Julie Nixon, 137
Elliot, Charles, 127–28
Ellsberg, Daniel, 105

emperors, 24, 59, 144, 145, 289,
  319, 326
  and dictators, 308
Engels, Friedrich, 92, 103
Europe, 22, 34, 53, 72
Exploration (journal), 170

factionalism, 89, 92, 128
Faggetter, Rachel, 132, 161
Fairbank, John King, 74, 75, 94,
  123, 158, 324
Fairbank, Wilma, 158
family, 82, 84, 89, 319
family farming, 195, 203, 216, 218,
  319
Fang, Percy, 197
Fang Lizhi, 199, 232, 239, 308
farmers, 32, 150, 187, 188, 301
  and Communist bureaucrats, 218
  and democracy movement, 332–
    333
  and land, 35, 217
  and Marxism, 332
  naturalistic world view of, 332
fascism, 79, 154
Federal Bureau of Investigation
  (FBI), 122*n*, 137*n*
Fei Xiaotong, 158
Feng Youlan
  A History of Chinese Philosophy,
    110
feudalism, 53, 135, 199, 231
Feuerbach, Ludwig, 109
Firing Line (TV program), 121,
  122*n*
Flowers on an Iron Tree (Terrill), 131
Flying Tiger Brigade, 255
Food
  centrality of, in China, 333
Ford, Gerald, 140, 161, 166
foreign policy, 16, 98, 99, 106, 113,
  123, 221, 322, 334
foreigners
  called "barbarians" (*ye man, da
    bizi*), 41
  Chinese attitude toward, 107,
    150, 181–82, 193, 266, 280,
    285, 309, 321

quest to understand China, 324–325
and Tiananmen Square massacre, 284–87, 291
France, 33, 95, 118, 145
freedom, 212, 226, 232, 239, 254, 318, 326, 329, 330, 336
bourgeois, 235, 246, 270
fear of Western, 323
political, 112, 247
of the press, 247
sexual, 175, 191, 316
French Revolution, 216, 232, 312, 317
Friedman, Edward, 153, 155, 156
Friedrich, Carl, 329
Fudan University (Shanghai), 240
Fujian Province, 34
Future of China, The (Terrill), 163, 170

Gang of Four, 146, 147, 154, 156, 174, 175, 178, 179, 208, 231, 304
trial of, 156–59, 177, 195, 197, 272
see also Jiang Qing
Gao Xin, 256, 287
Gao Yuan, 79, 83
Born Red, 65, 82
generation gap, 231–32, 247
geography of China, 16
Goebbels, Joseph, 302
Goldwater, Barry, 49
Gorbachev, Mikhail, 220, 250–51, 252, 253, 254, 255, 271, 289, 312
Great Britain, 42, 46, 51, 69, 143, 145, 323
and Hong Kong, 81, 196
see also Opium War
Great Leap Forward, 14, 17, 32, 33, 34, 38, 70, 147
criticisms of, 62
failure of, 37
Great Wall, 227, 242
Guan Yin, 258–59
Guangdong Province, 46, 78

Guangxi Art Institute (Nanning), 181
Guangxi Province, 135
Guangzhou, see Canton
Guilin, 134, 135
Guo Moruo, 104–5, 150–51
Guomindang, see Nationalist party, 40

Hai Rui Dismissed from Office, 62, 64, 87–88
Han Chinese, 35, 330
Han dynasty, 59, 127
Han Xu, 96
Hangzhou, 129, 288
Harland, Bryce, 130
Harriman, Averell, 51
Harvard University
anti-Vietnam War movement at, 64, 84, 116
Chinese students at, 181, 191
Hatem, George, 316
He Chunyi, 207
Hebei Province, 65, 79, 82
Hefei, 199, 239
Henan Province, 167
hierarchy, 27, 218, 223, 226
Hill, Ted, 106, 107
Hirohito, Emperor, 66
Hitler, Adolf, 87, 135
Ho Chi Minh, 145, 196
Holbrooke, Richard, 162, 163
Holt, Bob, 68
Hong Kong, 24, 56–57, 61, 80, 95, 100, 182, 311, 315
British acquisition of, 46
and China, 43, 47, 193, 222, 226
and Cultural Revolution, 80–81
future of, 192, 196, 202
Hu Qili, 199, 251, 253
Hu Sheng, 174
Hu Shi, 27
Hu Yaobang, 199–200, 202, 219, 231, 246, 307, 311, 313
death of, 233, 234, 236, 239, 240, 243, 312
funeral of, 234–35, 237, 239

Hua Guofeng, 139, 171, 178, 283
    arrest of Gang of Four, 157
    as Mao's successor, 143, 144,
        146–49, 152
    and nationalism, 192
Huang Hua, 95, 97, 122
Hubei Province, 76, 126, 224
Hughes, Richard, 106
human rights, 169, 170, 192, 239,
        327
Humphrey, Hubert, 67
Hunan Province, 29, 30, 33, 46,
        108, 116, 135, 139, 147, 156,
        199, 212
Hungary, 14, 70, 220, 267
Huntington, Samuel, 75
Hurley, Patrick, 68

Iacocca, Lee, 231–32
Ibsen, Henrik
    A Doll's House, 63, 89
ideology, 17, 32, 59, 67, 85, 98, 99,
        122, 135, 163, 211
    return to, 293
    shift away from, 149, 174, 175,
        179, 317, 335
Idi Amin, 87
Immigration and Naturalization
    Service, U.S., 136
imperialism, 30, 37, 46, 79, 82,
        142, 218, 221
    American, 24, 49, 53–54, 67,
        102
    British, 43, 52
    Chinese, 222, 223
    Japanese, 222
India, 36, 39, 44, 99, 159–60, 332,
        333
individualism, 103, 212, 220, 265,
        318, 333, 336
    lack of, in China, 160, 175, 319–
        320, 322, 325, 326
    movement toward, in 1980s,
        174, 218, 234, 295, 321, 322,
        328, 329
Inner Mongolia, 167, 223
intellectuals, 301
    Chinese vs. Indian, 159

International Club (Peking), 105,
        107
International Women's Day, 190
"Internationale," 308
internationalism
    in China, 55, 74, 85, 98, 227, 328
Isaacs, Harold, 324, 325

Japan, 27, 60, 105, 192, 193, 221,
        226, 328, 335
    attack on China, 30, 31, 165
    trade with, 39
    and United States, 50
Ji Pengfei, 107
jia (household), 89, 294, 295, 319,
        322, 326, 329, 333
Jia Jing, Emperor, 88
Jiang Qing, 55–56, 62, 80, 134, 223
    contradictions of, 91
    criticisms of, 76, 88, 101, 139,
        152–53, 177
    and Cultural Revolution, 197
    and Deng Xiaoping, 130
    on Deng Xiaoping, 149, 178
    early life of, 63
    fall of, 146
    and Mao Zedong, 30, 61, 63–64,
        87, 90, 94, 125–26, 142, 144,
        147, 197
    marriage of, to Tang Na, 89
    as successor to Mao, 138
    trial of, 156–59
    see also White-Boned Demon, The
        (Terrill)
"Jiang Qing and the Chinese
    Political System" (Terrill), 196
Jiang Shengde, 182–83
Jiang Wen, 158
Jiang Zemin, 311, 322
Jiangsu Province, 230, 284
Jiangxi Province, 71, 129
Jilin University (Changchun), 281
Jinggangshan, 61
Johnson, Lyndon, 23, 49–50, 94,
        97
Joint Liaison Group of All Capital
    Circles, 253
Journey to the West, 90

Kalb, Bernard, 119
Kang Sheng, 88
Kang Youwei, 326–27
Karnow, Stanley, 128
Keatley, Robert, 113
Kellett-Long, Adam, 42, 50
Kennedy, John F., 49, 50, 96, 97
  and China policy, 118
Kennedy, Senator Edward, 95, 96,
  97, 113, 123, 137
Khmer Rouge, 168
Khrushchev, Nikita, 53, 54, 69, 87,
  148, 238, 250, 256
  critique of Stalin, 22, 70, 156
  on Great Leap Forward, 34
Kierkegaard, Sören, 193
Kim, Charles, 243–44, 308
Kim Il Sung, 79
King, Martin Luther, 267
Kissinger, Henry, 94, 96, 97–98,
  105
  and Mao Zedong, 120
  and opening of China, 113, 116,
    117–18, 119, 120, 122, 123
  and U.S. China policy, 140–41,
    162
  view of China, 136
  on Zhang Wenjin, 164
  and Zhou Enlai, 102, 106, 116,
    120
Koppel, Ted, 292, 306
Korean War, 34, 36, 49, 51, 53, 69,
  117, 164, 168
  Chinese Communists in, 14, 111
Kublai Khan, 24

land
  contract system in, 216
  ownership of, 35, 150
  vs. industrial assets, 188
landlords, 29, 77, 82, 332
language
  Chinese, 116, 324–25
  Russian, 38, 77
Lao Yujun, 248–49
Lao Zi, 27
law, 154, 173, 205–8, 210, 228, 238
Lee Kuan Yew, 138

Lei Feng, 37–38, 39
Leland, Timothy, 136
Lenin, 14, 30, 33, 70, 72–73, 92,
  199, 228, 317
Leninism, 79, 154, 179, 194, 216,
  335
  definition of, 196
  and Marxism, 51, 70, 196, 209,
    227, 314
  and preservation of power, 54,
    271, 314, 327
Li, Pastor, 187–88
Li Lu, 246, 250, 252, 281n
  Moving the Mountain, 281n
Li Peng, 258, 304, 309, 311, 325
  and democracy movement, 235,
    244, 245, 249, 253, 255, 266,
    280, 287, 290, 292, 295, 302,
    312, 313
  on imperialism of West, 322
  and reform, 229–30
  resistance to, 305, 313
  and Western culture, 323
  and Zhao Ziyang, 313
Li Pingfen, 203, 210–11
Li Rui, 153, 154
Li Xin, 154
Li Yanning, 168, 197–98
Li Zhao, 235
Liberation, 13, 15, 17, 28, 32, 35,
  45, 107–8, 215, 277, 330
  fortieth anniversary of, 232
  proclamation in Tiananmen
    Square, 18, 19
Liberation Army Daily, 64
Lifton, Robert J.
  Revolutionary Immortality, 86n
Lilley, James, 286
Lin Biao, 62, 126, 157, 158, 238
  death of, 127, 134
  and Mao Zedong, 70, 72, 77, 87,
    94, 115, 135, 147
  and PLA, 125–26
Lin Ling, 216, 229
Lin Luoyi, 38
Lin Mu, 299–303, 307, 327, 329n
Lin Ping, 141
Literarny Listy, 73

Liu Binyan, 37, 83, 247, 294, 297
Liu Fusheng, 135
Liu Guogeng, 292
Liu Luxin, 236–37, 268
Liu Shaoqi, 55–56, 60, 66–67, 108,
    156, 224
  in Cultural Revolution, 69, 72,
    80, 82, 83, 88, 89, 91, 93, 128,
    129, 200
  How to Be a Good Communist, 60
  and Jiang Qing, 157
  and Mao Zedong, 33, 60–61, 62,
    63, 70–71, 74, 92, 94, 127
  rehabilitation of, 159
Liu Tao, 89
Liu Xiaoyan, 294
Liu Yunruo, 80
Lodge, Henry Cabot, 68
Long March, 30, 33, 59, 60, 63, 72,
    101, 126, 149, 199
Lord, Bette Bao
  Legacies, 199
Lord, Winston, 116
luan (chaos), 28

Ma Qingguo, 234, 238–39, 240,
    249, 254, 255, 258, 298, 303
Ma Yuzhen, 114
MacLaine, Shirley, 163
Malraux, André, 54–55, 60–61
  Man's Fate, 60
Manac'h, Etienne, 95–96, 118
  La Chine, 96n
Manchuria, 228, 240, 259
Mao: A Biography (Terrill), 153,
    236–37, 238, 268, 310
Mao Anqing, 88
Mao Zedong, 57, 59, 92–93, 179,
    254, 318, 329
  and battle for succession, 125–
    129, 138, 146–49
  belief in Marxism, 53, 90
  birth of, 29
  on birth rate, 47
  and Buddhism, 212
  and Chiang Kai-shek, 23, 60
  and class struggle, 86, 138, 332
  On Contradiction, 31

and cult of personality, 86–87,
    109, 330
death of, 17, 137, 142, 143–44,
    146, 150, 157, 169, 331
and Deng Xiaoping, 34, 149,
    215, 268, 310, 311
early life of, 29–31, 232
education of, 30
final years of, 124, 131, 134
"Foolish Old Man Who
    Removed the Mountains,
    The," 31, 99
foreign policy of, 98, 99, 113,
    140, 221, 222
funeral of, 144–45
and Gang of Four, 157
and Hong Kong, 80
and Hua Guofeng, 146–47
"In Memory of Norman
    Bethune," 99
and individualism, 232
and Jiang Qing, 63, 75, 158
and Kang Youwei, 326–27
and Khrushchev, 87, 148, 250
and Leninism, 196
and Lin Biao, 125–28
and Liu Shaoqi, 34, 55–56, 60–
    61, 70, 80, 82, 126
On New Democracy, 31
and Nixon, 85, 120, 137, 163
on old vs. new culture, 26
and opening of China, 113, 116,
    119, 121
physical appearance of, 30–31
as poet, 59, 61, 87, 120, 137,
    152–53
on political power, 277
On Practice, 31
Quotations, 64n, 70
re-evaluation of, 155–56, 223–24
"Report on an Investigation of
    the Peasant Movement in
    Hunan," 30
return to Chinese traditions, 85–
    86
and Russia, 34, 54, 62, 189, 334
"Serve the People," 31, 99
and smoking, 61–62

"Snow," 59–60, 61
and Stalin, 34, 51, 148
and Taiwan, 34
theory of hegemony, 221, 222
and Tibet, 226
and United States, 34, 51, 69
victory of, 13, 18, 19, 22, 24, 316
and Vietnam War, 53–54, 68, 69,
    98, 111
view of Russia, 73–74
view of United States, 34, 51,
    53–54
Works, 77
see also Cultural Revolution;
    Great Leap Forward
Maoism, 17, 43, 44, 47, 51, 85,
    130, 133, 134, 135, 144
failure of, 179, 192, 194, 195,
    217, 219
Marco Polo, 129
Marcos, Imelda, 270
Marshall, General George, 23
Marshall Mission, 23
Marx, Karl, 14, 30, 62, 72–73, 92,
    103, 131, 199, 225, 228, 317
Das Kapital, 167
*Eighteenth Brumaire of Louis
    Bonaparte, The*, 82
Marxism, 27, 37, 38, 46, 48, 60,
    72, 86, 93, 191
campaigns for study of, 135
and Chinese view of history,
    332
and Christianity, 43–44
definition of, 196
and democracy, 170
and economic life, 187, 216
failure of, 154, 211–12, 228, 233,
    237, 294, 317, 329, 330
and isolation of China, 329
and Leninism, 51, 70, 196, 227
and modernization, 57, 131
and rebellion, 91
and socialism, 227
"true" vs. "false," 153
see also class struggle; Mao
    Zedong: belief in Marxism
Massacre in Beijing, 281n

May Fourth Movement, 27, 33, 53,
    92, 152, 189, 322
and Communist party, 27
seventieth anniversary of, 232,
    245, 246
McMahon, William, 95, 96, 97,
    118
Meade, Peter, 289
Meisner, Maurice, 154, 155
Menon, Krishna, 36
military, 14, 125, 229, 293, 302
and democracy movement, 251,
    255, 257, 259–60
see also People's Liberation Army
Mill, John Stuart, 73
Mills, Harriet, 324, 325
Ming dynasty, 13, 62, 333
missionaries, 24, 44, 324, 325
Miyamoto, Kenji, 66–67
modernization, 111, 176, 177, 201,
    203
and communism, 112, 131, 150,
    215, 217
investment in, 222
and Marxism, 57, 131
and nationalism, 192, 193
social, 159
and urbanization, 132, 133
and youth, 217
Mongolia, 127, 222
Monkey King, 90–91
Mount Emei, 187
Mussolini, 135

Nan Fang Ribao (Southern Daily;
    Guangzhou), 310
Nankai University (Tianjin), 155,
    234, 239, 258, 298–99
Nanking, 31
National Geographic, 185, 203
National Liberation Front, 67, 68
National People's Congress, 232,
    256–57
nationalism, 17, 46, 49, 69, 192–93,
    290, 308, 325–26, 335
and Chinese foreign policy, 167,
    221
cultural, 330

Nationalist party (Guomindang),
27, 30, 53, 120, 142, 158, 190,
223, 292, 317, 330
cooperation with Communists,
126
loss of Chinese mainland, 13, 38,
48, 69, 334
treatment of Communists, 79
see also Chiang Kai-shek
Nehru, Jawaharlal, 36
New Culture Movement, 27
New Republic, The, 72, 146
New York Times, The, 107, 113,
142, 152, 159, 166–67, 191
Newsday, 107, 113
Newsweek, 171
Ni Weiguo, 230–31, 304–5
Nie Rongzhen, Marshal, 235
Nightline (TV program), 292, 306
Nikodim, Archbishop, 45
Nixon, Richard, 96, 97, 98–99,
102, 105, 106
arrival in China, 120
and communism, 118
and opening of China, 16, 85,
113, 116, 117–19, 122, 123,
136, 137, 162, 163, 221
resignation of, 140
and student protesters, 241
view of China, 94, 136, 166
normalization, 161–63, 164, 171
North Korea, 78–79, 137, 246,
334
North Vietnam, 49, 53, 68, 121,
137
Northwest University (Xian),
308
nuclear weapons, 14, 22, 34, 40,
54–55, 84, 105, 124, 335

Oksenberg, Michel, 162
Old Bachelor Wang, 63
opium trade, 39, 40, 51, 99
Opium War, 39, 51, 69, 191, 231,
315
Orwell, George
Animal Farm, 173
1984, 173

Palmerston, Lord, 46
Pan Haiqing, 214, 220
Paris Peace Conference (1919), 27
Pascal, Blaise
Pensées, 324
paternalism, 17, 18, 333
Paulsen, Friedrich
System of Ethics, 232
Peace Corps, 65
Pearl of Scandinavia (cruise ship),
173, 184, 230, 234, 241, 242
Pearl River, 47, 52, 69
peasants, see farmers
pedicabs, 26, 262–72
passim, 317
Peking, 15, 22–28
in 1989, 261–62
burning of Summer Palace in,
24
change of name to Beijing, 163–
164
Communist changes in, 24–28
description of, 24–33
Forbidden City in, 13, 24, 42,
229
foreigners in, 41–43
Mao's entrance into, 13
Muxidi Bridge in, 265, 280
Palace Hotel in, 261–308 passim
in 1970s, 100, 129
streets of, in 1980s, 180
underground trains in, 133
Xin Qiao Hotel in, 24, 25–26,
28, 40, 53, 114, 167, 172,
197
Yanjing Hotel in, 151–52
Peking Aeronautics Institute, 80
Peking University, 76, 77, 88, 100,
104, 110
Peng Dehuai, 62, 88, 126
Peng Hua, 105, 106, 113
Peng Zhen, 64, 88
Pentagon Papers, 105
People's Daily, 55, 56, 70, 91, 106,
107, 127, 151, 154, 199, 225,
332
April 26 editorial in, 243, 245,
247, 257, 260

and democracy movement, 241,
    242, 244, 245, 246, 247, 248,
    253–54, 257, 282
  Mao's refusal to read, 60
People's Liberation Army, 64, 65,
    126, 127, 190, 290
  and April 27 demonstration, 244
  and Mao Zedong, 62, 125
  and student protesters, 250, 259–
    260
  and Tiananmen Square massacre,
    262, 264, 266, 275, 279, 283,
    284, 293, 300, 303, 310
People's Publishing House (Hebei
    Province), 236
People's Republic of China, 14
  embassies in Europe, 14–15
  eradication of venereal disease in,
    316
  founding of, 25, 72
  "guests" of, 104
  invitations to scholars from,
    104–5
  leadership of, 148
  recognition of, 123–24
  thirty-fifth anniversary of, 195,
    196
  travel in, 22, 104
  and United Nations, 52, 124
  unity of, 334
Ping-Pong diplomacy, 97, 98, 99,
    107
PLA, see People's Liberation Army
Poland, 61, 70, 73, 136, 220, 240,
    309, 311
Politburo, 89, 126, 129, 147, 148,
    157, 235
  and Cultural Revolution, 16, 69,
    82
  members of, 167, 199, 229, 251,
    284, 285
  and military, 125
politics
  American vs. Chinese, 321
  Chinese, 111, 153, 203
  and economics, 203, 219, 290
  and personality, 196–98
  and religion, 109

population, 13–14, 124, 184, 333,
    334–35
Portuguese, 46
power, 17, 154, 317, 321, 323, 329,
    331, 334
PRC, see People's Republic of
    China
Provisional Students' Federation,
    234

Qiao Guanhua, 130
Qin dynasty, 59, 144
Qin Jiwei, 256
Qin Shi Huang, 139, 148
Qing dynasty, 13, 23, 30, 52, 222,
    326
Qing Ming festival, 138–39, 146
Qinghua University, 108
Qiu Yehuang, 79

Reader's Digest, 189
Reagan, Ronald, 163, 166, 167,
    168, 200
Red Army, 126, 199, 316
Red Crag, 79
Red Flag, 135
Red Guards, 65, 66, 79, 81–82,
    100, 128, 181, 201
  after Cultural Revolution, 133–
    134, 191
  and Chinese Communist party,
    252
  and Deng Xiaoping, 71
  female, 78
  idealism of, 90
  and Mao Zedong, 64, 83, 91, 92,
    320
  and public affairs, 84, 85
  and universities, 76
  see also Cultural Revolution
reform, 152, 229
  and Chinese Communist party,
    249, 312, 313
  and democracy, 200
  economic vs. political, 219–20,
    302
  legal, 205
  political, 219, 231, 246, 250, 307

reform (*cont.*)
  and revolution, 215–20
  and socialism, 200, 216, 219
  and student movement, 312, 313
  two kinds of, 302
  see also Deng Xiaoping: reforms
    of
Reischauer, Edwin, 96, 97, 118,
  136
religion, 43–46, 109, 159, 187,
  211–13
  see also Christianity
ren kou (population; lit., "human
  mouths"), 333
revisionism, 70–71, 73
  Soviet, 67, 70, 79, 80
rock concerts, Chinese attitude to,
  327–28
Rodin, Auguste, 73
Romania, 322, 331
Roork, Lin, 67
Roosevelt, Eleanor, 51
Roosevelt, Franklin D., 210
Rosenthal, A. M., 142
Roy, Stapleton, 188–89
Royal Viking Star (cruise ship), 173,
  175, 182, 192, 205
Russia-China split, 54, 91, 97, 335
Russian Revolution, 22, 30, 31, 33–
  34, 70, 317

Saddam Hussein, 87
Saigon, 59, 68–69, 196
Samson, Valerie, 284–85
Schell, Orville, 248
Schram, Stuart, 155
science, 27, 152, 189, 232, 239
SERI, *see* Social and Economic
  Research Institute
Sex, Chinese Communist view of,
  174–75
Shaanxi Province, 109, 111
Shandong Province, 76, 89, 101,
  134
Shanghai, 33, 129, 133, 169, 177–
  178, 182–85
  democracy movement in, 288
  exclusion of Chinese in, 51, 182

founding of CCP in, 27, 30
Japanese attack on, 63, 90
Mao Zedong in, 61–62
Shanghai Academy of Social
  Science, 177
Shanghai Communiqué, 162
Shanxi Province, 147, 149
Shen Chunyi, 107, 171–76, 193,
  200–201
Shen Tong, 232, 245, 249–50, 252,
  288
Shenyang, Democracy Forum wall
  in, 288
Sichuan Academy of Social Science,
  216
Sichuan Province, 33, 101, 167,
  185–92, 200, 202, 203, 204*n*,
  205, 333
  1988 visit to, 210, 211, 214, 225
  see also Chengdu
Sichuan University (Chengdu), 231
Sihanouk, Prince, 129
Singapore, 222, 240
Smedley, Agnes, 322
Smith, Adam, 73
Snow, Edgar, 49, 87, 104, 114, 118
  The Long Revolution, 87*n*
Social and Economic Research
  Institute (SERI), 232, 233,
  252–53, 258, 287
socialism, 13, 32, 53, 71, 73, 234
  Afro-Asian, 37
  Chinese, 39, 64, 70, 75, 86, 101,
    135, 216, 226
  "Eurasian," 72
  and modernization, 215
society, Chinese
  contradictions of, 102
  as mechanism, 29
Solomon, Richard, 196
Song dynasty, 59
South Africa
  and China, 39, 40
south China, vs. north China, 47
South Vietnam, 48, 69
Soviet Union
  and China, 16, 21–22, 30, 33–34,
    54, 67, 73–74, 98, 110, 120,

164, 166, 168, 250–51, 271, 284, 318, 330, 335
Chinese attitude toward, 53
disintegration of, 334
and Korean War, 14
reform in, 220
religion in, 45
republics of former, 322
socialist realism of, 27
travel in, 21–22
Srinivasan, Thambi, 41–42
Staley, Tony, 69
Stalin, 31, 34, 72
and Khrushchev, 22, 70, 87, 148, 156
Stalinism, 18, 39, 197, 216, 233, 335
Stevens, Wallace, 248
Strong, Anna Louise, 61, 82, 91, 92, 148
Su Fei, 316
Su Shaozhi, 256
suicide, 78, 231
Sukarno, Madame, 55, 56
Sun Longji, 35
Sun Muzhi, 179–80
Sun Yat-sen, 27, 31, 44, 48, 69, 193, 194
Sun Yat-sen, Madame, 31
Sun Zi
    The Art of War, 289
Sunday Times (London), 106

Taiwan, 96, 113–14, 124, 141, 142, 161–62, 167, 192, 193
and mainland China, 55, 157, 193, 215, 222, 226, 292
Nationalists on, 24, 31, 38, 335
treaty with (1954), 162
Taiwan Strait, 34, 51–52, 162, 168
Tan Changhua, Judge, 204–8
Tan Zhenzhou, 240, 259, 260, 303–304, 332–33
Tang dynasty, 59, 87, 103, 108, 330, 333
Tang Mingzhao, 65–66, 114
Tang Na, 63, 89–90
Tang Tsou, 155, 156

Tangshan earthquake, 143, 331, 332
Taoism, 44, 187, 332
Tarnoff, Peter, 68
Tawney, R. H., 95, 116, 329
Taylor, Charles, 28–29, 41
Taylor, George, 118
technology, 84, 178, 232
television, 151, 158, 171, 188–89, 309, 313
    Chinese Communist propaganda on, 292
    and Tiananmen Square demonstrations, 249, 250, 292
Temple of Heaven, 24, 309–10
Terzani, Angela, 132
    Chinese Days, 181
Thailand, 165
Third World, 36, 37, 45, 98, 142, 222, 245, 302, 334
Thomson, James, 96–97, 136
Thought of Mao Zedong, 16, 62, 9?
Thurston, Anne, 79, 135
ti (cultural essence), 323
Tiananmen Square, 43, 156, 193, 204, 336
    April 27 rally in, 243–44, 246, 308, 319
    and Asian Games, 315
    description of, 264
    Gate of Heavenly Peace at, 265, 271
    Goddess of Democracy in, 258–259, 265, 269, 278, 318, 326
    Great Hall of the People in, 38, 39, 60, 114–15, 119, 125, 129, 234, 235, 247, 250, 265, 281
    hunger strike in, 247, 248, 249, 250, 252, 253, 254, 256, 257, 258, 259, 312
    Mao Zedong in, 13, 14, 19
    Mao's funeral in, 144
    Mao's mausoleum in, 224, 237
    massacre in, 18, 261–96, 331
    and May Fourth Movement, 27
    Monument to the People's Heroes in, 139, 235, 243, 249, 264, 266, 273

Museum of Chinese History in, 38, 39
Museum of the Chinese Revolution in, 38, 39, 266, 278
1976 demonstrations in, 139, 146, 172, 199, 233
portrait of Mao in, 265, 269
rallies in, 23, 91, 234, 243, 245
Tianjin, 155, 258
Tianjin Daily, 236
Tibet, 35, 78, 86, 222, 223, 226, 271, 289, 334
Time, 171
Toffler, Alvin
Future Shock, 167
Topping, Seymour, 107, 113, 142
Toronto Globe and Mail, 28
totalitarianism, 35, 36, 73, 100, 293, 294, 308, 309
tourist industry, 151
trade, interregional, 150
trade unions, 107
travel in China, 155, 185, 219
Treaty of Nanking, 51
treaty ports, 51, 52
Truman, Harry S., 23, 49, 53, 117, 119
Twenty-One Demands, 27

Ulam, Adam, 94
United Nations, 52, 66
and China, 96, 97, 98, 113, 124, 142
United States
and Chiang Kai-shek, 23–24, 51
and China, 16, 22, 34, 51–52, 69, 96, 113, 118–20, 124, 136, 166
Chinese attitude toward, 48–53, 200–202
and Cultural Revolution, 140
demonstrations against, 23, 43
elections in, 320–21
policy in East Asia, 68, 166
and Soviet Union, 119, 120, 141–42, 162, 163, 168
and "two Chinas," 31, 98, 119, 141, 142, 161–63

wars with China, 168
see also Vietnam War
urbanization, 131–32
Utley, Freda, 322

Vanguard, 106
Vietnam
and China, 68, 74, 97, 145, 165, 166, 173, 222, 225, 277, 334
U.S. withdrawal from, 140
Vietnam War, 61, 67, 120–21, 124, 136, 328
and China, 23, 53–54, 59, 74, 75, 82
expansion of, 22
and U.S. detente with China, 16, 99
see also Harvard University: anti-Vietnam War movement at
Vincent, John Carter, 74–75
Voice of America, 288

Wall Street Journal, The, 113, 189, 254
wan sui ("long life"; lit., "ten thousand years"), 66, 320
Wang Dan, 232, 248, 252, 253, 256, 288
Wang Gaolong, 216
Wang Guangmei, 55, 56, 80, 88, 157
Wang Hairong, 129, 130, 162, 165
Wang Hongwen, 146, 147
Wang Juntao, 232, 252, 256, 258, 287
Wang Ruoshui, 70, 91, 154, 225, 301
Wang Shaoguang, 255n
Wang Yongdi, 186–87, 188
Wang Zhenglong, 177–78
warlords, 28, 30, 31, 165
Washington, George, 53
Washington Post, The, 116, 117
Watergate, 140
Wedemeyer, General Albert, 68
Wei Jingsheng, 170, 171, 172–73, 176, 232, 327
Wen Hui Bao, 178

West
and China, 16, 22, 36, 42, 51–52,
94, 99, 328
Chinese attitude toward, 46, 49
impact of, 24, 51, 74, 75, 227,
231
three seminal concepts of, 188
Whampoa Military Academy
(Canton), 126
White, Theodore
Thunder Out of China, 28
White-Boned Demon, The (Terrill),
196–98, 236, 237–38
Whitlam, Gough, 95–96, 97, 99,
105, 106–7, 108
elected prime minister of
Australia, 120–21
1973 visit to Mao, 130
and opening of China, 114–16,
118, 119, 123, 124, 149
Wilkinson, Endymion, 159
Wilson, Sir David, 42–43, 46
Wong, Keith, 208, 209
workers
factory, 35, 214
and job security, 151, 214
and shareholding, 214, 216, 219
support for student protesters,
249, 253, 255, 288, 291
World Student Christian
Federation, 85
World War I, 189, 232
World War II, 15, 24, 31, 66, 145,
167
Wright, Richard
The God That Failed, 56
Wu, Empress, 87
Wu Gang, 153
Wu Zuguang, 318, 319
Wuer Kaixi, 251, 252, 253, 256,
288, 311
Wuhan, 129, 133, 199
Wuhan University, 299, 300
Wuxi, 109, 116, 118

Xian, 103, 108, 109, 140, 148, 149,
308
Xiang Jiachuan, 205–8

Xiao Yang, 83, 84, 214, 215, 217,
288
Xichang, 187
Xie Fuzhi, 66
Xie Qimei, 141, 161–62
Xin Qiao Hotel (Beijing), 24, 25–
26, 28, 40, 53, 114, 167, 172,
197
Xinjiang, 222, 334
xinli anwei (comfort for the spirit),
301
Xu Yiyong, 198

Yan Jiaqi, 245–46
Yan'an, 30, 60, 61, 63, 64, 90, 101,
103
Yang Bingzhang, 76–79, 100–101,
181, 185, 201
Chinese Politics, 78
Yang Kaihui, 88, 89, 152
Yang Shangkun, 255, 257, 287, 312
Yangzi River, 152, 181, 323
Yao Wenyuan, 62, 146, 147
Yao Yilin, 229, 284, 313
Ye Qun, 126, 127
Yellow Emperor, 109
Yenching University, 103
Yi people, 204*n*
yong (practical function), 323
Young Men's Christian Association
(YMCA), 43
Yu Guangyuan, 154, 156
Yuan Ming, 236
Yuan Weigong, 200, 283–84

Zablocki, Clement, 162
Zhang Chunqiao, 146, 147, 154,
158
Zhang Hanzhi, 146*n*
Zhang Ling, 211
Zhang Shaohua, 88
Zhang Wenjin, 164, 166, 167, 197,
198
Zhang Zhidong, 316–17, 323, 328
Zhao Fusan, 44–46, 74, 101–2,
212, 321, 322, 326
Zhao Ziyang, 167–68, 200, 202,
219, 229, 230, 232, 307, 311

Zhao Ziyang (*cont.*)
  and Chinese Communist party,
    216, 310
  and democracy movement, 245–
    246, 250, 251, 252, 253, 255,
    256, 258, 262, 264, 287, 289,
    304, 313
  on Deng Xiaoping, 289, 312
  fall of, 257
  at funeral of Hu Yaobang, 234–
    235, 241
  and succession to Deng
    Xiaoping, 313
  visit to Washington, 167–68,
    200
Zhejiang Province, 115
zheng yi (justice), 223
Zhongguo (middle country), 39, 40
Zhongnanhai compound, 65, 229,
    243, 244, 249, 258, 290, 309,
    312
Zhou Enlai, 33, 94, 95, 96, 102,
    224, 255
  African tour of, 36

  biography of, 197
  and Cultural Revolution, 71, 72,
    83, 128
  death of, 138, 230
  early life of, 71–72, 239
  foreign policy of, 98, 99, 106,
    113, 114–15, 123, 140, 221
  funeral of, 138
  illness of, 129, 130, 139, 184, 230
  and Lin Biao, 126–29
  memorials to, 139
  and opening of China, 113, 119,
    162
  physical appearance of, 115
  on Taiwan, 113–14
  and United States, 97, 98–99
Zhou Nan, 103, 105, 106, 111–12,
    114, 116, 117, 142, 315, 323,
    324
Zhou Yiliang, 223, 307
Zhu Bingchun, 254
Zhu De, 82, 143, 224
Zhu Rongji, 288
Zhu Yasheng, 282, 305–6

PHOTO CREDITS